MATTERS OF TESTIMONY

MATTERS OF TESTIMONY

Interpreting the Scrolls of Auschwitz

Nicholas Chare and Dominic Williams

berghahn
NEW YORK · OXFORD
www.berghahnbooks.com

First edition published in 2016 by
Berghahn Books
www.berghahnbooks.com

© 2016, 2017 Nicholas Chare and Dominic Williams
First paperback edition published in 2017

All rights reserved. Except for the quotation of short passages
for the purposes of criticism and review, no part of this book
may be reproduced in any form or by any means, electronic or
mechanical, including photocopying, recording, or any information
storage and retrieval system now known or to be invented,
without written permission of the publisher.

Library of Congress Cataloging-in-Publication Data
Chare, Nicholas, author.
Matters of testimony: interpreting the scrolls of Auschwitz.
   pages cm
   Includes index.
   ISBN 978-1-78238-998-9 (hardback: alk. paper) -- ISBN 978-1-78533-352-1 (paperback) -- ISBN 978-1-78238-999-6 (ebook)
   1. Birkenau (Concentration camp). 2. Sonderkommandos--Poland--Oswiecim--Biography. 3. Holocaust, Jewish (1939-1945)--Poland--Oswiecim--Personal narratives. 4. Auschwitz (Concentration camp) I. Williams, Dominic, author. II. Title.
   D805.5.B57C43 2015
   940.53'1853858--dc23
                                                                    2015013049

British Library Cataloguing in Publication Data
A catalogue record for this book is available from the British Library

ISBN: 978-1-78238-998-9 (hardback)
ISBN: 978-1-78533-352-1 (paperback)
ISBN: 978-1-78238-999-6 (ebook)

Contents

List of Figures		vi
Preface		vii
Introduction	Matters of Testimony	1
Chapter 1	Matters of History	30
Chapter 2	Zalman Gradowski: Literature in the Death Factory	60
Chapter 3	Scattered Selves: The Stories of Leyb Langfus	93
Chapter 4	Final Arrangements: Zalman Lewental's Histories of Resistance	125
Chapter 5	Characters and Letters: Chaim Herman and Marcel Nadjary	154
Chapter 6	The Camera Eye: Four Photographs from Birkenau	183
Conclusion	Crossing the Circle of Flame	214
Bibliography		223
Appendices		237
Index		245

Figures

Figure 1.1	Pencilled list in Polish, found with Zalman Lewental's account. The shooting of 460 members of the SK is recorded on the right-hand side.	48
Figure 3.1	Photograph of the penultimate page of the lost manuscript by the 'anonymous' author, Leyb Langfus.	94
Figure 3.2	Detail of page [22] 27 from *The Deportation*. The title of Chapter 4 can be made out in the middle of the image.	99
Figure 3.3	Detail of page [99] 111, inserted loose at the end of *The Deportation*.	107
Figure 3.4	Detail of a page from the account 'The 3000 Naked Women'. The words *nisht beobakhtet* appear followed by white space on the fourth line.	109
Figure 4.1	Page from Zalman Lewental's manuscript. The symmetrical stain indicates that it is the central page of a signature. Page numbers 56 and 70 are visible in the top left and bottom right corners of the sheet.	129
Figure 4.2	Detail from Zalman Lewental's manuscript. The text discusses events in 1939. Part of what seems to be a title is readable at the top. The page number 93 is visible in the top left corner.	144
Figure 5.1	Page 2 of Marcel Nadjary's manuscript.	168

All images courtesy of the Auschwitz-Birkenau State Memorial Museum

Preface

Matters of Testimony centres upon a set of manuscripts written over seventy years ago by members of the Sonderkommando who worked in the crematoria at Birkenau. These writings, commonly referred to as the Scrolls of Auschwitz, were then carefully buried beneath ashes and earth in the hope they would one day be discovered. The grounds of the crematoria, of necessity, became the initial site for this unique archive of barbarism. These remarkable witness accounts, furtively written by men trapped at the core of a 'death factory', while distinctive in many ways are also like all Holocaust testimony in that they require responsibility and sensitivity of their readers. The Scrolls were therefore sometimes daunting to engage with. They provide eyewitness accounts of the most horrendous events and pose complex, at times very troubling, questions about the nature and limits of testimony. The physical documents, distressed and fragmentary, seem haunted by their authors and the circumstances in which they wrote. They are unnerving to touch.

The Scrolls comprise demanding material, and our readings of them have emerged from complex, usually exceptionally fruitful, and even occasionally fraught, sets of discussions and negotiations between us over materials and meanings. Some chapters include more input by one or other of us, but the book is a genuine collaborative enterprise. The primary responsibility for research and writing was taken by Nicholas Chare for chapters 1, 5 and 6, and Dominic Williams for chapters 2, 3 and 4. This reflects the particular skills and expertise, linguistic and analytic, that we could contribute to this project. However, as the chapter on Lewental with its close reading of the physical properties of one of the manuscripts by Dominic, or the literary analyses performed by Nicholas of the 'enduring tongue' in the chapter on Gradowski and in the final paragraphs of the chapter on Langfus demonstrate, there is often crossover between approaches and chapters. Each chapter is the product of discussion between us, and the revisions and final form were a combined effort. This arises from our, perhaps unique as far as collaborations go, shared background in both comparative literature and art history. Our living across disciplines, in terms of both teaching and research, has been a key to the success of this endeavour. We hope that this book therefore stands as a positive example of what transdisciplinary scholarship can achieve.

We wish to thank the British Academy and the Elisabeth Barker bequest for their help in facilitating much of the research behind this book. We are indebted to the Auschwitz-Birkenau State Museum and, in particular, to Wojciech Płosa and Agnieszka Sieradzka for assistance during our visits to archives there. We are also grateful to the staff at the Jewish Historical Institute in Warsaw, especially Michał Czajka and Agnieszka Reszka; at Royal Holloway Library, especially Russell Burke; and at the Wiener Library, London. Bruce Levy of the United States Holocaust Memorial Museum kindly helped us with our enquiries about the *Shoah* archive. Our work benefited greatly from the advice of Justin Clemens, Aurélia Kalisky, Marcel Swiboda and Miriam Trinh, who read and commented on draft chapters. Nikos Papastergiadis and Chrisoula Stamoulis are to be thanked for generously translating Marcel Nadjary's letter into English for us, and Alex Emmanuel provided invaluable commentary and translations of Nadjary's post-war account. Krzysztof Majer speedily helped us with last-minute queries about Polish. Thanks to Daniel Heller for his advice on the Betar movement in interwar Poland, and to Ruth Marcus for dealing with specific questions on Zalman Gradowski. Nasser Hussain, Robert Stanton and James Ward offered keen-eyed and -eared stylistic advice. Many other individuals contributed to the genesis of this book. We are deeply appreciative of the intellectual and, often, practical support of Suzannah Biernoff, Sara Chare, Esther Chare, Bryan Cheyette, Maria-Luisa Coelho, Vanessa Corby, D. Ferrett, Anne Freadman, Cathy Gelbin, Benjamin Hannavy-Cousen, Jemma Hefter, Eva Hoffman, Anne Karpf, Peter Kilroy, Silvestra Mariniello, Milena Marinkova, Maria Mileeva, Jane Moody, Angela Mortimer, Peter Otto, Sue Vice, Emma Wilson and Roy Wolfe. Particular gratitude for their encouragement and selfless sharing of insights goes to Griselda Pollock and Dan Stone. We are also obliged to Tag Gronberg for inviting us to Birkbeck to present work-in-progress. Additionally, Jacqueline Rose is owed considerable appreciation for encouraging further research into the Scrolls of Auschwitz. Without her wise words of inspiration, this project would not have happened.

We are very grateful to Marion Berghahn who first encouraged us to submit a proposal for the book and was then a source of support throughout its production. We are also grateful to Chris Chappell, Charlotte Mosedale, Nigel Smith, Ann Przyzycki DeVita and Molly Mosher at Berghahn Books for their help at various times during the production process.

Technicalities

Very occasionally in the endnotes [NC] or [DW] appears at the end of a body of text by one or other of us writing as an individual.

The crematoria at Auschwitz-Birkenau have been described by two numbering systems. The one used by the Auschwitz museum and most historians (which also appeared on the designs) includes the crematorium at Auschwitz I Stammlager, which it counts as 'Crematorium I'. The other is that used by the Sonderkommando themselves, which counted only the four crematoria in Birkenau. We have adopted what we think is the simplest and clearest method to distinguish these two systems. The Sonderkommando used Arabic numerals for the crematoria, and we have maintained these numbers in the same form in our quotations. In all other places, following the most common practice, we number the Birkenau crematoria II–V, using roman numerals. Thus, the crematorium that was burnt during the October uprising will be referred to as 'Crematorium 3' in direct quotations from the SK, and Crematorium IV elsewhere.

In quoting from often badly damaged texts, it is sometimes necessary to indicate gaps in the manuscript (where words have not been deciphered), and also where conjectures have been included. We have tried to make it as intuitive as possible, but explain the use of symbols here:

*****   For a lacuna (gap). This symbol gives no indication of how big this gap is. In most cases the line numbers in the reference give an indication of it size.

×××   One word missing.

< >   Angled brackets indicate a conjecture. If the reference is to the MS, it is our own. If the reference is to an edition, it is to its editor's.

^ ^   Words inserted into the original text by the original author.

[ ]   Words between square brackets are our own additions, unless otherwise indicated.

Where other editions have used other symbols, we have standardised them to our practice.

Transliterations from Yiddish follow an adapted version of the YIVO standard. Ber Mark tried as much as possible to preserve the spelling of the original manuscripts, and we wish to respect that decision. We have used the standard YIVO transliteration for letters to reproduce the spelling as given in the manuscript, or if we have not been able to view it, as given in the Yiddish transcription: thus often 'zeht' where YIVO has 'zet', 'fervandelt' for 'farvandelt', etc.[1]

In giving the names of the Sonderkommando, we have used the Polish transliterations for the three Polish Jews' surnames, because it is the established spelling in the case of Gradowski, it is consistent, and it is most likely the version they used for themselves most often. Yad Vashem holds forms from Gradowski's niece and Lewental's brother using these spellings for their own names. For Marcel Nadjary we employ the English spelling used by his wife, which was also presumably his own. Other sources use an extremely wide variety of different spellings. We include all the alternatives of which we are aware here. This does not include typographic errors or errors of transcription (e.g. those made by the transcriber of Claude Lanzmann's interview with Filip Müller).

זלמן גראַדאָווסקי   Zalman Gradowski, also Salman, Salmen, Załmen, Zelman, Gradovski, Gradovsky.
לייב לאַנגפוס   Leyb Langfus, also Lajb, Leib, Lejb, Langfuss.
זלמן לעווענטאַל   Zalman Lewental, also Salman, Salmen, Załmen, Zelman, Levental, Leventhal, Lewenthal, Loewenthal, Löwenthal.
Μαρσέλ Νατζαρή   Marcel Nadjary, also Nadjar, Nadjari, Nadsari, Nadzari, Natsaris, Natzari.
Chaim Herman, also Haïm, Hermann.

Note

1. There is one exception to this. We do not follow Mark's decision to transcribe Zalman Lewental's spelling using *yuds* where standard spelling would use *vovs*: thus, for example, '*in*' for '*un*'; '*ints*' for '*unts*' (YIVO '*undz*'). This would make the transliteration much harder to follow. Moreover, since both letters when handwritten are basically vertical lines, the only difference between them is length, which often becomes simply a matter of judgement. Many times what Mark transcribes as a *yud* could plausibly be read from the manuscript as a *vov*.

Introduction
Matters of Testimony

Discoveries

In February 1945, in the weeks after the liberation of Oświęcim by the 60th Army of the First Ukrainian Front, the massive complex of Auschwitz-Birkenau was proving difficult to manage. The Red Army, preoccupied with securing its position against German attempts to recapture the valuable industrial zone of Silesia, had few resources to spread across the camp's multiple sites. The grounds of Birkenau were littered with debris and rubbish. Luggage lay in the cars of a train left on the unloading ramp, and was also strewn over the ground nearby. The departing SS had set fire to storehouses, and blown up the crematoria. The snow was beginning to melt, leaving everything in a sea of mud, and revealing more of what had been left behind: mass graves and burnt human remains. Around six hundred corpses had been found inside blocks or lying in the snow, and needed to be buried. Of the seven thousand prisoners who had been liberated on 27 January, nearly five thousand were in need of some kind of treatment. Soviet medical officers and Polish Red Cross volunteers came to the camp to care for them.[1]

Andrzej Zaorski, a 21-year-old doctor stationed in Kraków, was one of these volunteers. He arrived at Auschwitz a week or two after its liberation, where, as he recalled twenty-five years later, he was lodged in the commandant's house. He found a richly illustrated book among the papers left behind. The author, an SS-man, described the birdlife in the vicinity of the camp, and thanked the commandant for permission to carry out observations. In the trees round the camp, Zaorski noticed, there were lots of bird boxes. Preoccupied as he was with the business of treating former inmates, he remained in the grounds of Auschwitz I, the Stammlager, at first. By the time he had arrived, all of the ex-prisoners had been moved there and housed in its barracks, leaving Birkenau and Monowitz deserted. They were clearly having difficulty adjusting to their new status as patients, as they would hide their bread under their mattresses and would try to escape if told they were being taken for a bath.

After a few days, Zaorski and some fellow volunteers found time to visit the Birkenau site three miles away. He caught sight of heaps of ashes behind the ruins of Crematoria II and III, with groups of people rooting though them. They ran off as the doctors approached. On top of one heap, Zaorski found a sealed half-litre glass bottle containing a bundle of papers.

> I opened the bottle and took out from it some sheets of graph paper, superbly preserved. They were folded up in the form of a letter. On the outermost sheet of paper, out of which a makeshift envelope had been made, could be seen the address of the Polish Red Cross. On an inner part of the letter was written another address, this time to the actual addressee in France ... Because the letter was folded and rolled up in paper, and was not in a sealed envelope, I unrolled a few sheets of paper written in French. It was a personal letter to a wife ... The author of the letter described the terrible fate and experiences which had befallen him as one of the workers in the crematoria, forced by the Germans to be in the crematorium team. He stated clearly that he would certainly die, just like all his colleagues and predecessors forced to do the same work. He gave her a set of instructions about life after the war along with some bank details. He asked her never to return, never to travel to Poland.[2]

The team which the letter's author, Chaim Herman, described was mostly known by the name *Sonderkommando* (the 'special squad').[3] Zaorski may have been the first to discover one of many documents hidden by its members in the grounds of the crematoria. As his testimony indicates, locals were desperate enough to consider digging around in human remains looking for valuables in this unguarded site, and so other discoveries may simply have been thrown away.[4] But more documents were found and preserved during the course of 1945, albeit in a rather haphazard fashion, with discoverers free to treat them according to their own lights. Zaorski thought of his find as a letter that should be sent on to its destination, and gave it to the French embassy in Warsaw. In contrast, representatives of the Soviet Extraordinary Commission for the Investigation of German Fascist Crimes were interested in finding evidence. On 5 March 1945,

Shlomo Dragon, a former member of the Sonderkommando who had escaped from the death march from Auschwitz, provided them with a notebook and letter he had dug up near Crematorium II. The letter was signed by Zalman Gradowski. The commissioners ignored Gradowski's plea to contact his relatives in New York, and took the documents back to the Soviet Union.[5]

Amateur hunters also preserved some of the documents they found, seeing in them either the potential to turn a profit, or perhaps simply interesting junk worth hoarding. A young Polish man found another manuscript in early 1945, and sold it to Chaim Wolnerman, a Polish Jew who was preparing to leave his home town of Oświęcim for Palestine. Wolnerman worked out from a simple number code in the text that the author's name was Zalman Gradowski. This manuscript also asked its finder to contact relatives in America, which Wolnerman did.[6] In April 1945, Gustaw Borowczyk, another native of Oświęcim, returned from Germany where he had been working as a forced labourer, and while 'visiting' Birkenau disinterred a ledger containing an account in Yiddish, a language he could not read. He put it in the family attic, where it stayed until 1970.[7]

By the time other documents were unearthed, a museum had been set up on the site of the camp, but only gradually did it take control of the process of discovery. In 1952, Franciszek Ledwoń unearthed an exercise book while he was cutting the grass around Crematorium III. After passing through several different hands with several claims to ownership made upon it from competing interests, it probably ended up in the Jewish Historical Institute in Warsaw.[8] In the early 1960s, a more systematic search was made, again in the grounds of Crematorium III, with two finds carefully logged and their situations recorded. On 28 July 1961, a bracelet and two manuscripts were found together, one a diary from the Łódź ghetto, and the other a commentary signed by Zalman Lewental; on 17 October 1962, an exercise book also signed by Lewental, some unsigned loose sheets of paper, and a list. In 1970, Gustaw Borowczyk's brother Wojciech brought in the notebook that he had found in the attic, and both brothers completed reports about how they had discovered it.[9] The following year, Andrzej Zaorski also gave testimony about how he had found Chaim Herman's letter. Efforts were also made in the early 1970s to find the manuscript discovered in 1952, but it had gone missing.[10] When a group of students cutting the grass around Crematorium III stumbled across a manuscript in Greek, on 24 October 1980, that mistake was not repeated: the museum was the undisputed place to which to take it. A reader of Greek was found who identified the author as Marcel Nadjary.[11]

'Out of all these recovered items, the most noteworthy that a cultural history could have overall, to the shame and misfortune of all of us, only tiny fragments have been published so far', Nachman Blumental lamented in 1966.¹² Although he named no one, one of the figures at whom Blumental was directing his ire may have been Ber Mark, who had replaced Blumental as director of the Jewish Historical Institute in Warsaw. Mark had been given the post as a more reliable communist, although he combined being a loyal party member with attempting to rebuild Jewish life in Poland and maintain ties with Jewish communities elsewhere. By the later 1960s such a balancing act was becoming increasingly hard to pull off: Jewish communists were subject to public and aggressive criticism, and Mark had begun to fantasise at least about immigrating to Israel. Mark devoted much of his post-war life to the history of the Shoah, in particular obsessively producing account after account of the Warsaw Ghetto Uprising.¹³ By 1966, the year of his death, he was close to completing a work he had entitled *Megiles Oyshvits*, the Scroll of Auschwitz, which was to include one text by Zalman Gradowski, both of those by Zalman Lewental and the anonymous manuscript found in 1952. His widow Esther was supposed to see the book through to publication in Poland, but the 'anti-Zionist' campaign beginning in March 1968 made that impossible.¹⁴ Esther Mark, like many of the staff at the Jewish Historical Institute, was forced to leave Poland for Israel, where she undertook more research and identified the 'unknown author' as Leyb Langfus.¹⁵ Also in Israel, Chaim Wolnerman, having had great difficulty finding a publisher for his manuscript, eventually decided to bring it out himself. Wolnerman's book and the Marks' book both appeared in 1977, making no reference to each other.¹⁶

In the meantime, the Auschwitz museum had published two editions of the Sonderkommando writings in quick succession: 1971 and 1973. The first edition provided Polish translations of the same set of texts as the Marks' edition, as well as of Chaim Herman's letter. All of the 1962 find was attributed to Zalman Lewental, and no author was ascribed to the 'anonymous' manuscript. The 1973 edition also included the notebook brought in by the Borowczyks.¹⁷ With the increasing absence of Yiddish specialists in Poland, the museum drew upon the talents of Roman Pytel, a philologist whose primary expertise was in Aramaic, to decipher the text. The author had not signed his notebook, which he had entitled *The Deportation*, but was named 'Leyb' in the story. The museum concluded that he was Leyb Langfus, although they have not taken any notice of Esther Mark's attribution of other texts to him.

By 1977, then, all the writings discovered up to that point had been published in some form, but translations into other languages happened quite patchily, often at one remove. Apart from a direct translation of selections from Gradowski's writings, the only English translations of the Scrolls are of the first Polish Auschwitz edition, and of the Hebrew version of the Marks' book.[18] Only Polish and German versions exist of *The Deportation*. No English translation of Nadjary's letter has been published. Although interest in the writings, especially those of Zalman Gradowski, has increased in the twenty-first century in other countries, knowledge of them is still quite limited in the anglophone world.[19] Accounts of these documents are often little more than descriptions. We know of no account published before 2013 that even mentions that the authorship of some texts is disputed.[20] Our book is the first in any language to provide a detailed engagement with all of the Scrolls of Auschwitz, something scholars seem to have been reluctant to do before. Such reticence is consonant with widespread uneasiness about the status of the Sonderkommando themselves.

The Sonderkommando

The 'Special Squad' was a Nazi euphemism for the group of prisoners tasked with processing the bodies of those gassed in the Auschwitz main camp and in Birkenau. Different tasks were given to different specialists. '*Schleppers*' or '*Leichenträger*' pulled bodies from the gas chambers. 'Dentists' extracted gold teeth. 'Barbers' cut hair from the dead women's heads. '*Heizer*' ('stokers') were responsible for burning the corpses, either in the ovens or in pits. What many saw as the worst task, which may have been called the '*Aschenkommando*' ('ash squad'), involved grinding up the ashes into dust and disposing of them.[21] Other general duties included sorting clothes and effects before they were sent to the nearby warehouses of 'Kanada', and general upkeep of the crematoria. When it was discovered that their presence helped to keep victims calmer, they also had to stay with them while they undressed.[22]

The role and composition of the Sonderkommando changed a great deal over time, but there is one clear cut-off point falling at the beginning of December 1942. Almost no one who was in the SK before this time seems to have survived. Before it, groups of mainly Slovak Jews were recruited on an ad hoc and then somewhat longer-term basis to dispose of freshly gassed bodies, and to dig up and burn corpses of those buried when the ovens had broken down. The ad hoc groups were probably eliminated after carrying out their tasks. The final group seems to have been liquidated in its entirety in early December 1942.[23] The group who replaced them included Leyb Langfus and Zalman Gradowski, as well as a number of other men from central and north-eastern Poland. Like Langfus and Gradowski, most members were recruited within days of arrival, when they were disoriented and least likely to resist, but some spent time in the camp before joining them. Zalman Lewental, for example, arrived in Auschwitz in early December 1942, but was only transferred to the Sonderkommando in January 1943.

Up to the spring of this year, the SK had mainly been working in the two 'Bunkers', farm cottages converted into gas chambers, with the bodies burnt in pits nearby. In March, the crematoria started to come into use, bespoke buildings combining undressing rooms, gas chambers and ovens. By this time, the squad had taken on a relatively settled form. In July 1943 they were moved from Block 2 of camp BIb to Block 13 of camp BIId, which, along with Block 11 for the penal group, was surrounded by a wall. Although they were supposed to be kept isolated from the rest of the camp, there are enough accounts of contact between them and other prisoners to indicate that it was sometimes possible, if risky, to cross that boundary.[24] Members of the Sonderkommando wore civilian clothes with a red stripe on them, and had their hair closely cropped. They had far fewer people to a block than the Birkenau standard, and much better access to washing facilities. There are plenty of reports of them being beaten, but sometimes the SS saw the wisdom of letting them get on with their jobs. Some SS men seem to have called their Kapos, and perhaps others of them too, by their first names.[25] The Sonderkommando were much better fed than other prisoners, largely because they could scavenge what was left by the groups who were murdered in the crematoria.[26]

As transports from different countries came to Birkenau, new members were recruited. French Jews were brought in during the spring of 1943, and a number were impressed into the SK. One of them was Chaim Herman. After transports from Greece started to arrive, a large contingent of Greek Jews was drafted in April 1944, strong and fit but mostly with no understanding of German. They were often given the most arduous tasks. Marcel Nadjary was among them. While periodic selections and expansions did take place, these were not the four-monthly liquidations of legend. The skills acquired by experienced members of the SK were too valuable for that.[27] All of the authors named above survived into the autumn of 1944. When nearly half a million Hungarian Jews were brought in and killed at Birkenau over the summer of 1944, all of them had to take part.[28]

All of the writers also seem to have been involved in some way in the plans for an uprising, a convoluted and difficult process that never managed to realise its aims, often stymied by events, and suspected by the camp administration. In July 1944, most of the SK were brought to live as well as work in the crematoria to prevent contact with other parts of the camp. When a revolt did break out, it was more of a desperate, divided scramble from men about to be killed than the coordinated action that had been discussed.[29] They had managed to acquire some weapons, but it is not clear that any of them were actually used. The squad of each crematorium acted differently. The men of Crematoria IV and V who had been picked to be liquidated attacked the SS. Some attempted to run away; others ran into Crematorium IV and set it on fire. The SS were able to maintain control in the courtyard and in Crematorium V. The men in Crematorium II killed a Kapo, ran out of their building, cut the wire and escaped. They were tracked down and killed in the countryside nearby. All of the writers (with the possible exception of Gradowski) were part of the squad for Crematorium III, who, unclear what was happening, tried to stick to the plan to revolt later that day.[30] About 450 members of the SK were killed in the uprising or in retaliation for it, Gradowski among them. All the other writers survived, still working within the remaining crematoria that were operational, but also eventually responsible for dismantling them after the order had come to stop the gassings. 160, probably including Herman, Langfus and Lewental, were killed at the end of November.[31] About one hundred members, one of them Marcel Nadjary, managed to mingle with the group evacuated from Auschwitz and force-marched towards Mauthausen. Around two thousand men are thought to have worked in the Sonderkommando at one time or another. Eighty or so survived.

The Sonderkommando have been objects of fascination for many people for a long time, but more often as part of myths and fantasies of collaboration, or revenge, or both. Early portrayals of them were often of wretchedly self-interested individuals who sold their souls for an extra few weeks of life.[32] Although survivors of the Sonderkommando produced testimony from early on, this was often mixed with other legends about them, or indeed contributed to legends. Two early examples are Ota Kraus and Erich Kulka's compilation of evidence *The Death Factory* and Miklós Nyiszli's memoir of the time he had spent in Auschwitz. Kraus and Kulka's *Death Factory* included first-hand testimony from Filip Müller, but also described the SK as 'apathetic and insensitive'. The 'expression on their faces changed radically until they all appeared brutalized'.[33] Nyiszli had assisted Mengele with autopsies as well as acting as doctor to the SK, and generalised from his four months' experience to assert, for example, that there had been twelve squads of Sonderkommando dating back to 1941. His descriptions of the SK's luxurious lifestyle may also be something of an exaggeration.[34]

Primo Levi's 'The Grey Zone' (1986) relies heavily on Nyiszli's testimony to consider the moral status of the Sonderkommando.[35] In this essay, the Special Squads provide a major example of ethical ambiguities and challenges generated by Jewish actions during the Holocaust. For

Levi, they formed a moral quandary to be discussed alongside Chaim Rumkowski, the head of the *Judenrat* in the Łódź ghetto.[36] The members of the Sonderkommando were used as forced labour by the Germans and were consequently not straightforward collaborators. Levi recognised that the use of Jewish prisoners to maintain the gas chambers and to man the ovens enabled the Nazis to economise their workforce and to distance themselves from the 'most atrocious tasks' that accompanied their crimes.[37] He also perceived the creation of the Special Squads to form another means by which the Nazis could humiliate and degrade their Jewish victims.

For Levi the squads were abject, forced to act out the Nazi belief that the Jewish people would bow to 'any and all humiliation'.[38] The members, as representative of the Jews as a whole, are therefore figured as submissive, as forming obedient servants to their Nazi masters. Levi appears to judge the squads negatively yet also affirms that judgment falters when assessing their actions. There is therefore a telling tension within the essay. Levi at once condemns the Sonderkommando, finds them repellent, and betrays a sombre compassion for them. The acts of squad members prompt what he describes as 'convulsed questions' (*domande convulse*).[39] There is, for him, therefore something gut-wrenching about the SK. At least initially, they generate a visceral rather than cognised response. In this context, his sustained engagement with their experiences can be understood as a remarkable effort to overcome this instinctive repulsion and guardedly reflect on them.

Levi's equivocal meditation regarding the status of squad members is powerful and thoughtful, yet also, we would suggest, limited in scope. He refused to judge the squad members as collaborators, or to use them as an excuse to erase differences between victim and perpetrator, but his sense of who they were and what they felt was restricted. He was obviously familiar with the existence of writings by the Sonderkommando, describing 'diary pages written feverishly for future memory and buried with extreme care near the crematoria', yet he does not appear to have read them.[40] His account seems to be based in large part on the partial descriptions given in Miklós Nyiszli's book. For Levi the only testimony that the Sonderkommando were therefore capable of producing would be 'a lament, a curse, an expiation, and an attempt to justify and rehabilitate themselves'.[41] They could not, he implies, reflect on their situation, or serve as witnesses. They lived 'in a permanent state of complete debasement'.[42] At the same time, however, he acknowledges the squads composed testimony intended for a future audience and recognises that they were assiduous in concealing it.

Gideon Greif's collection of interviews with survivors of the Sonderkommando, *We Wept without Tears*, is a vital resource for moving beyond the understanding that Levi exemplifies. Greif's primary concern is to humanise the Sonderkommando and defend them from the attacks made upon them in earlier accounts, even those of Levi. He often stresses his personal relationships with the surviving members, including direct addresses to them and expressing a desire to make his words their memorial. He includes pen portraits of each of them, emphasising their human qualities, their virtues, and the ways that they were able to form and build relationships after the war.[43] Greif's readings of the Scrolls are equally informed by this concern, making use of them to show how the SK were not unfeeling automata, or, in the more difficult parts, at times even apologising for what is written there.[44] He fails to give sufficient consideration to the fact that the writings are not simply records of the SK's souls, but are consciously formed works that are made with a purpose – to reach the outside world. His sensitivity and sympathy have been vital to his work interviewing former members, and his book provides a wealth of information about the SK based on those interviews. Nonetheless, his approach may be too defensive and apologetic, still too much of a reaction to early misrepresentations of the SK.

Gideon Greif's book was published in Hebrew in 1999, but only translated in 2005. That same year saw the publication of Eric Friedler, Barbara Siebert and Andreas Kilian's *Zeugen aus der Todeszone*. This, the only full-length historical study of the Sonderkommando, has also helped to establish the facts and dispel some myths, but shows little interest in reflecting on ways in which greater knowledge of the SK and their writings might enable us to better address Primo Levi's moral questions, or affect our approaches to testimony, or even enhance our general understanding of the extermination camps and how they operated.[45] The fact that this book remains untranslated into English, and the length of time taken to translate Greif's collection of interviews, indicate the reluctance there has been, especially in anglophone scholarship, to probe further into these crucial questions.

As some of the few survivors to have been present at gassings, the Sonderkommando have at times been granted a chance to recount what they saw. Members of the SK bore witness at major trials in Poland and Germany.[46] In accounts which see the gas chambers as absolutely central to the Final Solution, the Sonderkommando's testimony has been particularly significant, not least in Claude Lanzmann's film *Shoah* (1985). As Adam Brown has argued, however, even here the ambiguous position of the SK comes out in Lanzmann's expectation that they should re-enact harrowing moments of their past, in a kind of expiation for their actions.[47] Filip Müller is a key witness for Lanzmann, as one of those who saw and indeed entered the gas chambers. But his witnessing has to take place retrospectively, produced and guided by his interviewer. For Lanzmann, breaking through consciously relayed narratives is what leads to true moments of witnessing, of incarnation. Indeed, even Müller's voice is taken out of his own conscious control, slowed down to match the images Lanzmann has filmed.[48]

Lanzmann's unwillingness to grant the Sonderkommando the capacity to represent and reflect on their conditions has been even more evident in the controversies over the four photographs taken by one member of the SK, identified only by the first name Alex. Images that recurred again and again in different contexts, these photographs remained more or less unanalysed until the beginning of the twenty-first century, with essays by Dan Stone and Georges Didi-Huberman. Didi-Huberman's expansion of his essay into a book, *Images malgré tout*, was as a response to attacks on his analysis by Lanzmann and his followers, who argued that the photographs failed to represent the Final Solution, and were 'images without imagination'.[49]

What recurs in discussions of the SK, therefore, is the idea that they could not reflect on their situation, or serve independently as witnesses. In this book, we want to argue that that is exactly what they could do. We will argue that the Scrolls are an important, and under-read, archive of Holocaust writing.

Holocaust Writing

Some aspects of the Scrolls are unique, and much of this uniqueness stems from the status of the Sonderkommando: the better conditions under which they lived and the relatively higher standing that they enjoyed probably helped them in some way to maintain a sense of identity. They had the energy to produce testimony. At the same time, the tasks that they were given, and the fact that they had no expectation of coming out alive, took a massive psychic toll on them. This latter factor comes out in their writings, in ways close to Primo Levi's expectations. But simply to focus on these two aspects is to ignore many of the ways in which they can be compared to other kinds of Holocaust writing. Firstly, the Sonderkommando operated like other prisoners in the camp, and their writing was only possible because of the elaborate networks of exchange by which products could be obtained, the system of *organising*. Prisoners from the Kanada Kommando had to provide them with paper, pen and ink.[50] Even light was a scarce resource: their *Stubedienst* had to arrange a bunk for writers that was near a window. The task of finding materials that would preserve the texts once buried was given to a number of members of the Sonderkommando, who searched constantly for wax to seal them in packages.[51]

Secondly, the Sonderkommando were only one group attempting to attest to what was happening in Birkenau. Even scratching one's name into a surface was an attempt to bear some kind of witness. But prisoners did much more than this. Famously, some prisoners escaped with reports on what was taking place in the camp.[52] Others kept secret lists, or hid or copied official records and photos.[53] Drawings and art representing camp life were concealed on site, or in some cases smuggled to the outside world.[54] Songs were sung, adapted, or written from scratch.[55] Yisroel Levental's song 'Fun Oshvientshim' has a chorus which asks 'Why did I come to Auschwitz?' and proclaims it better to die than to eat 'Auschwitz bread'. It does give some elements of information: what happened on arrival, the violence and threats of the Kapos, even mentioning the crematoria. But its tenor is to place experiences in the camp in a form which helps to make them bearable, to offer perhaps a modicum of rueful humour. The chorus especially would suggest that it was there to be sung communally.[56] Some prisoners even wrote poetry in Auschwitz, not usually to make a record of events, but rather to escape from its environment. Ruth Klüger's poetry, some of which was composed mentally and memorised in Auschwitz before being written down afterwards, 'constituted for her a mode of keeping her sanity in the camps', putting her experiences into some regular form, and expunging from them the presence of the perpetrators.[57] Three poems, written by an unknown woman in the Czech family camp, were given just before its liquidation to a Kapo, and then passed on to Erich Kulka. Here, using profoundly Christian imagery, the writer pours scorn on her tormenters and stares her future death in the face, while also asserting her ability to keep up some cultural life within the family camp.[58]

Each of these kinds of writing and recording took a different form, a result of the variety of positions occupied by different groups in the camp. The specificities need to be noted, but comparisons can be drawn too. This extends to writing produced at different sites. Alan Rosen notes that in earlier scholarship, the emphasis on the camp experience and the great, usually insurmountable, difficulties of writing there meant that for a long time Holocaust writing was only seen as beginning after the war had ended.[59] Much work has now recognised the significance of writings produced in the ghettos and in hiding. Recent scholarship has also noted continuities between pre-war historical practice and the work done in the ghettos, and continuities between that and the work of survivor-historians in the immediate aftermath.[60] It is also possible to see some continuity between ghetto and concentration camp, even with the sites of extermination. Many of the feelings associated with the camps – of powerlessness, of absolute vulnerability to arbitrary acts of violence, of squalor, hunger, dirt – were part of the ghetto experience. Analogies can be drawn between writing projects in the ghettos and in the camps. The compilation and archiving of documents by Oyneg Shabes in Warsaw was massively more extensive than what prisoners in Auschwitz were able to carry out, but the impulse to collect and record had much in common. The archivists of the Białystok Ghetto, working somewhat more chaotically than in Warsaw, were not professional historians, but rather were directly involved in armed resistance. For the Sonderkommando too, writing and resistance were inextricably intertwined. The chronicles of the Łódź ghetto were 'compiled in one of the offices of the ghetto administration', although without the knowledge of the Germans.[61] Being able to testify in Auschwitz was also often the result of being in a 'privileged' position.

Diaries written in ghettos or in hiding vastly outnumber those written in the camps. But some do exist. In concentration camps in Germany and Holland, diaries were occasionally kept, usually by prisoners higher up in a camp's social order.[62] Fela Szeps wrote in the Grünberg camp, and was even able to try out and assess different modes of writing.[63] Leon Weliczker Wells's book *Death Brigade* is adapted from a diary he seems to have kept in the Janowska Road camp.[64] Ghettos were also places where the process of extermination was recorded. Escapees from Treblinka and Chełmno came to Warsaw and bore witness there.[65] An escapee from Ponar testified to the archivists of Białystok.[66] Such testimony was not exclusively produced in the ghettos. Kazimierz Sakowicz, a bystander rather than a victim, but at great personal risk nonetheless, kept a diary of the shootings in the Ponar forests. He too buried it.[67] Prisoners in Chełmno managed to write letters in Yiddish and Polish recording what happened there. Some of them also produced a lengthier document describing what happened at the site, and calling for revenge.[68]

Poets in ghettos wrote about extermination. Władysław Szlengel's Skamandrite lightness of touch extended even to 'The Little Station of Treblinka' and its final image of an advertisement urging: 'cook with gas'.[69] And some poems were found in extermination camps. In his investigations for the Central Committee for Jewish History, Nachman Blumental discovered a bundle of paper in the ruins of Chełmno, a strange cycle of poems that he interpreted as a satire on the Germans. He also noted down songs that were associated with death camps, such as a version of '*Mayn shtetele Belz*' which was adapted to refer to Bełżec.[70] Two poems given to the commission had been found in the pocket of an M. Shenker (first name not given) in Treblinka. He may have written them within the camp itself. 'I am ashamed' ("*Kh shem zikh*") expresses the shame he feels to be alive when his wife and child are dead. Shenker's 'Sleep my child' ('*Shlof mayn kind*'), another poem mourning the death of his child, and

Aron Liebeskind's 'A lullaby for my little boy in the crematorium' ('*A viglid far mayn yingele in krematoryum*'), also possibly written in Treblinka, have similarities with the ghetto lullabies which Frieda Aaron discusses.[71]

None of this is to argue that making distinctions in time and space is meaningless. Zoë Waxman's differentiation between the literature of the ghettos and that produced in camps still stands,[72] as does the gulf in experience noted by Alexandra Garbarini between someone writing at the beginning of 1942 and someone in 1943.[73] But it is to say that thin, fragile continuities did exist, that enabled some testimony, perhaps only in rare and bizarre circumstances, to continue to be written. This testimony needs to be read.

Currently, as we have said, there seems to be a reluctance to provide readings of the Scrolls of Auschwitz. Such a position is understandable. Tom Lawson notes his own feeling of shame in talking of the Sonderkommando,[74] and subjecting their writings to literary analysis might seem perverse. George Steiner says of Chaim Kaplan's *Warsaw Diary* ('Scroll of Agony') that 'the only decent "review" … would be to re-copy the book, line by line'.[75] Gideon Greif's lengthy quotations from the Sonderkommando's writings in the introduction to his book, some of them extending over a page, often with barely any commentary at all, seem to enact what Steiner recommends. Other scholars such as Saul Friedländer might also be said to follow him. There are a number of useful introductions to and summaries of the writings of the Sonderkommando available, especially those by Nathan Cohen and Susan Pentlin.[76] But they usually do not have the space (and perhaps the inclination?) to say anything more about them. Even creative responses to the Scrolls often take a documentary-collage approach, quoting from them directly without comment.[77] This situation is beginning to change. Philippe Mesnard and Pavel Polian have shown the value of considering Gradowski's writing as literature.[78] David Roskies too has recognised Gradowski's literary ambitions.[79] Tom Lawson makes brief but thoughtful comments on some of the SK writings.[80] Dan Stone has credited the Sonderkommando with the agency to write works of history rather than simply record their experiences.[81] Alexandre Prstojevic writes powerfully and persuasively that the Sonderkommando writings are 'varied in their form and style, but all marked by the desire to go beyond bare facts'.[82] This book will follow these examples, and those provided by scholars of other texts from camps and ghettos.[83] We provide complex readings of the Scrolls, ones which show that they require, and repay, careful attention. The fact that they can be placed in a network of writings – not the same, but nonetheless comparable – suggests to us that they do have a wider significance, that they can be read in dialogue both with other primary texts and with other modes of reading Holocaust testimony. That does not mean that they simply sit comfortably within these modes of reading, however.

Being inside the Event

The existence of the Sonderkommando writings has major implications for arguments concerning the Holocaust's unsayability or unrepresentability. The Holocaust or Auschwitz, Dominick LaCapra affirms, has, until recently, 'been a privileged term for the unnameable'.[84] LaCapra's qualifier indicates this view has come under increasing pressure.[85] The Sonderkommando writings challenge the idea of unrepresentability, both through their context of production and through their form and content. Ways in which these writings call into question Dori Laub's assertion that during the Holocaust '*the event produced no witnesses*' have already been explored.[86] Laub argues that the Holocaust could not be attested to from within as 'the very circumstance of *being inside the event*' made it unthinkable that someone 'could step outside of the coercively totalitarian and dehumanizing frame of reference in which the event was taking place, and provide an independent frame of reference through which the event could be observed'.[87] Laub has recently been criticised for failing to display the independence, the retrospective objectivity, he perceives as necessary for witnessing to take place.[88]

The Sonderkommando writings, as will become clear in subsequent chapters, are certainly partial. They are written in unconcealed hatred of Nazi perpetrators. Calls for vengeance are a common theme. They are also fragmentary in terms of their overview of events. They provide no direct account, for example, of the atrocities committed by the *Einsatzgruppen* against the Jews from 1941 onwards. The writings also do not *observe* events, Laub's use of the term implying passive detachment. The authors of the 'Scrolls of Auschwitz' were active, if unwilling, in the smooth running of the crematoria. Their accounts were clagged by mass death. This is possibly one of the reasons why Laub, while acknowledging the existence of the manuscripts (he writes of diaries written and buried in the ground), dismisses them.[89] His main rationale for ignoring them, however, is because:

> the degree to which bearing witness was required, entailed such an outstanding measure of awareness and of comprehension of the event – of its dimensions, consequences, and above all, of its radical *otherness* to all known frames of reference – that it was beyond the limits of human ability (and willingness) to grasp, to transmit, or to imagine.[90]

The terms Laub employs here, describing experiences beyond the human capacity to comprehend or communicate, evoke psychological trauma. In Cathy Caruth's well-known definition, trauma is a missed experience. The traumatic event 'is experienced too soon, too unexpectedly, to be fully known and is therefore not available to consciousness until it imposes itself again, repeatedly, in the nightmares and repetitive actions of the survivor'.[91] Trauma is therefore an experience that waits to be claimed.[92] Laub describes it as 'an event that could not and did not proceed through to its completion, has no editing, attained no closure, and therefore, as far as its survivors are concerned, continues into the present and is current in every respect'.[93] It is only through the work of the analyst, the listener, that a traumatic event can finally be accessed and articulated. The hearer acts as 'the blank screen on which the event comes to be inscribed for the first time'.[94]

Laub's thinking in relation to the way trauma can be alleviated emerges from his experiences working as a psychoanalyst and also as an interviewer for the Video Archive for Holocaust Testimonies at Yale. The witness accounts he discusses are those of the (then) living. Only a survivor has the occasion, the opportunity, to speak about, and thereby partially overcome, the traumatic experiences they have been subject to. There was no scope within the Holocaust for any comparable psychotherapy to take place. Psychiatrists, such as Viktor Frankl, who were caught up in the destruction of Europe's Jews were preoccupied with surviving rather than attending to the psychic needs of fellow inmates.[95] In the chapters that follow, however, we will argue that the plain pages used by the authors of the 'Scrolls' occasionally provided a 'blank screen' comparable to the analyst. Writing, we will show, became a space through which traumatic experiences could be articulated and, to a degree, managed. Sheets of paper 'listened'. The words committed to them provided a source of psychic sustenance to each author. They helped to prevent the kind of loss of subjectivity that Laub has claimed rendered attesting from within impossible.[96]

Oral and written testimonies are usually differentiated. Comparing video and literary testimony, Lawrence Langer contends that reading a retrospective account of events which seeks 'to carry us "back there" is an order of experience entirely different' from video testimony.[97] Video testimony fosters situations in which, through a 'complex immediacy', the voice reaches us 'simultaneously from the secure present and the devastating past'.[98] Langer provides the example of the video witness Barbara T., who vanishes 'from contact with us even as she speaks, momentarily returning to the world she is trying to evoke instead of recreating it for us in the present'.[99] This description is reminiscent of Laub's example of a woman being interviewed for the Yale Video Archive who, while relating her memories of Auschwitz, was suddenly 'fully there'.[100] Video testimonies therefore generate situations in which something akin to what Claude Lanzmann describes as 'incarnation' occurs.[101] They produce instances in which the past is relived rather than simply recounted. The past ceases to be past, is presenced in the present. In our Conclusion we examine the Sonderkommando writings in relation to Lanzmann's ideas about incarnation and the archive.

For Langer, written testimony is too staged, too thought through, to compare with accounts as raw as those produced in interview situations. Writing always portrays rather than embodies the past.[102] The Sonderkommando manuscripts are no different from the retrospective written accounts Langer has in mind in that they employ style, imagery, chronology. They are representational and narratological. The writings produced at Birkenau, however, are also of their moment. They speak from the world of the death factory. They can therefore be said to carry that world within them in ways retrospectively produced accounts cannot. The literary techniques they exhibit were designed not to carry a reader back (or not solely to do that) but also to carry experiences forward. The authors strove to convey a past lived as their present to another present, a future present they would not live to see. The understanding of temporality employed by Langer to make sense of oral testimony is therefore difficult to reconcile with these writings.

We are not suggesting that because of the context of their production the Sonderkommando writings are somehow superior to video testimony. The kind of hierarchy imposed by Langer is questionable in its usefulness, and reversing it serves no worthwhile purpose. The chapters that follow nevertheless make clear that qualities ascribed to oral accounts are also present in the writing. There is a comparably complex immediacy in the manuscripts. Although they were not instant responses to specific events, occasionally the time of writing comes close to collapsing into the times it is describing. This occurs in a particularly poignant way in the last notations made by Langfus, which are discussed in Chapter 3. It is also markedly present in Lewental's history of the Sonderkommando uprising, written in haste shortly after the failed revolt, which we examine in Chapter 4. During moments such as these, re-presentation comes close to presentation *tout court*. In his discussion of Holocaust representation, Berel Lang suggests that if we assume in any representation 'a construct that substitutes the representation for an original, then since no representation can ever *be* that original, representations will also never quite be adequate'.[103] There is always a gap between event and account, and between word and thing. Lang, however, does acknowledge that diaries come near to bridging this gap. He suggests that 'the diary comes as close as representation can to performing the events it cites rather than to describing them; it is an act in, if not fully of, the history it relates'.¹⁰⁴

The Sonderkommando writings are not diaries but they do come close to performing rather than representing occurrences.¹⁰⁵ To suggest that like the diaries they are in but not fully of the history that they relate would, however, be wrong. Several of the writings openly look to be history or to shape how history will be written. All the writings display a degree of historical awareness. The letter by Herman discussed in Chapter 5, for instance, shows concern with how the actions of the Sonderkommando will be perceived and interpreted in the future. In Chapter 1 we also consider how the materiality of the manuscripts additionally renders these documents 'of' the history they relate (although not in a way Lang would necessarily recognise). The extant manuscripts literally have traces of the events that occurred at Birkenau embodied in them. Lang suggests the literal rather than the abstract is the opposite of the representational.¹⁰⁶ The Sonderkommando writings therefore form representations yet possess additional qualities that are not representational. In this context, the chapter on Langfus identifies a strong affective register at work in some of his accounts. He gives a feel for events as well as relaying facts about them. This leads his account to possess an urgent affective intensity, which although incited by the representational dimensions to his writings cannot be equated with them.

Finding the Words

Crucial to working through trauma is finding words for feelings or words able to transmit feelings. Judith Herman describes the difficulty of those who have experienced trauma finding 'a language that conveys fully and persuasively what one has seen'.¹⁰⁷ She might also have added 'what one has felt'. LaCapra proposes that 'trauma brings about a dissociation of affect and representation: one disconcertingly feels what one cannot represent; one numbingly represents what one cannot feel'.¹⁰⁸ Langfus, however, is able to use representation, the figurative powers of language, to realise a kind of reconciliation between words and affects. He therefore engages in working through of the kind recommended by LaCapra, who suggests that:

> when the past becomes accessible to recall in memory, and when language functions to provide some measure of conscious control, critical distance and perspective, one has begun the arduous process of working over and through the trauma in a fashion that may never bring full transcendence

of acting out (or being haunted by revenants and reliving the past in its shattering intensity) but which may enable processes of judgment and at least limited liability and ethically responsible agency.[109]

From within the crematoria, Langfus begins this gruelling process. LaCapra has suggested that denying the Holocaust's representability and, consequently, the idea that the experience of it can be worked through, leads to foreclosure regarding issues of moral agency in contemporary and historical testimonies.[110] This is no doubt why no scholarship has so far examined how some of the authors of the Sonderkommando documents exhibited 'ethically responsible behavior, including consideration for others' in their accounts.[111] In Chapter 3, Langfus's efforts to formulate an ethically considered response to the nightmare situation he found himself in, his striving to perfect a suitable style to express events, are analysed, and his approach to witnessing in this context is compared with that of Gradowski. The ethical quandary Gradowski wrestles with in his account of the murder of a group of women is examined in Chapter 2. Gradowski struggles to do justice to the women's experiences. Agency of the kind identified by LaCapra can therefore be detected in several of the writings. It can also be located in the four photographs taken by Alex of the cremation pits and a group of women on their way to the gas chamber, which are analysed in Chapter 6. Alex displays a similar sense of responsibility coupled with discomfort to Gradowski.

The last photograph Alex took, one of treetops obscured by bright sunshine is almost abstract in appearance. It is close to non-representational and may signal a refusal to index aspects of the killing process. Doubts in the capacity of representation or in its appropriateness feature repeatedly in the Sonderkommando testimonies examined here. Retrospective debates surrounding the Holocaust's representability are therefore prefigured in accounts from within the event. Nadjary, for example, states that '<the dramas that> my eyes have seen are indescribable'.[112] His sentiments anticipate those of Lang, who has argued in the context of Holocaust representation that for some subjects or contents 'no artistic form may be adequate'.[113] Despite his assertion, however, Nadjary continued to search for words to describe what he had experienced. The authors in the Sonderkommando may have questioned representation's capabilities, yet they never abandoned it altogether as their varied efforts at witnessing powerfully demonstrate. Some of their endeavours, such as Gradowski's startling address to the moon discussed in Chapter 2, are remarkably audacious works of literature.

The implications of many of these writings for long-standing beliefs about representability are therefore considerable. A degree of caution nevertheless needs to be exercised. The Sonderkommando were in a unique position within Auschwitz-Birkenau and, as subsequent chapters show, their accounts attest to this. Too often debates about representation are grounded in a homogenous sense of the event. The Sonderkommando, however, specifically bear witness to the horrors of the 'exterminatory universe'. Although some comparisons are possible, it is vital that we make them with a clear sense of the difference between their writings and those of *'l'univers concentrationnaire'* – the 'concentrationary universe' (to use David Rousset's term for the concentration camps).[114] Many theorisations of Holocaust testimony focus on the latter rather than the former. Giorgio Agamben's discussion in *Remnants of Auschwitz* of the figure of the *Muselmann*, 'that to which no one has borne witness', forms a major recent example of this general tendency.[115]

In his preface to *Remnants of Auschwitz*, Agamben does reference the Sonderkommando manuscripts. He draws attention to Lewental's remarks in the Łódź addendum about how unimaginable the horrors he has witnessed are, as a means to demonstrate how Auschwitz generated circumstances in which 'a reality that necessarily exceeds its factual elements' came into being.[116] In a passage not cited by Agamben, Lewental makes a similar observation to his readers about the historical situation at Auschwitz: 'You do not want to <be>lieve in the truth and later you will not believe the true fac<ts> and la<ter you will probably look for> various excuses'.[117] Agamben's focus on the bio-political dimension of the concentrationary universe means that he ignores the importance of language as resistance in the death factory. Philippe Mesnard and Claudine Kahan have examined Agamben's unscrupulous use of Lewental's addendum, detailing how he fails to properly contextualise it and makes loose use of quotations.[118] For Mesnard and Kahan he is also at fault for neglecting the specific horrors of the extermination camp and collapsing the two discrete, if interrelated, camp universes together.[119] The Sonderkommando worked not to attest to the *Muselmänner*, emaciated, near lifeless inmates of the concentration camps, hopelessly subsisting rather than actively staying alive. The writers from the death factory attested instead to victims who were frequently 'overflowing with ardour for life'.[120] They therefore challenge the stereotype of the lethargic, emaciated victim of which the *Muselmann* forms the extreme.

The Sonderkommando regularly witnessed the deaths of these alert, spirited victims, assisting in the destruction of all traces of them. In this environment, each word the Sonderkommando authors committed to paper, each character, as a sign of life, life writing, resisted Nazi efforts at destruction. At times these efforts were designed to preserve self-identity. In Chapter 2, we examine how, through his elaborate description of the process of incineration of bodies, which he links with the extinguishing of the future creative potentials of individuals, Gradowski bears witness to a crucial dimension of the death factory while simultaneously attesting to his powers as a writer, expressing, preserving his own creativity. In Chapter 4, we trace how Lewental, by contrast, was more focused on the lives of others. His account of the Sonderkommando uprising uses words to provide memorials to specific individuals, to safeguard their memories.

The power that even rudimentary writings can possess in this context is brought to the fore in Chapter 5 in which the letters of Chaim Herman and Marcel Nadjary are briefly compared with testimony produced by the last working party of Jews at the extermination camp of Chełmno. All the Sonderkommando writings were composed in fear of dying. Each author knowingly exploited language's capacity for maintaining something of their life after their death. Writing as representation, for them, therefore promised posthumous escape and a substantial victory over Nazi efforts to erase all traces of their crimes. It also provided a means by which to record those crimes. The documents were predominantly composed as deliberate testimony. The chapters that follow seek to explore all these aspects of the 'Scrolls of Auschwitz' and to demonstrate various ways in which they provide a compelling argument for refusing to regard the event as beyond representation.

Having discussed the circumstances in which they were found in this Introduction, we begin with a consideration of the material state of these documents as an aspect of their status as testimony. We move on to consider the most striking of the writers from a literary perspective, Zalman Gradowski. We then show that the other Yiddish writers in the SK also repay close reading: Langfus for affective and ethical dimensions, Lewental for historical and memorial. Next we consider the letters of Herman and Nadjary, which add an extra dimension in relation to understanding the group dynamics of the SK and considering issues related to masculinity. The theme of resistance, and of the power of writing to contribute to it, runs through all these chapters. Finally, we draw upon all of our previous readings to revisit the SK photographs and show that a greater familiarity with the Scrolls reveals aspects that have not been covered by the debate set up by Didi-Huberman.

Notes

1. Andrzej Strzelecki, *The Evacuation, Dismantling and Liberation of Auschwitz* (Oświęcim: Auschwitz-Birkenau State Museum, 2001). The footage taken immediately after liberation by Alexander Vorontsov is included in the film *The Liberation of Auschwitz* (dir. Irmgard von zur Mühlen, 1986). Jacek Lechandro, 'From Liberation to the Opening of the Memorial', <http://en.auschwitz.org/m/index.php?option=com_content&task=view&id=227&Itemid=13&limit=1&limitstart=1>.
2. Andrzej Zaorski, 'Relacja', AŻIH 301/7182. The 'book' that Zaorski found was almost certainly a journal article, perhaps put into a format to present to Rudolf Höss. Günther Niethammer, 'Beobachtungen über die Vogelwelt von Auschwitz/Ost-Oberschlesien', *Annalen des Naturhistorischen Museums in Wien* 52 (1942): 164–99. Niethammer's activities in Auschwitz have inspired a recent novel, Arno Surminski, *Die Vogelwelt von Auschwitz* (Munich, Langen Müller Verlag, 2008).
3. Because we use the word Sonderkommando so much in this book, we will not italicise it. We will also use 'special squad' and 'SK' to refer to them. Although SK was sometimes used to refer to the *Strafkompanie*, the penal work group, it does seem to have also been used for the Sonderkommando.
4. Chaim Wolnerman recalls attending a town meeting in Oświęcim which discussed trying to stop children robbing graves. Those present argued that assistance to the poorest families would help to reduce it. 'Araynfir', in Zalman Gradowski, *In harts fun gehenem* (Jerusalem: Wolnerman, n.d. [c.1977]), 2–3. Andrzej Zaorski expressed considerably more disgust, calling them 'human hyenas' (AŻIH 301/7182). A recent treatment of these sorts of incidents is in Jan Tomasz Gross and Irena Grudzińska Gross, *Golden Harvest: Events on the Margin of the Holocaust* (Oxford: Oxford University Press, 2012).
5. Gideon Greif, *We Wept without Tears: Testimonies of the Jewish Sonderkommando in Auschwitz*, trans. Naftali Greenwood (New Haven, CT: Yale University Press, 2005), 165. Ber Mark, *Megiles Oyshvits* (Tel Aviv: Yisroel-Bukh, 1977), 260–61.
6. Wolnerman, 'Araynfir', 3–4.
7. Wojciech Borowczyk and Gustaw Borowczyk, reports of 5 Nov and 14 Nov 1970, APMO Wspomnienia Tom 78A. Another document found in the grounds of the crematoria in this early phase was not written by the SK, but was rather a diary of a teenage girl in the Łódź ghetto. It was discovered by Zinaida Berezovskaya, a Red Army doctor, in spring 1945, and kept in her family until 2008. Rywka Lipszyc, *The Diary of Rywka Lipszyc*, ed. Alexandra Zapruder (San Francisco, CA: Jewish Family and Children's Services Holocaust Center, 2014). See also <http://www.rywkadiary.org> and <http://jfcsholocaustcenter.org/diary-rywka-lipszyc/>. We briefly discuss the significance of how this diary was hidden in Chapter 3, endnote 2.
8. Jan Kucia, 'Relacja', 2 April 1974, APMO Wspomnienia Tom 73, 156644/420. There was no consistent policy of keeping manuscripts in the archive at Auschwitz itself until the mid-1950s at the earliest. Jonathan Huener, *Auschwitz, Poland, and the Politics of Commemoration, 1945–1979* (Athens: Ohio University Press, 2003), 142.
9. Wojciech Borowczyk and Gustaw Borowczyk, reports of Nov 1970.
10. The location of it is still unknown (Żydowski Instytut Historyczny, personal communication).
11. Franciszek Piper, 'Protokoł', Nov 1980, APMO, Wspomnienia Tom 135.
12. Nachman Blumental, *Shmues vegn der Yidisher Literatur unter der Daytsher Okupatsye* (Buenos Aires: Tsentral Farband far Poylishe Yidn in Argentine, 1966),

178. At the time he was writing, only two shorter texts had been published: the anonymous author's manuscript in 'W otchłani zbrodni', *Biuletyn Żydowskiego Instytuta Historycznego* 9–10 (1954), and Zalman Lewental's commentary on the Łódź ghetto diary in Janusz Gumkowski and Adam Rutkowski (eds), *Szukajcie w popiołach*, trans. Szymon Datner (Łódź: Wydawnictwo Łodzkie, n.d. [1965]).

13. Joanna Nalewajko-Kulikov, 'Trzy kolory: szary: Szkic do portretu Bernarda Marka', *Zagłada Żydów* 4 (2008): 263–84. Bernard Mark, 'Dziennik (grudzień 1965 – luty 1966)', trans. Joanna Nalewajko-Kulikov, *Kwartalnik Historii Żydów* 226(2) (2008): 156–92. Dovid Sfard, 'Prof. B. Mark', *Mit zikh un mit andere: Oytobiografishe un literarishe eseyen* (Yerushalyim: Farlag 'Yesushalayim Almanakh', 1984), 375–79.

14. Joanna Nalewajko-Kulikov, 'The Last Yiddish Books Printed in Poland: Outline of the Activities of Yidish Bukh Publishing House', in *Under the Red Banner: Yiddish Culture in the Communist Countries in the Postwar Era*, ed. Elvira Grözinger and Magdalena Ruta (Wiesbaden: Harrassowitz, 2008), 133. On the anti-Zionist campaign, see Leszek Głuchowski and Antony Polonsky (eds), *1968: Forty Years After, POLIN: Studies in Polish Jewry* 21 (2008). In addition to Esther Mark, a number of other people mentioned in this book were forced out of Poland at this time: Dovid Sfard and Yehoshua Wygodzki (Chapter 2) and Adam Rutkowski and Adam Wein (Chapter 4).

15. On the basis that Esther Mark contributed research to this project and may indeed have been involved with it all along, we will sometimes refer to the book as the Marks' edition.

16. This is a little surprising, as Dovid Sfard, who was a long-time friend of Ber Mark, wrote a short foreword to the Wolnerman edition. 'Eynike zikhroynes vegn Zalman Gradowski', in Gradowski, *In harts fun gehenem*, 6–8.

17. Jadwiga Bezwińska and Danuta Czech (eds), *Wśród koszmarnej zbrodni: Notatki więźnów z Sonderkommando w Oświęcimiu* (Oświecim: Wydawnictwo Państwowego Muzeum w Oświęcimiu, 1st edn 1971; 2nd edn 1973).

18. Zalman Gradowski, 'The Czech Transport: A Chronicle of the Auschwitz Sonderkommando', trans. Robert Wolf, in *The Literature of Destruction: Jewish Responses to Catastrophe*, ed. David Roskies (Philadelphia: Jewish Publication Society, 1989), 548–64; Ber Mark, *The Scrolls of Auschwitz*, trans. Sharon Neemani (Tel Aviv: Am Oved, 1985); Jadwiga Bezwińska and Danuta Czech (eds), *Amidst a Nightmare of Crime: Manuscripts of Members of Sonderkommando*, 2nd edn, trans. Krystyna Michalik (Oświęcim: State Museum at Oświęcim, 1973).

19. See for example: Carlo Saletti (ed.), *La voce dei sommersi: Manoscritti ritrovati di membri del Sonderkommando di Auschwitz* (Venice: Marsilio, 1999); Georges Bensoussan, Philippe Mesnard and Carlo Saletti (eds), *Des voix sous la cendre: Manuscrits des Sonderkommandos d'Auschwitz-Birkenau* (Paris: Calmann Lévy/ Mémorial de la Shoah, 2005); Zalmen Gradowski, *Au coeur de l'enfer: Témoignage d'un Sonderkommando d'Auschwitz, 1944*, trans. Batia Baum (Paris: Kimé, 2001); Teresa Świebocka, Franciszek Piper and Martin Mayr (eds), *Inmitten des grauenvollen Verbrechens: Handschriften von Mitgliedern des Sonderkommandos*, trans. Herta Henschel and Jochen August (Oświęcim: Verlag des Staatlichen Auschwitz-Birkenau Museums, 1996); Zalman Gradowski, *V serdtsevine Ada: Zapiski, naidennie v peple vozle pechei Osventsima*, trans. Aleksandra Polian (Moscow: Gamma Press, 2011). This last Russian edition is the only one to revisit the original manuscripts after the Marks and the Auschwitz museum. Translations of Gradowski's writings have also appeared in Czech, Dutch, Hebrew and Spanish.

20. Dan Stone, 'The Harmony of Barbarism: Locating the Scrolls of Auschwitz in Holocaust Historiography', in *Representing Auschwitz: At the Margins of Testimony*, ed. Nicholas Chare and Dominic Williams (Basingstoke: Palgrave Macmillan, 2013), 27 n. 3.
21. Filip Müller uses the term '*Aschenkommando*', but we have not seen it elsewhere. *Sonderbehandlung: Drei Jahre in den Krematorien und Gaskammern von Auschwitz*, literary collaboration with Helmut Freitag (Munich: Steinhausen, 1979), 222.
22. The most comprehensive history of the Sonderkommando is given by Eric Friedler, Barbara Siebert and Andreas Kilian, *Zeugen aus der Todeszone: Das Jüdische Sonderkommando in Auschwitz* (Munich: Deutsche Taschenbuch Verlag, 2005). Useful summaries are given by Angelika Königseder, 'Das Sonderkommando', *Der Ort des Terrors: Geschichte der nationalsozialistischen Konzentrationslager*, ed. Wolfgang Benz and Barbara Distel, vol. 5: *Hinzert, Auschwitz, Neuengamme*, ed. Königseder (Munich: Verlag C.H. Beck, 2007), 152–53; Franciszek Piper, '*Sonderkommando* Prisoners: Details of their Living Condition and Work', in *Auschwitz 1940–1945: Central Issues in the History of the Camp*, ed. Wacław Długoborski and Franciszek Piper, trans. William Brand, 5 vols (Oswiecim: Auschwitz-Birkenau State Museum, 2000), vol. 3, 180–97. Aside from Gideon Greif's book of interviews *We Wept without Tears*, testimony from Sonderkommando appears in: Miklós Nyiszli, *Auschwitz: A Doctor's Eyewitness Report*, trans. Tibère Kremer and Richard Seaver (London: Penguin, 2012), trans. of *Dr Mengele boncolóorvasa voltam az Auschwitzi krematóriumban*, 1946; Filip Müller, *Eyewitness Auschwitz: Three Years in the Gas Chambers*, trans. Susan Flatauer (Chicago: Ivan R. Dee, 1999), trans. of *Sonderbehandlung: Drei Jahre in den Krematorien und Gaskammern von Auschwitz*, 1979; Marcel Nadjary, *Khroniko, 1941–1945* (Thessaloniki: Etz Khaim, 1991) (no English version available); Leon Cohen, *From Greece to Birkenau: The Crematoria Workers' Uprising*, trans. Jose-Maurice Gormezano (Tel Aviv: Salonika Jewry Research Centre, 1996) (original French manuscript unpublished); Rebecca Camhi Fromer, *The Holocaust Odyssey of Daniel Bennahmias, Sonderkommando* (Tuscaloosa: University of Alabama Press, 1993); Jan Południak, *Sonder: An Interview with Sonderkommando Member Henryk Mandelbaum*, trans. Witold Zbirohowski-Kościa (Oświęcim: Frap-Books, 2009), trans. of *Zonder: Rozmowa z członkiem Sonderkommando Henrykiem Mandelbaumem*, 1994; Shlomo Venezia, *Inside the Gas Chambers: Eight Months in the Sonderkommando of Auschwitz*, trans. Andrew Brown (Cambridge: Polity, 2009), trans. of *Sonderkommando: Dans l'enfer des chambers de gaz*, 2007.
23. Piper, '*Sonderkommando* Prisoners', 180–83.
24. Yehuda Bacon, Mordechai Ciechanower, Sam Itskowitz and Shmuel Taub were all able to make some contact with the SK. USC VHF 26983 Yehuda Bacon (esp. segs. 218, 228–29); Mordechai Ciechanower, *Der Dachdecker von Auschwitz-Birkenau*, trans. Christina Mulolli (Berlin: Metropol Verlag, 2007), 164–67; USC VHF 15815 Sam Itskowitz (segs. 25–26); Shmuel Taub, 'A bintl troyerike zikhroynes', *Maków Yizker Book*, 289–90. See also: Gideon Greif, 'Between Sanity and Insanity: Spheres of Everyday Life in the Auschwitz-Birkenau *Sonderkommando*', in *Gray Zones: Ambiguity and Compromise in the Holocaust and its Aftermath*, ed. Jonathan Petropoulos and John K. Roth (New York: Berghahn Books, 2005), 57.
25. Greif, 'Between Sanity and Insanity', 52. See also: USC VHF 1770 Leon Welbel (seg. 80).

26. Although Miklós Nyiszli writes of the SK feasting on what victims had brought with them (*Auschwitz* 23–24), some members also give accounts of times when they were hungry and thought obsessively about food. USC VHF 1770 Leon Welbel (seg. 74).
27. A number of historians, including Sybille Steinbacher, still repeat this myth. Sybille Steinbacher, *Auschwitz: A History*, trans. Shaun Whiteside (London: Penguin, 2005), 103. Gideon Greif lists seven selections in the history of the SK; in only one of these were they liquidated in their entirety. *We Wept without Tears*, 347 n. 34. The origin of the story has been attributed to Miklós Nyiszli – Nyiszli, *Im Jenseits der Menschlichkeit: Ein Gerichtsmediziner in Auschwitz*, trans. Angelika Bihari, ed. Andreas Kilian and Friedrich Herber (Berlin: Karl Dietz, 2005), 167 n. 39 – but it may also have been a rumour that circulated in the camp, perhaps inspired by the early history of the SK. Leon Cohen recalled being warned not to join as he would be eliminated after three or four months. Cohen, *From Greece to Birkenau*, 29. Rudolf Höss also claimed that he had been given instructions by Adolf Eichmann to regularly eliminate groups. Rudolf Höß, *Kommandant in Auschwitz: Autobiographische Aufzeichnungen*, ed. Martin Broszat (Munich: Deutsche Taschenbuch Verlag, 2013), 242. However, as Claude Lanzmann put it, they were actually 'skilled workers' ('*Facharbeiter*'), and so it was to the camp administration's advantage not to keep killing them. Transcript of interview with Filip Müller, 107 (PDF downloadable from <http://www.ushmm.org/online/film/display/detail.php?file_num=4745>).
28. Randolph L. Braham, 'Hungarian Jews', in *Anatomy of the Auschwitz Death Camp*, ed. Gutman and Berenbaum, 463–66.
29. Henryk Świebocki categorises it as a 'mutiny in the face of imminent danger'. *Auschwitz 1940–1945*, vol. 4, 245–49.
30. Danuta Czech, *Auschwitz Chronicle*, trans. Barbara Harshav, Martha Humphreys and Stephen Shearier (New York: Henry Holt, 1990), 725–26; Friedler, Siebert and Kilian, *Zeugen aus der Todeszone*, 270–80; Igor Bartosik, *Bunt Sonderkommando: 7 października 1944 roku* (Oświęcim: Państwowe Muzeum Auschwitz-Birkenau, 2014), 15–33. Leon Welbel was close to Crematorium V. USC VHF 1770 Leon Welbel (segs. 124–25). Filip Müller was close to Crematorium IV. *Sonderbehandlung*, 250–53. Zalman Lewental and Marcel Nadjary were in Crematorium III. Zalman Lewental, 'Fartseykhenungen', in Ber Mark, *Megiles Oyshvits*, 411–16; Marcel Nadjary, *Khroniko, 1941–1945*, 58–60.
31. Langfus is often listed as among the dead of 7 October, but see Chapter 3 for our reasons for not accepting this claim.
32. Gideon Greif has provided an exhaustive account of the historiography of the Sonderkommando. *We Wept without Tears*, 75–83. There is also a cultural history of their representations. We simply do not have the space to discuss this aspect here, but see: Adam Brown, *Judging 'Privileged' Jews: Holocaust Ethics, Representation, and the 'Grey Zone'* (New York: Berghahn Books, 2013); Dominic Williams, 'The Dead Are My Teachers: The Scrolls of Auschwitz in Jerome Rothenberg's *Khurbn*', in *Representing Auschwitz: At the Margin of Testimony*, ed. Nicholas Chare and Dominic Williams (Basingstoke: Palgrave Macmillian, 2013), 58–84; Dominic Williams, 'Figuring the Grey Zone: The Auschwitz Sonderkommando in Contemporary Culture', (forthcoming). We will also engage with this history of representations at greater length in a further book, provisionally entitled *Figuring the Grey Zone: Representations of the Auschwitz Sonderkommando 1944–Present*.
33. Ota Kraus and Erich Kulka, *The Death Factory: Document on Auschwitz*, trans. Stephen Jolly (Oxford: Pergamon Press, 1966), 152.

34. Nyiszli, *Auschwitz*, 23–25, 144.
35. Primo Levi, 'The Grey Zone,' *The Drowned and the Saved*, trans. Raymond Rosenthal (London: Abacus, 1989), 22–51.
36. On this subject, it is noteworthy that as well as the considerable emphasis placed upon testimonies by the Sonderkommando in *Shoah*, Claude Lanzmann also originally intended to include footage of his extensive interviews with Benjamin Murmelstein (a member of the *Judenrat* at Theresienstadt) in the film. These interviews were subsequently used in the standalone film *The Last of the Unjust* (dir. Claude Lanzmann, 2013).
37. Levi, 'The Grey Zone', 37.
38. Ibid.
39. Ibid., 41. For the Italian original see Levi, *I sommersi e i salvati* (Torino: Einaudi, 1986), 43.
40. Ibid., 35.
41. Ibid., 36–37.
42. Ibid., 36.
43. E.g. Greif, *We Wept without Tears*, 87–88, 122–24, 286–87.
44. Ibid., 22–32, esp. 30–31.
45. Levi, for example, is only referred to in passing because of his suicide (321). Their eagerness to establish the facts may lead them to too great a confidence about what can be known about the SK. For instance, attributing the four photographs to Alberto Errera has less of a firm basis than they seem to believe (see our discussion in Chapter 6). Their narrative of the Sonderkommando revolt is also rather too keen to smooth out any discrepancies between sources: Greeks and Poles give very different accounts of who played prominent roles in the uprising. Compare Zalman Lewental's list of the leaders with those given by Leon Cohen and Marcel Nadjary. Cohen, *From Greece to Birkenau*, 51–53. Nadjary, *Khroniko*, 58.
46. Most notably, the trial of Rudolf Höss in Kraków in 1947 and the Frankfurt Auschwitz Trial of 1963–65.
47. Adam Brown, *Judging 'Privileged' Jews*, 124–30.
48. Ziva Postec, 'Editing *Shoah*', <www.zivapostec.com/Shoah.php> (accessed 6 Feb 2014). See our Conclusion for a more detailed discussion.
49. See Chapter 6 for a detailed discussion of this controversy.
50. Friedler, Siebert and Kilian, *Zeugen aus der Todeszone*, 265.
51. Greif, *We Wept without Tears*, 165, 247, 361 n. 62.
52. Most famously the Vrba-Wetzler report, but also the Rosin-Mordowicz Report. Miroslav Karny, 'The Vrba and Wetzler Report', in *Anatomy of the Auschwitz Death Camp*, ed. Yisrael Gutman and Michael Berenbaum (Bloomington: Indiana University Press, 1994), 553–68.
53. Clandestine lists of various kinds were kept by Otto Wolken, Jan Olszewski, Izydor Łuszczek and Vlasta Kladivová. Tadeusz Joachimowski buried the record books of the 'gypsy camp' in a bucket in its grounds. They were dug up in 1949. Ludwik Lawin and Tadeusz Kubiak made copies of official photos, which were buried near one of the Construction Board buildings, and retrieved in 1946. *Auschwitz 1940–1945*, vol. 3, 260–65.
54. See, for example: Jürgen Kaumkötter et al. (eds), *Kunst in Auschwitz/Sztuka w Auschwitz* (Bramsche: Rasch Verlag, 2005); David Mickenberg, Corinne Granoff and Peter Hayes (eds), *The Last Expression: Art and Auschwitz* (Evanston, IL: Mary and Leigh Block Museum of Art, Northwestern University, 2003); Agnieszka Sieradzka

(ed.), *Szkicownik z Auschwitz/The Sketchbook from Auschwitz* (Oświęcim: Państwowe Muzeum Auschwitz-Birkenau, 2011).
55. Alan Rosen, *The Wonder of their Voices* (Oxford: Oxford University Press, 2010), 110–19.
56. AŻIH 226/326. This poem or song, along with a Polish translation by Marek Tuszewicki, is published in Agnieszka Żółkiewska (ed.), *Słowa pośród nocy: Poetyckie dokumenty Holokaustu* (Warsaw: Żydowski Instytut Historyczy, 2012), 186–89.
57. Andrés Nader, *Traumatic Verses: On Poetry in German from the Concentration Camps, 1933–1945* (Rochester, NY: Camden House, 2007), 33, 67.
58. Otto Dov Kulka, *Landscapes of the Metropolis of Death*, trans. Ralph Mandel (London: Penguin, 2013), 52–55. The poems are translated by Gerald Turner.
59. Alan Rosen, 'Introduction', in *Literature of the Holocaust*, ed. Rosen (Cambridge: Cambridge University Press, 2013), 15–16. Rosen only refers to the Sonderkommando writings and songs as exceptions.
60. Samuel Kassow, *Who Will Write Our History?: Rediscovering a Hidden Archive from the Warsaw Ghetto* (London: Penguin, 2007); Laura Jockusch, *Collect and Record!: Jewish Holocaust Documentation in Early Postwar Europe* (Oxford: Oxford University Press, 2012). Kassow sees a clear continuity between Emmanuel Ringelblum's pre-war historical work and his activity in the Warsaw Ghetto. Laura Jockusch traces the continuities between Ringelblum and post-war survivor historians (see esp. 34–36).
61. Lucjan Dobroszycki, 'Introduction', *The Chronicle of the Łódź Ghetto 1941–1944*, ed. Dobroszycki, trans. Richard Lourie, Joachim Neugroschel et al. (New Haven, CT and London: Yale University Press, 1984), xvii.
62. Renata Laqueur, *Schreiben im KZ* (Bremen: Donat Verlag, 1991).
63. Alexandra Garbarini, *Numbered Days: Diaries in the Holocaust* (New Haven, CT and London: Yale University Press, 2006), 149–57.
64. Leon W. Wells, *The Death Brigade (The Janowska Road)* (New York: Holocaust Library, 1978).
65. Kassow, *Who Will Write Our History?* 287–93, 309–10.
66. <http://www.jhi.pl/en/resistance_and_the_holocaust/international_academic_conference_being_a_witness_to_the_holocaust/75>.
67. Kazimierz Sakowicz, *Ponary Diary 1941–1943: A Bystander's Account of a Mass Murder*, trans. uncredited (New Haven, CT and London: Yale University Press, 2005).
68. Reuven Dafni and Yehudit Kleiman (eds), *Final Letters: From the Yad Vashem Archive* (London: Weidenfeld and Nicholson, 1991), 119–22; Shmuel Krakowski and Ilya Altman, 'The Testament of the Last Prisoners of the Chelmno Death Camp', *Yad Vashem Studies* 21 (1991): 105–24.
69. Władysław Szlengel, *Poeta Nieznany*, ed. Magdalena Stańczuk (Warsaw: Bellona Spółka Akcyjna, 2013), 218–19. For readings of Szlengel see: Bożena Shallcross, *The Holocaust Object in Polish and Polish Jewish Culture* (Bloomington and Indianapolis: Indiana University Press, 2011), 17–35; Frieda W. Aaron, *Bearing the Unbearable: Yiddish and Polish Poetry of the Ghettos and Concentration Camps* (Albany, NY: SUNY Press, 1990), 20–27, 39–53.
70. Blumental's work is discussed in some detail in Jockusch, *Collect and Record!*, 84–120. See also: Mark L. Smith, 'No Silence in Yiddish: Popular and Scholarly Writing about the Holocaust in the Early Post-War Years', in David Cesarani and Eric J. Sundquist (eds), *After the Holocaust: Challenging the Myths of Silence* (London: Routledge, 2012), esp. 58–59.

71. Blumental, *Shmuesn*, 148–65. Aaron, *Bearing the Unbearable*, 119–30. Liebeskind seems to have been moved from Treblinka to Sachsenhausen, where he gave the song to Aleksander Kulisiewicz. Shirli Gilbert, *Music during the Holocaust: Confronting Life in the Nazi Ghettos and Camps* (Oxford: Clarendon, 2005), 151 n. 17. It should be noted that "*Kh shem zikh*" has also been listed as a poem written in the Warsaw ghetto. Żółkiewska, *Słowa pośród nocy*, 335. No explanation is given, however, as to why this edition does not accept Blumental's account of the provenance.
72. Zoe Waxman, *Writing the Holocaust: Identity, Testimony, Representation* (Oxford: Oxford University Press, 2006), 7–87.
73. Garbarini, *Numbered Days*, 93.
74. Tom Lawson, *Debates on the Holocaust* (Manchester: Manchester University Press, 2010), 243–44.
75. George Steiner, *Language and Silence: Essays on Language, Literature and the Inhuman* (New Haven, CT: Yale University Press, 1998), 168.
76. Nathan Cohen, 'Diaries of the Sonderkommando', in *Anatomy of the Auschwitz Death Camp*, ed. Yisrael Gutman and Michael Berenbaum (Bloomington: Indiana University Press, 1998), 522–34; Susan L. Pentlin, 'Testimony from the Ashes: Final Words from Auschwitz-Birkenau Sonderkommando', in *The Genocidal Mind*, ed. Dennis B. Klein et al. (St Paul, MN: Paragon House, 2005), 245–62. See also: Waxman, *Writing the Holocaust*, 81–84. David Patterson makes a number of references to Gradowski in *Along the Edge of Annihilation: The Collapse and Recovery of Life in the Holocaust Diary* (Seattle and London: University of Washington Press, 1999). These are often useful observations but, as Waxman points out, Patterson gives no real consideration to the different circumstances in which Gradowski was writing compared with the other diarists he cites (*Writing the Holocaust*, 54–55).
77. Jerome Rothenberg, *Khurbn and Other Poems* (New York: New Directions, 1989); Dieter Schlesak, *Capesius, der Auschwitzapotheker* (Bonn: Dietz, 2006); Elliot Perlman, *The Street Sweeper* (London: Faber, 2012). Pierre Cholley's oratorio *Le Chant des rouleaux* (2005) includes extracts from Gradowski that are spoken rather than sung. Michael M. Lustigman, *The Kindness of Truth and the Art of Reading Ashes* (New York and Bern: Peter Lang, 1988) might be best grouped with these sorts of responses.
78. Philippe Mesnard, 'Ecrire au dehors de soi', *Des voix sous la cendre*, 215–43. Pavel Polian, 'I v kontse tozhe bilo slovo … (vmesto predisloviya)', in Gradowski, *V serdtsevine Ada*, 47–53.
79. David Roskies, 'Wartime Victim Writing in Eastern Europe', in *Literature of the Holocaust*, ed. Alan Rosen (Cambridge: Cambridge University Press, 2013), 29–31.
80. Lawson, *Debates on the Holocaust*, 244–45. Lawson focuses almost exclusively on the texts included in the Marks' edition, and this causes him to insist too heavily on their saying little about the process of extermination. However, his point that they are providing interpretations and not simply records is an important one.
81. Stone, 'The Harmony of Barbarism', esp. 23–26.
82. Alexandre Prstojevic, 'L'indicible et la fiction configuratrice', *Protée*, 37(2) (2009): 35.
83. See especially David Roskies, *Against the Apocalypse* (Cambridge, MA: Harvard University Press, 1984), 196–224, as well as the texts cited above by Frieda Aaron, Nachman Blumental, Alexandra Garbarini, Samuel Kassow, Andrés Nader and Bożena Shallcross.
84. Dominick LaCapra, *History, Literature, Critical Theory* (Ithaca, NY: Cornell University Press, 2013), 19.

85. Giorgio Agamben's *Remnants of Auschwitz*, for example, argues strongly for refusing the logic of the Holocaust's unsayability as it unintentionally repeats Nazi biopolitics by paring an aspect of human life, bare life, from language. Giorgio Agamben, *Remnants of Auschwitz: The Witness and the Archive*, trans. Daniel Heller-Roazen (New York: Zone, 1999), 157. See also Karyn Ball, *Disciplining the Holocaust* (New York: SUNY, 2008) and Naomi Mandel, *Against the Unspeakable: Complicity, the Holocaust and Slavery in America* (Charlottesville: University of Virginia Press, 2007).
86. See Nicholas Chare, 'The Gap in Context: Giorgio Agamben's *Remnants of Auschwitz*', *Cultural Critique* 64 (2006): 62, Nicholas Chare, *Auschwitz and Afterimages* (London: I.B. Tauris, 2011), 86–87, and Dan Stone, 'The Harmony of Barbarism', 22–23.
87. Shoshana Felman and Dori Laub, *Testimony: Crises of Witnessing in Literature, Psychoanalysis, and History* (New York: Routledge, 1992), 80–81.
88. See Thomas Trezise, *Witnessing Witnessing: On the Reception of Holocaust Survivor Testimony* (New York: Fordham University Press, 2013), 8–39.
89. Felman and Laub, *Testimony*, 84. The Sonderkommando manuscripts have frequently been referred to as diaries (see Chapter 5).
90. Ibid.
91. Cathy Caruth, *Unclaimed Experience: Trauma, Narrative, and History* (Baltimore, MD: Johns Hopkins University Press, 1996), 4.
92. For useful summaries and critiques of Caruth's conception of trauma, see Ruth Leys, *Trauma: A Genealogy* (Chicago: Chicago University Press, 2000), 266–97; and Trezise, *Witnessing Witnessing*, 40–62.
93. Felman and Laub, *Testimony*, 69.
94. Ibid., 57.
95. For an account of Frankl's time at Auschwitz and Dachau, see Viktor E. Frankl, *Man's Search for Meaning: An Introduction to Logotherapy*, 3rd edn (New York: Touchstone, 1984).
96. Felman and Laub, *Testimony*, 82.
97. Lawrence Langer, *Holocaust Testimonies: The Ruins of Memory* (New Haven, CT: Yale University Press, 1991), 20.
98. Ibid., 21.
99. Ibid., 20.
100. Felman and Laub, *Testimony*, 59.
101. For Lanzmann's views on incarnation as truth to traumatic experience, see Claude Lanzmann, 'Le lieu et la parole', in *Au sujet de 'Shoah': Le film de Claude Lanzmann*, ed. Michel Deguy (Paris: Belin, 1990), 414.
102. Langer, *Holocaust Testimonies*, 19.
103. Berel Lang, *Holocaust Representation: Art within the Limits of History and Ethics* (Baltimore, MD: Johns Hopkins University Press, 2000), 19.
104. Ibid., 22.
105. See our discussion of diaries in Chapter 5.
106. Lang, *Holocaust Representation*, 51. See also Lang, 'The Representation of Limits', in *Probing the Limits of Representation: Nazism and the 'Final Solution'*, ed. Saul Friedländer (Cambridge, MA: Harvard University Press, 1992), 300.
107. Judith Herman, *Trauma and Recovery: From Domestic Abuse to Political Terror* (London: Pandora, 1994), 2.
108. Dominick LaCapra, *Writing History, Writing Trauma* (Baltimore, MD: Johns Hopkins University Press, 2001), 42.
109. Ibid., 90.

110. Ibid., 93.
111. Ibid., 91.
112. MS page 5. A Greek transcription of this manuscript is published in Nadjary, *Khroniko, 1941–1945*, 11–23. We use the numbering given to the manuscript pages by the Auschwitz museum. This mistakenly jumps from page 9 to page 11, without a page 10. All translations of Nadjary's letter are courtesy of Nikos Papastergiadis and Chrisoula Stamoulis.
113. Lang, *Holocaust Representation*, 123–24.
114. David Rousset, *L'univers concentrationnaire* (Paris: Éditions de Minuit, [1946] 1981). For a discussion of the potential limits of the usefulness of the term 'concentrationary universe' in relation to Holocaust representation, see Michael Rothberg, *Traumatic Realism: The Demands of Holocaust Representation* (Minneapolis: University of Minnesota Press, 2000), 115–16. See also the analysis of Rousset's term in Griselda Pollock and Max Silverman, 'Introduction. The Politics of Memory: From Concentrationary Memory to Concentrationary Memories', in Pollock and Silverman (eds), *Concentrationary Memories: Totalitarian Terror and Cultural Resistance* (London: I.B. Tauris, 2013), 2–5.
115. Agamben, *Remnants of Auschwitz*, 41.
116. Ibid., 12.
117. Zalman Lewental, 'Hesofe tsum Lodzher ksav-yad', in Ber Mark, *Megiles Oyshvits*, 433.
118. Philippe Mesnard and Claudine Kahan, *Giorgio Agamben: À l'épreuve d'Auschwitz* (Paris: Éditions Kimé, 2001), 23–27.
119. Ibid., 30.
120. Ibid.

Chapter 1

Matters of History

'From now on we will bury everything in the earth.'¹

Teeth

In the final months of the operation of the 'death factory' at Auschwitz-Birkenau, during the same period that the Sonderkommando were composing and concealing their accounts of mass murders, they also hid quantities of teeth in the grounds of the crematoria.² Zalman Gradowski writes that many teeth were buried: 'we, the workers of this kommando, specifically scattered [*tseshotn*] them over the entire area, as many as we could, so that the world could find living signs [*lebedige simonim*] from millions of murdered people'.³ The choice of phrasing here is noteworthy: with the idea of teeth returning as living entities, the text connotes the legends of Cadmus and Jason, who scattered dragons' teeth that came to life as warriors.⁴

Georges Didi-Huberman reads the depositing of physical remains as a means to ensure that 'one day the earth itself could bear witness, archaeologically, to what had happened'.⁵ An aim of the Sonderkommando was certainly to provide hard evidence of the crimes they had witnessed. Teeth enamel, which consists mostly of inorganic material, is the toughest substance in the body. The mineral elements in teeth make them highly resistant to fire, although changes to them will occur if they are subjected to extreme temperatures.⁶ Their resilience makes them an obvious choice of substance to choose as material evidence.⁷ The size of teeth – small, easily concealable – also makes them a wise option.

One of the tasks of the Special Squads was to make the bodies of those who had been gassed disappear. They were instructed to 'burn them, pound their ashes into dust'.⁸ It seems, from Gradowski's description, that for him, and possibly others, burying the teeth was a considered attempt to leave something approaching a *siman muvhak* (distinguishing mark) of individuals in circumstances where identifying the dead was rendered impossible. Another reason, as is clear from the implicit reference to Jason in his account, was to spur revenge. Avenging the deaths of those murdered was, as will be discussed further in Chapter 5, an abiding concern of the squads, a source of psychological sustenance for them.

The teeth are alluded to in the Sonderkommando documents yet they are not usually mentioned or considered in conjunction with them. It is, however, obvious from Gradowski's reference that they should be. They formed part of the same project – an attempt to bear witness to horrendous crimes. The decision to hide teeth in the grounds of the crematoria can therefore inform our understanding of the manuscripts. The teeth, for example, work to corroborate the writings. As will be returned to, they index the killings in a way that writing cannot. Buried alongside the testimonies, the teeth lent physical substance, material facticity, to descriptive passages about mass murder. The Sonderkommando obviously hoped both sets of evidence, physical and textual, would be discovered and considered in tandem.

The teeth, however, as a form of proof, would comprise testimony to murder, testimony retrospectively regarded as unnecessary by some. Claude Lanzmann, for one, believes that providing evidence of the Shoah buys into the logic of negationist thought. Georges Didi-Huberman fell foul of this line of reasoning when he chose to explore the testimonial significance of the four photographs taken at Birkenau by a member of the Sonderkommando; these form the focus of our discussion in Chapter 6. Lanzmann steered the status of these images towards that of evidence and was thereby able to suggest that they acted as proof for that which has no need to be proven.⁹ In a response to the criticism directed at him, Didi-Huberman drew attention to the way the eccentric judgement of proof advanced by Lanzmann and his disciples renders the practice of history, based as it is upon an evaluation of evidence, perverse.¹⁰ This attitude towards substantiation, towards substances of history such as photographic archives, was justified by Lanzmann because archival images lack imagination.¹¹

The archive, for Lanzmann, is an unfeeling repository of information, a collection of facts that can attain the status of truth.¹² This would seemingly apply to the teeth. The calcified remains, an archive cataloguing murder, are made up of mere stuff. The aims behind burying teeth may, however, have gone beyond simply concealing and preserving evidence of atrocity, and hoping this would provoke revenge. The teeth each formed interred traces of distinct identities. Spencer Rogers explains in *The Testimony of Teeth* that 'from teeth alone it may be possible to derive considerable information as to the individual's provenience in terms of early environment, food habits, occupational activities, and medical history'.[13] Rogers goes on to state that 'because of their durability and variability [teeth] provide a highly valuable resource for personal identification'.[14] This is not to suggest that members of the Sonderkommando believed that one day the teeth could be used to discover the identities of specific victims. They would have realised that the immense scale of the killings rendered such acts impossible. It is, nonetheless, conceivable that the men who buried quantities of teeth appreciated their capacity to 'remember', their metonymic potential.

Rogers postulates that 'teeth are a dead person's most assured physical link with his [*sic*] pre-mortem past'.[15] A person's teeth archive aspects of their life after death. The hoped for recovery of the teeth after the war would not have led to the re-establishment of the identity of unknown victims but it would have given a sense of the kinds of people who had been killed, their ages and backgrounds. Each tooth would communicate a trace of an individual existence. It is possible the Sonderkommando recognised the biographical potential of teeth in a similar way to how forensic investigators conceive of a biography 'fossilized into the morphology and texture of bones'.[16] In reality, however, after the liberation of the camp copious quantities of physical remains were discovered, including bone fragments and whole bodies. This caused the teeth buried by the Sonderkommando to go unremarked. They vanished amidst the vast quantities of physical remnants buried and scattered in the grounds of the crematoria and their environs.[17] The writings did not share this fate. Their importance was sufficiently appreciated that many were recovered and preserved or, at least, transcribed. Their historical significance was recognised.

Hidden Histories

Zalman Lewental's testimonies, a lengthy account of the resistance movement at Auschwitz and an addendum to an anonymous manuscript detailing conditions and events in the Łódź ghetto, draw attention to the perceived future role of the historian in examining and interpreting the mass murders perpetrated by Nazis. Lewental recognises the unique perspective the Sonderkommando can provide on the murders, writing:

'surely everyone is interested to know what happened to us, because without us no one will know what happened and when'.[18] As will be discussed at length in Chapter 4, he recognises himself as a historian. His aims are primarily historiographic rather than literary. During his discussion of the burial of documents by the Sonderkommando he states: 'you will find many ***** because we must, until now, until the ***** events ***** transmit everything, ordered chronologically and historically, to the world'.[19] Lewental wishes to compose a narrative that describes events in the temporal order in which they happened. He has a conception of how history should be written.

Dan Stone has drawn attention to how remarkable it is to read the work of a historian writing from within an extermination camp, suggesting that Lewental's words 'produce in the historian today a chilling realization that he or she is being addressed by a colleague from the heart of Auschwitz'.[20] His analysis of how issues raised in Lewental's writings foreshadow later, still ongoing, debates about Jewish collaboration comprises a powerful argument for their contemporary relevance to a historian of the Holocaust.[21] Stone, however, may not exhaust the insights these testimonies and those of the other writers of the 'Scrolls of Auschwitz' can provide for historians. He reads Lewental as providing a 'sober (and sombre) discussion of the hard facts'.[22] Historiography in general has been perceived as a practice that professes 'to privilege "hard" facts or material remains over "softer", ephemeral traces [of the past]'.[23] The documents by Lewental, and the other Sonderkommando testimonies for which the original manuscripts survive, are both accounts of facts and artefacts. Their artefactuality, moreover, contributes to, and cannot be divorced from, the facts they communicate.

History is usually conceived of as a process of narrative making which identifies a story that has already happened, and narrates that story, an act that produces a text, written or otherwise, that comprises the retrospective narrative.[24] Alun Munslow supplements this description of the historian's practice with the category of 'expression', which refers to the form of representation that a narrative may take.[25] Representation is, as Griselda Pollock succinctly summarises, 'something refashioned, coded in rhetorical, textual or pictorial terms'.[26] In this sense, the past never is in history. History is a narrative about the past 'fashioned by historians'.[27] The Sonderkommando manuscripts are no exception. They describe events that have already happened in a variety of different ways, using distinct forms of fashioning. They are, however, markedly dissimilar as histories from the kinds of historicising practised by Stone, or Ber Mark, or in this book. The authors of the documents are writing while the events that they are describing, that they are a part of, are still unfolding. The implications of this cannot be minimised.

Lewental orients his account of the past towards a post-war future that he envisages from within a present of historical significance. His ability to foresee that future is, of course, itself noteworthy. The present he writes from is preserved, in part, in the physical materials that comprise his manuscripts. Here, we wish to focus on the historical significance of the materiality of the extant Sonderkommando manuscripts that are held in the archives of the Auschwitz-Birkenau State Museum.[28] In literary studies, there has been a growing awareness of the insights the physical characteristics of texts can provide. James Daybell, for example, has demonstrated how giving attention to material form productively complements literary analyses of Early Modern English letters.[29] Despite this rise in interest in material matters, the materiality of the documents produced by members of the Sonderkommando, their physical characteristics and conditions, comprises a layer of their textuality that is seldom discussed or appreciated.[30] The physical dimension to the surviving Scrolls harbours testimonial insights of significant value for the historian.

Like the practice of history described by Munslow, this requires recourse to representation, to giving voice to artefacts. In *Mengele's Skull*, while discussing forensics as an art of persuasion, Thomas Keenan and Eyal Weizman state that in classical rhetoric one skill that was practised involved having objects address the forum, those present in the public square during a debate. They suggest of such objects that 'because they do not speak for themselves, there is a need for translation, mediation, or interpretation between the "language of things" and that of people'.[31] This requires resorting to prosopopoeia, a practice that 'endows inanimate objects with a voice'.[32] For Keenan and Weizman, this technique of animating the inanimate echoes the role of the forensic investigator who gives voice to material traces as mute witnesses: who tells their story for them.

The Sonderkommando documents can be read as engaging in prosopopoeia in relation to the teeth buried alongside them. They speak for these mute physical remnants. The documents themselves, however, also possess wordless aspects, such as the different kinds of papers and pigments which, taken together, form the matter of writing. The mute dimension to the manuscripts also includes the patinas they have accrued. Additionally the containers the documents were concealed in to protect them when they were buried exhibit a comparable silence. These types of writing (in the expanded sense of the term) also contribute to the historical record and can, and should, be construed as histories. All these frequently overlooked materials form part of, give form to, the documents, despite a tendency to focus only on their words. There is a disquieting propensity, for example, to detach the words from the inks that form them, the pages that support them. These materials are perceived as means to communicative ends rather than communications that merit attention in themselves. Attending to how words have been appended to a page is, however, informative.

The account of the Sonderkommando uprising written by Lewental is composed in faded black ink in the apparently unlined pages of a notebook. Lewental's other, shorter manuscript can only be viewed as a photographic reproduction as the original is currently undergoing conservation. It is written in a dark ink. The curved corners of the fragmentary pages suggest they too had come from a notebook. Leyb Langfus's *The Deportation* is written in fountain pen in a small ledger. He appears to have used inks of different colours, penning his account over a period of time, as the colour of the script varies from ultramarine to periwinkle to faded grey. There is also a solitary calculation in pencil, an addition which appears to bear no relation to the rest of the document. It may be the only writing in the hand of the ledger's first owner. Additionally, there is a section of script in *The Deportation* where the pen has scratched the paper because Langfus's supply of ink appears to have run out. Two loose leaves from an address book were found within the pages of the ledger. One of these, to be discussed in Chapter 3, contains a draft for the final sentences of the main text. It is written in a now greyed ink. Marcel Nadjary's letter looks to have been composed on plain white paper. It is written in what now appears as blue-black ink. Finally there is a list of groups of people, from various places including the Sonderkommando itself, who were killed at the crematoria in October 1944. The list is written in pencil on a long, thin piece of paper with perforations still intact at the top, suggesting it came from a pad from which sheets could be torn with ease. The page has been pulled from the binding rather than torn out along the perforations. The account by Gradowski that is held at the the Medical and Military Museum in St Petersburg can be studied in facsimile at the Auschwitz museum. It is formed of two parts, a notebook and a letter, both written in ink.

The different kinds of paper and of writing utensils used to produce these manuscripts demonstrate the relative ease with which the Sonderkommando were able to source such materials although their supply was never guaranteed. From the accounts that have survived, there were obviously far more documents produced by members of the squads than were subsequently discovered.[33] It appears there was a period of frenzied creativity, in terms of writing, over the summer months. This was evidently made possible by the still steady influx of prisoners to Birkenau into the late summer of 1944. The list of transports details arrivals from, for example, Slovakia and Terezín. It is possible some of the materials used in manuscripts such as *The Deportation* were sourced from the possessions of these inmates. The presence of items such as fountain pens, inks, notebooks, in their belongings gives indications as to their class and literacy. The subsequent ownership of these personal effects by the Sonderkommando signals their comparatively privileged position within the prisoner hierarchy at Auschwitz. The extant documents demonstrate that the capacity for resistance, written or otherwise, was a product of concessions granted the Sonderkommando. They had access to materials unavailable to most inmates.

The extant manuscripts discussed here are written in three languages. The majority are in Yiddish, Nadjary's letter is in Greek, and the list is in Polish. Additionally, Gradowski's account includes preliminary matter written in Polish, Russian, French, German and English. This preamble to his account comprises a single sentence translated into the five languages: 'Take interest in this document, which contains very important material for the historian'.[34] Gradowski here, like Lewental, frames his writing as being of historical importance. In this context, the choice of languages in Gradowski's prelude and in the writings of the Sonderkommando as a whole are important. The linguistic diversity is easily remarked when looking at the original documents but can become lost in translation. The handwritings of all the authors are distinctive. The Yiddish writings, for example, use cursive Hebrew script and are therefore visibly different from the Greek alphabet employed by Nadjary. The characters of the documents, their distinct calligraphies, vanish when they are typeset. Typefaces homogenise, transforming dissimilar scripts into the same standard lettering.

Handwriting is associated with personality. Each person's style of writing 'displays a particular combination of character forms which gives that handwriting much of its individuality'.[35] The cursive distinctiveness of each of the authors of the manuscripts that have survived is plain to see. Langfus possesses the most curvaceous and florid script. Lewental's characters, by contrast, are thinner, his sentences more regimented, straighter on the page. The letters in Langfus are upright, Lewental's hand sometimes slopes. Nadjary's style of writing is broad and uneconomical in comparison with these two, averaging six or seven words per line. Collectively, as indexes of specific personalities, these writings graphically challenge the assertion of Dori Laub that the Holocaust created a world 'in which one *could not bear witness to oneself*.[36] The distinct scripts reflected back to those who wrote them – who they were, that they were. Laub argues that the Holocaust produced a situation 'in which the very imagination of the *Other* was no longer possible'.[37] Writing by hand, however, provides a means by which to affirm identity.[38] The space of the page, in its otherness to the writer, provides a means by which to assert subjectivity. It grants visible recognition of individuality. The words that address the paper, through their characteristic scripts, therefore possess potency in the original that cannot be found in transcription.

Remnants of Actions

The writings also convey other information about the authors and the conditions under which their texts were produced. In her essay, 'The Forensic Examination of Documents', Audrey Giles describes how handwritings can vary involuntarily for reasons such as 'difficult writing positions, use of alcohol or drugs, stress, or tiredness'.[39] Gradowski draws explicit attention the difficult conditions in which he labours: 'I am writing these words in a moment of the greatest danger and agitation'.[40] The uneven script in Nadjary's letter provides a telling example of such agitation, of the kind of involuntary variation referred to by Giles. It does not appear to have been produced in the same carefully organised way as Gradowski's and Langus's major writings, but seemingly ad hoc and in more of a hurry.[41] On the most legible page of his letter, for instance, the writing undulates, the second and third lines particularly rippled. Nadjary's wavy sentences diverge markedly from, for instance, Langfus's precise jottings or Lewental's even and regular, disciplined lines. His penmanship also lacks their regularity of scale. The size of the script shrinks considerably as the writing carries down the page. It flows and ebbs. The letter is visibly of a different order to the lengthier accounts written in Yiddish.

This is not to say that there are no signs of agitation in the other documents. In Langfus's *The Deportation*, as already mentioned, there seems to be a moment where the ink thins and gives out, yet the author does not stop and wait for a new supply. He carries on, his nib scratching characters into the paper. These abrasive inscriptions, still clearly legible in raking light due to the force with which they were made, show that there is limited ink, that sourcing writing materials is difficult even from a position of qualified privilege. The motivation for Langfus to continue writing at this point rather than waiting for a new supply of ink can only be speculated at. He may have been afraid he would lose his train of thought, his flow, he may have been anxious to complete the document as quickly as possible, or a combination of these two. There are also variations in the size of the writing in *The Deportation* but of a different kind to Nadjary's letter. These changes occur at the tops and bottoms of pages as Langfus reduces his script to make as much use as possible of the paper in his possession. This economy signals recognition of how precious paper is. The difficulty of sourcing writing materials is not referenced in Langfus's account. It deals with more pressing matters. Changes in the handwriting, nevertheless, bear silent witness to the sometimes scarcity of items such as ink and paper. The account's visible compaction, its cramped, hemmed in script, also strikingly echoes the stifling conditions in which Langfus wrote. The arrangement of the words on the page, circumscribed by dire circumstances, comes across as cautiously frantic. The crammed ledger appears to betray its author's careful desperation to attest.

The forcefulness of Langfus's writing as the ink he is using is coming to an end can be understood as a kind of testimony. Continuing to write in this situation, to carve letters into the paper, may signal anxiety or determination, or an amalgamation of these motivations. In Lewental's main account, there is a section of text in which the characters SS stand out.[42] Their substantiality in contrast with the surrounding lettering, words, is plain to see. The abbreviation was either retraced or it was written with more pressure. Either way, greater energy was visibly expended in penning these two letters. This forceful moment evinces either a desire for precision or, perhaps, an expression of hatred. Given the dominant outward emotion in the Sonderkommando was that of vengefulness towards their Nazi oppressors, the vehemently penned letters may well be the product of loathing. The handwriting possesses feeling in a way typescript cannot capture (even if retrospectively identifying specific emotions and stimuli with certainty in the original is not possible). The extant manuscripts index not just the personalities of their authors. They also manifest the affective circumstances in which they were written. This affective register operates in excess of the overt narrative.

The feelings of Langfus or Lewental as exhibited in the documents, as extrapolated here, are not fact. The character of all handwriting is overdetermined and uncertain. The feelings, however, can function to tinge facts. Hayden White has written of how Primo Levi's figurative prose brings feeling to fact.[43] The handwritings can be seen to form a comparable source of emotional vitality. Their flourishes and stresses bring a figurative aspect to the graphic. The form that the writings possess can be studied in detail, the inkless striations in *The Deportation*, for instance, are clearly visible, yet their feelings are not concrete. The lack of analytical objectivity that necessarily accompanies attending to the emotional tenors of the manuscripts may make their value to some historians appear questionable, particularly in the context of the Holocaust where, as Stone has observed, the field is 'methodologically quite staid'.[44] The events at Birkenau were, however, keenly felt.

Lewental writes of the struggle to preserve emotion, to hold onto repugnance, in the early days of the work of the Sonderkommando. He states that there were only a few 'individual <people> who did not in any way allow themselves to be influenced by the habit, did not allow it to become completely easy, did not get carried away'.[45] Many members of the Sonderkommando evidently became, or professed to become, numbed to the horror. In such a situation, feeling itself becomes an act of defiance. The production of the documents formed one way to foster such emotion. The act of writing, as much as the words produced by it, constituted a vital means for expressing feeling. The recognition that emotions were present, informing the curls and pressures of each script, is crucial. It has historical importance. Only by attending to the actual manuscripts can some aspects of these states of mind be adequately retraced.

Words can describe emotions, stand for them, and refer to them. The play of forces of hand, pen and page that involves each word, however, comprises another equally compelling register of feeling. There is, for example, a fierce sense of pride evident in the way Nadjary carefully spells out ἙΛΛΆΣ or HELLAS in his letter (see Figure 5.1 in Chapter 5). The rest of the script is cursive but this word is in block capitals. Writing it like this has necessitated the pen repeatedly leaving and returning to the page. Given the difficulties it seems Nadjary had writing this document, the attention he devotes to this name, a term for his homeland, is remarkable. The word accrues affective value through its visible difference from the surrounding script. Printed words are too discrete to vehicle sentiment, nationalist or otherwise, of this kind. It is emotion that is embodied in traces of gestures, expenditures of energy, and time taken, as indexed by the handwriting. Fully appreciating the value of Nadjary's letter as a historical document requires attending to the temperaments of the writing.

This attention is frequently bound up with the process of trying to read some of the more damaged parts of these manuscripts. In its not-quite decipherability, its promise of being readable and resistance to being spelled out, the writing becomes something else. Staring at fragments of words and trying to find the letters that would join them together into sense, or to distinguish between what marks were made from human intention and what by dirt and damp, retracing the route taken by the pen, give rise to an eerie feeling. Craig Dworkin writes that in reading a near-illegible text 'the reader is repeatedly made aware of the most minute aspects of visual perception, which the habitual reader can usually afford to ignore: the general situation of the reading space, the sculptural dimensions of the book, and the physicality of the reader's entire body, which can no longer be ignored in an illusion of direct mental engagement with the writing'.[46] At such times it is not so much the meaning of the words that calls up a response in the researcher, but precisely those moments when the words only exist as marks, records of gestures made. One body is responding, or attempting to respond, to another.

Reading the 'Scrolls of Auschwitz' in this way requires attending to their sub-narrative dimensions, inhabiting the writings, retracing the motions of the hands that composed them. Rebecca Schneider has suggested that if a gesture recurs across time, is reiterative, it may pulse with multiple temporalities.[47] The act of following the steps taken by a hand that was writing, reproducing its motions in the present, may lead to a situation in which then and now imbricate. Schneider argues that 'an action repeated again and again and again, however fractured or partial or incomplete, has a kind of staying power – persists through time – and even, in a sense, serves as a fleshly kind of "document" of its own recurrence'.[48] Repeated gestures of this kind potentially provide affective insights and therefore have an evidentiary status. The feelings behind the handwritings in the manuscripts cannot, we have already acknowledged, be identified with certainty although it is clear that they are there.

The precarious status of the emotions present in the documents may not necessarily be negative. Dominick LaCapra has strongly argued for an empathic response towards Holocaust testimony. LaCapra perceives it 'as a counterforce to numbing' that tries 'in limited ways, to recapture the possibly split-off, affective dimension of the experience of others'.[49] This kind of empathic response involves responding to the traumatic experience of others without appropriating their experience.[50] LaCapra terms this process 'empathic unsettlement'. It does not involve merging or identification with the suffering of others, rather it comprises a knowing through intimate distance. Empathic unsettlement implicates the self in the past.[51] It generates a limited affective understanding, providing an insightful, yet imperfect, feel for the feelings of others. The historian who is open to the emotional tenor of the handwritings of the Scrolls can gain awareness of this kind. It is, of necessity, partial and subtle.

Frames of Reference

The Scrolls were all buried within containers of various kinds. These vessels are now mostly lost. Zalman Gradowski's manuscripts that are now in Russia were buried in an aluminium canteen manufactured in Germany.[52] The canteen has been preserved alongside the documents in St Petersburg. Gradowski's *In the Heart of Hell* was concealed inside a tin box that was unearthed. This box has disappeared.[53] Chaim Herman's letter was hidden in a bottle that was subsequently discarded. Langfus's *The Deportation* was in a broken glass container when it was exhumed.[54] This damaged receptacle was presumably thrown away. The notebook, known for many years as 'The Anonymous Manuscript', was buried in a jar.[55] The manuscripts by Langfus and Lewental that were interred together were wrapped in oilcloth and protected by a large glass jar, also referred to as a water flask with a tin lid.[56] Its whereabouts are not known although a photograph exists of it. Lewental's addendum and the Łódź manuscript were secreted in a mess tin. This can no longer be located. Nadjary's letter was stashed in a thermos flask placed in a leather briefcase. These have both been preserved by the Auschwitz museum.

The objects that the Scrolls were buried within have attracted little interest to date. They were mundane items that served a simple function, to protect the writings. These everyday objects were temporarily pressed into service as elaborate dust jackets, designed to safeguard the documents they enclosed. Once the manuscripts were discovered their purpose was at an end, they were out of the frame. The materials used to fashion these wrappers are, however, significant. They were evidently sourced from the possessions abandoned in the undressing room by those sent straight to the gas chambers from transports or, in the case of the mess tin, and possibly the canteen, from camp supplies.[57] If the bottles and jars were carried to the gas chamber then presumably they still contained food taken to provide sustenance on the journey to the camp. The briefcase may well have carried papers felt to be important, possibly also the blank pages Nadjary wrote on. He could have composed his letter opportunistically, motivated to act spontaneously by the contents of the case. His method of protecting his writing was one of the most ingenious yet may have been impromptu.

The varied containers that held the writings are worthy of attention in that they form part of the story of those documents. The manuscripts could not have survived without protection of this kind. In this, the receptacles become comparable to the zone of shadow Didi-Huberman discusses in relation to two of the photographs surreptitiously taken by the Sonderkommando member Alex. This shadow, which is formed by walls of the crematorium, is sometimes removed in reproduction through cropping. Didi-Huberman denounces this practice as it deprives the pictures of their phenomenology, 'everything that made them an *event* (a process, a job, physical contact)'.[58] Removing the shadow 'is almost to insult the danger that [Alex] faced and to insult his cunning as *résistant*'.[59] The overlooking of the modes of concealment of the Scrolls, the effort and resourcefulness involved in their safeguarding, is not of the same order as ignoring Alex's perilous actions. Nevertheless, the lost jars and bottles, the preserved canteen and flask, speak of desire and determination to leave behind communications. These modest objects also harbour affective force.

Additionally there is a significant phenomenological import of the kind described by Didi-Huberman attached to these materials if efforts are made to contextualise their interment. This import, like that of the photographs, can be imaginatively reconstructed. The careful placement of documents in different repositories, the cautious burial of the containers with their precious consignments while undertaking 'work' close to sentry posts, can be envisioned. The location where Nadjary's briefcase was discovered, for instance, is carefully recorded. It was a position which would have been shielded from the view of the main camp complex, with the crematorium providing cover. Nadjary's chosen spot was, however, relatively close to a guard tower. There was therefore an obvious danger involved in burying documents. The artefacts the manuscripts were concealed in do not tell this story for themselves. They are mute. It is, however, possible to mindfully re-enact the circumstances in which these objects were deposited in the grounds of the crematoria, and thereby speak on their behalf.

Andrzej Zaorski, the doctor who discovered Chaim Herman's letter in February 1945, responded in just this kind of way. In his account of finding it in a bottle on top of a pile of ashes, he surmised that it was designed to travel outside the boundaries of the camp. The ashes were intended to be dumped in the river Soła, and Zaorski suggested that the bottle was placed among them intentionally. Once in the river, the bottle would then have floated away, to be found and fished out. In his speculating, Zaorski attempted imaginatively to reconstruct the ingenuity with which Herman approached the task of communicating with his family from inside the crematoria.[60] Whether the conjectures are correct is questionable, given that Herman refers in the letter to his intention to bury it.[61] The container and what it contained, however, were prompts to a creative reconstruction of past events.

Once concealed beneath ash and soil, the papers, metals, silica and textiles did not remain inert. They reacted and changed. In the case of Nadjary's briefcase, the time the glass of the thermos was pressed tight against the leather has left the brown skin of the bag impressed by a spectral image of the flask. It has caused a series of cream-coloured ridges to appear along the length of the case. This ghost image is reminiscent of the impressions left upon the paper of the Łódź diary by the ornate piece of metalwork that Lewental buried with it. This bracelet was made in the Łódź Ghetto and shows scenes from it. Lewental would seem to have chosen this artefact precisely because of its representative potential. He looks to have deliberately accumulated material about the ghetto which could then form an archive. The diary, in this instance, would speak for the bracelet. The bracelet, however, like the writing was a form of documentation. The burial of the bracelet, like that of the teeth, demonstrates recognition by members of the Sonderkommando that documents are things, but things also document.

Remastering Testimony

The documents all display discolouration, some of it caused by disintegrating materials, chemical reactions. They all exhibit what Jane Bennett terms 'vital materiality'. Bennett formulated this expression as a means to think of things 'as actants rather than as objects'.[62] The vital materiality of the writings has led them to degrade. Ink has faded and blurred because of humidity in the storage containers. Paper is decayed because the alum-rosin sizing agent reacted with moisture, generating highly corrosive sulphuric acid while the manuscripts were buried. Sizing is a process used to make paper hydrophobic; it enables pages to accept ink without it spreading and blurring. This process, however, also reduces the resistance of the paper to deterioration. Fostering legibility reduces paper's lifespan. The degeneration of the writings has led the Auschwitz museum to work hard to conserve the documents. These efforts have, historically, not always worked as well as they might. The manuscripts by Langfus and Lewental that were discovered together in 1962 had been damaged by damp, rendering approximately 40 per cent of the text illegible. The pages were dried and then laminated. This conservation process involved inserting each page between tissue and sheets of cellulose acetate, and then placing it in a heated press to fuse the plastic together. The procedure strengthened the individual sheets of paper and literally made them untouchable.

The laminated documents are hard to read. Despite the presence of tissue, there is still a gloss, a luminous 'noise', which interferes with visibility. The tissue also veils the writing on each page, visibly mutes it. Additionally, it is probable that the plastic, which is impressed into the paper, is degenerating as cellulose acetate is unstable. There is visible evidence of this in the bubbling and warping that some of the plasticised sheets exhibit. The decision to preserve the manuscripts in this way must therefore, retrospectively, be considered a bad one. The museum had abandoned this way of treating documents by the time Nadjary's letter was happened upon in 1980. The letter was, however, also conserved. Its sheets have been reconstructed. At the time of its discovery, the pages of the letter had tears along their edges. These have now been filled and mended. The paper was also curled, discoloured at its peripheries by detritus and foxing. It has now been flattened and bleached so that it is more even in colour – a near-constant beige. The letter was not simply preserved, maintained in the physical form in which it was disinterred, it was also restored. Procedures that are irreversible were used to make the paper 'whole' again. The ink that has faded to illegibility can never be recovered, yet the paper now has minimal discolouration and possesses sharp edges and no gaps.

The museum is also conserving the other manuscripts in its possession. If the Nadjary letter is treated as a template then this is cause for considerable concern. Langfus's *The Deportation* and Lewental's addendum both exhibit deterioration and imperfections which comprise a crucial aspect of their testimonial value. It is an aspect that has now, to a considerable extent, been lost in Nadjary's letter. It is, however, perversely preserved in the laminated documents. These protect each page's imperfection by way of their impenetrable marring. The staples that held together the notebook Lewental wrote in were corroded because of the humidity, and this caused rust to spread to the paper and eat into it making it appear burned. The iron oxides produced holes and also substantial brown blotches reminiscent of Rorschach tests. The destructive effects of the staples are duplicated in facing pages leading the fissures in the paper to occasionally possess symmetry that coincidentally resembles an unsettling visage. If the manuscript had been discovered later it is likely it would have been treated in similar fashion to the letter, with discolouration minimised and breaks mended.

The decay that the manuscripts each exhibit is, however, a crucial part of their story. It indexes their necessary concealment. The patina that many of the pages of the ledger containing *The Deportation* have accrued is also not insignificant. Gradowski refers to writings lying 'in pits, soaked in blood, bones not always entirely burnt, and bits of flesh'.[63] Its burial in these conditions has led the manuscript to bear physical traces of the murders committed at Birkenau. The contact it had with wet soil once the jar it was stowed in had broken has left it tinged with the crimes the Nazis sought to conceal. *The Deportation* carries more than descriptions of murder. It forms a resting place. The pages are impressed with evidence of crimes, stained by the dead. The forensic investigator Edmond Locard wrote of the microscopic debris that formed trace evidence as a 'mute witness'.[64] This testimony, however, can be made to speak if it is examined and its importance recognised. Locard goes on to define dust as 'an accumulation of debris in a state of pulverisation'.[65] The 'dust' that clings to the pages of the ledger comes from the scene of a crime against humanity.

The driving force behind the museum's ongoing restoration programme is likely to be an inability to 'tolerate a creative work that has been diminished in its intelligibility'.[66] The tears and stains that mark the documents are perceived to mar them. They act as impediments to legibility. The historical importance of the manuscripts lies solely in the written accounts they bear. The aim is therefore to make accessing these words as easy as possible. Nadjary's letter was evidently folded to fit into the thermos. In its original condition this was obvious. Now, however, each page is flush. Nelly Balloffet describes paper that has not lain flat as acquiring 'a memory of the folds'.[67] This memory in Nadjary's letter has now been suppressed. The restoration process is, intentionally or not, amnestic. In the determination to remember more clearly, a material forgetting occurs.

The alternative to the purity of communication that the Auschwitz museum seems to want to achieve is not to choose some other moment at which the documents existed and try to get back to that state, but rather to acknowledge the different temporalities that are embedded in them: not just the moment when they were written, or when they were concealed, or when they were found, but also the whole history of how they were treated and what that tells us of the memory of the Shoah in Poland. Of course, that does not preclude recognising the differences between these moments and at times perhaps attempting to reconstruct and focus on one of them rather than another; but it also means that no other moment is just interference that simply needs to be seen through or edited out.

When Lewental framed his account as a work of history, he did not envisage that another text would be written upon, across, through the same pages he had penned. The damage caused by the moisture and staples, however, does constitute another kind of historical narrative. It is one that merits recognition and respect. The material stories borne by the extant manuscripts describe the effects of their concealment and reinforce the dire conditions that made such secrecy necessary. Some documents also carry remnants of crimes. Conservation practices threaten to stifle these powerful embryonic narratives. The unrestored documents embody a moving symbiosis between two forms of narrative. The materiality of the manuscripts informs, inflects the writing. In the context of trauma, LaCapra has argued against modes of representation that 'in their very style or manner of address tend to overly objectify, smooth over, or obliterate the nature and impact of the events they treat'.[68] He suggests that any acceptable account of 'traumatic experiences must in some significant way be marked by trauma or allow trauma to register in its own procedures'.[69]

A manuscript such as *The Deportation* or Lewental's account of the Sonderkommando revolt, through its contingent caesuras, its broken prose, demonstrates the kind of fidelity to traumatic experience that LaCapra demands. Trauma 'creates a gap or hole in experience' that is mirrored by the perforated style of the manuscripts.[70] The 'noise' in these accounts should therefore not be treated as a deficit but as a vital means of communicating the catastrophic nature of the events endured by the Sonderkommando. When Stone suggests Lewental's 'texts are hardest to read, with many gaps', he is not only referring to practical but psychic adversity.[71] The fissures in the writings, the ink that has bled and blurred, the fractures in the paper, combine to figure trauma for the reader. The ruptures also disrupt narrative coherence. Narrative, as James Young notes, seems to 'resolve' violent events, to transform them into accounts that hang together rather than acknowledging them as things that stand apart, defying description. He suggests that 'once written, events assume the mantle of coherence that narrative necessarily imposes on them, and the trauma of their unassimilability is relieved'.[72] The physical phenomena we are referring to prevent the narratives from readily assuming this salvific status. The materiality of the writings acts to prevent their traumatic content from being allayed. This materiality is one that is muffled by invasive restoration and dulled when the documents are read in transcription. The traumatic history of the manuscripts is embedded within them. Their physical condition is of interest.

Touching the Past

LaCapra associates archival research with 'excessive objectification, purely formal analysis, and narrative harmonization'.[73] The historian who engages in such activities is conceived here as someone who sifts through documents, extracting pieces of information which are then coolly combined into a coherent account of the facts of an event. This detached approach leads to the production of histories that are unfaithful to traumatic experiences. Many historians, however, would argue that it is impossible to write history without this distance. History, as discussed earlier, is a representational practice, one that requires operating at a remove from the past. The historian figures from out of the gap between present and past. There are still some historians who believe that 'history is "concealed" in the facts and that telling a history is a matter of digging out and making explicit what is already there'.[74] The majority, however, would concede that history is created rather than discovered. It emerges from out of a representational practice that produces knowledge of the past based on justified beliefs. History is a 'textual substance' that involves 'authorial assumptions and narrative choices'.[75]

The Sonderkommando manuscripts from Birkenau, however, as already mentioned, form narratives, histories, written from within the still unfolding events they reference. The physical materials out of which the accounts are composed comprise historical artefacts with evidential significance. The manuscripts were created from out of stuff with historical import. Munslow avers that 'only if historians believe they can escape "back to the past" would they seriously doubt that they write explanatory narratives in the here and now'.[76] He also suggests that 'the only way a historian can conflate the past *with* history is by ignoring the situation that the past *and* history are ontologically distinct'.[77] The writers of the Scrolls, however, think from a future that is yet to arrive: 'Let the future judge us on the basis of what I have written'.[78] They envisage the horrific events they are caught up within becoming the past, yet know that past is still their present. The histories they compose therefore pose a challenge to how the writing of history is conventionally conceived. Writing about Lewental's work of history in the present, for example, is obviously to look back at the past. We write from a distinct moment. Lewental himself, however, occupies a complex position in relation to the separation of past and present, of the past and the history of the past.

The past and the process of history writing, the past and history, collided for a brief span of time at Birkenau. Munslow contends that 'the past can be arbitrarily located in physical objects but the notion of "pastness" does not inhere in them – it is a nature, a quality, or a worth imposed upon them and which we call "history"'.[79] The writings of the Sonderkommando and the teeth they buried, however, were regarded as a yet-to-become past that formed a kind of history and that would also be used for the production of later histories. Lewental could be said to have written a history of his present. The histories brought into being in the grounds of the crematoria at Birkenau refer to events that have already happened. They are created retrospectively, yet never entirely so. The examination of the significance of the handwritings, for example, demonstrates how even as past times were being committed to paper, narrative choices being made, the present was also becoming history. The difficult conditions of the production of the documents were being graphically recorded at the same time as words were describing an earlier period. History and the past conjoin, for instance, in the strained script of Nadjary's letter. The presence of the present in the ink, a nascent history, cannot be pared from the past it refers to. In a different way, history and past also come close to fusing in Langfus's 'Notes', discussed at length in Chapter 3.

The anonymous list detailing the arrival of transports at the gas chamber, which was buried with manuscripts by Langfus and Lewental, forms another example of how writing can constitute a space in which past and history blend and clash. This list gives the order in which a series of mass murders were committed at Birkenau in October 1944. It is seemingly a simple set of facts, a basic narrative composed retrospectively, that details crimes. The way the list is reproduced in *The Scrolls of Auschwitz* reinforces such an interpretation.[80] The visual appearance of the list, however, shows ways in which it also provides commentary on contemporary circumstances (Figure 1.1). It begins on 6 October (Mark misreads this as the 9th) with the specifics of a transport of eight hundred men from Germany. There are then twenty-six further lines, each detailing

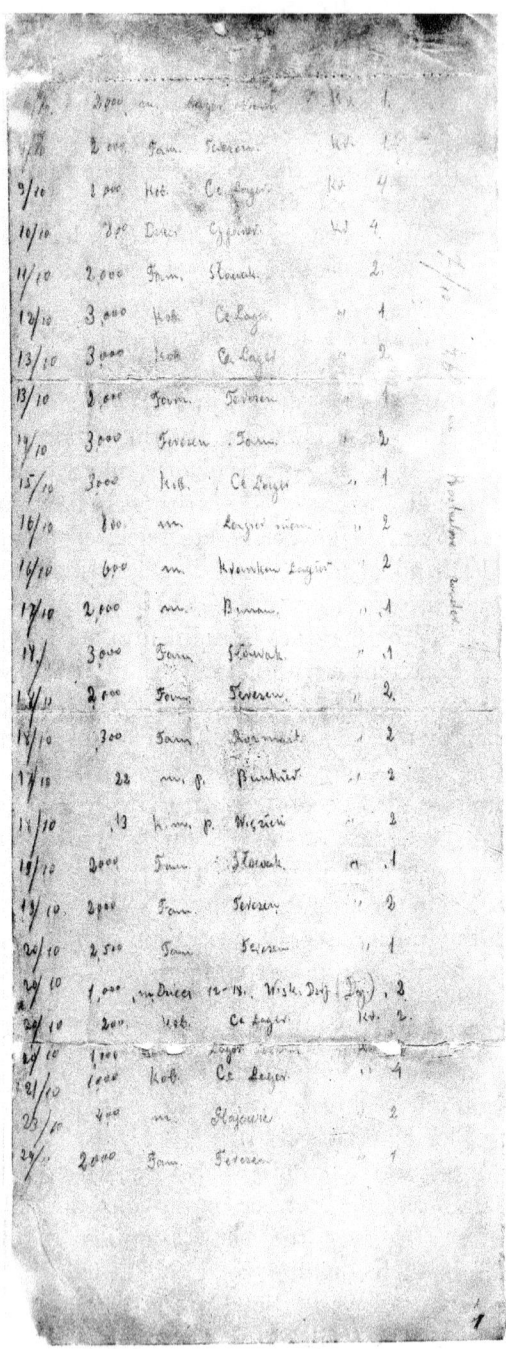

Figure 1.1. Pencilled list in Polish, found with Zalman Lewental's account. The shooting of 460 members of the SK is recorded on the right-hand side.

the date of arrival and make-up of a particular transport, and also in which crematorium they were murdered. It ends on 24 October with a transport of two thousand people, families from Terezín. These horizontal lines, written in chronological order from earliest to latest, fill the bulk of the sheet of paper. There is, however, another line of information written perpendicular to them. This line gives the particulars of the execution of 460 members of the Sonderkommando on 7 October.[81]

The line appears to have been added as an afterthought. It should be second on the list in terms of chronological order. It is, however, visibly detached from this linear history. It is out of sequence, carefully, deliberately divorced from that series. There was still room to add the line at the bottom of the list. The writer, however, chose not to, chose instead to turn the page. The reader must repeat this action, physically tilting the paper to help to decipher the line. This motion forms a kinetic affirmation of the difference of the Sonderkommando from the other inmates on the list. The placement on the page of the details of the Sonderkommando deaths also visibly attests to the group's differential status – apart yet a part. Through the way he recorded this information, the member who wrote this list reveals how the Sonderkommando perceived their relationship to other prisoners. His actions index his present situation even as he records events in the past. In the list, history and past, present and former, intersect. The effects of this extraordinary fusion of past and history can be felt in the present. In handling the documents, there is a powerful perception of encountering the past. Fiona Candlin claims in *Art, Museums and Touch* that touching timeworn artefacts can produce 'a deep sense of intimacy and emotional involvement'.[82] Holding the manuscripts, studying these ravaged materials, seems to provide a tentative, unprompted conduit of this kind: one to Birkenau back then.

Sublime Historical Experience

As part of *Sublime Historical Experience*, Frank Ankersmit describes situations in which an experience of the past becomes possible in the present. This experience is unmediated. During his explanation of Richard Rorty's conception of language and its relation to experience, Ankersmit suggests that 'language and the world are as closely tied together as the two sides of a sheet of paper, and there is just as little room for the autonomy (and the priority) of experience as there is between the front and the back of that sheet'.[83] The use of paper as the figure through which to explain this relationship is telling. Paper, wood pulp, organic material, is of the physical world. It is usually used for the inscription of words, providing a ground upon which, and through which, language can emerge. Paper is also, of course, always already of significance. Ankersmit ably demonstrates its figurative potential here. The blank sheet still signifies – it signals civilisation, technological advancement, or, here in Ankersmit, the relationship between signs and their referents.

The paper, however, is not merely an expression of language. Judith Butler's subtle reflections on the relationship between matter and signification are informative in this context. Butler argues that the materiality of bodies is not 'simply and only a linguistic effect which is reducible to a set of signifiers'.[84] The signifier is itself material. Butler goes on to suggest that materiality 'is bound up with signification from the start'.[85] Materiality and signification are indissoluble. There is, however, a tendency to overlook some signifiers as insignificant. In relation to the Sonderkommando manuscripts, for example, the words have been read as what matters. They are viewed as dissociable from the ink, from the traces of physical energy and force, of affective vigour, that sustained them for so long beneath the ash and soil. It is this ink that, in significant part, caused history to suffuse the accounts of the past that the authors of the documents were composing. The ink draws history and past together. It is also what pulls the historian, in the present working in the Auschwitz archive, towards the past.

Ankersmit does not share Butler's (or Rorty's) conception of language. He favours ink unaccompanied by words, thoughtless, unformed matter. Ankersmit believes substances such as paint (and, presumably, pen and ink) can provide 'an authentic experience of the world', one dissociated from language.[86] They provide a means of cultivating transparency between language and reality. Ankersmit argues that 'the loss of the past *is* this loss of transparency in the relationship between language and reality'.[87] If a sublime indeterminacy in the relationship between language and reality is brought about then 'at that very moment the past makes its entrance in our minds'.[88] It could be said that such a situation of indeterminacy is fostered by the manuscripts from Birkenau. They represent the past to us yet their modes of representation are that past. The manuscripts possess a dimension that is beyond representation, that is not narration or narratable. This non-narrative element forms the catalyst for sublime historical experience.

In such experiences, subjectivity is temporarily placed in abeyance, ceases to be, causing a person to be overwhelmed by feeling or experience.[89] Ankersmit contends that intense pain can lead to a comparable 'movement toward an experience without a subject of experience'.[90] These forms of experience comprise moods, feelings. They are, for Ankersmit, beyond language.[91] Ankersmit believes that it is language, or rather its loss, which renders the registration of this affect possible. In this context, the Sonderkommando documents can be seen to enact a staging of this loss through their gaps and inky bleeds. They are not, however, an illustration of Ankersmit's idea. They do not simply represent what sublime historical experience 'looks like'. Their blurred and pitted surfaces nurture such an experience.

Ankersmit does not believe historical documents can afford or cultivate sublime histories. He states 'the experiential basis that documents undoubtedly present permit[s] the historian to develop a construction of the past but not a *re*-construction of the past (as it actually has been)'.[92] He adds that documents 'may function as *evidence* for a certain conjecture of what the past may well have been like but can never amount to a revelation of its actual nature because we can never check these conjectures against the past itself'.[93] His preferred example in terms of cultural artefacts that can generate the conditions for sublime historical experience is an artwork, *Arcade with a Lantern* by Venetian painter Francesco Guardi, which he claims grants him access to the mood of the *Ancien Régime*, one of boredom.[94] For Ankersmit, 'sublime historical experience is the experience of the past breaking away from the present'.[95] Past and present are not yet discrete categories. There is not yet 'any distance between the two of them'.[96] The past is, however, coming into being. In such a moment, 'the past is then born from the historian's traumatic experience of having entered a new world and from the awareness of irreparably having lost a previous world forever'.[97]

Ankersmit does not believe the Holocaust forms an event of this kind. It did not constitute a crisis in which Western civilisation 'experienced the traumatizing loss of an old world because one was forced to enter a new one'.[98] He contends that 'there is no evidence, as yet, that the Holocaust has been such a traumatic experience in *this* sense'.[99] This makes the event different from, for example, the mediaeval past or the French Revolution. The Holocaust did not produce a collective trauma in which civilisation felt it was permanently leaving a previous identity behind, instituting a gap, producing a past for itself. This interpretation of the collective effects of the Holocaust is highly questionable. Ankersmit's deductions about the impact of the event are hampered by his homogenising tendencies. For him, civilisation either is or is not traumatised by a historical event. There is no room for nuance. There is no admission that the French Revolution, for example, probably had no noticeable impact on the self-identity of many in Europe, hardly registered for them. There is no acknowledgment that for Europe's Jews, a crucial element in its civilisation, the Holocaust did form a historical rupture, a sublime historical experience. There is no recognition that, as Alon Confino examines, for many living in the 1930s and 1940s comparing the rise of Nazi Germany with the French Revolution occurred with regularity.[100] Confino also suggests that the Holocaust is now regarded, like the French Revolution, as a 'historical novum'.[101]

A number of thinkers have described the Holocaust as instantiating a historical rupture. Arthur Cohen argues powerfully that the event should be understood as productive of a tremendum. The tremendum is 'the abyss of the historical'.[102] It is 'a horror that exceeds the category of horror and is, for that reason, inadmissible to some, even to many, whereas the horror acknowledged by all (the dropping of atom bombs or the use of genetically deforming contaminants in Vietnam) is in part neutralized and divested of its horror'.[103] Jean-François Lyotard similarly argues that a chasm exists, one registered through art. Art persists after Auschwitz yet it has changed character, attesting in the present only to doubt in its own procedures. After Auschwitz, 'it does not say the unsayable, but says that it cannot say it'.[104] The unsayable here is the sublime, the excess to thought that is the disaster of the Holocaust. For Lyotard, the catastrophe has irrevocably shaken art's self-belief, a contention that the analyses of the Sonderkommando writings in subsequent chapters will implicitly bring into question.

Ankersmit, however, refuses to admit this catastrophe, this horror. He does not, will not, recognise that for many in Europe the Holocaust did generate a new historical consciousness. This emerging consciousness, this emergent trauma, is already signalled in the Sonderkommando manuscripts. Lewental writes with knowing disbelief of what he has witnessed at 'the very heart of civilised Europe'.[105] He declares that 'an abyss [*obgrund*] has opened'.[106] His history is produced from within this abyss, this gulf opening between the before of the event and its aftermath. Ankersmit's rejection of the Holocaust as conducive to sublime historical experience enables him to avoid the tough issue of how the capacity for some forms of culture to facilitate the emergence of the past in the present relates to arguments around the event's unsayability.

If the Holocaust is admitted to be a sublime historical experience, then manuscripts such as the writings produced at Birkenau may assume a comparable status to the artworks discussed by Ankersmit; as remnants of past events they carry its atmosphere with them, within them. The manuscripts, Lewental's and the others, all potentially provide 'the fissures of sublimity in web of meaning and context' that Ankersmit suggests are necessary for historical experience to occur.[107] The documents occasionally form a gap in context, their considerable affective charge overwhelming the reader. At such moments, the writings are felt rather than read. Ankersmit contends that 'the mood of a time is something we can only hear and not see – although it is no less real for that'.[108] He encounters paintings as if they were music, believing moods resonate through their chromatics. Munslow says of Ankersmit's view of historical materials, 'the past is always with us in its relics, atmospheres'.[109] The stains and tinges of the Sonderkommando writings, the words obscured and diffused to oblivion, provide such an atmosphere, as does the feel of fragile pages beneath the fingers.

The gaps the writings contain produce a 'narrative of dislocation', of ruptures and breaks, comparable in effect to those identified by Confino in Saul Friedländer's *The Years of Extermination*.[110] Friedländer builds his history around individual Jewish testimonies of the unfolding genocide. He includes extracts from Gradowski. It is a history constructed in short sections, a fractured history. For Confino, Friedländer incorporates gaps as a historiographic strategy to signal that his history is 'partial', that the events described 'cannot quite be captured'.[111] The incomplete, yet powerful, insights that the individual testimonies can afford readers is suggested by Friedländer's assertion that they 'are like lightning flashes that illuminate parts of a landscape'.[112] The choice of simile is instructive: lightning flashes reveal and obscure, produce blindness and insight. Documents that prompt this kind of challenge to perception do conceivably comprise 'fissures of sublimity' of the kind Ankersmit describes.

Ankersmit explains in the context of world views before and after the French Revolution that 'when thus moving from one representation to another, one had to pass, if only for a moment, through the terrible void between individual representations and to experience the nakedness of momentarily having no self-representation at all'.[113] This void is where 'sublime historical experience may announce itself'.[114] In the Sonderkommando manuscripts, the brittleness of the writings, their imperfections and indecipherable passages, contribute not just towards a fidelity to traumatic experience, they also signal a crisis in identity representation. The authors of the documents try to make sense of the horrors in their midst, try to fathom their role in relation to them. Their efforts form forceful accounts of what Primo Levi, as discussed in the Introduction, called 'the Grey Zone'. This zone cleaved identity. The writers of the manuscripts, as will become clearer in subsequent chapters, struggled at times with how to understand and represent their grim actions and, by extension, themselves. They therefore used writing as a means to search for self-representation. This hesitant self-representation, as alluded to earlier, is present as much in the energetic loops and twists of the scripts forming words as it is in the words themselves. The material aspects of the writings enable readers to access the mood, the horror, of the historical moment in which they were composed – in a manner comparable, in some ways, to the sublime historical experience that Ankersmit finds in artworks.

Traces of Crimes

In the United Kingdom, documents take the form of two kinds of evidence. They can be defined in law 'either as chattel – a substance such as a paper or parchment bearing an inscription, or else as statement – the inscription on the substance'.[115] This definition is informative in relation to the 'Scrolls of Auschwitz'. They are, as this chapter has sought to demonstrate, evidentially significant at the level of both substance and statement. These two aspects provide evidential traces of past events. In 1910, Locard famously stated that 'every contact leaves a trace'.[116] This idea became known as Locard's exchange principle. The principle is 'that when someone commits a crime they always leave something at the scene which was not there before, and take away with them something that was not on them when they arrived'.[117] These materials deposited and removed from crime scenes are referred to as trace evidence.

The criminal does not usually intentionally provide trace evidence. Such vestiges are generated unawares. It is commonly the victims of crimes who, if they are able to, intentionally strive to indicate who is responsible for a particular wrongdoing. This was the aim of the Sonderkommando in composing and then burying their writings and also in interring teeth alongside them. The teeth form proof of the existence of murdered people. Charles Peirce uses murder as an example of indexicality.[118] For him, the body of the murder victim consists of a sign that there is a murderer.[119] The writings cannot function as an index in this way. There are limits to what they can signify. Recognising this deficiency, the Sonderkommando therefore supplemented their descriptions of the operation of the death factory with physical remains generated by it.

The writings are, however, also indexical. The handwritings, as described earlier, gesture towards mental states, emotions. Damage accrued by the manuscripts also records their circumstances of production and how they survived into the present. These material dimensions, as indexes, bear witness in ways as valuable as the words that will be analysed in subsequent chapters.[120] The insights they provide exceed that of simple evidence. They do more than document. They also serve to incarnate the past, to materialise it. Lanzmann has spoken of revisiting the scenes of Nazi crimes in order to 'relive' what occurred there.[121] The manuscripts do not produce an impossible recall of this kind. Scholars who come into contact with them, nonetheless, are left with unsettling impressions, subtle traces of what it was like to live amidst the horror of murder. The academic is not a criminal, yet Locard's exchange principle helps to make sense of their experience of inspecting the writings, of studying their materiality which forms a kind of writing in itself. After such an encounter, the reader takes away an unnerving, perturbing, powerful sense of Birkenau that was not there before.

Notes

1. Zalman Lewental, 'Fartseykhenungen', in Ber Mark, *Megiles Oyshvits* (Tel Aviv: Am Oved, 1977), 420 (92.10). (For an explanation of the numbering system included in brackets, see Chapter 4 p.151 n. 21.)
2. The term 'death factory' was first used to describe Auschwitz-Birkenau by Erich Kulka and Ota Kraus. See Kraus and Kulka, *The Death Factory* (Oxford: Pergamon Press, 1966), trans. of *Továrna na smrt*, 1946.
3. Zalman Gradowski, 'Fartseykhenungen', in Mark, *Megiles Oyshvits*, 347.
4. The word used for sign, *simen*, has a range of references as well as 'sign': trace, mark and even mnemonic. It is also used in the Talmud to refer to distinguishing marks, including those used to identify a dead body.
5. Georges Didi-Huberman, *Images in Spite of All*, trans. Shane B. Lillis (Chicago: University of Chicago Press, 2008), 110.
6. Spencer L. Rogers, *The Testimony of Teeth: Forensic Aspects of Dentition* (Springfield, IL: Charles C. Thomas, 1988), 88.
7. A member of the Sonderkommando, a cook called Leon, did, however, construct a concrete box in which he concealed not just teeth but also hair, one of the most fragile parts of the body, taken from the dead. Leon also included a prayer shawl, a set of phylacteries and a prayer book. This box has never been located. See Ber Mark, *Megiles Oyshvits* (Tel Aviv: Am Oved, 1977), 259.
8. Lewental, 'Fartseykhenungen', 386 (12.16).
9. For a discussion of Lanzmann's position, see Didi-Huberman, *Images in Spite of All*, 89–119.
10. Ibid., 90.
11. Ibid., 92.
12. Ibid., 96.
13. Rogers, *The Testimony of Teeth*, v–vi.
14. Ibid., vi.
15. Ibid., 4.
16. Thomas Keenan and Eyal Weizman, *Mengele's Skull: The Advent of a Forensic Aesthetics* (Frankfurt: Sternberg Press, 2012), 19.
17. See, for example, the photographs reproduced in Danuta Czech, *Auschwitz Chronicle*, trans. Barbara Harshav, Martha Humphreys and Stephen Shearier (New York: Henry Holt, 1990), 799, 802.
18. Lewental, 'Fartseykhenungen', 418 (86.17–19).
19. Ibid., 420 (92.8–9). ***** indicates a gap in the text of the manuscript of variable size. See the Preface for a full key to textual symbols.
20. Dan Stone, 'The Harmony of Barbarism: Locating the "Scrolls of Auschwitz" in Holocaust Historiography', in *Representing Auschwitz: At the Margins of Testimony*, ed. Nicholas Chare and Dominic Williams (Basingstoke: Palgrave Macmillan, 2013), 25.

21. Ibid., 25.
22. Ibid., 25.
23. Rebecca Schneider, *Performing Remains: Art and War in Times of Theatrical Reenactment* (Abingdon: Routledge, 2011), 14.
24. Alun Munslow, *Narrative and History* (Basingstoke: Palgrave, 2007), 22.
25. Ibid., 25.
26. Griselda Pollock, *Vision and Difference: Feminism, Femininity and the Histories of Art* (London: Routledge, 1988), 6.
27. Munslow, *Narrative and History*, 9.
28. We were unable to secure permission to visit and view the writings by Zalman Gradowski that are held in the Medical and Military Museum in St Petersburg, Russia.
29. James Daybell, *The Material Letter in Early Modern England: Manuscript Letters and the Culture and Practices of Letter-Writing, 1512–1635* (Basingstoke: Palgrave Macmillan, 2012).
30. Earlier explorations of the significance of the materiality of the Scrolls can be found in Chare, *Auschwitz and Afterimages: Abjection, Witnessing and Representation* (London: I.B. Tauris, 2011), 77–91; Chare, 'On the Problem of Empathy: Attending to Gaps in the Scrolls of Auschwitz', in *Representing Auschwitz: At the Margins of Testimony*, ed. Nicholas Chare and Dominic Williams (Basingstoke: Palgrave Macmillan, 2013), 33–57.
31. Keenan & Weizman, *Mengele's Skull*, 28.
32. Ibid.
33. Ber Mark mentions a deposition by Henryk Porębski that refers to thirty-six caches of documents but speculates that this may not comprise the total number concealed. Mark, *Megiles Oyshvits*, 259.
34. Gradowski, 'Fartseykhenungen', 288. When Aleksandra Polian examined this document in 2007, she was only able to make out a few of these words in French and German, and none at all in Polish. Zalman Gradowski, *V serdtsevine Ada: Zapiski naidennye v peple vozle pechei Osventsima* (Moscow: Gamma, 2011), 57 n. 1.
35. Audrey Giles, 'The Forensic Examination of Documents', in *Crime Scene to Court: The Essentials of Forensic Science*, ed. Peter White (Cambridge: Royal Society of Chemistry, 1998), 108.
36. Shoshana Felman and Dori Laub, *Testimony: Crises of Witnessing in Literature, Psychoanalysis, and History* (New York: Routledge, 1992), 82. Emphases in the original. All emphases are in the original unless otherwise stated.
37. Felman and Laub, *Testimony*, 81.
38. Compare Alexandra Garbarini's claim that diaries produced by Jews during the war can be read as 'efforts to maintain a sense of an individual self, even as that possibility was being erased'. However, Garbarini focuses less on the practice of writing and more on what that writing records. Alexandra Garbarini, *Numbered Days: Diaries and the Holocaust* (New Haven, CT: Yale University Press, 2006), 9.
39. Giles, 'The Forensic Examination of Documents', 111.
40. Gradowski, 'Fartseykhenungen', 349
41. Additionally, Nadjary may not have had easy access to a suitable surface for writing on in the crematoria. In such a situation, ledgers and notebooks provide their own support in a way that loose leaves of paper do not.
42. MS page 30b.
43. Hayden White, 'Figural Realism in Witness Literature', *parallax* 10(1) (2004): 123.

44. Dan Stone, 'Introduction: The Holocaust and Holocaust Methodology', in *The Holocaust and Holocaust Methodology*, ed. Dan Stone (New York: Berghahn Books, 2012), 8.
45. Lewental, 'Fartseykhenungen', 391 (38. 12–15).
46. Craig Dworkin, *Reading the Illegible* (Evanston, IL: Northwestern University Press, 2003), 57.
47. Schneider, *Performing Remains*, 37.
48. Ibid.
49. Dominick LaCapra, *Writing History, Writing Trauma* (Baltimore, MD: Johns Hopkins, 2001), 40.
50. Ibid., 41.
51. Ibid., 102.
52. Bernard Mark, 'O rękopisie Załmena Gradowskiego', in *Wśród koszmarnej zbrodni: Notatki więźniów z Sonderkommando odnalezione w Oświęcimiu*, ed. Jadwiga Bezwińska and Danuta Czech (Oświęcim: Wydawnictwo Państwowego Museum w Oświęcimiu, 1971), 69. A photograph of the canteen and manuscript is included in this text (ibid., 70). For the English edition, see Jadwiga Bezwińska and Danuta Czech (eds), *Amidst a Nightmare of Crime*, trans. Krystyna Michalik (Oświęcim: State Museum at Oświęcim, 1973), 71–74.
53. Chaim Wolnerman describes it as a box or can (*'ablekhene* [sic] *pushke'*), and says that he bought the document from the person who discovered it, but mentions nothing more about the box. Chaim Wolnerman, 'Araynfir', in Zalman Gradowski, *In harts fun geheynem* (Jerusalem: Wolnerman, n.d.), 3–4.
54. Carlo Saletti, 'À propos des manuscrits des membres du *Sonderkommando* de Birkenau', in *Des voix sous la cendre* (Paris: Le Livre de Poche, 2005), 27. Reports by Wojciech Borowczyk, 5 November 1970, and Gustaw Borowczyk, 14 November 1970, Tom 76A, Auschwitz State Museum Archives.
55. Jan Kucia, 'Relacja', 2 April 1974, APMO Wspomnienia Tom 73 156644/420.
56. See *Amidst a Nightmare of Crime*, 125; Saletti, 'À propos des manuscrits', 25
57. Inmates arriving at Auschwitz were usually ordered to leave their luggage either in the railway cars or near the train but some evidently ignored these instructions and carried a few possessions with them. For a description of the arrival process at Auschwitz, see Simone Gigliotti, *The Train Journey: Transit, Captivity and Witnessing in the Holocaust* (New York: Berghahn Books, 2009), 186–90.
58. Didi-Huberman, *Images in Spite of All*, 36.
59. Ibid.
60. Andrzej Zaorski, 'Relacja', 11 March 1971, AŻIH 301/7182.
61. It is possible Herman changed his plan spontaneously. Leon Cohen's account of the burial of letters to relatives in the grounds of the crematoria (including, presumably, Herman's) would, however, also suggest otherwise. See Cohen, *From Greece to Birkenau: The Crematoria Workers' Uprising*, trans. Jose-Maurice Gormezano (Tel Aviv: Salonika Jewry Research Centre, 1996), 60.
62. Jane Bennett, *Vibrant Matter: A Political Ecology of Things* (Durham, NC: Duke University Press, 2010), 10.
63. Gradowski, 'Fartseykhenungen', 347.
64. Edmond Locard, 'The Analysis of Dust Traces: Part 1', *The American Journal of Police Science* 1(3) (1930): 276.
65. Ibid., 278.

66. Nicholas Stanley-Price, 'The Reconstruction of Ruins: Principles and Practice', in *Conservation: Principles, Dilemmas and Uncomfortable Truths*, ed. Alison Richmond and Alison Bracker (Oxford: Elsevier, 2009), 32.
67. Nelly Balloffet, *Preservation and Conservation for Libraries and Archives* (Chicago: American Library Association, 2005), 84.
68. LaCapra, *Writing History, Writing Trauma*, 103.
69. Dominick LaCapra, *History and Memory after Auschwitz* (Ithaca, NY: Cornell University Press, 1998), 110.
70. Ibid., 21.
71. Stone, 'The Harmony of Barbarism', 24.
72. James Young, 'Interpreting Literary Testimony: A Preface to Reading Holocaust Diaries and Memoirs', *New Literary History* 18(2) (1987): 404.
73. LaCapra, *Writing History, Writing Trauma*, 99.
74. Munslow, *Narrative and History*, 86.
75. Ibid., 114. See also Sande Cohen, *History Out of Joint: Essays on the Use and Abuse of History* (Baltimore, MD: Johns Hopkins University Press, 2006), 103–25.
76. Ibid., 97.
77. Alun Munslow, *A History of History* (Abingdon: Routledge, 2012), 64.
78. Gradowski, 'Fartseykhenungen', 347.
79. Munslow, *A History of History*, 110.
80. Mark, *Megiles Oyshvits*, 370.
81. There is also a small spelling mistake in this line: 'rostrzelone' instead of 'rozstrzelone' (shot/gunned down). The error is indicative either of Polish not being the writer's first language, or of their level of education, or of their haste.
82. Fiona Candlin, *Art, Museums and Touch* (Manchester: Manchester University Press, 2010), 71.
83. Frank Ankersmit, *Sublime Historical Experience* (Stanford, CA: Stanford University Press, 2005), 74.
84. Judith Butler, *Bodies that Matter: On the Discursive Limits of 'Sex'* (New York: Routledge, 1993), 30.
85. Ibid.
86. Ankersmit, *Sublime Historical Experience*, 6–7.
87. Ibid., 177.
88. Ibid.
89. Ibid., 226.
90. Ibid., 229.
91. Following Butler's line of thinking in relation to matter and signification, it might be better to say, contra Ankersmit, that such experiences actually form a different register to language, one that is affective rather than representational. We touch upon the question of affect in Chapter 3.
92. Ibid., 113.
93. Ibid.
94. Ibid., 275.
95. Ibid., 265.
96. Frank Ankersmit, *Meaning, Truth, and Reference in Historical Representation* (Ithaca, NY: Cornell University Press, 2012), 203.
97. Ankersmit, *Sublime Historical Experience*, 265.
98. Ibid., 351.
99. Ibid.

100. Alon Confino, *Foundational Pasts: The Holocaust as Historical Understanding* (Cambridge: Cambridge University Press, 2012), 6–14. Confino's book is a sustained examination of ways in which the study of the Holocaust and the French Revolution can inform each other.
101. Ibid., 6.
102. Arthur A. Cohen, *The Tremendum: A Theological Interpretation of the Holocaust* (New York: Continuum, 1993), 98.
103. Ibid., 31.
104. Jean-François Lyotard, *Heidegger and 'the jews'* (Minneapolis: University of Minnesota Press, 1990), 47.
105. Lewental, 'Fartseykhenungen', 421 (24.2).
106. Ibid. (24.10).
107. Ankersmit, *Sublime Historical Experience*, 280.
108. Ibid., 274.
109. Munslow, *A History of History*, 162.
110. Confino, *Foundational Pasts*, 56. Citing Ankersmit's quotation from Huizinga, Confino also argues that the 'historical sensation' that both discuss can be gleaned from diaries in 'the materiality of the written page, the pen, and the act of writing in the direst circumstances' (60).
111. Ibid., 57.
112. Saul Friedländer, *The Years of Extermination: Nazi Germany and the Jews, 1939–1945* (London: Phoenix, 2008), xxv.
113. Confino, *Foundational Pasts*, 57.
114. Ibid.
115. Colin Tapper, *Cross & Tapper: On Evidence*, 10th edn (London: Reed Elsevier, 2004), 62.
116. Peter Cobb, 'Forensic Science', in *Crime Scene to Court: The Essentials of Forensic Science*, ed. Peter White (Cambridge: Royal Society of Chemistry, 1998), 3.
117. Angela Gallop and Russell Stockdale, 'Trace and Contact Evidence', in *Crime Scene to Court: The Essentials of Forensic Science*, 47.
118. Charles S. Peirce, 'On a New List of Categories', *Proceedings of the American Academy of Arts and Sciences* 7 (1868): 287–98; 290.
119. For a discussion of Peirce's idea of the index in relation to his example of murder, see Anne Freadman, *The Machinery of Talk: Charles Peirce and the Sign Hypothesis* (Stanford, CA: Stanford University Press, 2004), 5–31.
120. Here we differ from James Young's rather exclusive attribution of an 'indexical relation to the events they signify' to the 'physical materiality' of such texts as the Sonderkommando manuscripts. Young argues that these documents gain their 'evidentiary authority' from their physical state rather than from 'repeated attestations from within the narrative'. Young, 'Interpreting Literary Testimony,' 420–21. As the other chapters will show, the words too can be seen to have an indexical relationship with the events they describe.
121. LaCapra, *History and Memory after Auschwitz*, 122.

Chapter 2

Zalman Gradowski

Literature in the Death Factory

Questions

This man Gradowski – is this not a subject to ponder? In the most terrible circumstances of the Sonderkommando, where he saw wandering reach its end, where he himself, with his own hands, we can say, closed the doors of kilns in which lay the bodies of those gassed – this man *wrote*. Wrote lyrically, colouring his account poetically; we might say, he played at being an author – and here we need to distinguish the function of a report-writer and of someone who writes with finesse: because that is exactly what Gradowski does! This diary acquires additional power from the artfulness of the author's writing. But there arises a *problem*, a psychologically troubling one.[1]

Yehoshua Wygodzki's astonishment sums up what must be the reaction of most readers to Zalman Gradowski's writings. Here are not facts and figures hastily jotted down, nor scribbled and desperate messages to loved ones, nor inarticulate expressions of suffering. Instead, he writes in a 'vibrant literary Yiddish,'[2] 'laden with pomp and pathos.'[3] His texts are 'poetic';[4] they might even be '– hard to say though it is – *beautiful*.'[5] Zalman Gradowski, writes Pavel Polian, was 'not just one of the most heroic figures of the Jewish Resistance, not just a chronicler, rebel and optimist, he was also a man of letters!'[6] And yet, as Wygodzki's puzzlement also indicates, many readers are unsure how to react to the literary dimension of Gradowski's testimony. 'How did it happen that a man, after carrying out *that sort* of work, could sit down to write, and write *like this*?' Wygodzki asks.[7] Other readers have answered the question by avoiding it. It may just be his habitual way of writing, suggests one.[8] Others treat it is a hindrance to conveying the stark reality of the crematoria,[9] and many simply ignore it altogether in pursuit of the vital facts.[10]

We believe that avoiding thinking about Zalman Gradowski's way of writing is not an adequate response to the problem Wygodzki raises. Instead, as both Philippe Mesnard and Alexandre Prstojevic argue, the literary dimension is crucial to Gradowski's being able to testify in the first place.[11] Mesnard suggests that Gradowski's style was a mode by which he could stand outside himself and his situation and look back on them.[12] We read it as moving in both directions. The literary forms which Gradowski found for his accounts were not only ways to frame his experience as if from the outside. They were also means to get the accounts to the outside, like the containers in which the manuscripts were buried. Like the containers too, the literary forms had to be what he could find on the inside: drawn from the history that he brought with him, reliant upon whatever bodily condition that he could maintain, suitable for fitting into the times and spaces away from his 'work' and the oversight of the SS. As with the material states of the documents and their containers, therefore, the style is itself evidence. It testifies to the kind of man who was in Birkenau, and what being there did to him; and also to the conditions in which he found it possible to write, and to which he had to adapt how he wrote.

Such an approach has to credit the fact that members of the Sonderkommando had a modicum of agency, some sense of themselves, even an ability to interpret the environment in which they were living and dying. This inevitably calls into question both the prevalent images of the SK and more general assertions that the Shoah was an 'event without a witness'.[13] This chapter provides ample evidence to call for a rethinking of these positions. We show that in his first manuscript, Gradowski was able to use literary means to imagine a witness for his writing, and to shape his experience into a meaningful whole which that witness could make sense of. Our approach also requires us to acknowledge that Gradowski was making choices in how to portray events, and even to ask whether he might have chosen other ways to do so. The reading that we provide of Gradowski is not an entirely uncritical one, therefore. In his second manuscript we examine the gendered imagery in two of its three sections: one taking the form of a lengthy address to the moon, and the other telling of the women of the Czech family camp, murdered on the night of 7/8

March 1944. Here we ask whether his way of writing is able to respond adequately to people, especially women, who stand on the threshold of the gas chamber. We ask difficult questions of Gradowski's prose, not sparing it. This is the greatest compliment that we can accord to him as a writer.

Traces of a Life

Of the scribes of the Sonderkommando, Zalman Gradowski is the person about whom we know the most. He gives some information about his family in the prefaces to his writings. He came from a fairly prominent family in Suwałki, which is mentioned in the town's yizker-bukh a number of times. Dovid Sfard, his brother-in-law, conveyed his memories to Ber Mark and in a foreword to one of Gradowski's texts. And a number of survivors from the Sonderkommando identified Zalman Gradowski as a leader of the uprising of 7 October 1944.

Haim Zalman Gradowski was born between 1908 and 1910 in Suwałki in the north-east of Poland, situated after independence in a wedge of territory between East Prussia to the west and Lithuania to the east. He was the eldest son of a family that was well respected in the community, and may have received some religious education at the Łomża yeshiva, but probably less than his two brothers.[14] He went to work as a clerk in his father's tailoring business; his brothers acquired rabbinic qualifications.[15] Dovid Sfard thought that 'he expected to be something different and something more than what he was', and that he only felt sure of himself when talking about two things: God and Zionism.[16] The Suwałki yizker-book shows him active in both religion and politics. Zalman worked with his brothers at the Tiferes Bokherim ('the glory of youth'), where young working men could read and discuss basic religious texts, and played a part in other charitable organisations.[17] He was also a member of Betar, the Zionist youth movement of Vladimir Jabotinsky's revisionist party. When Jabotinsky took his party out of the World Zionist Congress in 1933, a group of revisionists led by Meir Grossman split from him to remain within it. Unlike most Betarists, Gradowski was amongst them, and became the leader of the Grossmanite faction in Suwałki.[18] Sfard describes Gradowski's ambitions to be a writer, although the pieces he wrote, mostly expressing love of Zion, were 'sentimental', with 'too much affectation [*melitse*] and too little concrete description'.[19]

At some point in the mid-1930s, Gradowski married Sonia (Sarah) Zlotoyabko from another prominent merchant family in the much smaller town of Łunna, south-east of Grodno.[20] They appear not to have had any children. He and her brother were apparently making plans to emigrate for Palestine, but these were curtailed by the outbreak of the Second World War. Suwałki was occupied by the Germans, and Zalman and Sonia fled to her family town, which was under Soviet control.[21] After 1941, when the Germans invaded the Soviet Union and set up a Jewish ghetto in Łunna, Gradowski served on the Judenrat, with responsibility for sanitation.[22]

He, his wife and their families were deported in November 1942 to the transit camp in Kiełbasin, and in early December to Auschwitz. His mother, his sisters, his wife, his father-in-law and his brother-in-law were killed on 8 December. Within days of his arrival, Gradowski was recruited into the Sonderkommando. According to Yaakov Freimark, he worked in Crematorium IV and each day would put on tallis and tfilin and say kaddish for the dead, crying out that he was a sinful man.[23] He was a leading figure in the resistance among the Sonderkommando, and took part in the uprising of 7 October 1944. Freimark reports that he was captured and tortured to death.[24]

These brief details strongly suggest that Gradowski's life in the Sonderkommando was not completely disconnected from his life beforehand. He had had experience as an activist and an administrator, and it is likely that he was able to use some of this in planning and leading the uprising. Moreover, the link between his writing and his activism was maintained. Before the war, he wrote in support of Zionism. In Birkenau, he wrote as part of the resistance. That is not to underestimate the huge gulf between these two parts of his life, but it does show that it is appropriate to draw on what we know of his life beforehand to inform our readings of his texts. The religious element in his identity is clearly to the fore in Yaakov Freimark's memories of him in Birkenau, and in some of the ways that his writing has been read. We believe that his Zionism, which was not always straightforwardly compatible with being strictly religious, also needs to be taken into account.[25] Revisionist Zionism produced some striking writers, including Jabotinsky himself, and it makes sense to read Gradowski alongside them.[26] His writing is certainly not of the kind of aggressive modernism exemplified by Uri Zvi Greenberg or Ya'acov Cohen, but some of the interest in violence shown by Revisionist poets speaks to Gradowski's ways of writing. Where they used violence as a literary strategy, a way of breaking from established conventions to forge a new kind of Hebrew poetry, Gradowski used literary means to deal with violence, not revelling in it, certainly, but hardly constrained by notions of taste. For Gradowski, writing in the highly rhetorical way that he adopted was a call to a future reader, but it was also an assertion of self, showing his ability to rise above the conditions in which he was placed in order to become a writer. His style allowed some distancing, enabling him to invest in the patterning and structures of words and thus not to need to hold back from some of the most difficult subjects. The emotional investment in the words is bound up with other kinds of investment: a belief in himself as a writer-spokesman for his people; a complex of emotions of guilt, empathy and desire on confronting victims at the threshold of the gas chamber; the need to express and fight against the psychic damage caused by handling the dead.

As the introduction explained, two caches of documents by Gradowski were found in 1945. The one found by the Red Army contains two parts written at quite different times: a notebook written in late 1943 and a letter dated 6 September 1944, explaining the history of the text. It was buried amongst ashes, which he thought would not be disturbed, and then concealed in another location when the ashes were removed. The notebook has a very similar note added at the end, presumably also written in September 1944, saying that the rest of the text was written ten months earlier.[27] This would indicate that the notebook is the earliest piece of writing by Gradowski that we have, and the letter is the latest. In between he wrote at least two parts of the three-part manuscript found in 1945 and sold to Chaim Wolnerman. This document includes a description of the selection of the Sonderkommando carried out in February 1944 and the liquidation of the first group from the Czech family camp on the night of 7/8 March 1944. These two parts each have a prologue saying that Gradowski has been in Auschwitz for fifteen months and sixteen months respectively, which dates them to March and April 1944. The third part is not dated, but is thematically tied to the April 1944 section, so is likely to have been written at a similar time. This chapter will discuss these documents in more or less chronological order, looking first at the St Petersburg manuscript and then at the Yad Vashem one.

The Exhortation

> Come to me you happy citizen of the world, who lives in that land where there still exist happiness, joy and pleasure, and I will tell you how modern-day common criminals have turned a people's happiness into unhappiness, changed its joy into everlasting mourning – destroyed its pleasure for ever.
>
> Come to me you free citizen of the world, where your life is assured by human morality and your existence guaranteed by law, and I will tell you how these modern-day criminals and common bandits have crushed the morality of life and annihilated the laws of existence.
>
> Come to me you free citizen of the world, whose land is encircled by modern-day Great Walls of China, where the claws of these pitiless demons were not able to reach, and I will tell you how they have locked a people in

their demonic arms and clamped their pitiless claws with sadistic brutality into their throats till they have choked and annihilated them.[28]

These are the first three paragraphs of a text relating the story of a transport from the Kiełbasin camp to Auschwitz.[29] Another three paragraphs start exactly like this, and the address to the reader continues over something like the first sixth of the account. It is clear that care and effort have been put into this section, perhaps even more than into the narrative of the journey itself. The prose is highly rhetorically patterned. Words are repeated in sequence and paired with their opposites in the first paragraph ('happiness', 'joy', 'pleasure'); pairs of words are inverted in the second ('life' and 'morality'; 'existence' and 'law'), and an entire sequence is reversed in the third ('claws', 'pitiless', 'demons'). Between the paragraphs as well, terms are repeated, varied and built upon ('happy citizen', 'free citizen'; 'modern-day common criminals'; 'annihilated').[30] From an examination of photographs of the manuscript, it is also very likely that Gradowski spent more time over the opening passages than the rest. Some of the reason for this is obvious: writing his testimony down was a race against time, which is probably why it was left unfinished.[31] However, its neatness suggests a process of drafting, either mentally or quite possibly on other pieces of paper, as Leyb Langfus seems to have done (see next chapter). And yet this is effort put into a part that contains little concrete information; in fact the Auschwitz museum's edition of the text leaves it out completely.[32]

Rather than conveying information, therefore, Gradowski seems to be concerned with building a connection between reader and writer, creating a state of psychological preparedness and an understanding of the people whose fate he is describing. The self-consciously literary patterning is part of what achieves these effects. The contrasts and inversions in this passage are used to show how his own life is almost the exact opposite of the lives of his readers. They have 'happiness'; he only has 'unhappiness'. They unthinkingly enjoy the 'morality' and 'law' whose absence leaves him defenceless. But even this absolute opposition allows some bridge between writer and reader, some means for the experience Gradowski describes to be communicated. He is living in a world that is so much the reverse of his readers' that it is effectively a mirror image, and therefore they can look to their own world to understand his. The repetition itself builds up to a climax, from destruction of pleasure to annihilation of law and finally to the annihilation of a people. This is a rhetorical effect, increasing suspense until the final revelation of what has happened, but it also seems to indicate a greater readiness for the writer to deliver his message, and for the reader to receive it, or even in some sense to see it. The next paragraph continues to play variations upon the previous terms, but the frame changes slightly:

'Come to me ... and I will tell you *and also show you*' (289, emphasis added). As Gradowski continues, he seems to be expecting to conjure up the scene before the reader's eyes.

Indeed, conjuration might be a good way to characterise much of what Gradowski is trying to achieve in this introduction. In its repetitions it comes across as a kind of ritual, a spell, in which he is not simply attempting to provide visions to his readers, but even to summon them up before himself, so that he has a witness to whom he can speak. And even the converse: expecting to be dead by the time his text is found, Gradowski has to summon himself up before the reader, as a kind of ghost. Each figure, reader and writer, is a ghost to the other, never coinciding. The ghostliness is made explicit in a paragraph in which Gradowski presents himself as an individual who has undergone specific experiences, as well as the narrator tasked with the responsibility of speaking for all of the dead.

> Come with me, with the lone, single still living child of the people of Israel, who was torn from his home and with his family, friends and acquaintances found temporary rest in clay graves.

The reference is to the transit camp at Kiełbasin. Within the same paragraph, he moves to Auschwitz:

> And there I was appointed by these demons watchman at the gates of hell [*Un dortn bin ikh fun di tayvlonim als shoymer bay di toyern fun gehenem geshtelt gevorn*], through whose doors there passed and still pass millions of Jews from all of Europe ... They <entrusted> me with their last life-secrets. <I> accompanied them to the last step of their lives. Until they were locked in ***** Angel of Death and disappeared from the world for ever. They told me about everything, how they were torn from their homes and underwent a chain of agonising suffering until they reached their final destination as victims of the devil. (290)

The shift from 'he' to 'I' in this paragraph marks a new role for the first person in this introduction.[33] Before, Gradowski has only used the first person as a narrator. At this point, the first person is the protagonist in the narrative. And yet this is an 'I' that seems to have lost part of its humanity, self-dramatised as having become demonic, part of the administration of hell, without any human connections with any others. So this 'I' is actually precisely the narrator: he is the figure who has come into being because of what has happened to him at Auschwitz. In his demonic position he is able to hear everyone else's secrets, sucking them out of them with their last breath. The parallels between the narrator and the victims who tell him their last secrets extend figuratively to the reader too. The narrator has been 'torn from his home' just as the people who spoke to him have. In exactly the same way, the reader is told to say farewell to his wife and child, to his friends and acquaintances, because he will want to 'erase [his] name from the family of man' and will find his 'blood has frozen'.

> Tell them, that if your heart is turned into <a stone>, your brain is swapped for a cold, calculating machine and your eye forms a mere piece of photographic equipment [*vet ... dayn oyg bloyz a fotografishn aparat bildn*], then you will not come back to them.[34] (291)

The knowledge in this document will damage the person who hears it. Like some magical manuscript found unwittingly, it will summon up a figure from hell who will curse the reader.

This position is in some ways overblown – a mixture of myths and fairy tales about dangerous knowledge passed on by some strange seer, witch or magician, and a Romantic hero who has come too much in contact with evil. But we would contend that these kinds of images form a vital resource upon which Gradowski can draw. Imagining himself as a ghost, or a demon, is not only a sign of psychological damage from being asked to carry out unholy tasks and the guilt that ensues, or from being marked out for death. It also allows some coping with these feelings and functions as a narrative strategy, so that the story can be told in some kind of order. Picking up on the image of the camera, the narrator assumes powers made possible by his demonic persona.

> Come with me, let us rise up on the wings of a steel eagle and we will hover over the wide, tragic European vista and from there through microscopic lenses we will be able to observe [*baobakhten*] everything and penetrate everywhere. (292)

Together, reader and narrator descend to the transit camp itself and move around it (293). They go out onto the road and spy in the distance a group walking from Grodno to Kiełbasin (294–95). And eventually, as the Jews march to the station and are put onto trains, the narrator seems to be able to cross freely from one carriage to another, inviting the reader to 'take a tour of these moving cages' with him (306).[35] Whenever someone looks through a window, he can see too. Indeed, some of the effects could aptly be described as cinematic, an image Gradowski himself uses to describe the experience of being trapped in the train cars and looking out at the world (306).[36] In this text, Gradowski seems to be present in two ways: as the body that is trapped in one carriage with his family on the transport, and as the ghostly narrator who, from the point of view of one dead, about to die or representing the dead, can take on a far wider perspective.

This is not the only register in which Gradowski writes. He also includes a rather more straightforward analysis, framed as a reply to the reader's question as to why the Jews did not resist. It is this explanation that is followed by a claim of successful understanding and empathy: 'I believe that you understand us very well now, and even share our feelings in the present moment' (299). Nonetheless, the very presence of a reader, able to pose the question that Gradowski answers, has been made possible by the introductory paragraphs before it. Equally, the principle by which he is able to tell the story of the transport is established through the narrative persona that he assumes.

The Journey

Even when he begins to tell the story of the transport to Auschwitz, Gradowski does more than explain what happened to him and his family. He uses his journey as a literary device, permitting him to survey the condition of Jews in Poland.[37] Simone Gigliotti argues that the form of witnessing called upon by the Holocaust train journey is a more embodied one, based on touch and smell, proximity and not seeing. As her range of examples shows, this clearly does speak to many people's experiences.[38] There are sections of the journey where Gradowski discusses the suffering of those on the train. However, as the comparison to being in a cinema indicates, this is a highly visual description, occasionally supplemented by sound but little else. The passengers look anxiously out at different places to try to get a sense of where they are going and what is happening to Jews there. Having been forced onto the train at Łososna, the first major city they arrive at is Białystok.

> A klaxon sounds from a factory chimney. A reminder of life, a greeting from our brothers and sisters (who give up their efforts and labour there), and now find themselves in the arms of the great factory buildings and give up their energy, hard work and strength for the bandits who are taking us away now. They are working in return for the hope that this will be a protective wall for them. (310)

Phrases from the introductory pages are replayed in this passage, invoking the arms of demons and the wall behind which the reader is protected. Here, however, the arms and the wall are one and the same: the walls of the factory, evoking the uncertainty as to whether this place is a refuge or a site where they will die, or some combination of the two.

Further on in the journey, the train comes close to Treblinka, a site whose function the passengers clearly know all too well.

> We are approaching a station well known to Jews, Treblinka, which, according to various reports we have received, has swallowed up and destroyed the majority of Jews in Poland, as well as from abroad. (310)

The narrative here reaches a traditional moment of tension, with the passengers fearfully awaiting the turn down the branch from Małkinia to Treblinka, and overcome with relief when they do not.[39] But the relief only wins out temporarily. The fate of all the Jews of Poland is quickly returned to, symbolised particularly by the station at Warsaw: 'You see no trace now of a Jew at Warsaw, a station once filled with Jews' (313).

As they carry on from Warsaw, despair is replaced with a modicum of hope at the sight of Jewish slave labourers (signalling life), undercut by the puzzling signs of bystanders at smaller stations.

> The large yellow stars could be made out. Proof of groups of Jews still living and working. Everyone has gained consolation and hope. But it is notable what you can see at every station we stop at: you notice people standing and signalling to the travellers, and making signs with their hands. They draw their hands over their throats, or point at the ground. (318)

Finally, they arrive in Silesia, an area they clearly know much less well, and so are not able to identify particular cities. This is mirrored by the uncertainty about what is going to happen to them, which might involve slave labour in a mine, but they are not completely sure whether this is the fate awaiting them or if they can withstand this kind of work.

> It feels that this is the heart of Poland's golden, black earth. Each man is oppressed by the thought of being thrown into the deep subterranean coal mines – and who knows if he will be able to sustain his physical strength or if he will be able to cope with the conditions to which his all-too-familiar masters will subject him. (322)

Again, the idea of work is presented in imagery that makes it difficult to distinguish from death. This serves as a key image for the journey, encompassing what seem to be the two alternative fates both for the passengers and for Poland's Jews: slavery or death, with the difference between them hard to distinguish. The factories will swallow them just as Treblinka has swallowed the Jews. Poland as a whole seems to be swallowing up its Jews.

What Gradowski provides here works in quite a complex way. Through a dramatic narrative with moments of tension and of relief he gives some sense of the physical stresses upon the deportees as well as rather more on their fears and uncertainties, but also makes a sustained attempt to address the totality of the crime through an overview of the situation of Jews in Poland. This is an impressive literary achievement. Whereas Dori Laub has said that victims of the Shoah were unable to see it as a totality, and that they had no witness to whom they could appeal,[40] Gradowski's text seems precisely to be aiming at seeing something of the whole, and at conjuring up a witness to whom he can speak. He is not interested in simply speaking for himself, but rather wishes to sum up what the experience of all of the Jews of Poland has been. Gradowski's writing shows that both making a witness present and the attempt to think in general terms are enabled by literary devices.

Indeed, this function for his message seems to be greater than letting the future know what has happened in Auschwitz. The section on Auschwitz itself takes up about one-third of the text, finishing abruptly at the point where a group is selected, probably for the Sonderkommando. Gradowski describes the splitting of the transport into three groups and the first day of his group's induction into the concentration camp. The style is much plainer, with only occasional addresses to a reader, and some meditations on the significance of being split from one's family, on being tattooed with a number, and on hunger. The rules of the camp are given repeatedly. Towards the end, the text is more damaged, and it is also hard to tell if it is deliberately repetitive, somewhat rambling or even perhaps consisting of descriptions that are drafted and redrafted. There are two very similar sections on the importance of keeping one's shoes, two that describe music in the camp in a very similar way, and a number of speeches that, although they do seem to be assigned to different speakers, also say very similar things. In particular, there is a repeated scene in which the men are told that their families are dead, which also follows a similar pattern.[41] These may indicate the psychological difficulty of adjusting to this utterly inhospitable place, being told repeatedly the same things and not fully able to take them on board. But they certainly do not give the impression of literary patterning that Gradowski is able to make of the train journey.

Gradowski left the writing unfinished and buried the manuscript in November 1943, and this may well be because he believed there was a substantial risk of being found out, or of a large-scale selection taking place. But aside from this, the comparative plainness, the sense of its not being as polished a piece of writing as the earlier part of the text, and the fact that it stops immediately at the point where the men are selected for the Sonderkommando, might all suggest that Gradowski was much less able to make use of literary elements in his writing when discussing 'the heart of hell', even if from within it he could use them to testify about other places. The idea might be reinforced by the fact that on each telling of the deaths of their family, the response is astonishment that someone could even find the words to say these things. However, even if this was true, he returned to these topics only four months later, writing in perhaps an even more high-flown manner in the document acquired by Chaim Wolnerman.

The Moon

This second document, written in spring 1944, is focused much more tightly on events in Auschwitz-Birkenau. As stated above, two of its three parts deal with the selection among the Sonderkommando in February, and the liquidation of the family camp in March 1944. But rather than changing his mode of writing, Gradowski relies even more than previously on a high literary style to describe them. This is particularly evidenced by the fact that the other part is framed as a lengthy address to the moon.[42]

Elie Wiesel presents a brief reading of this section as an escape, as a sign that Gradowski could no longer face the reality that he was part of and needed to think about something else.[43] That fantasised element is certainly to the fore at the beginning, in which the 'majestic arrival' of the moon and her retinue and their passage through 'her kingdom, the deep blue night sky' is awaited by the writer 'like a loyal slave' whose eyes are 'riveted, hypnotised' ('*tsugeshmidt, farhipnotizirt*') by the sight of her (22). But if the moon is any kind of escape, the text acknowledges its impossibility by placing this view of her in the past.[44] The writer shifts into the present, and goes through a set of reactions to the moon. He denounces her for shining on indifferently while his people are being slaughtered, and even for failing to give them darkness in which to hide. He asks why she is still shedding her light on the perpetrators, and finally says that the world is not worthy of her light, but she should serve as a memorial candle for his people.

> May your eternal ray, may your mournful light always shine at the grave of my people. May this be their yahrzeit-candle, which you alone can still provide for them. (31)

The moon serves as a useful literary device, to an even greater extent than the train journey. She becomes a figure around which everything else is patterned, providing a set of contrasts that make sense of his situation: past and present; above and below; inside and outside; light and darkness. The devastation of the Jews of Poland is expanded to the whole of Europe, linked together by the moon. Addressing her, the speaker is able to discuss how she sees trains come from all over Europe, down to the specifics of the four crematoria of Auschwitz-Birkenau.[45]

The French edition of *In the Heart of Hell* makes reference to the religious significance of the moon, and some of this may be playing through Gradowski's address. The editor refers to the *kiddush levana*, the blessing said between three and fourteen days after a new moon.[46] Gradowski's moon does not really work in the same way. It is an image of remoteness and unmovedness, nothing like the way that the *kiddush levana* finds reassurance in the moon's being out of reach: 'Just as I leap toward you and cannot touch you, so may none of my enemies be able to touch me to do harm'.[47] If the reference is there, it is a negative one. For Gradowski, the moon's untouchability signifies, more or less, her indifference towards these Jews being within their enemy's grasp.

Other religious meanings of the moon do, however, seem pertinent here. The contrast between the last and first paragraphs suggest a moon that has become much more Judaised: ending with a moon that sits *shiva* (in mourning), or that serves as a *yahrzeit* (memorial) candle, as opposed to one that is the object of a kind of courtly romance. But they do not seem to us to be the central way that the text is working. There are a range of references to the moon in Yiddish literature which go beyond the religious. In S.Y. Abramovitsh's *Fishke der Krumer*, the narrator, Mendele Moykher Sforim, addresses the moon twice, first in a drunken, more comic register, while making direct reference to the *kiddush levana* blessing, and then in a more poetic vein in which, calling the moon his mother, he can cry out about his (and the Jews') suffering, and drop the performance that all is well.[48] Sholem Asch's novella *Dos shtetl* (1909) ends with moonlight picking out the snow-covered gravestones in the Jewish cemetery, as well as uniting all elements of the shtetl into one harmony of Jewish life.[49] Early twentieth-century Yiddish poets often used imagery of night-time solitude, sometimes in poems explicitly called 'A Moonlit Night'.[50] There are also references to the moon in Yiddish literature dealing with death and destruction. In the American poet H. Leivick's pogrom poem *Di shtal* (1920), one figure addresses the moon and stars, which did not shine during a pogrom, and answer that they do not know what happened.[51] Uri Zvi Greenberg's early poetry returns repeatedly to an image of dead soldiers hanging on barbed wire, the cleats in their boots gleaming in the moonlight.[52]

While we are not advancing these as the precise references Gradowski is making, each of them does resonate with his writing, even the modernists Leivick and Greenberg. Gradowski's address to the moon, therefore, can be read as part of a specifically Jewish tradition. But it also makes sense as part of a wider European tradition. While other kinds of poetry do include addresses to or an obsession with the moon – Jules Laforgue would be one example – it is the use made by Romantic writers that fits best with Gradowski's approach. In the Yiddish examples above, the only poet or narrator who addresses the moon himself is Abramovitsh's Mendele. In European Romantic poetry, such as that of Juliusz Słowacki, Heine, Leopardi and Keats, apostrophes to the moon are common.[53] In Goethe's poem 'An den Mond', for example, addressing the moon spans time and space between estranged lovers: both of them can see the moon, the only thing that links them in their separation.[54] The moon is a way of figuring the possibility of communication between two people who are apart. For Gradowski, it offers a way of figuring himself as an individual, apart from the camp in which he is imprisoned, and at the same time as someone connected to others, able to communicate with the outside.

Like the image of the moon, the figure of apostrophe is archetypally Romantic, used by writers to define themselves as poets.[55] As Jonathan Culler puts it: 'One who successfully invokes nature is one to whom nature might, in its turn, speak. He makes himself poet, visionary'.[56] Apostrophe allows Gradowski to assert himself as someone endowed with poetic power, capable of bearing witness. Romantic ideas of the poet as spokesman for his nation to all of humanity, and even as the last remnant of his people, can be discerned behind this position.[57] Such an approach to writing is of a piece with his politics, his attraction to the romantic nationalism of Revisionist Zionism. Yaakov Shavit writes about the Poet-Visionary that Revisionists wanted to lead them, based on Adam Mickiewicz's role as Poland's national poet. By the late 1930s, Uri Zvi Greenberg was often hailed as that figure.[58] In his writings, Gradowski also attempts to embody this role, drawing on the Romantic ideas of literature that Greenberg rejected. Like Adam Mickiewicz's Konrad in his monologue the Great Improvisation,[59] the writer curses the world and then finds a way for it to make sense, and seems to believe that he can bend it to his will through performing the role of the poet. Through the force of his words, an imprecation against the moon turns into seeing it as a memorial. He can re-signify what the world means. However, the moon still cannot do anything positive. All that is possible is that the world is marked as a set of signs that testify to the destruction.[60]

The moon's essential passivity, along with many of the traits we have been discussing so far (framing her as a queen or a lover, or even as a candle or a mourner), makes it a feminine figure, and her gender plays an important part in this section.⁶¹ The contradictions of wanting her to go away and then calling her back are partly smoothed out by carefully crafted transitions, but also made sense of by the dynamic of a love affair, which figures much of the speaker's relationship to the moon. The uncertain success of this calling out to the moon, which is also calling to the outside world and perhaps to the realm of literature too, is projected onto a feminine figure, which is indifferent and unmoved, unlike the male writer who faithfully stays with his people and has the power to represent them. Especially in an environment that only consisted of men, in which being female equalled being marked for immediate death, a feminine figure that stands for the past and for the outside takes on a very freighted significance. The moon's femininity is also linked to the fact that the victims in Gradowski's manuscript are primarily women.

The Czech Transport

It is not easy to trace the relationship between the three sections of the Yad Vashem manuscript in a linear way. Each section has a prologue, suggesting that even though they were kept together they were designed to function separately, with at least the potential to be split up and buried in different places, or to endure being split after their discovery. The three texts might be described as different modules, and this makes it hard to read them as parts of one greater whole. This is particularly evident in the slightly unsatisfactory way that they sit together in the same book. Chaim Wolnerman's Yiddish edition has the SK selection as the last part. The 2009 French edition has it as the middle.⁶² The address to the moon certainly has the feel of a beginning. It is the shortest, and unlike the other two sections it is not divided into chapters. It brings the reader into the situation in a relatively gentle way, and even sets the tone for saying that this subject needs to be written and read about. The account of the Czech transport has the greatest sense of being an ending, with the address to the reader at the end being a clear call to action of some kind. But the two sections also seem to flow into each other, with the lunar imagery of the first being picked up and threading through the second. The third part, then, does not seem to fit anywhere. This is only true, however, if it must have a linear form, with one part dovetailing with another. Following the connections in moon imagery is only one of the paths we might take.⁶³

Nonetheless, as we have noted, there is much that links 'A Moonlit Night' with 'The Czech Transport'. The moon plays an important role in the beginning of this account too, which tells of a well-known incident:

the liquidation of the Czech family camp in March 1944.[64] As with 'A Moonlit Night', the first chapter, 'The Night', begins with everyone gazing at a moon which signifies peace and love. But in this story, the moon is not the same for Jews and non-Jews. For the latter there is a moon of love and sweetness, for the former a cruel, icy, indifferent moon (38–39).

Once again, the moon allows Gradowski to make a contrast between those inside and those outside Auschwitz, but it also unites the inmates of the family camp into a whole. In the following chapter, he can then move seamlessly between the different experiences and memories of women within the Czech family camp: a not-yet-sixteen-year-old schoolgirl who is a talented pianist (43–44), a twenty-year-old bride-to-be (45–46), a young mother (46–49), and an older mother, fifty and aged by troubles rather than by the passage of time (49). Every one is female, representative of a set of archetypally feminine life experiences. There are discussions of men, but at much less length: two descriptions of a young man and a young father, which quickly shift back to a description of a mother (51–52). This is rounded off with another reference to the moon:

> Silent, frozen, the moon remained untroubled and calm, and waited along with them for the murderers and criminals, and the holy ceremony, where they would bring five thousand innocent lives to sacrifice to their god. (53)

Turning to plainer prose for his next chapter, Gradowski explains the context in which this liquidation took place, the history, to some degree, of the crematorium and of resistance that took place there, particularly mentioning the killing of Oberscharführer Josef Schillinger.[65] He goes on to discuss the arrangements made to minimise resistance from the family camp, including splitting the families up a few days before, and telling them that they will be taken to work elsewhere. He then turns back to the viewpoint of the people in the family camp, following especially the women taken to the grounds of Crematorium II. The moonlight illuminates both their departure and their arrival, and unites them with the men to whom they say farewell, and the men who greet them in the crematorium's ground: the members of the Sonderkommando.

As they leave the family camp, the women are able to look back and have a final glimpse of their menfolk. 'In the glowing of the light, both their glances meet each other. Their hearts beat in time in fear and terror' [*In dem obshayn fun dem likht, trefn zikh di blikn beyde. Zeyer hartsn klapn ritmish in shrek un moyre*] (64). The light of the moon, the meeting of the glances, and the sharing of feelings are brought together in the rhythms of Gradowski's prose, which in the first sentence especially read like lines of regular verse. Another chapter follows them as they travel towards the crematorium, and realise that they are being taken to their deaths. Their thoughts are addressed to the world, in a similar way to the first section's address to the moon. When the women are taken out of the trucks, the conjunction of moonlight and glances plays out again:

> They allow themselves, freely, without resistance, to be gathered [*zey lozn zikh … arobnemen*] from the trucks – and fall as in a swoon, as cut sheaves [*vi obgeshnitene zangen*] straight into our arms. Here, take me, my dear brother, by the hand and accompany me on the little left to me of this journey from life to death. We take them, our beloved sisters, our dear, tender ones, we take their arms, we walk silently, step by step, our hearts beat in time [*di hertse unzere ritmish klapn*]. We suffer and bleed along with them, and we feel that each step that we make is a step further from life, and approaches death. (68–69)

There is a dreamlike atmosphere here. The images of harvesting, present in the 'cut sheaves' and possibly also in the verb used for 'gather' (which most commonly means 'take' but can also mean 'harvest') disturbingly naturalise this event: a gentle falling that contrasts with descriptions of prisoners being tipped out of a truck like gravel, or with Filip Müller's account of the same incident, in which people were driven from the trucks under a 'hail of blows and cries'.[66] Gideon Greif uses this scene as evidence that the Sonderkommando were not heartless brutes, but it reads in some ways as a fantasy on Gradowski's part, one that the writing itself might be said to acknowledge. This is what he wishes he could have done, rather than what he was able to do. The words spoken by a woman to an SK member are not put into quotation marks, unlike those in the next chapter. And although the account does specifically say that members of the SK were lined up in order to help them off the trucks, the situation does not seem to match with the beginning of the next chapter, where the narrator says that they met the women in the undressing room, and 'stared frozen at them' (70). The Sonderkommando man and the woman are united not quite by a bodily response to each other, but by a rhythm which is like that of Gradowski's prose, a poetic coming together of hearts as symbols as much as bodily organs.

> And before going down into the bunker, into the deep, before they make the first step on the stairway to the grave [*dem ershten trit af dem trepl fun dem keyver*] they give their last look to the sky and moon, and a sigh escapes instinctively from deep in both their hearts alike. In the glow of her light [*obshayn fun ir likht*] there shine tears from the sisters who are led, and a tear stands frozen in the eye of the brother [*farglivert blaybt shteyn a trer bay dem bruder*] who accompanies her now. (69)

This part amalgamates references to two earlier parts of this section: the beginning, with two lovers gazing at the moon with tears that come from their hearts (38), and the looks exchanged by the women on the trucks and those left in the family camp. The moon, therefore, stands again and again for the uniting of people: lovers and members of family. The fantasy here is that it will do the same for the Sonderkommando and the women, and that they will have the same relationship as lovers or as family.[67]

The sentence from the next chapter only makes grammatical sense as a follow-on from this sentence:

> Into the great hall, into its depths, in whose midst stand twelve pillars, which support the weight of the building, and is now harshly flooded with electric light. (70)

This almost has the effect of an enjambment: the pause before entering the underground undressing room which does not come to a full stop, and therefore emphasises the movement that comes after. The move from outside to inside contrast two different kinds of light: moonlight which unites Sonderkommando and woman, and the electrical light which seems to hold them apart.

> In the hall, the giant grave, there shines now a new light. They now stand arranged [*oysgeshtelt*] on one side of this great hell, these alabaster-white women's bodies [*alabaster vays froyen-kerper*] and wait, wait for the doors of hell to open and grant them passage to the grave. We the men, still in our clothes, stand now opposite them, and watch, frozen [*farglivert*]. We cannot grasp now if this image is reality, or if it is simply a dream. Have we fallen somewhere into a naked woman-world [*froyen-velt*], and here soon a demonic game will take place with them, the women here? Or have we fallen somewhere into a museum, into an art studio and the women, of different ages, with these grimaces of every expression, with this quiet weeping and sighing, have specially for the artist, for his art, come here? (73)

The first sentence of this paragraph is clearly a deliberate echo of the first sentence of the chapter, so their light is contrasted with the electrical light of the room. By a chain of contrasts, then, the light from the moon is linked to the whiteness of the women's bodies. This does not necessarily work as the bodies being equated to the moon, but it is certainly one possible way to make sense of the contrasts. Like the moon, the light from the bodies is reflected. They both come from a feminine source and both are 'calm' (73).

Moreover, just as the moon itself is remote, the women too are portrayed as if at a distance. All the way through this paragraph they are described as objects as much as people: in the first half of the paragraph, '*froyen*' ('women') is given only as part of the compound nouns '*froyen-kerper*' and '*froyen-velt*'. Only in the sentences describing the fantasy worlds that they seem to have fallen into are they described straightforwardly as 'women'. '*Oysgeshtelt*' can mean 'in order, lined up', but also 'on display'. Gradowski is grasping for terms of reference to make sense of this nakedness, or terms that he thinks a reader would be able to understand. But, like the moon, the women seem to be in part the objects of a kind of literary exercise. They are studies, sketched as in a room of plaster casts.

Even when they do interact with the members of the Sonderkommando, there is something unreal about their actions. Is it really plausible that women who had only recently been separated from their families would come and ask the Sonderkommando to undress them, to feel hands on them that substitute for their lovers?

> A few fall on us, as if drunk, as if in love, throw themselves into our arms and ask us, with embarrassed glances, to undress them. They want to forget everything now, they don't want to think about anything now. With the world of yesterday, with its morality and principles, and ethical concepts, they have, with the first step on the stairway to the grave, made their accounting. ... Their bodies, they alone, they feel still, they sense still. ... And therefore they want that their young bodies, which strongly pulse with life blood, the hand of an unknown man, who is now the nearest dearest there, to touch, caress their bodies now [*Un deriber viln zey, az der yunger kerper, velkher shprits mit blut fun lebn shtark, zol di hand fun a fremdn man, velkher iz yetst der nonster libster do, barirn, tsertlen zeyer kerper yetst*]. And in this way they will feel as if the hand of their lover or husband were stroking or caressing their bodies inflamed with passion. (72)

A very complex set of feelings is in play here, and this is in some ways a moving moment, but part of what makes it moving are the possible failures as well as the attempt at empathy. Indeed, the awkwardness of the key sentence describing their desire might hint at the difficulty of conjuring up this scene. '*Kerper*' ('body') is given in the nominative, as if it is to be the subject of some verb that never arrives, before it is repeated as the object of '*barirn*' and '*tsertlen*' ('touch' and 'caress'). The narrator is trying to understand what these women might be feeling, but it seems hard to separate this attempt at understanding, and the desire to comfort them, from a sexual response to their bodies. Although this itself might be in part a way to relate as one human to another, it also seems a fantasy of what they might want from him. Gradowski does mention other ways that the women act, asking after their families, enquiring how easy a death it is or wanting not to be seen naked. But this is the passage that rounds off this particular scene, before trucks with more victims arrive, and this is the passage that seems to pulse with the greatest emotion. Perhaps it functions as a way of dealing with the guilt of being in the Sonderkommando, wanting to believe that the women see them not as perpetrators or collaborators, but as brothers or husbands. Gradowski tries to make plausible an attraction that seems unlikely, and yet contains within itself signs of guilt, sexual desire, the wish to connect with the victims and even with his readers as potential witnesses.

The sexual energy in these passages is noteworthy as it again draws attention to the distinct experiences of members of the Sonderkommando in contrast with most other inmates. Hermann Langbein discusses the absence of sexual urges in the majority of prisoners.[68] Alvin H. Rosenfeld also suggests that sexual desire was usually held in abeyance. For him, because of this, 'one of the characteristics of Holocaust writings at their most authentic is that they are peculiarly and predominantly sexless'.[69] This characterisation, however, is not applicable to Gradowski's aching prose. His writing is therefore in keeping with Elie Cohen's observation that for prisoners in a good state of nutrition 'the sexual drive was indeed of importance'.[70]

The energy that comes from being relatively well fed, and perhaps a partly sublimated sexuality too, also inform his ability to reflect upon his own experiences. There is some ambition here, some risk taking, the desire to tell a kind of truth and to think about the sexual element in this encounter, an attempt not just to sentimentalise and make easy the deaths of the women or even the role of the Sonderkommando, but also to think through how the SK might regard the victims. Gradowski seems to be willing to take the risk of saying how he is attracted to the women, even if it is partly diverted through a claim that they are attracted to him.

Other accounts which touch on the element of desire in response to women undressing just before they are gassed do exist. Richard Glazar, part of the equivalent of the Sonderkommando at Treblinka, makes some reference to a sexual response to naked bodies as well as disavowing it.

> Usually, looking from a corner past piles of clothing, I can see the last of the naked backs as they head for the 'hairdressers.' But today the barracks are still full. Into half of the building, along one entire wall, naked bodies are pressed together – an enormous mural [*ein riesiges Bild*], a fresco of bottoms, bellies, arms folded over breasts, undone hair. Along the opposite wall are piles of clothing, some smaller, some larger. The body odor clogs your nose and your mouth and stings your eyes. The screams of children pierce through the bedlam into your ears.

'Hey, you,' one of the Red thugs jars me out of my crippling daze and points me at my work. As I slowly bend over the clothes, my eyes still staring straight ahead, he winks, leans over to me, and yells into my ear in Polish, very slowly and clearly, to be sure I understand: 'Well, well, has one of your dreams from out there in life come true, seeing a whole roomful of naked broads?'[71]

Glazar presents his own feelings mainly as pity and disgust, although he too reaches for artistic terms to try to discuss it. When a member of the Red commando (the squad responsible for collecting the clothes and effects of victims) interprets Glazar's fascination as voyeurism we are encouraged to take this as a sign of his own, crude, inhuman feelings.

Yehuda Bacon in video testimony tells a story which he heard in turn from Kalman Furman, a member of the Sonderkommando. 'What they have done when a woman transport came and there was a very beautiful woman, they left her to the very end and *they* took off their clothes, I mean, as if they gave her a kind of better treatment.'[72] Here, an 'aesthetic' appreciation of female beauty manifests itself in what seems unambiguously sexual behaviour. But in this dreadful context, aesthetics and sex might operate differently. Appreciating women in an aesthetically 'disinterested' way,[73] seeing them with detachment, hints of psychic damage, seeing them in some sense as objects, already dead. Shlomo Venezia describes one woman in strikingly similar terms to Gradowski's image of the room of plaster casts, except for the fact that she is dead: 'one day, among the corpses brought out of the gas chamber, the men found the body of an incredibly beautiful woman. She had the perfect body of ancient statues'.[74] In turn, Bacon seems to see the SK removing their clothes as a kind of salute, an expression of fellowship. In this environment, and as witnesses to how naked women were used as objects of sadistic pleasure by SS men,[75] it is not completely implausible that some of the Sonderkommando might have taken sexualised ways of relating to women as more humanising than they might seem to us.

Gradowski's sexualisation of the women could be read, therefore, as an attempt to show them as living, breathing human beings.[76] To us as readers, there is something disquieting in this approach, but we also wish to understand what it was trying to achieve. Gradowski writes of himself imagining them as dead, even as they are alive: 'I stand now by a group of women, ten to fifteen in number, and a wheelbarrow will contain all their bodies, all their lives in a wheelbarrow of ashes' (75). Writing of them after their deaths and attempting to give some sense of them as living beings must have required an immense effort of the imagination, one that perhaps could not have been carried out without a great belief in his powers as a writer. But the risk is that it becomes more of an occasion for him to show the power of his writing and to assert his selfhood than to respond to other human beings. It becomes a rhetorical figure, prosopopoeia, like his apostrophe to the moon.[77] His own desires – to be a writer, to speak for the dead, to be seen as their brother and not their enemy, perhaps even to be desired – take over his attempts to convey what the women themselves felt.

That is not to say that Gradowski presents them as nothing but objects. To some degree, the narrative does acknowledge the women's agency and ability to assert themselves, even as they go to their deaths. They too can produce words of defiance. In the following chapter, 'The March to Death', the women pour scorn on the SS and predict their defeat (78–79). As they enter the gas chamber, they sing the Internationale, *HaTikvah*, the Czech Anthem and the Partisan Song (82–89). The narrative structure even starts to follow what they do rather than the different stages of their annihilation, with each song given a separate chapter. Each song also shakes the confidence of the SS somewhat, albeit only briefly.

A short, stark chapter, only one paragraph long, 'Pouring In the Gas' (92), follows two silhouettes in the moonlight as they move from one gas entry chute to another, hearing the groans within. Rather than showing the effects of their actions in the gas chamber, Gradowski then shifts to the story of what happened in Crematorium III, where the men of the family camp fail to rise up as was hoped, and are also gassed. This seems to be based on Gradowski's own experience, as the narrator and the rest of his squad are moved over to this building, but it also holds the narrative in suspense, before it reaches its grisly climax. There is much less emotional investment in the men as victims, as the somewhat more distanced chapter titles, and the disappointment that they fail to revolt, also show (94–99). As the SK open a gas chamber (which seems to be the one in Crematorium II), the structure returns to a descent ever deeper into the inferno, with three chapters entitled 'In the Bunker', 'Preparations for Hell', and 'In the Heart of Hell'. Here there occur some of the most extraordinary passages of Gradowski's writing. He is clearly determined to describe every part of the process, from the opening of the doors of the gas chamber to the burning of the bodies in the ovens.

> Our eyes are riveted, hypnotised [*tsugeshmidt, farhipnotizirt*] by this sea of naked dead bodies, which has now appeared before us. We have now caught sight of a world of nakedness. They lie fallen, intertwined, twisted together like a tangled skein, as if the devil before their deaths had played a special devilish game with them, and laid them out in such poses. Here lies one completely stretched out on top of the bodies. Here two hold onto each other and sit together by the wall. Here only part of a shoulder sticks out, and the

> head and feet are pressed into other bodies. Here you see only a hand, a foot sticking out into the air, and the whole body lies in this deep naked sea. You see only parts of human bodies on the surface of this naked world.
>
> In this great sea of nakedness heads float about. They cling to the surface of the naked waves. It seems as if they are swimming in the great sea's depths and only the heads look out from this deep naked abyss.
>
> These heads – dark, fair, brown – are the only individual parts that break out of the universal nakedness. (101–2)[78]

The emphasis on seeing is important here. Gradowski is trying as far as possible to make this scene visible to the reader, supplementing the vivid present tense of much of his account with constant repetitions of 'here' and 'you see' [*du zest*]. That effort is still bound up with making this a literary description, inventing metaphors for what he sees, and making meaning even out of this tangle of bodies. He uses sea imagery both to convey something of what this mass of bodies looks like, but also to convey how the individuality and lives of the women he has so passionately described have been extinguished, as if washed away. He is even prepared to read the heads sticking out of the mass as traces of that individuality in opposition to the abyss of the bodies, referring back to his description of different hair colours when they were alive: 'so many full heads of hair: dark, brown, fair, and also a few grey' (70). Describing the men as 'riveted, hypnotised' also uses the same words by which he describes his reaction to the moon (22).

But the Sonderkommando cannot stand there for long. They must begin the process of disposing of the bodies.

> We must deaden our feeling hearts, dull every feeling of grief in ourselves. We must forswear [*farshrayen*] the horrific suffering in us, which like a storm sweeps through every part of our bodies. We must turn into robots [*oytomatn*], which see nothing, feel nothing and understand nothing. (103)

This description is close to the effect that Gradowski describes his tale will have on the reader in the St Petersburg manuscript. Here we see what that knowledge has done to him. But it is clear that this affectless state is what his writing is fighting against. He wants to see and feel, just as he wants his readers to do as well. Becoming robots like this simply makes the process of getting rid of the bodies more efficient.

At the Heart of Hell

The closing passages to the section on the extermination of the Czech family camp are intricately interrelated. There is a devilish attention to detail in the segments on how bodies are prepared for the ovens and then burnt, the division of labour, the order and duration of the process by which a being, a body, is reduced to cinders. This reinforces the reality that this is insider testimony. Only someone at the heart of hell could possess such an intimate knowledge of the operations of a death factory.

> They are laid out on the iron 'burial' board [*ayzernem ta'are bret*]; then the hell-mouth is opened and the board is pushed [*arayngerukt*] into the oven. The hellish fire extends [*tsit … oys*] its tongues like open arms and snatches up the body just as though it were a treasure. First to catch light is the hair. The skin swells up into blisters and splits in a few seconds. Now the arms and legs begin to move – this is the blood vessels tightening and this moves the limbs. The body in its entirety is now blazing strongly; the skin has split, the fat flows and you hear the sizzling of fire burning. You no longer see a corpse – only a chamber of hellish fire, in the middle of which lies … something. The stomach splits. The guts and entrails quickly spill out of it, and in minutes there is no trace of them left. The last to burn is the head; from its eyes two little blue flames now flicker – these are the eyes burning with the brain inside [*dos brenen di oygn mitn tifn markh aroys*], while from the mouth the tongue also still burns now. Twenty minutes for the entire procedure. And a body, a world, has been turned to ashes. (104)[79]

The lengthy, lavish even, description of the destruction of a body forms material for the kind of envisioning that Gradowski desired of his readers. He gives the matter, the actions, sights, and sounds, from out of which to imagine the burning of a body: the sizzling, cracking, running and spurting that accompanies physical dissolution, including the stunning image of two little blue flames glimmering in the eye sockets. Here he is not simply telling us what he has seen; he is, as he promised in his first manuscript, *showing* it to us.

The elaborate description, however, does more than merely summon the imagination of his readers. The depiction of the absenting of a body, through its significant anatomical detail, its focus on parts – the skin, the stomach, the entrails, the intestines, the brain – also oddly materialises that body. This serves at least two purposes. Lending the burning body substance in this way redoubles the impact of its ultimate reduction to nothing. It gives the fire more to consume than would a pared account. It also works to demonstrate the power of literary language in the face of destruction. When the section that follows this one is taken into consideration, it is possible to read the burning description as a kind of meditation on language. The section that comes after describes another two bodies that have been loaded onto the 'burial' board: 'two human beings, two worlds, who had their place among humanity; who lived and existed, acted and created' (104).

The creative capacity of these victims is one shared by Gradowski. He expresses this aspect of his humanity through his writings. One role he has chosen for himself in what remains of his life is to be a writer. Given the repeated emphasis on how the ovens reduce worlds to nothing, it does not seem implausible that he saw his words as a way to cheat the flames, to endure. In the striking imagery of the burning bodies, a sight that transfixes the viewer, it is the tongue, a means to speech, which burns to ashes last of all. In this context, the writings he composed and concealed can be read as resisting oblivion like the enduring tongue. A trace of Gradowski's world will survive in and through his literary endeavours.

The horrific detail is also expressly included for another purpose: it does not spare his readers as it is designed to anger and disgust them. The account of the murder of these inmates from the family camp ends shortly afterwards, with Gradowski conveying the hope that his words will act as tinder to vengeance such that readers will have the courage to intervene in this process of mass murder.[80] The readers are implored to see to it 'that its flames devour those who kindled it' (106). The gruesome description of a body's dissolution, obliteration, is therefore designed to inflame conscience and lead to action. Creativity here also ensures that Gradowski as 'world' possesses a posthumous capacity to act in the world.

Final Thoughts

The last surviving piece that Gradowski wrote is the letter buried with the St Petersburg manuscript.[81] He explains what he did with this manuscript, and that he expects a revolt to happen soon. The different style in which it is written is striking. It is much less assured, much plainer, and far less of an attempt to be a literary piece. This may indicate a change that had happened to Gradowski: less able to invest in the power of literature, perhaps? It is of course very likely that he was pressed for time too. The high literary style that he cultivated did not come naturally to him. He needed time to be able to structure his words in this way. More than this, however, it bespeaks a need to provide an account of himself as an individual, adding more of his own story. Like the prologues to each section of the Yad Vashem manuscript, this letter now provides a frame for his text in which he speaks more as himself. Each of these frames includes the names of his family, acting as their memorial. They also help to make the tone here much more personal, and much less prophetic. Gradowski needed to speak sometimes in a more subdued and less stylised way, as well as in the poetic register of the majority of his writings. The fact that he did this would indicate that he himself saw it as a performance. It may have been necessary to adopt this role to tell what he had witnessed. But it may also have allowed him to avoid talking about himself.

Pavel Polian points out that this is the only document that Gradowski signs with his full name. In one of the prologues from *In the Heart of Hell* he includes his initials. In the other, he uses a simple number code for the letters of his name. Since Gradowski clearly wanted the reader to be able to identify him, Polian suggests, quite rightly we think, that he must have been trying to conceal his name in case the documents were discovered prematurely. In September 1944, this seems no longer to have concerned him. Polian wonders, again quite plausibly, if this was because he thought the revolt could break out at any moment.[82] But, of course, Gradowski had been naming a group of people throughout these prologues: the dead members of his family. Signing his name so straightforwardly means that he takes his place among them. It probably indicates that he expected soon to be dead.

The reading of Gradowski's texts that this chapter has presented is certainly not the only one that is available. Connections between his writing and the religious side of his experience, such as his ties with the Łomża yeshiva, could certainly be explored more fully. We have also not been able to include the third section of the Yad Vashem manuscript in our discussion. There is, therefore, much more to be said about Gradowski, and his writing should invite many more readers, and many more readings. From our selection, this chapter has tried to show that an interconnected literary and political reading of his work is possible. Gradowski's connections with Revisionist Zionism suggest a way of reading him as taking up the role of a poet for his people, at times glorying in that role, while also at others recognising it as a role. This position enables writing of an astonishing eloquence and power, making use of what in other circumstances might be seen as an overwrought mode that gives him the means to describe, to organise and to evoke a set of experiences that he urgently needed to communicate to the outside world. In doing so, many of the conventional understandings of Holocaust writing (that the Shoah went unwitnessed, that its victims lost all sense of self, that they were essentially sexless) must be thrown into question. However, doing justice to this writing requires not simply reading it in a celebratory or apologetic way. Gradowski's use of women as his archetypal victims is a sincere attempt to memorialise them. But it is also a use of them as material, a way to assert himself as alive and able to testify, as a subject, as a writer, as a man.

In the crematoria of Birkenau, to find any way of writing was an extraordinary achievement, and to demand that Gradowski manage not only that but also match our ethical demands of it is, of course, unreasonable. Nonetheless, Gradowski's writing did not just result from the physically exhausting and psychologically wounding environment in which he lived. It is also a measure of the literary and political attitudes that he brought with him to Birkenau. Other members of the Sonderkommando, from different backgrounds, wrote in quite different ways, and comparing how the communication of horror was achieved by other authors is informative. Gradowski therefore only offers one possibility of testimony. The other Sonderkommando have something to say as well. It is important that as readers we do not focus simply on the most striking of the writers. As our chapters on the other Sonderkommando writings will show, they too have much to teach us.

Notes

1. Yehoshua Wygodzki, 'A vort fun a gevezenem asir', in Zalman Gradowski, *In harts fun gehenem* (Jerusalem: Wolnerman, n.d. [c.1977]), 11.
2. Ber Mark, *Megiles Oyshvits* (Tel Aviv: Yisroel-Bukh, 1977), 263.
3. Philippe Mesnard, 'Écrire au-dehors de soi', in *Des voix sous la cendre: Manuscrits des Sonderkommandos d'Auschwitz-Birkenau* ed. Georges Bensoussan, Philippe Mesnard and Carlo Saletti (Paris: Calmann-Lévy/Mémorial de la Shoah, 2005), 238.
4. Kateřina Čapková, 'Das Zeugnis von Salmen Gradowski', *Theresienstädter Studien und Dokumente* (1999): 107. Nathan Cohen, 'Diaries of the Sonderkommando', in *Anatomy of the Auschwitz Death Camp*, ed. Yisrael Gutman and Michael Berenbaum (Bloomington: Indiana University Press, 1998), 525.
5. Dan Stone, 'The Harmony of Barbarism: Locating the Scrolls of Auschwitz in Holocaust Historiography', in *Representing Auschwitz: At the Margins of Testimony*, ed. Nicholas Chare and Dominic Williams (Basingstoke: Palgrave Macmillan, 2013), 26.
6. Pavel Polian, 'I v kontse tozhe bylo slovo (vmesto predisloviya)', in Zalman Gradowski, *V serdtsevine Ada: Zapiski naidennie v peple vozle pechei Osventsima*, trans. Aleksandra Polian (Moscow: Gamma Press, 2011), 52.
7. Wygodzki, 'A vort fun a gevezenem asir', 11.
8. Cohen, 'Diaries of the Sonderkommando', 525.
9. David Roskies, who credits him with few abilities at all as a writer, asserts that 'his literary means were limited, but his insights were not', as if the means by which Gradowski wrote simply stood in the way of those insights. 'Wartime Victim Writing in Eastern Europe', in Alan Rosen, ed., *Literature of the Holocaust* (Cambridge: Cambridge University Press, 2013), 43. See also his rather dismissive comment that Gradowski 'cultivated what he believed to be a literary style'. David Roskies (ed.), *The Literature of Destruction: Jewish Responses to Catastrophe* (Philadelphia: Jewish Publication Society, 1989), 518. Krystyna Oleksy says that 'the style might suggest

a carelessness about the facts', a worry that can be assuaged by attention to the facts of the case, although her article is actually quite attentive to how Gradowski writes. 'Salman Gradowski: Ein Zeuge aus dem Sonderkommando', *Theresienstädter Studien und Dokumente* (1995): 133.

10. A number of scholars writing about Gradowski seem to take little interest in his literary ambitions. See, for example, Susan L. Pentlin, 'Testimony from the Ashes: Final Words from Auschwitz-Birkenau Sonderkommando', in *The Genocidal Mind*, ed. Dennis B. Klein et al. (St Paul, MN: Paragon House, 2005), 245–62; Zoë Vania Waxman, *Writing the Holocaust: Identity, Testimony, Representation* (Oxford: Oxford University Press, 2006), 81–84.
11. Mesnard, 'Ecrire au-dehors de soi'. Alexandre Prstojevic, 'L'indicible et la fiction configuratrice', *Protée*, 37(2) (2009): 37–39.
12. Mesnard, 'Ecrire au-dehors de soi', 239.
13. As discussed in the Introduction.
14. Dovid Sfard talks of him being given a yeshiva education. 'Eynike zikhroynes vegn Zalman Gradowski', in Zalman Gradowski, *In harts fun gehenem* (Jerusalem: Wolnerman, n.d. [c.1977]), 6. This does not completely square with the information in the Suwałki yizker book, which specifically states that Gradowski's brothers went to the Łomża yeshiva, and does not mention Zalman (see following note). The records of the Łomża yeshiva from 1927 list two students whose names match these brothers. Ben-Tsion Klibansky, 'Unique Characteristics of the Łomża Yeshiva Students after WWI', *Landsmen: Quarterly Publication of the Suwalk-Lomza Interest Group for Jewish Genealogists* 19(1–2) (2009): 6–14. The list includes 'Awraham Gradowski', aged 20 (no. 62), and 'Moishe Grodowski' [*sic*], aged 14 (no. 196), both from Suwałki. Avraham's age is almost certainly incorrectly recorded here: his date of birth on the JDC refugee list in Vilnius is given as 1911 (see note 20). Even so, this would imply that Zalman did not complete a full yeshiva education. On the basis of the low average age of students at this yeshiva, Klibansky suggests that it served as both a preparatory and senior yeshiva. One way of resolving the conflicting evidence would be to surmise that Zalman attended Łomża only at the preparatory stage.
15. Sfard, 'Eynike zikhroynes', 6. Avraham/Ever and Moishe are both given the title Rabbi. *Yizker-bukh Suvalk un di arumike shtetlekh* (Nyu-York: Suvalker relif komitet in Nyu-York, 1961), 367–69. Their father is given a short biographical entry in Yehoyesh Zawoznicki, 'Portretn fun lomdim, askonim un nedivim in Suvalk', *Yizker-bukh Suvalk*, 451. The Polish business directory of 1929 lists two Gradowskis in Suwalki as tailors (157).
16. Sfard, 'Eynike zikhroynes', 6.
17. Yehoyesh Zawoznicki, 'Di toyre-yugnt in Suvalk', *Yizker-bukh Suvalk*, 369.
18. Shloime Ryman, 'Betar', *Yizker-bukh Suvalk*, 407. On Revisionism, see Walter Laqueur, *The History of Zionism*, 3rd edn (London: Tauris Parke, 2003), 338–83. On Betar specifically, and especially in parts of Poland outside Warsaw, see Daniel K. Heller, *The Rise of the Zionist Right: Polish Jews and the Betar Youth Movement, 1922–1935* (Ph.D. diss., University of Stanford, CA, 2012).
19. Sfard, 'Eynike zikhroynes', 6.
20. R. Zlotojablko is listed as a merchant in imported goods in the 1929 Polish business directory (137). He owned the largest grocery store in town. <http://kehilalinks.jewishgen.org/Lunna/Urban.html>.
21. Gideon Greif, *We Wept without Tears: Testimonies of the Jewish Sonderkommando from Auschwitz*, trans. Naftali Greenwood (New Haven, CT, and London: Yale University

Press, 2005), 247. Eliezer Eisenschmidt also confirmed this to Ruth Marcus (pers. com.). Other members of Gradowski's family fled elsewhere. In his prologue to 'The Czech Transport', Zalman mentions that one sister was arrested in Otwock, and both his brothers were arrested in Lithuania. An Abram Gradowski from Suwałki was recorded in the refugee list compiled by the JDC in Vilnius in 1940 (no. 7732). <http://74.127.32.5/multimedia/Documents/Names%20Databank/Vilna%20 Refugees/Vilna_AR33-44_00876_00181.pdf>.
22. Ruth Marcus, 'Lunna-Wola during the Second World War and the Holocaust' <http://kehilalinks.jewishgen.org/lunna/German.html>.
23. Mark, *Megiles Oyshvits*, 262.
24. In addition to the testimony given to Gideon Greif, a number of early works identified Gradowski as a leader of the uprising. Ota Kraus and Erich Kulka referred to him as 'S. Grandowski from Suwalk'. Kraus and Kulka, *The Death Factory: Document on Auschwitz*, trans. Stephen Jolly (Oxford: Pergamon Press, 1966), 259. Filip Müller also mentioned him in his discussion with Claude Lanzmann, although his name was transcribed as 'Grabowsky'.
25. None of the other people mentioned as being active in one sphere appear in accounts of the other. Zawoznicki, 'Di toyre-yugnt in Suvalk', 365–72; Ryman, 'Betar', 405–8.
26. Michael Stanislawski, *Zionism and the Fin-de-Siècle: Cosmopolitanism and Nationalism from Nordau to Jabotinsky* (Berkeley and Los Angeles: University of California Press, 2001), 116–237. Eran Kaplan, *The Jewish Radical Right: Revisionist Zionism and its Ideological Legacy* (Madison: University of Wisconsin Press, 2005).
27. It seems reasonable to assume that the last page of the notebook was written at the same time as the letter of 6 September. They give the same account of concealing the notebook among ashes and then digging it up again. It would be strange for there to be two such incidents. He was probably making sure that the retrospective part remained with the book, so that even if the letter was lost there would be some commentary to remain with it.
28. Zalman Gradowski, 'Fartseykhenungen', in Ber Mark, *Megiles Oyshvits*, 288. References to this book will appear in the main body of the text from now on.
29. The Russian edition of this text, based on a recent examination of the manuscript, includes one partially legible paragraph before these three: 'Come to me, man of the free world, a world without fences [*ograd*], and I will tell you how ***** was enclosed within a fence [*zaborom*] and shackled with chains'. Zalman Gradowski, *V serdtsevine Ada: Zapiski naidennye v peple vozle pechei Osventsima*. Trans. Alexandra Polian (Moscow: Gamma, 2011), 57.
30. Technically, these figures are: parallelism, chiasmus, anaphora.
31. The pressure of time seems to have been felt in phases: the final copy goes from small, neat handwriting with no crossings out, to progressively scrappier and hastier-looking writing up to the middle of the book, before returning to neater and smaller writing.
32. The text starts with the train's departure. Jadwiga Bezwińska and Danuta Czech (eds), *Wśród koszmarnej zbrodni: Notaki więźniów z Sonderkommando odnalezione w Oświęcimiu* (Oświęcim: Wydawnictwo Państwowego Muzeum w Oświęcimiu, 1971), 75 (in 2nd edn, 133).
33. Thanks to Josie Riddle-Browne for pointing this out to me [DW].
34. The rhythm, and the connotations, of this sentence seem to me to demand the translation of *'fotografishn aparat'* as 'piece of photographic equipment', but it is the standard Yiddish term for a camera [DW]. We consider this passage alongside Georges Didi-Huberman's reading of it in Chapter 6.

35. Alexandre Prstojevic also reads this passage as a fictionalisation of Gradowski's journey, allowing him to imagine the thoughts and feelings of people he could not meet. Prstojevic, 'L'indicible et la fiction configuratrice', 37.
36. In his later manuscript, Gradowski also describes personal memories as playing like films through the minds of detainees. Zalman Gradowski, *In harts fun gehenem* (Jerusalem: Wolnerman, n.d. [c.1977]), 43.
37. As Wolfgang Schivelbusch points out, railways unified both the space and time of a nation, making even distant towns appear close. *The Railway Journey: The Industrialization of Time and Space in the Nineteenth Century* (Leamington Spa, Hamburg and New York: Berg, 1986), 33–44. This helped to produce the ability to grasp a nation as a whole. Schivelbusch also places a great deal of emphasis on speed and detachment from the landscape. Wojciech Tomasik identifies a similar tendency in Polish literature. *Ikona nowoczesności: Kolej w literaturze polskiej* (Wrocław: Wydawnictwo Uniwersytetu Wrocławskiego, 2007). Leah Garrett finds a comparable strand in Yiddish literature which laments the disruptive effects of train travel, as well as having a particular awareness of the dangers of public space for Jews. But she also notes that writers saw trains as offering the possibility of contact with the wider world and between Jewish communities. *Journeys beyond the Pale: Yiddish Travel Writing in the Modern World* (Madison: University of Wisconsin Press, 2003), 90–122. Gradowski could be said to be drawing on all these strands in his writing.
38. Simone Gigliotti, *The Train Journey: Transit, Captivity, and Witnessing in the Holocaust* (New York and Oxford: Berghahn Books, 2009).
39. Eliezer Eisenschmidt also tells Gideon Greif that his father said that if they did not turn left they would not go to Treblinka. Greif, *We Wept without Tears*, 219.
40. Dori Laub, 'An Event without a Witness', in Shoshana Felman and Dori Laub, *Testimony: Crises of Witnessing in Literature, Psychoanalysis and History* (London: Routledge, 1992), 80–81.
41. *Megiles Oyshvits*, 325–45. It should be pointed out that Dan Stone still finds much to marvel at in this passage, especially Gradowski's meditation on music. Stone, 'The Harmony of Barbarism', 26.
42. Zalman Gradowski, 'A levonedike nakht', *In harts fun gehenem*, 22–31. References to this book will appear in the main body of the text from now on.
43. Elie Wiesel, 'The Holocaust as Literary Inspiration', in Wiesel et al., *Dimensions of the Holocaust* (Evanston, IL: Northwestern University Press, 1977), 11.
44. Oleksy, 'Salmen Gradowski', 128.
45. The fact that four are in operation is consistent with the idea that this was composed before the summer of 1944, since Bunker II ('the little white house') came back into action as Bunker V at this time.
46. Zalman Gradowski, *Au cœur de l'enfer: Témoignage d'un Sonderkommando d'Auschwitz, 1944*, trans. Batia Baum (Paris: Tallandier, 2009), 233–34 n. 5.
47. *The Koren Sacks Siddur*, trans. and commentary Jonathan Sacks (Jerusalem: Koren, 2009), 716. See also b. Sanhedrin 41b–42a.
48. S.Y. Abramovitsh (Mendele Moykher Sforim), 'Fishke der Krumer', in *Ale shriftn fun Mendele Moykher Sforim*, vol. 1 (New York: Hebrew Publishing Company, n.d.), 48–49, 63–64.
49. Sholem Asch, *Geklibene verk* vol. 1: *Dos shtetl* (New York: Ykuf Ferlag, 1947), 131.
50. Dovid Einhorn, 'In a Levone-Nakht', *Shtile gezangen* (Warsaw: Ferlag Progres, 1910), 20; Moishe Kulbak, 'A Levone Nakht', *Shirim* (Vilnius: Farayn fun di Yidish Literatorn un Zhurnalistn in Vilne, 1920), 8; Uri Zvi Grinberg, *Farnakhtengold*

(Warsaw: Farlag 'Di Tsayt', 1921), 5, 204, 205; Naftali Imber, *Vos ikh zing un zog* (Lviv: n. pub., 1909), 47–55.

51. H. Leivick, 'Di Shtol', *Ale Verk* vol. 1 (New York: Posy-Shoulson Press, 1940), 199–200. See David G. Roskies, 'The Pogrom Poem and the Literature of Destruction', *Notre Dame English Journal* 11(2) (April 1979): 103–7.
52. Dan Miron, 'Uri Zvi Grinberg's War Poetry', in *The Jews of Poland between Two World Wars*, ed. Yisrael Gutman (Hanover, NH: University Press of New England, 1989), 368–82.
53. John Keats, 'Ode to Nightingale' (1819); Juliusz Słowacki, 'Księżyc' (1825); Heinrich Heine, 'Nacht liegt auf den fremden Wegen' (1826); Giacomo Leopardi, 'Canto notturno di un pastore errante dell'Asia' (1830). In this aspect, David Roskies sees Gradowski as simply an epigone of Polish Romanticism. Roskies, 'Wartime Victim Writing in Eastern Europe', 43.
54. Johann Wolfgang von Goethe, 'An den Mond', in *Sämtliche Werke*, ed. K. Richter, vol. 2.1 (Munich and Vienna: Carl Hanser Verlag, 1987), 35–36.
55. Sara Guyer, *Romanticism after Auschwitz* (Stanford, CA: Stanford University Press, 2007), 25–45. M.H. Abrams, *The Mirror and the Lamp: Romantic Theory and the Critical Tradition* (Oxford: Oxford University Press, 1971).
56. Jonathan Culler, 'Apostrophe', *Diacritics* 7(4) (Winter 1977): 63.
57. Fiona J. Stafford, *The Last of the Race: The Growth of a Myth from Milton to Darwin* (Oxford: Clarendon Press, 1994). Stafford points out that the figure of 'the last of the race' was often a poet. Chapter 4, 'The Last Bards', 83–108. Nachman Blumental draws directly on this trope when he describes the people involved in the Treblinka uprising as 'the last of the "Mohicans"'. Nachman Blumental, *Shmuesn vegn der yidisher literatur unter der daytsher okupatsye* (Buenos Aires: Tsentral Farband far Poylishe Yidn in Argentine, 1966), 128–29.
58. Yaakov Shavit, 'Politics and Messianism: The Zionist Revisionist Movement and Polish Political Culture', *Studies in Zionism* 6(2) (1985): 233–35.
59. In this famous monologue, the figure of Konrad, imprisoned for his rebellion against the Russian rule, blasphemously calls out against God for failing to help the people of Poland, and lays claim to forge his people's consciousness in his own poetry. He begins by dismissing 'the crowd', but by the climax says that 'my nation is incarnate in my soul'. Adam Mickiewicz, *Dziady/Forefathers' Eve III*, Scene II.
60. This may also relate to the rather more practical needs of remembering where the testimonies were buried, turning the space in which the SK were imprisoned into a kind of mnemonic. Shlomo Dragon had to remember where these documents were buried. Greif, *We Wept without Tears*, 165.
61. Although yahrzeit candles can be lit by men and women, sabbath candles are lit by the women of the family.
62. The earlier, 2001 edition follows the same order as Wolnerman. Zalman Gradowski, *Au cœur de l'enfer*, trans. Batia Baum (Paris: Editions Kimé, 2001).
63. The choice to pursue this path at some length has meant that we do not have the space to discuss the third section of the Yad Vashem manuscript here.
64. Most famously, it has been described by Filip Müller, both in *Shoah* (dir. Claude Lanzman, 1985), and in his book *Sonderbehandlung: Drei Jahre in den Krematorien und Gaskammern von Auschwitz*, literary collaboration with Helmut Freitag (Munich: Steinhausen, 1979), 143–89. Miroslav Kárný thinks that Gradowski is a more believable witness than Müller, but Kárný's focus is on the broader question of whether there were plans for a revolt at this stage. He notes that Müller did not mention

in earlier testimony much of what he said about the incident in *Sonderbehandlung*. Miroslav Kárný, 'Fragen zum 8. März 1944', *Theresienstädter Studien und Dokumente* (1999): 9–42. For an extraordinary recent meditation on this same set of events, see Otto Dov Kulka, *Landscapes of the Metropolis of Death: Reflections on Memory and Imagination*, trans. Ralph Mandel (London: Penguin, 2013).

65. This is a much told story. Haya Bar-Itzhak counts fourteen separate versions, not including Gradowski's. Haya Bar-Itzhak, 'Women in the Holocaust: The Story of a Jewish Woman Who Killed a Nazi in a Concentration Camp: A Folkloristic Perspective', *Fabula* 50(1–2) (2009): 67–77. See also Kirsty Chatwood, 'Schillinger and the Dancer: Representing Agency and Sexual Violence in Holocaust Testimonies', in *Sexual Violence against Jewish Women during the Holocaust*, ed. Sonia Hedgepeth and Rochelle G. Saidel (Hanover, MA, and London: University Press of New England, 2010), 61–74.

66. Leyb Langfus, 'Di 3000 nakete', in Mark, *Megiles Oyshvits*, 364. Filip Müller, *Sonderbehandlung*, 169.

67. As Miroslav Kárný points out, the members of the family camp could just as easily have reacted to the SK as if they were Kapos. 'Fragen zum 8. März 1944', 34–35.

68. Hermann Langbein, *People in Auschwitz* (Chapel Hill: University of North Carolina Press, 2004), 402–3.

69. Alvin H. Rosenfeld, *A Double Dying: Reflections on Holocaust Literature* (Bloomington: Indiana University Press, 1980), 164.

70. Elie A. Cohen, *Human Behaviour in the Concentration Camp* (London: Free Association Books, 1988), 141.

71. Richard Glazar, *Trap with a Green Fence: Survival in Treblinka*, trans. Roslyn Theobald (Evanston, IL: Northwestern University Press, 1995), 67. Trans. of *Die Falle mit dem grünen Zaun: Überleben in Treblinka* (Frankfurt: Fischer Taschenbuch Verlag, 1992), 69–70.

72. USC VHF 26983 Yehuda Bacon (seg 227).

73. We mean to refer to Kant's concept of 'disinterestedness' here – a 'judgment that is indifferent to the existence of the object' (Ak. V 209). Immanuel Kant, *Critique of Judgment*, trans. Werner Pluhar (Indianapolis: Hackett, 1987), 51.

74. Shlomo Venezia, *Inside the Gas Chambers: Eight Months in the Sonderkommando of Auschwitz* (Cambridge: Polity, 2009), 97.

75. Otto Moll in particular is reported to have taken pleasure in torturing and killing naked women. Müller, *Sonderbehandlung*, 226–27. Leon Cohen, *From Greece to Birkenau: The Crematoria Workers' Uprising*, trans. Jose-Maurice Gormezano (Tel Aviv: Salonika Jewry Research Centre, 1996), 47. David Olère, *Le SS Moll abat et précipite des jeunes femmes dans une des fosses d'incinération du crématoire V* (drawing, pen and ink, 1945).

76. This is more or less the way that Krystyna Oleksy reads it. Oleksy, 'Salmen Gradowski', 130.

77. Susan Gubar provides a discussion of prosopopoeia as a desire to speak for the dead, but also failing to accomplish it. Susan Gubar, *Poetry after Auschwitz: Remembering What One Never Knew* (Bloomington and Indianapolis: Indiana University Press, 2003), 177–206.

78. My translation is somewhat more literal, but still quite close to Robert Wolf's translation. Zalman Gradowski, 'The Czech Transport', trans. Robert Wolf, in *The Literature of Destruction*, ed. Roskies, 562–63 [DW].

79. Again, I have followed Robert Wolf rather too closely to call this translation entirely my own. Gradowski, 'The Czech Transport', 563–64 [DW]. Note, however, that Wolf repeatedly holds back detail that Gradowski includes: For example, he translates '*der boykh platst*' as 'the belly goes', and '*di kishkes un di gederem loyfn shnel fun im aroys*' as 'bowels and entrails are quickly consumed' (563). The reticence of this translation, its suppression of Gradowski's visceral descriptive inclinations, is noteworthy. It suggests discomfort on the part of the translator, a feeling that the reader should be spared this level of physical detail. This, of course, opens up interesting questions related to the ethics of translation which we cannot explore here.
80. Wygodzki thinks there are no calls for revenge ('A vort fun a gevezenem asir', 10), but Oleksy points out that Gradowski does include them ('Salmen Gradowski', 127).
81. It should be noted that the Yiddish version in the Marks' edition is not the original, but rather a translation back into Yiddish from Polish. When Esther Mark was forced to move to Israel, in the process of transferring papers for the book, the photocopy of the original was lost. Mark, *Megiles Oyshvits*, 350 n. 45. However, a photo reproduction of the letter from the St Petersburg Medical Military Museum is available in the Auschwitz archive.
82. Polian, 'I v kontse', 46.

Chapter 3

Scattered Selves

The Stories of Leyb Langfus

The Death of the Author

An unsigned manuscript found in the area of Crematoria II and III in 1952 ends with the following exhortation to its reader (Figure 3.1):

> I ask that all my various descriptions and notes, signed Y. A. R. A., which were buried in their time, be collected together and they are located in various boxes and jars in the courtyard of Crematorium 2 and also 2 longer descriptions one entitled 'The Deportation' it lies in a pit ^of bones^ at Crematorium 1 and also a description entitled Auschwitz it lies among bones strewn on the south-west side of the same courtyard; afterwards I rewrote and expanded it and buried it elsewhere in the ash by Crematorium 2 and put it into order and publish it ^all^ together under the name 'Amidst the Horror of Murder'[1]

As Chapter 1 has shown, producing a document such as this was not simply an individual task. Each of the materials with which it was written – paper, pen and ink – needed to be *organised* from within the network of barter and exchange in the concentration camp. Equally, finding containers that would preserve the texts once buried – the jars and boxes mentioned here – was a shared responsibility.[2] Even writing the words

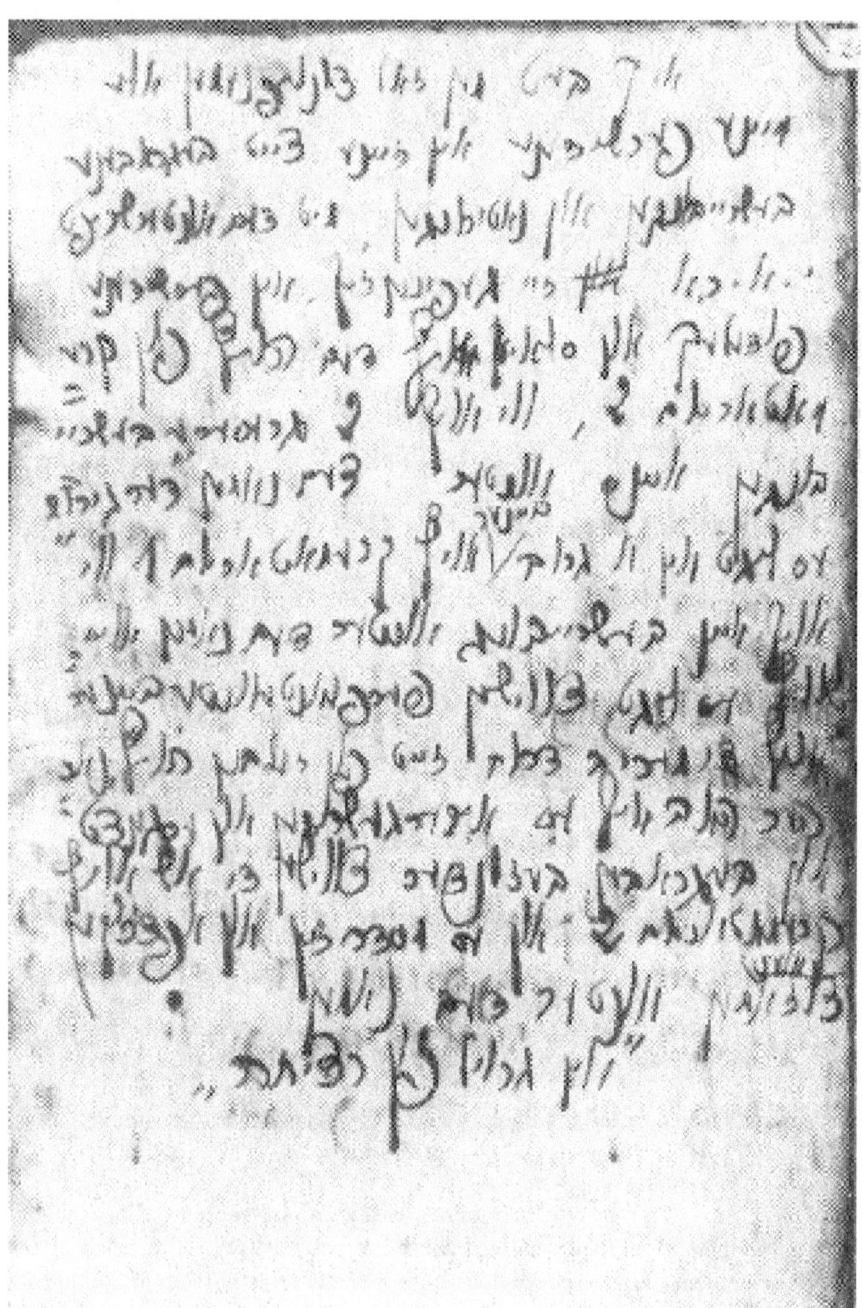

Figure 3.1. Photograph of the penultimate page of the lost manuscript by the 'anonymous' author, Leyb Langfus.

themselves seems to have had little greater importance than rewriting them; copying was vital as it doubled the chance of the information being found. Although one version of the manuscript 'Auschwitz' is enlarged ('*ergentst*'), it does not seem to take priority over the other: the locations of both versions are given. Writing transmits information about where more writing can be found. This long, snaking sentence, twisting to and fro between what the writer has done and what he asks the reader to do, binds reading and writing together, demanding the participation of whoever finds this document. The finder is given responsibility for looking for more manuscripts, for assembling them into one text, and for recognising them as all the work of one person. In a very real sense, the text calls upon the reader to bring the author into existence.

This chapter responds to that call by reading this manuscript, together with two others found in 1945 and 1962, as the work of one author: Leyb Langfus. But it also acknowledges its paradoxical nature: even at the point where he seems sure of his death and there is no need to conceal his identity, the author calls himself only by an acronym, and even that has not been found on any of the other documents discovered. Although the chapter will show that there are very good reasons to attribute them to one man, it will also address the significance of their anonymity, and the reasons why other scholars have ascribed them to a number of writers. It is no accident, we will argue, that the author remained nameless. Like his absenting himself from most of the action he describes, it was a significant decision about how to position himself in his own narratives. Moreover, the different forms – genres even – taken by his writings, which have led some to see them as the work of different hands, actually show that their author was making a range of choices about how to represent the events in which he took part. Taking seriously the idea that Langfus wrote all of these pieces, therefore, means acknowledging the living, thinking person who was behind them, and the ways in which his selfhood both continued through the different times at which he wrote, as well as the ways in which it was profoundly damaged and broken.

The Finds

The three documents we attribute to Langfus were found between 1945 and 1962. The first of these, a ledger entitled *The Deportation* ('*Der Geyresh*'), disinterred in the vicinity of Crematoria II and III in April 1945, is indisputably by Langfus. The narrator comes from Maków Mazowiecki, his wife at one point calls him 'Leyb', she is called Dvoyre and their son is called Shmuel. All of these details match those discovered about Langfus by Esther Mark. However, she appears not to have been aware of this book, as it did not come to the Auschwitz State Museum until 1970.[3] Esther Mark only attributed the two other anonymous finds to Langfus: an exercise book often called 'The Manuscript by an Unknown Author', found in the grounds of Crematorium III in the summer of 1952, and some loose sheets of paper found on 17 October 1962 buried alongside two other documents.[4] Mark's attribution of the first is borne out by the fact that the 1952 manuscript finishes with a statement from the author that he has buried other works in Crematoria II and III, among them one entitled *Der Geyresh*. Esther Mark also came up with an ingenious, albeit speculative, decoding of the only signature the author does offer, the acronym Y. A. R. A., by explaining it as a translation of the author's name into Hebrew.[5]

The find from 1962 includes an exercise book signed by Zalman Lewental, and the Auschwitz museum has assigned all of these texts to him. But, in addition to a list of transports in Polish, there were in fact two Yiddish manuscripts: the bound exercise book and some loose leaves. Even though as part of the process of preservation all the pages were detached from each other, so they are now all kept loose, the bound and loose parts are still clearly distinguishable. The staples, as discussed in Chapter 1, have stained the bound part brown, while the other pages have a very distinct green colour. These loose leaves are written in a different way (continuously rather than one way through the book and then back again), in a different ink, with different spelling and distinctly different handwriting. Ber Mark too distinguished the handwriting of these pages from Lewental's notebook, and believed them to be in the same handwriting as the 1952 find;[6] moreover the handwriting of *The Deportation* looks very similar to both of them. We therefore agree with Esther Mark that Leyb Langfus was the author of the two unsigned Sonderkommando documents known to her, and believe that these and *The Deportation* need to be examined together as Langfus's work.

Esther Mark was also able to research something of Langfus's biography, and this is mostly what we have to go on for an account of his life before Auschwitz. He was born around 1910 in Warsaw, and after a yeshiva education moved to the town of Maków Mazowiecki, about 50 miles north of Warsaw.[7] There, in 1933 or 1934 he married Dvoyre, daughter of Shmuel Yoysef Rozental, dayan (rabbinic judge) of the town. After his father-in-law's death, Langfus was elected in his place as dayan. They had one son, called Shmuel.[8] When the rabbi fled to Warsaw at the beginning of the war, Esther Mark claims that Langfus became spiritual leader of Maków.[9] However, there are only passing references to Langfus in the memorial book of Maków from 1969, only by surname, without much detail about him. He is identified as the man who became dayan in 1934, beating the candidate from the 'Hasidic side'.[10] The family was deported to Auschwitz via the transit camp in Mława, arriving in early December 1942. Langfus's wife and son were killed within a day or two of arrival, and he was conscripted into the Sonderkommando a few days later.[11]

He is mentioned, usually not by name but as the dayan or maggid (preacher) from Maków, in the testimonies of a number of survivors, including two of the best-known books of Sonderkommando testimony, those by Filip Müller and Miklós Nyiszli.[12] Mordechai Ciechanower also tells of his meetings with Langfus in his much more recent account.[13] Langfus attempted to be as observant as possible; testimonies mention him trying to keep kosher.[14] He was kept, as far as possible, from the work of handling bodies. Several testimonies mention him writing.[15] He also seems to have tried to play some part in the uprising of 7 October 1944, but survived it. Müller and Nyiszli describe him as being killed on 26 November 1944, which accords with the last dated entry in the writings.[16]

The accounts given by former members of the SK (and, indeed, the brief description Zalman Lewental gives of him too) paint a picture of a strictly and unbendingly religious man, who saw a divine plan even in what was happening in Birkenau, and only rarely expressed doubt.[17] But this picture is not easily borne out by the texts that Langfus wrote – powerful, disturbing and painful accounts of loss and suffering.[18] He shows a knowledge of Judaism, but does not always draw explicitly upon a religious framework to understand the events. Thus, although it might be possible to read his stories in a more religious way, we read his writing more as exploring ethical and affective modes of witnessing, purposely trying to get through to the future reader with an emotional connection, creating something like what Dominick LaCapra calls 'empathic unsettlement'.[19] Like Zalman Gradowski's, Langfus's writing has a literary dimension, therefore. His French translator claims that he is 'simply report[ing] the facts',[20] but there is considerably more to his testimony.[21] Rhetorical effects such as irony and hyperbole are deployed, sayings and proverbs in Yiddish are drawn upon and reworked, and the storytelling traditions of the Jews of the Pale of Settlement evoked. Langfus can be seen to have taken a good deal of care in structuring his pieces of writing, in ways that both draw upon narrative traditions within Yiddish, and that also meditate carefully upon the relationship of individual suffering and collective trauma.

The Deportation

This manuscript, the first of Langfus's writings to have been discovered, is also almost certainly the first of the surviving texts that he wrote.[22] Whereas the documents discovered later mostly tell of events in the Birkenau crematoria between 1943 and 1944, *The Deportation* gives an account of the liquidation of the ghetto in Maków Mazowiecki in November and December 1942. It begins with the announcement of the liquidation, and ends with the population of Maków being gassed. The text has been used by historians as a source of information about the ghetto in Maków, and has helped to establish the facts as they are known.

Maków had a Jewish population of about 3,700 out of about 6,700 inhabitants before the war. After the invasion of Poland in 1939, the area it was part of was annexed to the German Reich as *Regierungsbezirk Zichenau*, part of East Prussia rather than the Wartheland. After initial atrocities, the destruction of the synagogue and attempts to encourage Jews to flee over the German–Soviet border, Jews were confined to one part of Maków, which was eventually (between late 1940 and early 1941) surrounded by a fence. Most Jewish men were forced to work in labour camps in the area, but were then brought back to Maków for the deportation, announced in November 1942. The inhabitants were taken en masse on carts driven by conscripted Polish peasants to the town of Mława, a rail centre 50 miles north, before being taken by train to Auschwitz-Birkenau in early December.[23]

Langfus's text is therefore an important historical document, but not just for what is documented. How details and events are chosen, and how they are placed together is important. *The Deportation* begins with a date, 31 October, and the sense of a narrative that proceeds in a linear and relatively slow way: several pages are given over to the execution by hanging of twenty Jewish workers on the site of the synagogue. Following this, with the end of one page damaged and the beginning of another very hard to read, there is the announcement from the ghetto commissar Steinmetz that all inhabitants of the ghetto in Maków will be deported: the fit will go to a mine in Silesia, the unfit to Małkinia. Many pages after this are given over to discussing the reaction of Maków's Jews. This seems to be a continuous narrative, with the announcement being given immediately after the hanging, but other historical accounts show these to have taken place several months apart. The hanging of twenty Jews was in July 1942; the announcement in November.[24]

It is possible that the mass hanging is being referred to retrospectively in the narrative, and that the damaged part brings the reader back to the autumn of 1942. But the pace of the telling goes against this idea, and suggests that the extant part reflects what was written: an announcement immediately after an execution. This may simply stem from an error of memory on Langfus's part, or even from not being in Maków at the time, but placing these two events together makes sense if his text is approached as a piece of writing, concerned with conveying meanings as well as facts. Mass execution is compounded with an announcement of resettlement to draw out the latter's equivalence to the former, to show the powerlessness of those receiving the announcement, and to highlight the way the execution was a form of terrorising and cowing the people so that they would be less willing to resist other moves against them.[25]

This is only one small example of the decisions Langfus made about how to pace and structure his writing, decisions that are at work across the entirety of this text, even in the simple device of dividing it into chapters. The edition published by the Auschwitz museum does include chapter titles, but only six of them, with numbers that do not run in sequence: 1, 6, 10, 11, 12 and 17.[26] Rather than trying to identify the other chapters, however, or assuming that the titles occur in damaged parts, the editors suggest that 'the author may also have been making notes in a second notebook, which he hid in a different place'.[27] Such an implausible proposition can only stem from an idea that chapters are simply parts that do not need to add up to a whole: in other words that they each, independently, convey information, and that the structure they are part of does not need to be considered. In fact, other chapter titles are clearly

Figure 3.2. Detail of page [22] 27 from *The Deportation*. The title of Chapter 4 can be made out in the middle of the image.

identifiable in the manuscript. Numbers 2, 4 and 5 are all fairly easily decipherable (Figure 3.2), and there are plausible candidates for chapter titles for most of the ones missing between 1 and 17 (see Appendix A). Damage towards the end of the document becomes too extensive for us to be able to assess whether there are any chapter titles after Chapter 18. It may be that the last twenty-five pages were not divided in this way, but even this is not certain.

An examination of the content of the chapters and the divisions between them shows that, like chapters in most books, they serve a structuring function. The end of Chapter 5 draws it to a climactic close: 'the chaos of ××× had reached its culmination point'.[28] A short phrase that has a line to itself, and includes the word 'commission', would appear to be the title of Chapter 7 (the number may just about be discernible on that line). Following this title, there are lines that are very difficult to decipher, but include 'chapter on its own, which teaches the ××× highest degree of trickery'. Here Langfus would appear to be saying that he has clear reasons for his chapter divisions. There are particular points that he wants his readers to gain from these chapters, and they are structured and titled to highlight them. In most chapters, the title simply summarises what happens in this chapter. Titles may sometimes have been added retrospectively, such as the title for Chapter [9], 'Saying Farewell' (*gezegenung*), which is written at the top of page [42] 47 in much fainter ink than the following line; or Chapter 17, which started as 'In the Square', but was changed to 'To the Train' ([83] 88). At other times they look as though they are part of the run of writing, for example '5 In the Street', and 'Chapter 6 The Psalm'.[29] These two are emblematic titles: not summarising the whole chapter, but rather anticipating one moment within it, when people come out into the street and discuss their fears, and when prayer provides some way for feeling to be expressed.

There must, therefore, have been some element of forethought to the text in its final form. Langfus had probably been a prisoner in Auschwitz for some time before he began to write *The Deportation*. It is possible that he had a chance to think over his story before he began to commit it to paper. The final pages also show that he drafted some parts of it before writing it up in the notebook. The evidence thus suggests an element of planning in Langfus's writing procedure, as well as some improvisation. Going back and inserting titles indicates that he also reviewed what he wrote. These simple observations show how describing this and other Sonderkommando documents as diaries, as will be discussed further in Chapter 5, is a misnomer. Unlike the entries of a diary, which are usually separated according to the days when they are made, the division of Langfus's text into chapters was not dictated by the time when they were written. They were instead a structure that Langfus gave to his story. They may have served some mnemonic function, and may also have given him some framework by which to control emotionally very difficult material.[30] But they also guide readers through the events, and give them some meaning.

Figuring Separation

One striking example of the use of chapter structure in this book occurs early on, soon after the ghetto's liquidation is announced. Only one section of the book (at least in its legible parts) is given over to the narrator's own individual experience, and that of his wife and son ([14] 9–[22] 27). This section would appear to form Chapter [3]. The beginning, at the top of page [14] 9, is at the least a new paragraph, and is certainly starting a new topic from the previous page: the story shifts from a meeting discussing the possibility of resistance to Leyb's wife coming in off the street. The marks above this line look to have been added afterwards, and could even be the chapter heading. The end is clearly identifiable, with the title of Chapter 4 appearing below. Within this chapter, his wife expresses her fears for their son, who sensing her worry cries out and asks his father to do all he can to keep him alive. Leyb eventually feels he has to lie to him, and say that they will be able to hide in the attic, and escape to find refuge with a non-Jewish family. At the very end of the chapter, he describes himself standing by the bed while his son sleeps.

> My son's words rang in my ears: 'Daddy, I want to live, do everything you can so that I can stay alive. What can be done – I want to live so much.' I stood by my child's bed and studied every lineament of his face. I scrutinised the curve of his brow, his nose, ears, and even the nails on his hands. In case my fate will be sealed and we will have to part, whether living or dead, I must now give my eyes their fill of his features, so he will stay forever before my eyes. Deeply embittered, despairing and broken, I stood a long long time and felt my entire self [*mayn gantser ikh*] disappear in relation to my child. I imagined the utter bleakness of my life without my child. The hollow meaning of my existence, which would be blotted out from my life. And I shook convulsively from anxiety and fear of the days looming ahead. My mouth suddenly transformed itself into a spring, gently flowing with heart-rending words, torn from the most secret and hidden recesses of my soul, fiercely painful, powerfully piercing, deeply seething words, which worked upon me so suggestively that all forms of expression in the world seemed empty and meaningless compared to my catastrophe. An unquenchable pain and deepest hopelessness took hold of me and I embodied [*ferkerpert*] my great, terrible tragedy in one slow, broken sound, interr<upt>ed by deep sighs, of one single word that contained the entire horror of my fate: 'Shmuel, my little Shmuel,' which I cried out endlessly long. ([20] 25–[22] 27)]

This is a moment of crushing emotional pain for Leyb, which must have come back to Langfus as he wrote this passage. But examining and communicating these emotions seems to have been both necessary and possible for him, and he clearly spent time and effort trying to do so. In searching for the right expression, Langfus uses sequences of near-synonyms which suggest that the words of his description are not enough, and this has a parallel in the way all expressions become 'empty and meaningless'. But the fact that he keeps searching also fits with the way that language has power in this passage, from the effect that his son's words have on Leyb to the way the name Shmuel is used to express his despair and grief. Words have a material existence here, bound up with the bodies that they work through and work upon, escaping conscious control, coming out as a mixture of sounds and sighs, and allowing Leyb to embody (*ferkerpern*) his tragedy. The word 'Shmuel' is spoken slowly and repeatedly, as if, perhaps, the extended length of the vocable registers his unwillingness to let go of the child, a refusal to end the word preserving connection with what it refers to. That the name is painful to say, physically hurting the speaker, is affirmed through the sonic unevenness Langfus describes. The word tears, injures, the body from which it emerges.

And, it would seem, the word's potential to harm was what Langfus was drawing upon, reliving this pain in order to transmit some of it to his readers. He does not divorce the pain from literary or figurative use of language, however. It is precisely at the moment where Leyb loses his sense of self and control over his own body that the one metaphor of the passage appears: his mouth becomes a spring. This is language that is being used, considered, shaped, by Langfus as he is writing. Such shaping includes the fact that these pages appear at the end of a chapter, making them the climax of an overwhelmingly emotional episode, but also placing some boundaries upon it, bringing it to some kind of end. As Nathan Cohen notes, Langfus 'does not return to the subject of his personal vicissitudes, and abandons completely the use of the first person singular'.[31] Confining this personal element to one chapter might itself be a way of containing his feelings, ones that must be acknowledged, but that would be too difficult for him to sustain throughout his narrative project.

Nonetheless, this chapter also works within the sequence of chapters that surround it. Chapters 1 ('The First Announcement') and 2 ('Confusion and *****') present the official declaration of a 'resettlement' and the reaction to it. Chapter 4 ('A Fraudulent Hoax') shows how Steinmetz changed the initial declaration to persuade the inhabitants of the ghetto that their families would remain together. All take place in a public space, and form a narrative whole. Chapter [3] takes place in what seems to be the private space of one home. Placing Leyb and his family within this self-contained chapter sets them apart from the collectivity, whose story continues on either side of them, seemingly unaffected. But it also embeds them into the structure of the entire piece, working out the relationship between a part (a self, a family) and a whole (a community, even the Jewish people), which does not equate one with the other, or subsume one under the other, but rather allows both to coexist in an uneasy, but necessary connection.[32] Chapter [3] shows the emotional consequences of the announcement and reactions of the first two chapters being played out within one family, and also a private deception taking place in anticipation of the public deception of Chapter 4. It both personalises and individualises the initial situation, and shows the foundation for the way that Steinmetz is able to fool the Jews of Maków.

The need to return as little as possible to the personal and its dangerous attendant emotions is particularly evident in Chapter [9]. Here, the dayan from Maków Mazowiecki, last in a series of speakers including the head of the Judenrat, and the rabbi from the nearby town of Krasnosielc,[33] warns that they are probably going to their deaths.

> The most moving and bravest of the speakers was the last, the dayan of Maków. He dealt with the subject with complete frankness, warning against illusions and unwillingness to believe: people should be ready and prepared for the fact that they were taking us to an inevitable death. When leaving their houses they should say farewell to all their nearest [*zikh gezegenen mit ale nohntste*] … to their wives, to their children. We were all going to lay down our lives for our faith [*mir geyen ale af kidesh hashem*]. ([43] 48)

Quite understandably, Czech and Bezwińska take the author of this account and the dayan of Maków to be separate individuals,[34] but, as we have noted, a number of testimonies show them to be the same person.[35] As strange as it seems, it must be the case that Langfus is writing about himself in the third person.[36] While one cannot dismiss entirely the possibility that he writes in this way in order simply to sing his own praises in an ostensibly objective manner, it suggests another reading. Here the public figure of the dayan, who speaks for the entirety of the community, who knows what will happen to them and what they must do, is set apart from the figure of Leyb who is defined entirely by his family ties. However, although the dayan is set apart to some degree from the narrative voice, the two blend in the fact that his speech is given indirectly, that he predicts how the narrative will unfold, and even in the fact that his words are taken up in what appears to be this chapter's title: 'Saying Farewell' ('*gezegenung*') ([42] 47). So although ostensibly the unity of narrator and dayan is concealed, the narrative reveals it. The fact that he can now only appear in the text in the third person also figures the way Langfus becomes a writer of these events, in the main part feeling the need to absent himself from the narrative as a protagonist.

Dori Laub and Nancy Auerhahn observe:

> The word 'we' is often found in survivors' narratives. It is possible that its use sometimes reflects a high degree of social bonding … but often 'we' is a defense against saying 'I' with any feeling.[37]

While Laub and Auerhahn's claim does make some sense of the narrative strategy Langfus deploys, it must be remembered that at points he does use 'I', and seems to have built both its presence and absence into the structure of his account.[38] It appears almost exclusively in one chapter where he even goes so far as to describe his 'entire self' (literally 'entire I' [*gantzer ikh*]) as disappearing. Rather than simply avoiding individual feeling, he shows how it overwhelms the sense of self. Langfus is not simply acting out, or even recording, this situation, but meditating on it. The need to allow both personal and impersonal modes to coexist in this text suggests the need to preserve the tension of different kinds of selves (Leyb, the dayan). In other words, there are parts here that do seem to fit with common models of trauma (such as Laub's), but others that do not. He is perhaps traumatised, certainly psychologically damaged, by his suffering, but he is able, in some sense, to understand it as it is happening to him: in the middle of the event, rather than retrospectively.

A Corpus of Feelings

The impersonal and collective narrative voice of the rest of the chapters does not preclude the description of feelings, but rather gives rise to other methods of representing them. What Langfus hit upon was actually quite an unusual method of narrative: one that mostly dealt with people in a collective, and often – and most strikingly – described their emotional responses physically. Individual voices are heard, but usually without names assigned to them. They are described usually as 'we' or discussed in general terms: 'what each man felt', for example.

Emotional responses are almost always presented in bodily terms: feelings of breathlessness, hearts beating, hot anger burning through bodies.[39] These feelings, then, are grounded not so much in subjectivities (although this side is not denied) as in bodily sensations.

The family members came back from the Gemeinde. Their hearts were beating from walking so fast. They had difficulty breathing when they spoke. Their confusion, distraction and wild terrified eyes robbed the normal facial colouring from those around, and a chalk-whiteness came over their faces, even before they knew what had actually happened. ([20] 11)

Here, one set of physical states induces another set of physical states in the onlookers, prior to any intellectual understanding being achieved or words being spoken. The experience of reading this text works in a similar way: these descriptions of physical states can have an intense effect on the reader. What the bodies are doing is entirely imaginable. None of these physical states is unknown to a reader; none of them is about the sensation of intense pain or physical damage. They are, rather, reminders of living breathing bodies undergoing what was, already in the ghetto, an experience of vulnerability and powerlessness which caused intense anguish.

This must, we think, have been part of what Langfus was aiming at in recording the experience in this way. These are extraordinary attempts to communicate not just what happened but how it felt, made in such a way that that feeling might be recognisable. Whereas survivors frequently demonstrate the need to say that words cannot convey the sensations of cold or hunger that they underwent, Langfus had no hope that anything other than his words would survive. The words had to evoke whatever bodily presence the reader was to feel.[40]

This emphasis on embodiment in Langfus is quite different from Gradowski's physical descriptions. Although, for example, the wording to describe the rhythmic beating of hearts is not so very different from that of Gradowski, it serves another function entirely. Gradowski's bodies are either reanimated by his poetic power, or operate as symbols that can be made to mean on a 'higher' plane. Langfus is concerned with transmitting something of what it felt like to be those bodies. These collective sensations, operating at the physical level, might be described as 'affects': bodily responses that have not yet been fully processed or assigned meanings as specific emotions. Jill Bennett argues that artworks that draw upon affect can transmit something of an experience of pain or trauma to viewers without allowing simple identification with and appropriation of it.[41] We would suggest that at these points *The Deportation* works in a similar way, to disturb its readers without giving them a definable point of view to identify with.

Langfus's method of presenting the journey to Auschwitz is also very different from Gradowski's. Gradowski provides a dramatic and tension-filled account of the journey from Kiełbasin to Auschwitz, unified by his own role as narrator. Langfus's 'I' disappears during this journey; his account is given coherence by its structure. Everything begins to shrink. Hopes are mentioned a number of times, but always as being lost: smaller and smaller hopes that are progressively taken away. The narrative moves through a set of spaces that become increasingly bare and constricted: the deserted homes of the Mława ghetto, in which they are temporarily housed ([56] 61); the ruined mill in which they wait for the train ([79] 84–[83] 88); the freight cars into which they are crammed ([88] 93–[90] 95), and finally the gas chamber ([95] 106). The Jews of Maków are stripped of their homes, their possessions, their lives, and eventually even their bodies. The length of each episode also works as part of this structure, with a decreasing amount of time spent in each location: half the book takes place in Maków, a third in Mława, and the final twenty pages in Auschwitz.

Although much of the part describing the arrival and gassing at Birkenau is not readily decipherable, here too events can be fitted into a pattern, returning to themes and anxieties raised earlier in the book. The worry expressed close to the beginning, that their bones will find no rest ([9] 18), is in fact realised at the very end ([98] 109). Equally, the mention of Leyb's wife and child in the third chapter is matched by the mention of their deaths. Langfus does include a description of a gas chamber here, but once again this is done in a very different way from Gradowski. These are people that he knows, including his own family. At this point the first person singular briefly reappears.

> Falling down dead in such a confined space the people pressed against each other in 5 or 6 layers, one on top of the other to over a metre in height. Mothers were left sitting on the ground clutching their children, men and women hugging each other. Some were stuck in a bent over posture on account of the mass [*a teyl zenen gebliben tsulieb di mase shteyn in a ibergeboygte poze*], the legs standing up, and from the waist up lying down. Some were left completely blue under the effect of the gas, and some completely fresh, as if sleeping. One group did not go into the bunker. They were held in a wooden hut until 11 in the morning the next day. They heard the despairing voices of the people being gassed, and worked out exactly what was awaiting them. They witnessed everything [*zey hoben ales tsugezehen*]. They suffered the greatest pain in the world in that accursed night and half a day. Whoever has not lived through such a thing [*der vos hot nisht azelkhes iberlebt*] cannot have the slightest conception of it. As I later found out, my wife and son were among <them>. ([96] 107–[97] 108)

Unlike the sea of flesh that Gradowski describes, it is the differences between people that seem much more important to Langfus. Even when some descriptions are very similar, he emphasises their relationships, and the different ways that they are affected by the gas. The concern is for precision and discrimination. And while this devastating passage clearly indicates that Langfus has seen the gas chamber himself, it is not really centred on his experience. It is not clear who 'lived through' the events he describes. Is it Langfus himself or the people locked in the wooden hut? It is they who are presented as the people who 'witnessed everything', even if they did not actually see it: their knowledge of the murders is an acoustic rather than visual one. This claim finds an echo in Primo Levi's statement that the true witnesses were those who did not survive.[42] The suffering too is that of the victims, not his own. After the bare sentence in which he mentions his wife and child, Langfus moves on to the facts of the bodies being cleared from the gas chamber, and says nothing directly about his own feelings. They are both only imaginable and indescribable.

The narrative ends with a description of their bodies being burnt, with the ashes and bones ground up and scattered so that no trace of their existence remains. Two leaves from an address book on which some of this material has been written was inserted into the notebook, after part of it was copied and reworked in the notebook itself. Probably in the belief that he did not have time to copy everything written on these pages, it would seem that Langfus decided that they could serve as the end point of the story (Figure 3.3).

Figure 3.3. Detail of page [99] 111, inserted loose at the end of *The Deportation*.

> The murderer washed his bloody hands. ~~The fire~~ The frying and roasting of people [*dos preglen un broten zikh fun mentshen*] xxx made the air in the entire area greasy [*ferfestet* (sic – read as *ferfetst*) *di luft in gantsen umgend*]. As soon as people got out of the cars, they already smelt [*gefihlt dem reyekh*] the people burning. ([99] 111–[100] 112)

These lines show that even in the circumstances in which Langfus was writing, and even when describing the most abject moment for him, he was concerned with finding words that measured up to the event. There is a desire for precision; describing the process as simply 'fire' is not enough: he has to use both 'frying and roasting', showing how the bodies were burnt, using their own fat as fuel. There is a need to emphasise the grease with three words evoking it: '*preglen*', '*broten*', '*ferfetst*'. This is a horrific description of cooking flesh, carefully unsparing, also suggesting something of Langfus's own status as a witness. Smell, perhaps even touch, are evoked – proximal senses. Langfus lived in direct proximity to death, and the oiliness evoked in the passage literally adhered to him.

At the same time Langfus seems also to have felt the need not to say everything, or that some things, even if written down in these circumstances, should not be read. The word before '*ferfetst*', presumably the word for which it substitutes, is very heavily crossed out. We believe there is a case to be made that it is '*fershtunken*', which literally means 'stank out', but is also used to mean: 'contemptible'. Langfus is as precise as possible, but perhaps he does not want to denigrate or dehumanise those who have died. It is the burning of 'people' ('*mentshen*'), not bodies, that he describes. He calls the smell from the bodies '*reyekh*' – a neutral term. This is a piece written at speed, one letter running into another, leaving them not fully formed. But nonetheless, Langfus not only feels it is important to spend time being as precise as possible, but also to spend time making something he has written as illegible as possible. There is no other place in the book where he crosses anything out so forcefully. At this moment, he demonstrates a sense of moral responsibility towards those he is writing about, towards his writing. Morality is registered through the urgent vigour with which he has obliterated a word, through a moment of reflexivity preserved in a veil of ink, a brief yet tangible back and forth of the pen meant to undo a word already upon the page. This is remarkable considering the circumstances under which Langfus is composing his account. Indeed, considering these circumstances, it may be that it is not appropriate to try to work out what he wrote, that there is an ethical demand on readers *not* to read parts that Langfus clearly did not want to be read.

Scattered Selves: The Stories of Leyb Langfus • 109

'The 3000 Naked Women'

The Deportation is a story of one kind of suffering only ending as it gives way to another, even worse, kind, and must have been unbearably difficult for Langfus to write. But he writes with such scrupulousness that it makes sense to see him raising concerns about testimony that have occupied later scholars: who it is that can witness, what that witnessing should consist of, and how that knowledge can be conveyed.[43] Such concerns become much more pressing when his own position becomes more difficult, and he begins to tell stories from the time when he was in the Sonderkommando. The SK feature briefly in *The Deportation* as gas-masked functionaries, who clear the gas chamber and dispose of the bodies. In the two later episodes found in 1962, they play a more personalised and compromised role, meeting the victims before they enter the gas chamber, standing by while the victims turn to them in vain. Both of these pieces describe events from 1944, about the last moments of particular groups brought to the crematorium in which Langfus was working. 'The 600 Boys' gives a brief, three-page account of a group of 12- to 18-year-olds driven into the gas

Figure 3.4. Detail of a page from the account 'The 3000 Naked Women'. The words *nisht beobakhtet* appear followed by white space on the fourth line.

chamber with great violence while pleading for mercy from the SS and help from the Sonderkommando.⁴⁴ 'The 3000 Naked Women' is somewhat longer (ten pages), and tells the story of a group starved for three weeks in Block 25 of Birkenau before being brought to Crematorium II. Much of this story is provided by lengthy speeches given by the women, who explain what has happened to them and lament their fate.

Just as in *The Deportation*, for most of these stories Langfus does not place himself in the action, although he does provide some judgements and statements as a narrator. But he does mention himself once, on the penultimate page of 'The 3000 Naked Women' (Figure 3.4).

> I quickly disappeared, and what happened next I didn't *observe* [*dem vayterdig farloyf hob ikh shoyn nisht beobakhtet*], because in principle I was never present when Jews were driven to their deaths, because it <cou>ld <have> happened that the SS-men would have conscripted me for <their> <mu>rderous <purposes> at the crematorium.⁴⁵

Clearly, among descriptions of the Sonderkommando's failure to help the victims, asserting his presence only in so far as he was absent looks like an attempt to escape the taint of this group. But other readings are suggested by the strong emphasis placed on the word '*beobakhtet*'. Langfus left the rest of the line blank after this word and seems to have spaced the letters out rather more (the equivalent in Hebrew script of using italics). '*Baobakhtn*' does occur in Yiddish, but almost all authorities regard it as non-standard, and too Germanic (*daytshmerish*). Although Langfus's language is often very German-influenced, this use of the word, and the stress placed upon it, could perhaps have been calling upon its German origin, implying that this kind of seeing would place him alongside the German oppressors, even before being 'conscripted … for their murderous purposes'. This would be seeing as a violation of the victims (the German word *beobachten* can be used to describe surveillance), putting them at a distance, keeping them under control. And so we would suggest that it indicates Langfus's own awareness of the difficulties of his position as a witness. Not just that he is trying to preserve some sense of apartness from the crimes being carried out before him, being able to disclaim responsibility for them, but also that he is refusing certain ways of witnessing, *observing*, that might themselves be part of that system of crimes.

The same word appears four pages earlier in a very different context, a strangely abstract concatenation of phrases, when one of the Sonderkommando confronts the horror of these women's deaths.

They examined our faces to see if we had sympathy [*mitleyd*] for them. One man stood to one side and observed the abyss of deep [or abyss-deep?] solitude of these defenceless agonised souls [*beobakhtet dem tom tifen elend fun di dozike shutzloze ferpaynikte nefeshes*]. He could not control himself and burst out crying. One young girl said, Ah! That I have yet lived to see [*derlebt*] before my death an expression of sympathy [*mitgefihl*], a tear shed for our terrible fate, here in this murderers' camp, where people are tortured, beaten, made to suffer and killed, where we've seen our fill [*men zet zikh on*] of savage murders and wrongdoings without limit, where we become dulled and hardened [*ferglivert*] to the greatest suffering, where every human feeling [*gefihl*] withers, where a brother or sister falls before your eyes [*far dayne oygen*], and you don't even mark it with a sigh. That there should be a person who is moved by our bitter misfortune, who expresses his sympathy [*mitgefihl*] through tears. Oh! What wonderful vision is this? Something unnatural? My death will be marked by a sigh, a tear from a living Jew. There is still someone who will mourn us, and I thought that we would disappear from this world like abandoned orphans. I find in this young man some small consolation; among mere bandits and criminals, I have lived to see [*derlebt*] before my death a man who feels [*a mentsh vos fihlt*].[46]

What it is that the man has observed is certainly nothing concrete – an 'abyss', 'loneliness', 'souls' – and the syntactic relationship between these words is unclear. But it has a shattering effect on him, which the girl describes as 'unnatural': miraculous, impossible, wonderful and terrible at the same time.[47] She sees in his crying that he is someone who is able to feel, not just someone who can see. The two moments where she mentions people seeing the atrocities in the camp ('we've seen our fill of bloody murders and wrongdoings'; 'a brother or sister falls before your eyes') are also ones where there is no reaction. The kind of witness being demanded here is not simply one able to attest to the facts. They do not just need witnesses; they need mourners. The story, therefore, as well as being a form of witnessing of these women's last few hours, can be read as a meditation on what kind of witnessing is appropriate. Seeing the women die is less significant than being moved by their fate, and this is true of both the SK member who bursts into tears, and Langfus in his decision not to stay to the end. The fact that he recorded and attempted to transmit this story shows he may well have felt it would also hold true for his readers.

'Particulars'

After the highly emotional tones that characterise both *The Deportation* and the stories buried with Zalman Lewental's document, the most substantial section of the 1952 manuscript seems a very different piece of writing. In this section, to which he gave the title '*Eyntselheyten*' (particulars, details), Langfus plays no part at all in the scenes he describes. The 'particulars' are each paragraph-long anecdotes about events in the crematoria, details that seem to have struck him and were then compiled into a series, but left out of chronological order. Many of these have similar content to what he recorded in his two longer stories: the guilt-wracked behaviour of the Sonderkommando, the suffering of children, things said and done by people on the verge of the gas chamber, and the atrocities carried out by the SS. But the emotions of the narrator are much harder to discern.

> It was the end of summer 1944. They brought in a transport from Slovakia. All of them knew for certain that they were definitely going to their deaths. But they remained calm, got undressed and went into the gas chamber. Going naked from the undressing room into the gas chamber, a woman said: 'Maybe a miracle will still happen for us.'[48]

Langfus strips his description down to the bare facts, but the incident hardly seems to have been chosen because of the information it would convey. It is also very difficult to tell what judgement can be made of the woman: is it an admirable example of faith enduring to the end, or a case of someone refusing to give up false hopes? If it offers neither information nor a judgement, perhaps then it is the fact that it is such a striking, such an emotionally unsettling, piece to read that is important. It is plausible to think that witnessing this incident had an effect on Langfus too – in a similar way, perhaps, to the response of the Sonderkommando to one of the three thousand naked women. If Langfus recorded it because of his own reaction, he probably did so in order that it would also have an effect on whoever read it. The bareness and simplicity of the tale, the lack of commentary, and the structure, all help it to have that effect. Langfus, therefore, was selecting and crafting what he wrote so that it would create a feeling in his readers. This, over and above any information, was what he wanted to convey.

A number of other 'particulars' work in a similar way: the story of the prisoners who are happy to die as long as they are fed beforehand; the story of the child who calls a Sonderkommando a murderer and refuses to let him help her undress her little brother; the story of the Poles and the Dutch Jews who die singing the Internationale together. In yet others, however, the distance adopted by the narrator goes hand-in-hand with a form of judgement, subtly yet insistently present in each turn of phrase. In one story a young man (by implication a secular intellectual), convinces people who have been preparing for death that they will not be murdered.

His speech is given in part, finished with a contemptuous '*un azoy vayter*' – 'etcetera'.

> Only when the gas was thrown in did this preacher of morals and deeply convinced man of conscience come round from his naïveté [*oysgenikhtert fun zayn naivitet*]. His arguments, with which he had so forcefully calmed [*kreftig beruhigt*] his brothers, were shown to be an illusion with which he'd fooled himself [*a iluzye fun zelbst opnareray*]. But he grew wise too late [*er iz tsu shpet klug gevoren*].⁴⁹

This is not 'literary prose', but it is aiming at effects that might be called literary in its piling on of epithets, the apposition of '*opnareray*' (being fooled) and '*klug*' (clever), which draws upon a wide range of Yiddish sayings about '*naronim*' and '*kluge*'.⁵⁰ Tellingly, Langfus originally wrote '*tief ibertsaygt*' ('deeply convinced') before crossing it out and writing '*kreftig beruhigt*': he clearly felt that this semi-oxymoron, with its much more sardonic ring, suited his purposes more.⁵¹

> At the end of summer 1942 a transport arrived from Przemyśl. The young people as well as the policemen had all hidden daggers up their sleeves and wanted to throw themselves on the SS-men. But they were misled by their leader [*hot zey ferfihrt zeyer onfihrer*], a doctor, who hoped by restraining them to go into the camp along with his wife [*arayntsugeyn in lager mit zayn froy*], and intervened about this with the Oberscharführer, who reassured him. So he calmed them down. They got undressed and he was then forced to go along after them all into the gas chamber along with his wife [*mittsugeyn nokh zey ale in bunker arayn mit zayn froy*].⁵²

Very slight variations in wording do a good deal of work here. The clause expressing the doctor's hope and the sentence expressing what actually happened to him both end '*mit zayn froy*'. The slight pun '*ferfihrt*', '*onfihrer*' echoes also with '*obersharfihrer*'. '*Arayntsugeyn*' is played off against '*mittsugeyn*': going into the camp is more important to him than going with everyone else, but he ends up having to go with them after all. This is irony – and it seems to us to have been composed with some deliberation to be ironic.

The use of irony forms a new departure for Langfus. It potentially signals a shift of outlook. Claire Colebrook suggests that ironic texts gesture to their incompleteness. They are fragmentary, sharing the creative act with their readers. The writer withdraws authority from a given text when they operate in an ironic mode. They also 'often convey a sense of the incoherence of voice, or that one *cannot* say what is being said'.⁵³ In turning to irony, under the conditions remarkable in itself as a literary choice, Langfus may therefore display a further effort to distance or detach himself from the events he attests to and a growing acknowledgment of the difficulties of finding words to encapsulate experiences.

The fact that they are not in chronological order need not count as evidence that Langfus could not give a more coherent account of the workings of the crematorium, nor even that the particulars were jotted down as they occurred to him. The photocopy of the manuscript shows a very clean copy indeed, regularly spaced, with small and precise handwriting. There are nine crossings out and five points where a word or phrase is inserted over the space of twelve pages.[54] It is therefore probably a fair copy: Langfus wrote these incidents down in draft form and then transferred them to this book. The episodes are loosely chained together: one paragraph about the habits of an SS-man is followed by another about the others. A paragraph on children from Šiauliai is followed by one about a child being killed by an SS-man. The defiant last words of a rabbi from Vittel are paired with the defiant last words of a rebbetsin from Košice.

The arrangement therefore seems to be a deliberate one, making reference to pre-existing forms of storytelling, with specific literary effects. It is not necessary to draw upon clichés of Hasidic storytelling here: cycles of storytelling were by no means confined to Hasidic circles.[55] As Barbara Kirshenblatt-Gimblett has described it, stories told in the bes-medresh (the house of study) between the two evening prayers of *minkhe* and *mayrev*

> are pre-formulated and relatively self-contained (they can be understood without reference to any preceding conversation or narration), [and so] there is a tendency for story-dominated events to be organized like beads on a string. Free association, one story triggering another, is an important feature of these events.[56]

The beginnings of Langfus's '*Eyntselheyten*' have a striking similarity to these formulas (see Appendix B).

> Traditional tales, both those told for their own sake and those used as illustration, typically begin with *a mol iz geven* (once there was), *in a shtetl iz geven* (in a *shtetl* there was), *iz a mol gekumen* (once [someone] came) and similar formulas.[57]

The fact that a number of survivors of the SK say that they called him the '*maggid*' (preacher, storyteller) is noteworthy in this context. Mordechai Ciechanower describes Langfus sitting in the Sonderkommando block, asking for stories from the rest of the camp and telling him stories in turn, to which he listened 'with bulging eyes': 'Last night there came a transport from this and that place'.⁵⁸ The 'Particulars' themselves, therefore, may have been stories that Langfus told before. The structure that he found for them also draws from the tradition of storytelling, as well as from a more general tendency in Jewish memory to use pattern rather than chronology.⁵⁹

But, as Alexandre Prstojevic also argues, it might be described as an ethical decision not to do so.⁶⁰ Chronology could be seen as an attempt at making sense of events that do not make sense in any order. The '*eyntselheyten*' (particulars, details, literally 'singlenesses') would be subsumed into some whole, a narrative whose protagonists would have to be the perpetrators, with the victims relegated simply to bit parts. Instead, they are allowed to exist individually, however briefly, each one of them making a singular appearance, only once.

Differences

Whereas, as will become clear, both Zalman Lewental and Zalman Gradowski have a recognisably consistent approach to their texts, Langfus seems to vary his way of writing to a very great degree. The pithy, epigrammatic writings in 'Particulars' are very different from the far more emotive and pathos-ridden tone of *The Deportation* and the two stories buried along with Lewental's writings. Some themes might be said to carry over: there is a concern in all three finds with the experience of children, which is consistent with the fact that Langfus was the only writer of the Scrolls who had a child die in Birkenau. And the style too has some common features: most noticeably, the tendency to use strings of similar-meaning adjectives and nouns. But nonetheless, the differences are great enough that it is not surprising that the Auschwitz museum attributed them to different authors. Although the evidence for them all being by the same author is persuasive, it is, admittedly, not completely certain. Nonetheless, it is worth taking the risk, in order firstly to respond to the author's request in the 1952 manuscript that all his writings be collected together, and secondly because the possibility that one person might write in such different ways, and what this might mean, needs to be considered.

It is probably evidence of texts being written at different times. *The Deportation* would seem to be the first text Langfus wrote, in so far as the 1952 manuscript references it. The two pieces buried with Lewental's manuscript probably discuss events that happened in October 1944. The 1952 find would appear to include the most recent material, as it finishes with the date 26 November 1944. The difference in time may therefore have brought about a different mental outlook: shifting from the pathos of his town and family's experiences to a sensibility worn down by constant exposure to death, and perhaps, therefore, more prone to veiling its emotional responses. It is also possible that the circumstances of writing were different. The likelihood is that *The Deportation* was written at least in part in Block 13 of the men's camp, whereas the other documents were certainly put into their final form in the crematorium, after the SK were relocated there in June 1944. The styles might reflect the location: one written in a place more part of a wider life, with some contact between the isolated block and the camp; the other two in the very site of extermination.

The variety is also, however, the result of a choice. Langfus was able to think about his subject matter and different means by which it could be represented, and decide which seemed most suitable. The narrative of *The Deportation* is effective because it is so extensive, because it follows a collective, because there is almost nothing that takes it away from being the simple story of how the entire Jewish population of a town was eradicated. 'Particulars' works because it is about individuals at singular moments of their lives. Each piece of writing considers what kind of pattern to fit the individuals into. Each of them uses its structure to do so. They are evidence not only of the events that they report, but also of the man who wrote them, considering carefully where to place himself, how to structure his stories, and how to evoke responses in his readers.

Finally, attending to the range of his writings brings to the fore how his approach was distinct from Zalman Gradowski's. Whereas Gradowski's testimony relied on his self-image as a poet-prophet who could give shape to his experiences and speak for other victims, Langfus adapted his modes of writing to different circumstances, and was more circumspect in his presentation of others' thoughts and feelings. Gradowski is, as we have noted, a highly visual writer: he wants to show his readers, to make them see. Especially in 'The 3000 Naked Women', Langfus questions seeing, putting forward other modes of witnessing that might be just as effective, or more appropriate. Langfus also seems to have tried to write about individuals in a way that did not make them straightforwardly stand for a wider whole. Langfus, perhaps, retains the individual 'world' of a victim in ways Gradowski's more general approach cannot achieve. He also holds back his words, measures them, in a way that bespeaks a maturity that may be missing in Gradowski. This is not to suggest that the latter is immature as an author. It is, however, to acknowledge what Greif observes, that his writings, with their accompanying emotions, are those of a young man, both in age and outlook.[61] Langfus may be similar in age but his attitude as it manifests itself through his choice of language, his literary style, is less bold, more careful – perhaps, even, more ashamed. Gradowski does not seem to have had any qualms about his writing. Langfus sometimes seems to not wish to write of these things but he has to.

In this context, the final section of the compositions in the exercise book discovered in 1952, 'Notes' ('*notitsen*'), is particularly significant. The fragment begins by describing Nazi efforts to conceal the mass murders that they have perpetrated through dismantling the crematoria and burning documents. Langfus, however, in noting these activities, in writing about them, strives to counteract the efforts to erase all evidence of atrocity. His testimony will shortly be concealed amidst rubble and remains.

Langfus knows his time is short here, realising that he too forms a kind of evidence, one the Nazis will not neglect to destroy. He begins writing this coda to the other compositions on 25 November, looking back to events from the past month and a half. It can be read as a kind of last will and testament. He is asking the reader to grant a final wish, to gather together, edit and publish his body of works, works he has bequeathed to a future reader, to a future he knows he will not see. The power of this final composition cannot be overstated. In the final days, hours, of his life, Langfus's thoughts turned to writing and to his writings. Resisting the Nazis' efforts to erase their crimes is obviously at the forefront of his actions.

The section, however, potentially reveals something more about Langfus as an author. Writing, it seems, is more than a means to attest to events, even when it only takes the form of 'notes'. It is a way to assert the self in the most trying, the most horrific, of circumstances. The brief piece was written over two days and comprises two separate acts of putting pen to paper. After the appeal for his works to be collectively published as 'Amidst the Horrors of Murder', four final sentences are added:

> We are now going to the 'sauna,' the 170 remaining men. We are sure that they are taking us to our deaths. They have selected 30 men to remain in Crematorium 4.
> Today is 26 November 1944.[62]

Langfus had evidently retained hold of the exercise book until the last possible moment. He continues to note his existence in it, to maintain that existence. Writing was obviously a vital activity to him. In the midst of mass death, it was a sustaining force, a way to affirm life, his own and those of his envisaged readers. For this reason, he would not abandon it until the last.

It also, as we have demonstrated, provided a means for trying to cope with the horrors that surrounded him, to chronicle and compartmentalise mounting atrocities. The writings as a whole show cumulatively that these dreadful events changed Langfus. These changes meant that the mode of writing he employed shifted through time, responded to transformations in the man himself. The scattered documents do represent discrete identities, personalities, even as they are written in the same hand. They show that surviving at Auschwitz for a prolonged period, working in the Sonderkommando, did not produce a homogenous individual experience. Tracking these changes, the emerging irony, the conscious understatement, is painful. Langfus, understandably, appears close to cynicism in the later writings.

The final composition, however, in its temporal complexity, also shows how Langfus retained a kind of positivity. He did not give up on himself. The continual shift in the fragment of prose between the present of his impending death and the future of the discovery of 'Notes', demonstrates his belief that a different world is coming and something of his, of him, will carry forward to it. The reader he imagines (addressed directly twice with requests) is one who will show interest in his works and be mindful of his entreaty to collate and transcribe them. In this chapter, we have partially followed Langfus's request, treating the assorted compositions as the work of a single author. We have allowed his name to function as the unifier of sometimes stylistically very different texts. This has permitted us to track how shifting circumstances within Auschwitz impacted on subjectivity. Combining the writings in this way, attributing them to an individual, should not detract from the varied, variable selves that were, and are, named Leyb Langfus.

Notes

1. Leyb Langfus, 'In groyl fun retsikhe', in Ber Mark, *Megiles Oyshvits* (Tel Aviv: Yisroel-Bukh, 1977), 361. Although the whereabouts of the original MS are not known, a photocopy was made. APMO Tom 73 156644/420. This translation follows the punctuation of the MS, including having no quotation marks around 'Auschwitz'.
2. More of a sense of this network of responsibility is given by the finding of the diary of Rywka Lipszyc. This diary was discovered in the grounds of the crematoria, and so was probably hidden by members of the Sonderkommando. However, Rywka appears to have survived the initial selection, and her effects were most likely processed in the Canada section of Auschwitz. This would seem to indicate that the workers in Canada passed the diary to the SK, presumably because they knew that the SK were burying documents. If so, then producing and archiving testimony was a collective project shared not only within the Sonderkommando but also with other prisoners in Birkenau. Rywka Lipszyc, *The Diary of Rywka Lipszyc*, ed. Alexandra Zapruder (San Francisco, CA: Jewish Family and Children's Services Holocaust Center, 2014). See

also <http://www.rywkadiary.org> and < http://jfcsholocaustcenter.org/diary-rywka-lipszyc/>.
3. See the Introduction.
4. Esther Mark also assigned to him the list, written in Polish, of deaths in October 1944. Esther Mark, 'Dergentsung tsu di yedies vegn dem mekhaber "anonim" un zayne ksav-yadn', in Mark, *Megiles Oyshvits*, 276–77. The reason for this attribution is not clear, but may be the fact that Shmuel Taub mentioned that Langfus was keeping lists of transports. Shmuel Taub, 'A bintl troyerike zikhroynes', *Sefer zikaron lekehilat Makov-Mazovyetsk* (Tel Aviv: Komitet fun makover landsmanshaftn in Yisroel un Amerike, 1969), 290 (henceforth, *Maków Yizker Bukh*). We do not believe there is enough evidence to assign an author to this document with any confidence, but the quirk of spelling Buna as 'Bunau' may link it to Zalman Lewental. See Chapter 4.
5. She suggested it stood for 'Yehuda Aryeh Regel Arukha'. Yehuda and Aryeh are the Hebrew equivalents of the Yiddish name Leyb, and Langfus (literally 'long leg') becomes in Hebrew '*regel arukha*'. Mark, 'Dergentsung tsu di yedies vegn dem mekhaber "anonim"', 278.
6. The translator Roman Pytel apparently believed the unknown author of the 1952 manuscript to have the same handwriting as Lewental. Jadwiga Bezwińska and Danuta Czech, 'Wstęp edytorski', in *Wśród koszmarnej zbrodni: Notatki więźniów z Sonderkommando odnalezione w Oświęcimiu*, ed. Bezwińska and Czech (Oświęcim: Wydawnictwo Państwowego Muzeum w Oświęcimiu, 1971), 8. The handwriting of the two authors is so distinct that we can only surmise that he was basing this comparison on the loose leaves found with Lewental's notebook, i.e. with the part that we (following the Marks) believe was written by Leyb Langfus.
7. Esther Mark states that Langfus went to the Sandomierz yeshiva, but her source for this claim is unclear ('Dergentsung tsu di yedies vegn dem mekhaber "anonim"', 278). It is possible that she bases it on a reading of Zalman Lewental's account of the SK, which mentions this yeshiva (44.15), but the MS is too damaged to see who it says studied there.
8. At the time Esther Mark identified Langfus as the author of these documents, the main sources of information available to her were the Maków yizker-book, and three testimonies which she listed as being in 'the Ber Mark archive'. It has not been possible to trace these testimonies: neither the Jewish Historical Institute in Warsaw nor the Goldstein-Goren Diaspora Research Center in Tel Aviv appear to have them. Two of them were by people who contributed to the memorial book: Mordechai Ciechanower and Shmuel Taub. The last was from the head of the Judenrat in the Maków ghetto: Abram Garfinkiel. 'Dergentsung tsu di yedies vegn dem mekhaber "anonim"', 276–81.
9. Esther Mark says that this was Shmuel-Yoysef Rozental, but other records show this must have been Yitshok Tsvi Adalberg, some of whose correspondence was preserved in the Ringelblum archive. ARG II 217 (Ring II/119). Janusz Szczepański, *Dzieje społeczności żydowskiej powiatów Pułtusk i Maków Mazowiecki* (Warsaw: Pułtuskie Towarzystwo Społeczno-Kulturalne and Towarzystwo Miłośników Makowa Mazowieckiego, 1993), 148. See also the following note.
10. Ben-Tsion Rozental, 'Makov shel mayle', *Maków Yizker Bukh*, 394. This election was brought about by the death of Shmuel-Yoysef Rozental. This presumably means that Langfus was not a Hasid. Note, however, that according to Leon Salomon, Langfus's nephew (the son of Langfus's wife's sister), Shmuel Yoysef Rozental was an Alexander Hasid (seg. 8). Salomon's account of Langfus's marriage, election as dayan and the

birth of their child is close to the information provided by Esther Mark and the yizker-bukh. USC VHF 46403 Leon Salomon.

11. Danuta Czech's *Auschwitz Chronicle* only lists one transport from Mława, which arrived on 6 December 1942, of whom 2,094 were gassed and 406 men admitted as labourers. Danuta Czech, *Auschwitz Chronicle*, trans. Barbara Harshav, Martha Humphreys and Stephen Shearier (New York: Henry Holt, 1990), 280. However, testimonies seem to indicate other ones. Some of the difficulties with Czech's list of transports will be discussed in Chapter 4. Shlomo Dragon (80359) also came to Auschwitz from Mława. According to his testimony, he arrived on 7 December 1942, and was inducted into Sonderkommando on the evening of the 9th, starting work on 10 December. Gideon Greif, *We Wept without Tears: Testimonies of the Jewish Sonderkommando in Auschwitz*, trans. Naftali Greenwood (New Haven, CT: Yale University Press, 2005), 130.

12. Miklós Nyiszli, *Auschwitz: A Doctor's Eyewitness Account*, trans. Tibère Kremer and Richard Seaver (London: Penguin, 2013), 140–42; Filip Müller, *Sonderbehandlung: Drei Jahre in den Krematorien und Gaskammern von Auschwitz*, literary collaboration with Helmut Freitag (Munich: Steinhausen, 1979), 104–6, 262–63. It should be noted that in the German original, Müller specifies that he is from Maków. The English translation omits this detail. Filip Müller, *Eyewitness Auschwitz: Three Years in the Gas Chambers*, ed. and trans. Susanne Flatauer (Chicago: Ivan R. Dee, 1999), 66–67, 161–62.

13. Mordechai Ciechanower, *Der Dachdecker von Auschwitz-Bikenau*, trans. Christina Mulolli (Berlin: Metropol, 2007), 164–67. This German translation uses '*Religionslehrer*' for the original Hebrew's '*dayan*'. Mordechai Ciechanower, *Mirakhok kokhav minatsnats* (Tel Aviv: Yad Vashem, 2005), 199–203. (I have relied heavily on the German translation to guide me round the Hebrew text. [DW])

14. Greif, *We Wept without Tears*, 247; Nyiszli, *Auschwitz*, 140; Müller, *Eyewitness Auschwitz*, 66. Both Nyiszli and Müller say that he only ate bread, margarine and onions. The strong overlap between Müller and Nyiszli here suggests that Müller's account may not be completely independent of Nyiszli's.

15. Greif, *We Wept without Tears*, 165, 247; Taub, 'A bintl troyerike zikhroynes', 290.

16. Greif, *We Wept without Tears*, 165, 246–47, 318–19, 330. Müller, *Eyewitness Auschwitz*, 66–67, 161–62. The Auschwitz museum edition states that Langfus died during the 7 October uprising. In the main, this seems to be based on Lewental including his name in a list of participants. But while it is true that some of those names are recorded as having died, there are three at the end for whom Lewental adds their current location. The last of these is Lewental himself. Langfus is specifically recorded as being 'today still in the crematorium'. A story is also sometimes told of Langfus blowing himself up in a gas chamber. Esther Mark simply says he was prepared to do so. This seems to be based on Shmuel Taub's account in the Maków yizker-book, where he says that Langfus told him that he was going to blow the gas chamber up. Taub, 'A bintl troyerike zikhroynes', 290.

17. Nyiszli, *Auschwitz*; Müller, *Eyewitness Auschwitz*; Greif, *We Wept without Tears*, 318–19; Ciechanower, *Der Dachdecker*, 1.

18. Compare the (admittedly retrospective) stories collected by Yaffa Eliach in *Hasidic Tales of the Holocaust* (New York: Oxford University Press, 1982), which almost always contain at least some affirmation of a divine order.

19. See Dominick LaCapra, *Writing History, Writing Trauma* (Baltimore, MD: Johns Hopkins, 2001), 36–42.

20. 'The language is simple and the author claims to do nothing other than simply report the facts', writes Maurice Pfeffer, his French translator. Georges Bensoussan, Philippe Mesnard and Carlo Saletti (eds), *Des voix sous la cendre: Manuscrits des Sonderkommandos d'Auschwitz Birkenau* (Paris: Calmann-Lévy/Mémorial de la Shoah, 2005), 32. Roman Pytel also claims that his writing is often clumsy, and causes unpleasant reactions in the reader. Roman Pytel, 'Od tłumacza', *Zeszyty oświęcimskie* 14 (1972): 14.
21. Compare Joan Scott's discussion of the importance of attending to the 'literary' in historical testimony. Joan W. Scott, 'The Evidence of Experience', *Critical Inquiry* 17(4) (Summer 1991): 794.
22. No published Yiddish text nor an English translation exists for this document. I have worked directly from the manuscript, also making use of the Polish translation: Lejb [—], 'Wysiedlenie', trans. Roman Pytel, *Zeszyty Oświęcimskie* 14 (1972), 15–62 (henceforth 'Wysiedlenie') [DW]. This text has been translated into German as: Lejb [Langfus], 'Aussiedlung', trans. Herta Henschel and Jochen August, in *Inmitten des grauenvollen Verbrechens: Handschriften von Mitgliedern des Sonderkommandos*, ed. Teresa Świebocka, Franciszek Piper and Martin Mayr (Oświęcim: Verlag des Staatlichen Auschwitz-Birkenau Museums, 1996), 73–129. We use the page numbering adopted in both these editions, with two numbers, the first in square brackets. The MS pages were originally numbered before being read. At this point it was discovered that some of the early pages were out of order. The number in square brackets indicates the reconstructed page order, as well as leaving out six pages of the manuscript (100–105) deemed undecipherable. The second number indicates the number actually written by the museum on the manuscript page.
23. Michał Grynberg, *Żydzi w rejencji ciechanowskiej 1939–1942* (Warsaw: Państwowe Wydawnictwo Naukowe, 1984), 18, 55–57; Szczepański, *Dzieje społeczności żydowskiej powiatów Pułtusk i Maków*, 150–56; Czech, *Auschwitz Chronicle*, 280. Useful summaries are provided by: Katrin Reichelt and Martin Dean, 'Maków Mazowiecki', *USHMM Encyclopedia of Camps and Ghettos, 1933–1945*, Vol. II, Part A, ed. Martin Dean (Bloomington: Indiana University Press, 2012), 15–17; 'Maków Mazowiecki', *Yad Vashem Encyclopedia of the Ghettos during the Holocaust*, ed-in-chief Guy Miron, co-ed. Shlomit Shulhani, 2 vols (Jerusalem: Yad Vashem, 2009), 450–51.
24. According to the Zichenau Gestapo records, the mass hanging took place on 9 July 1942: AŻIH 233/60. Akt. Zeichen II B2 2904/42. This is the only mass hanging they list in Maków, and it is the only one mentioned in testimonies. AŻIH 301/4480 Henia Mławska (mistakes date for 1941, but description matches Langfus's); USC VHF 15815 Sam Itskowitz; USC VHF 5384 Aron Blum; USC VHF 10853 Hersch Unger; USC VHF 29430 Moishe Silberman.
25. Jan Grabowski notes mass hangings in a number of ghettos in the Ciechanów region from the spring of 1942. The Gestapo specifically said that the purpose of such actions was to 'instil fear'. 'The Holocaust in Northern Mazovia (Poland) in the Light of the Archive of the Ciechanów Gestapo', *Holocaust and Genocide Studies* 18(4) (Winter 2004): 463–64. Mary Fulbrook observes the same pattern in Silesia: 'Public hangings appear to have taken place over a wide range of different locations at around the same time, around one month before major deportations'. Fulbrook, *A Small Town near Auschwitz: Ordinary Nazis and the Holocaust* (Oxford: Oxford University Press, 2012), 208.
26. 'Wysiedlenie'. In the Auschwitz museum edition, simply the title of Chapter 1 is given, but there is also a number 1 written before it in the MS. In the following

discussion, chapter numbers in square brackets indicate that the number is not legible in the MS. Other chapter numbers are.
27. 'Wysiedlenie', 10.
28. ××× indicates one word illegible. ***** indicates a gap of variable size. See the Preface for a full key to textual symbols.
29. Pytel translated this as 'W pochodzie' ('On the March'), but it clearly reads 'Der tilim' ('The Psalm').
30. One way to think about this might be with reference to Hanna Segal's reading of *Guernica*, as a piece that mobilises strong emotions, but seeks a structure in which they can be held. Hanna Segal, *Dream Phantasy and Art* (Hove and New York: Brunner-Routledge, 1991), 61, 71.
31. Nathan Cohen, 'Diaries of the "Sonderkommandos" in Auschwitz: Coping with Fate and Reality', *Yad Vashem Studies* 20 (1990), 284–85. This is not quite true, as we shall go on to show.
32. This revisits in a more elliptical and more pressing form, the difficulties of discussing self and community, which Yiddish semi-autobiographical writers worked through and meditated upon at the end of the nineteenth century. See Dan Miron, *A Traveler Disguised: The Rise of Modern Yiddish Fiction in the Nineteenth Century* (Syracuse, NY: Syracuse University Press, 1996); Dan Miron, *The Image of the Shtetl and Other Studies of Modern Jewish Literary Imagination* (Syracuse, NY: Syracuse University Press, 2000); and Jan Schwarz, *Imagining Lives: Autobiographical Fiction of Yiddish Writers* (Madison: University of Wisconsin Press, 2005). Marcus Moseley traces the origins of this dilemma. Marcus Moseley, *Being for Myself Alone: Origins of Jewish Autobiography* (Stanford, CA: Stanford University Press, 2006).
33. Reading 'krasnosheltser rov' instead of Roman Pytel's 'krasnashelder rov'. This removes the difficulty of explaining how a rabbi from Krasno in Ukraine would be in Maków.
34. 'Wysiedlenie', 36 n. 18.
35. In addition to Mordechai Ciechanower, Ben-Tsion Rozental and Shmuel Taub, Leon Salomon, Milton Buki and David Nencel all identified Langfus as the 'makover dayan'. USC VHF 46403 Leon Salomon. Buki was interviewed by Nathan Cohen ('Diaries of the "Sonderkommandos" in Auschwitz', 282 n. 13); Nencel by Andreas Kilian (Eric Friedler, Barbara Siebert and Andreas Kilian, *Zeugen aus der Todeszone: Das jüdische Sonderkommando in Auschwitz* [Munich: Deutscher Taschenbuch, 2008], 206).
36. Such a practice is not unknown in Holocaust chronicles, one of the most notorious being Shlomo Frank, who after the war revised his diary of the Łódź ghetto to conceal his own role as a ghetto policeman, often attributing his own experiences to 'a policeman' or 'the police'. But in this case, Langfus seems to have no pressing motivation to hide the role that he played within the community. Salomon Frank, *Togbukh fun lodzher geto* (Buenos Aires: Tsentral farband fun poylishe yidn in Argentine, 1958). On this see Robert Moses Shapiro, 'Diaries and Memoirs from the Lodz Ghetto', in Shapiro (ed.), *Holocaust Chronicles: Individualizing the Holocaust through Diaries and Other Contemporaneous Personal Accounts* (Hoboken, NJ: Ktav, 1999), 101–4.
37. Dori Laub and Nanette C. Auerhahn, 'Failed Empathy: A Central Theme in the Survivor's Holocaust Experience', *Psychoanalytic Psychology* 6(4) (1989): 383.
38. In his video testimony, David Nencel says a number of times that he does not like simply talking about 'I'. He presents this as an ethical stance, not the attempt to hide that Laub and Auerhahn claim it is. <http://www.google.com/culturalinstitute/asset-viewer/

testimony-of-david-nencel-born-in-rypin-1916-regarding-his-experiences-in-german-captivity-ghettos-in-poland-sonderkommando-in-auschwitz-and-mauthausen/jgHuY64vC0kWzA?hl=en&l.expanded-id=_gHpehtbnzcnHA>.
39. e.g. [3] 12, [6] 15, [7] 16, [12] 7, [36] 41, [40] 45, [60] 65, [63] 68, [65] 70, [68] 73, [82] 87. It is worth noting that a number of these are the passages that Pytel characterises as clumsy or overblown (see note 20 above).
40. This emphasis on physical experience being transmitted starts to call attention to the physical means by which it is transmitted: the document that Langfus's prospective reader might unearth.
41. Jill Bennett, *Empathic Vision: Affect, Trauma, and Contemporary Art* (Stanford, CA: Stanford University Press, 2005). Bennett succinctly outlines her understanding of affect in *Practical Aesthetics: Events, Affects and Art after 09/11* (London: I.B. Tauris, 2012), 20–26. For a persuasive reading of how affect might be mobilised in witness writing, see Milena Marinkova, *Michael Ondaatje: Haptic Aesthetics and Micropolitical Writing* (New York: Continuum, 2011), 63–92.
42. Primo Levi, *The Drowned and the Saved*, trans. Raymond Rosenthal (London: Abacus, 1989), 63–64.
43. See our discussion in the Introduction.
44. We will discuss this story in more detail in the Conclusion, in the context of Filip Müller's reading of it in the outtakes of *Shoah*.
45. Leyb Langfus, 'Di 3000 nakete', *Megiles Oyshvits*, 368.
46. Langfus, 'Di 3000 nakete', 366–67. Punctuation amended with reference to the manuscript.
47. Maurice Pfeffer translates '*umnatirlikh*' as '*surnaturel*' in order to convey something of this sense, but the word more commonly means something like 'strange' or 'unusual', and can have quite negative connotations. *Des voix sous la cendre*, 118.
48. Langfus, 'In groyl fun retsikhe', 354.
49. Langfus, 'In groyl fun retsikhe', 355.
50. See, for example, the collections of sayings in Ignats Bernshteyn, *Yidishe shprikhverter* (New York: Alveltlekhe Yiddisher Kultur-Kongres, 1983), 138–40; and Nokhem Stutshkov, *Der oytser fun der yiddisher shprakh* (New York: YIVO Institute for Jewish Research, 1950), 307–10.
51. APMO Wspomnienia Tom 73 autor nieznany 156644/420.
52. Langfus, 'In groyl fun retsikhe', 358.
53. Claire Colebrook, *Irony* (London: Routledge, 2004), 66. Emphasis in the original.
54. Some of these clearly are small revisions, but two involve crossing out a word that then occurs a little later. This would fit with a process of copying, where the copyist has jumped a little ahead. APMO Wspomnienia Tom 73 autor nieznany 156644/420.
55. See Joseph Dan's sceptical treatment of Hasidic storytelling as a tradition that can be distinguished from other kinds of Judaism. Joseph Dan, 'Hasidism: Teachings and Literature', *The YIVO Encyclopedia of Jews in Eastern Europe* Vol. 1 (New Haven, CT, and London: Yale University Press, 2008), 670–73.
56. Barbara Kirshenblatt-Gimblett, 'The Concept and Varieties of Narrative Performance in East European Jewish Culture', in *Explorations in the Ethnography of Speaking*, 2nd edn, ed. Richard Bauman and Joel Sherzer (Cambridge: Cambridge University Press, 1989), 291. Words in square brackets added.
57. Ibid. Italics and square brackets as in the original.
58. Ciechanower, *Der Dachdecker*, 165; Ciechanower, *Mirakhok kokhav minatsnats*, 201. The phrase Ciechanower uses for 'with bulging eyes' ('בעניים קרועות') connotes shock

rather than wonder. Of course, Ciechanower's memory of this incident may have been coloured by his knowledge of Langfus's writings.
59. See David Roskies, *Against the Apocalypse* (Cambridge, MA: Harvard University Press, 1984); and Yosef Yerushalmi, *Zakhor: Jewish History and Jewish Memory* (Seattle and London: University of Washington Press, 1996).
60. As he puts it, 'The mechanism of extermination that judges and historians attempt to reconstruct gives way to the intimate experience of the victims'. Alexandre Prstojevic, 'L'indicible et la fiction configuratrice', *Protée*, 37(2) (2009): 37.
61. Greif, *We Wept without Tears*, 30.
62. Langfus, 'In groyl fun retsikhe', 361.

Chapter 4

Final Arrangements

Zalman Lewental's Histories of Resistance

The erasures, the blanks, these have their own importance; and symbolic weight.

(Elie Wiesel, in reference
to the Scrolls of Auschwitz)¹

Facts

On 19 August 1944, a 26-year-old member of the Sonderkommando wrote the last words on the final page of a short manuscript. He turned back to the first page. At the top he wrote: '***** written from ***** the narrow circle Sonderko Crema 2 15-19/8 44 by <Za>lman Lewental Poland – Ciechanów'.² He drew a line under these words. He placed it in a half-litre glass jar along with two other artefacts: a diary by an inhabitant of the Łódź ghetto, and a bracelet made in, and showing scenes from, the ghetto.³ He buried the jar in the grounds of the crematorium. It remained there until it was dug up on 28 July 1961.⁴

This is a very different writing practice from both Gradowski and Langfus, one that calls for a different way of reading. Lewental is more interested in getting the facts down than expressing them eloquently, or movingly. He jots down the information in an abbreviated form.

Rather than placing himself among his family, he writes as part of the Sonderkommando, within their 'narrow circle': utterly cut off from the outside (as they had been since June), but also part of a tight-knit group, perhaps. He writes within a much shorter space of time. He has no qualms about identifying himself prominently and precisely. As we have seen with both Gradowski and Langfus, naming oneself as a writer like this was not a risk-free act. Perhaps, as someone younger, Lewental was less cautious than his older colleagues, but he may have been expecting the revolt to start, as was Gradowski two and a half weeks later.

Lewental wanted to preserve not only his own words, but also evidence from others. In fact, his writing was a commentary on the Łódź diary, which he presumably found in the effects of someone brought from Łódź and murdered in Crematorium III. As both Alexandre Prstojevic and Dan Stone have suggested, Lewental can be seen as a historian and archivist of the Sonderkommando.[5] In this he is clearly quite different from Langfus and Gradowski, who took up the responsibility for testifying through a writing practice that was more straightforwardly individual. Circumstances prompted him to write, in response to what he found, possibly because he was already part of the resistance.

There is one other fact about this document that makes it different from those written by Gradowski and Langfus. Even more than Langfus's *Deportation*, it is very badly damaged: by water seeping into the broken jar and, it would seem, from reacting to the bracelet wrapped round it. Only the top and bottom of each page is legible. The rest has not been deciphered. As we have argued in Chapter 1, this damage forms a text that can be read if the right strategy is adopted, but it also means that a different mode of reading must be applied to the words themselves. What is missing needs to be acknowledged, and the temptation simply to read across gaps to produce sense must be avoided. But this is not simply a matter of accepting loss. Taking into account the material state of Lewental's document might itself help to give it some form, as we hope to show in this chapter. We offer a new reconstruction of the order of Lewental's other, longer manuscript, written a few months later. Based upon this, we provide readings of its various parts, attending both to their distinct modes of writing, and to the changing degrees of damage undergone by different portions of the document. Finally, we return to Lewental's commentary of August 1944, to provide an overall assessment of his role as the historian of the Sonderkommando.

Lewental's Manuscript

Zalman Lewental's longer document was found in October 1962, after an archaeological-style dig that was deliberately searching for manuscripts buried by the Sonderkommando.[6] The features we noted for the 1961 find were true of this cache too. It was buried as a collection: Lewental's notebook, a set of pages written by Leyb Langfus, and a list of deaths in October 1944. It too had suffered extensive water damage. The glass jar in which it had been stored had not protected it from the damp. As discussed in Chapter 1, ink bled from the pages, which were stuck together, and the staples were badly rusted, the rust itself forming stain marks on the paper. In an attempt to preserve the document, the Auschwitz archive detached the pages from each other without making a record of their order. Because of the damage, and because Lewental had written first on the odd pages of the notebook before turning it over and writing back to the beginning on the even pages, they have had difficulties reconstructing the order in which it was written. The work of deciphering the manuscript was mainly undertaken by Salmen Seweryn Gostyński and Eugenia Kapczyc-Gostyńska, who were able to read from it the most comprehensive account we have of the Sonderkommando in Auschwitz.[7] Aside from some fragments about deportation, travel to and arrival at Auschwitz, and others about the history of Auschwitz, one part of the manuscript, the least badly damaged, told the story of the SK's attempts at resistance and revolt. It was possible to put this part into sequence, but where it stood in relation to the other fragments was much harder to decide upon. Three different editions produced between 1968 and 1977 gave much the same order for the story of the revolt, but differed quite considerably about where the other fragments should go.[8]

All of them relied upon the same methods: trying to follow the flow of what had been written, and identifying events and putting them into chronological order. The first of these is commonsensical enough, but for much of the text it is not possible as the words at the outer edges of each page are particularly badly damaged. The second method is understandable, and if the priority is to find out as much information as possible about what happened it makes some sense. But, as Langfus and Gradowski's writings show, writing in chronological order was only one strategy that the Sonderkommando men used. For their accounts of the expulsion from ghettos and transport to Auschwitz, they told their stories in sequence. For their accounts of what happened within the camp, they did not.

We believe that the order in which Lewental wrote can be reconstructed through a different set of methods, focusing on features of the manuscript pages rather than simply the words that could be read from them. The first, most obvious, feature was inexplicably overlooked by all three published editions: Lewental numbered the pages himself.[9] Although not all of these numbers are decipherable, many of them are, written in the top right or left corner of each page, in the same ink, and usually in the same state of legibility, as the rest of the text. Between pages 34 and 87, only five page numbers are entirely missing or are very difficult to read, with three others that are not completely clear. These numbers are on pages that are not badly damaged: the rest of the text is visible, and the other reconstructed orders are much the same for this part of the text. However, the numbers on other pages give them very different positions. The page all three editions put first is clearly numbered 93, and what the Marks call page 7 (and the Auschwitz museum page 4) has a number 100 written in its top left corner.

Far too many of the page numbers are illegible for them to provide the complete key to the original order. But by making use of them when examining the manuscript pages, it is possible to glean more information about the book in which they were bound. It is clear that pages 62 and 63 were the two sides of the last page of the exercise book, as 63 is written on the reverse of 62, but upside down. This is the point at which Lewental reached the end of his book, turned it over and started writing on the other sides. Since this is the last page of the book, we can also identify the signature (the group of sheets stapled together) which these pages go to make up: pages 49 to 76 all appear on the same seven sheets of paper, which were folded and stapled in the exercise book to make a signature of twenty-eight sides. Each sheet of paper has four pages that appear in the sequence of text, and the ones in the middle of the signature should have two consecutive pages on the same sheet but on opposite sides: this is true of the sheet on which there appear pages 56 and 57, and pages 69 and 70.

We would therefore expect the rest of the book to be constructed in a similar way, in signatures of a similar number of pages. And in fact there are four groups of sheets with quite distinct patterns of staining from their staples. All of the sheets bar one can be placed into one of four groups: two of seven sheets, and two of eight sheets. In each group, there is one sheet that has a symmetrical stain formed by one page pressing against the other while folded in two. For example, a trickle of rusty liquid has dried into mirrored ochre shapes on one sheet.[10] We would expect this sheet to be the middle sheet of each signature (Figure 4.1).

The final signature must form the middle section of Lewental's written text, since every page of the notebook has been written on.[11] The sequences before and after this middle (and therefore taken from the signature before the last one in the book) are also reasonably secure: we have continuous text for much of it and a large proportion of legible page numbers. Page

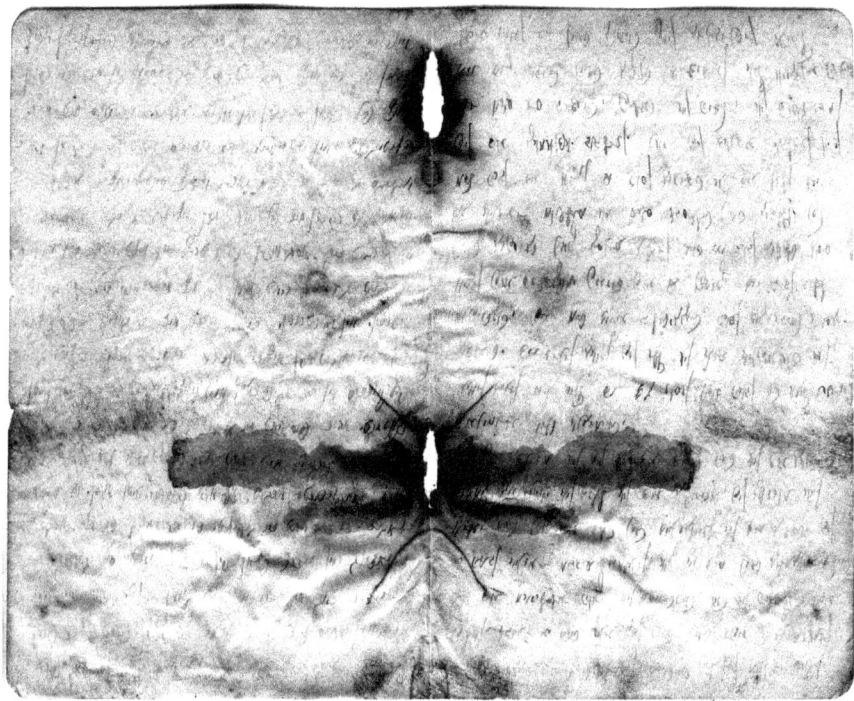

Figure 4.1. Page from Zalman Lewental's manuscript. The symmetrical stain indicates that it is the central page of a signature. Page numbers 56 and 70 are visible in the top left and bottom right corners of the sheet.

numbers 39 and 40 are clearly visible on one sheet, identifying it as the middle of this signature, as does the mirror-image staining around this sheet's staple holes. All other sheets have at least one page number on them, which allows us to put the sheets in order. Matching the staple stains means that we know the orientation of the sheet. Therefore, we can establish a page order for this signature with a good deal of certainty, and identify on them what we believe to be pages 32 to 47 and 78 to 93.

The other two signatures are much more damaged and difficult to read, but there are numerous blotches and marks that can be used to help identify a sequence. If similarly shaped stains of different sizes appear on a number of sheets, it makes sense for them either to grow or to shrink continuously rather than change size in no particular order. This is particularly true of the rust marks around the staples, which take very distinctive forms in different signatures. There are also many marks that are mirror images of each other on separate sheets, showing that their surfaces have been in contact. For one signature, almost every sheet shows a different pattern of dirt streaks radiating from the centre crease, a pattern which appears reversed on the sheet against which it was pressed.[12] A number of other features help to place sheets in sequence. The rust brown stain on the outer sheet of the second signature matches the stain on another page.[13] Three highly distinctive fangs of dirt appear on two adjacent sheets, the outer ones of each signature, albeit at different points on each page: one probably tore and moved up relative to the other.[14] Nicks on the top left edge of the cover decrease in size over the first three pages.[15] In combination with the page numbers that are still visible, and by following the same principle of grouping these sheets into signatures, we believe we can, therefore, identify very plausible sequences for them.

The order that we have reconstructed runs as follows:[16]

1–20	almost entirely undeciphered; some general remarks
21–24	what will be known about Auschwitz and who will tell it
25–29	arrival in camp (10 December 1942); learning that their families have been killed; grief and horror
30–34	Lewental's induction into the SK (25 January 1943); how the SK were recruited; their function
35–41	psychological questions: why they did not commit suicide, why they obeyed orders, why they did not escape
41–48	change of conditions: somewhat easier when Crematoria replace Bunkers (March 1944); start of discussion of resistance; individuals (Langfus and Gradowski); widening the sphere of resistance; acquiring gunpowder
49–53	escape plans and attempts: individual (Lewental, Handelsman, Warszawski) and perhaps more general; arrival of Russians from Majdanek (April 1944)
53–57	change of conditions: approach of Red Army; beginning of Hungarian transports (May 1944); tensions between SK and camp resistance; strengths and weaknesses of the Russians
57–61	plan to act on their own and force the hand of camp resistance; arrival of a transport (28 July 1944?) stymies plan; reactions
61–63	change in circumstances: new large scale plan delayed; individual plan also has to be called off
63–68	changes in circumstances: SK housed in the crematoria (c. June 1944), 200 SK taken to Gleiwitz and killed (September 1944); new plans have to be more cautious because of betrayal of Kapo Kamiński (2 August 1944); working with Russians, on own, with allies
68–72	announcement of selection of 300 from Crematoria IV and V; attempt to persuade camp resistance to carry out general revolt

	fails; a Russian gets drunk and fights an SS-man; Russians will join the 300 selected
72–77	events of 7 October 1944
77–82	who is left; reflections on what happened; honour to participants
82–83	discussions(?) with allies (unclear when), signature and date (10 October 1944)
84–92	reflections a few days later: what they managed to do, why they failed, how they will testify; list of names, signature
93–108	deportation from Ciechanów region to Auschwitz (17 November 1942 – 10 December 1942); gassing of majority of transport
109–115	further reflections on (or a story of another?) deportation, selection and gassing
116–124	undeciphered, apart from one page

What this new order confirms most strikingly is that the account was not, in fact, written in chronological order. Lewental wrote this document in distinct sequences, and these sequences are unlikely to have been planned beforehand. The first twenty pages are mostly undeciphered; the legible part starts with discussions of Auschwitz, moves on to Lewental's own experience of arriving there and being drafted into the SK, and then describes the planning and attempts at resistance that led to the revolt of 7 October 1944. After signing and dating this account on 10 October, Lewental then started writing again, firstly reflecting once more on the revolt. Only after writing this did he begin to tell the story of the deportation from the Ciechanów region to Auschwitz. How the document ends is also unclear.

The page that we count first in our order is very badly damaged, but it appears to have an underlined title at the beginning which looks like the Polish word 'październik' (October). If it is dated October, this suggests a very rapid process of writing. The date on page 83 is 10 October, only three days after the revolt. It may be that all of the text up to this point was written after the revolt, at great speed, in order to record what had happened.[17] Since Lewental wrote on only one side of each page to begin with, it is plausible to think that he did not anticipate filling the entire book, and only turned it over and used the other sides when he found that he had more to say and/or more time to say it in than he had anticipated. It might also indicate that he did not have the time to seek out extra materials. All of this is consistent with the idea that he wrote in a very short space of time.

This is writing produced under immense pressure, with little time for correction, and the style – telegraphic, note-like, often unwieldy in its syntax and rambling in its structure – indicates this. The writing also suggests someone who had a reasonably good fluency in spoken Yiddish but did not use it much in writing or reading. There are plenty of idiomatic expressions, but the sentence construction is rather unwieldy. Ber Mark and Roman Pytel point out that Lewental makes use of a fair number of Hebraisms, but his language also includes many non-standard Polonisms.[18] He repeatedly uses words in a loose way. 'Game' ('*shpil*') seems to have little more meaning than 'affair', for example. The SK's desire to revolt is phrased both as wanting to 'put an end to the game' (where game means collaboration) and 'start the game' (where game means the revolt). 'Material' also has numerous meanings, including weapons, possessions and information.[19]

Overall, then, Zalman Lewental did not have a sense of himself as someone well-versed in using Yiddish, unlike Gradowski the would-be writer, or Langfus the preacher and storyteller. Both of the extant pieces of writing from Lewental seem to have been responses to outside cues: finding the Łódź diary, and the Sonderkommando revolt. His second document may even have been prompted in its entirety by the revolt. Gradowski and Langfus appear to have made their home towns their priority; at least, this is what they wrote about first. Lewental may have only been able to write about his after examining the history of what had happened in Auschwitz. He was writing with a great sense of urgency, and probably did not have time to think about the order in which he wanted to place his text. His writing follows twists and turns that are comparable in some ways to free association: as something occurs to him he writes it down. The structure is more an index of the circumstances in which it was produced, and the mind that was placed in those circumstances. *How* these documents were written is a vital part of their testimonial and evidentiary function.

We will discuss this document more or less in the order that we believe it to have been written, dividing it into three sections. Beginning with the most damaged sections at the beginning of the document we argue that the gaps, often elided in published editions, need to be read as part of the text. We then go on to look at the least disputed sequence of the manuscript, that dealing with the Sonderkommando revolt. While the revised order does not have a major effect on our reading of this sequence, it does inform our interpretation of its dual function as both historical account and memorial to the Sonderkommando. Finally, in examining the description of the deportation, we will consider the significance of how this particular sequence of events is told, the consequences for some of the historical claims based upon Lewental's writing, and also what kind of writing Lewental might be said to have produced.

Lacunae (esp. pp. 1–20)

Reconstructing the order of pages brings to the forefront the parts that have remained undeciphered. Lacunae, gaps in the text, are indicated in the Auschwitz and Marks' editions by ellipses or dashes, with undeciphered pages simply omitted and no mention made of them. Cesare Brandi, the art restorer and theorist of restoration, argued that lacunae in paintings needed to be treated in such a way that the unity of the work of art could be preserved.[20] In a similar way, the lacunae in Lewental's work need to take their place as part of the structure of what he wrote. Simply presenting the parts that have been read, even while acknowledging some of their fragmentariness, pays too little attention to the fact that the text has some kind of shape, even if it was one that Lewental did not entirely consciously control. The gaps need to be made more present in order to space out the sections of the writing that we do have. Once this is done, there is less temptation to simply join parts together that cannot straightforwardly flow into each other and we can acknowledge more fully how much is missing, and how much we do not know of what is happening in this text. To some extent this is also true of the Langfus and Gradowski texts, but it has its apogee with Lewental.

The beginning of Lewental's manuscript is particularly significant in this respect. It is clear now that the text does not begin with the story of the deportation to Auschwitz, but so little has been deciphered from the first twenty pages that their content is mainly the object of speculation. On the page that we count first, the text below the title begins with a short sentence: '*vi <zogt?/halt?> di velt?*' ('what does the world say/how stands the world'), with the next sentence beginning: '*der malekh ha-movis*' ('the Angel of Death') (1.2–3).[21] The rest of the page, and many of those after it, have not been deciphered, but even this fragment suggests a very different kind of text to one that simply records the facts. Ten pages later, there are a few legible sentences about Jews being killed 'just because they were Jews' (12.5), and four after that a highly fragmentary page. We reproduce it in its entirety below, to give a sense of how these phrases relate to each other.

This rendering also gives a false impression of the page, because what lie in between these words are not blanks, but marks that hover just below the verge of legibility. It is perfectly possible to see that there are nineteen lines of writing, that words cover the entirety of the page, and often even to see how many words there are per line. Further work on this manuscript may well lead to more words being deciphered. Equally, what has been rendered perfectly intelligible is far more ambiguous. What we present in line 11 as 'terrible' (*gevaldign*) was read by the Gostyńskis as 'heroic' (*heldishn*).

[   ] may all the heavens be ink [   ]

[

[

[

[   ] were [   ]

[

[

[   ] written with blood in the world [   ]

[

[

[ ] terrible [   ]

[

[

[   ] in order to find out [   ]

[

[

[

[(17)

The choice to include this page in the Marks' edition and not in the Auschwitz museum edition fits the slightly different priorities these two editions had. The Auschwitz museum value these documents as historical resources, and so they have left out a page that does not provide any straightforward information. Ber Mark showed some interest in the literary qualities of the writing, and the striking phrases of lines 1 and 8 are probably the reason why he decided to include it. The previous four pages have not been deciphered; on the following page only twenty-two words have been. The words on this page float free of any clear context, reminding us of what we do not know, and demanding that we do our best to fill them. Close examination of the manuscript suggests that it may contain two more instances of '*zoln zayn*', running from lines 1 to 2, and at the end of line 2. If this is so, it suggests a much greater desire to write in a 'literary' way than either Mark or the Auschwitz museum accord to Lewental. The first half of this page seems to be concerned with writing, calling on the elements to bear witness, or to go into mourning, rather like Gradowski's address to the moon. The fragments of phrases call attention to how the words have been written, the necessary writing materials and the difficulty of writing, and express the need for them to go into the world.

Lewental may have used a much more rhetorical mode of writing at the beginning of his text, somewhat like Gradowski's, to call up a response in his readers, to channel his anger, or to screw his own courage up to write about the events that had just happened. This can only be suggested tentatively, since so much is hard to read at this point, and since Lewental's mode of writing follows such a winding path. It would make some sense for him to have started his writing with an overview similar to Gradowski's address to his reader at the beginning of the St Petersburg manuscript, but we do not really know what is on these first twenty pages. Could they consist entirely of the general lamentations and poetic writing that is all that has been deciphered? If that were so, we would have a very different view of Lewental as a writer. Could they comprise other information? If so, what might that be, and why did he put it first? Any understanding of this text must acknowledge that it is partial and vulnerable to radical revision.[22]

Lacunae, then, perhaps inevitably require us to speculate about what is missing. But they can prompt other kinds of reflection too. As we argued in Chapter 1, gaps in this manuscript have a vital testimonial function. They make us aware of the history and circumstances of the artefact, and also of what has been lost. Thinking through how other scholars have avoided, or engaged with, these gaps also provides understanding of their motivations and preoccupations. Nonetheless, although these are silences that can be listened to, they do not arise from or between Lewental's words. They are not silences where words have failed.[23] They occur where words used to be.

They are imposed on the text, interfere with his intentions, frustrate our attempts to get back to what he had to say, or to see what he could not say.

However, as Charles Hedrick suggests in his meditation on Late Antique inscriptions and erasures, the difference between the two may not be an absolute one.

> An erasure, we might say, is not the negation of writing, but rather an exaggerated form of it. Here the literate are confronted with the same truth that the illiterate have always known: this mark here, on the stone before me now, indicates something that is not there, and not apparent.[24]

Hedrick's point highlights the inevitable risks of communication from Lewental to whoever might find and read his manuscript. There is an inevitable gap between Lewental's experience and ours. It cannot simply be communicated, or imagined back to. It is worth remembering this, even as we try to work out what the SK were doing with their writings. Equally, Lewental does not seem to have been readily able to put his experiences into words. Unlike Langfus and Gradowski, we are only aware of silence from him before August 1944. That silence bleeds into the silence forced onto his first twenty pages by water damage. Those pages themselves might have shown Lewental working his way out of silence into being able to tell the story of the Sonderkommando.[25]

The Narrative of the Revolt (pp. 21–92)

Our revised order also makes some difference to the main story that has been gleaned from Lewental. Most simply, it brings together some pages to show that they are discussing a similar theme, and separates others to show that they are dealing with separate incidents. Both of these results are evident at the beginning of the run of decipherable pages, where Lewental first discusses writing about Auschwitz, and then describes his own arrival in Auschwitz.

The first continuously legible part, before any narrative elements, is a general discussion of Auschwitz, what is known about it and who will be able to tell about it:

> The history of Auschwitz Birkenau in general as a work camp and specifically as an extermination site for millions of people will, I believe, be more or less communicated to the world, partly by civilians and I believe that the world already knows these <details>. The rest, perhaps someone from the Poles

will survive, by them maybe, or from the camp elite who <occupy> the best positions and the most responsible. (21.1–8)

Against this, Lewental opposes the 'extermination process' (21.10–11) and seems to be suggesting that this will be less well known. The following two pages also call into question what these survivors will say about themselves. Those who survive, Lewental suspects, will say that they deserved to survive, even though all who did have compromised themselves (22–23). Page 23 contains the phrases 'no one knows', 'they won't know' and 'the smallest particle will be taken away' (23.11–13).[26] On the next page, after some discussion of the extermination process in general, which is highly fragmentary, Lewental introduces the 'well-known Sonderkommando', making mention of their work, the conditions in which they lived, and what 'we thought over the period' (24.12–15).

What is clear already is that Lewental is concerned both with what happened, and with who will be able to tell that story. Surviving Poles and camp elite will not be able to give the full history of Birkenau, and he as a member of the Sonderkommando has a story that also needs to be heard. In part this must be the process of extermination, but it may also be simply the story of the SK themselves: their conditions and work, but also, perhaps, what they thought. Although there are a number of sidetracks to his thought, Lewental is clearly introducing the account that follows with a consideration of history, and suggesting what it is that his account will add to what is known.

It is only after this that Lewental discusses his own arrival in Auschwitz. Our revised page order allows us to distinguish between the parts that describe the separate incidents of arriving in Auschwitz and being drafted into the Sonderkommando. Lewental first details the experience of coming to Auschwitz, which he dates as 10 December 1942. The transport undergoes a selection, and the men eventually realise that all their families are dead. Feelings of guilt and horror overcome them (25–29). Lewental then goes on to state that he worked in a number of different kommandos before coming into the SK on 25 January 1943.[27] After he has done this, he explains how the men were inducted into Sonderkommando, using the third person for the rest of this page and the next. The following page only contains a few words that are decipherable; on the page after he begins an account of how they became accustomed to the work (30–34). At points Lewental expresses an excruciating sense of guilt and shame. But at other points he seems able to step back and analyse the situation in which he was placed: the tactics used by the SS to deceive and achieve compliance, the psychology of those recently arrived in Auschwitz, and the reasons why the Sonderkommando carried out the function assigned to them.

> Outwardly you convince yourself you don't care about your own life, you don't care about your own person, but simply for the general good, for survival, for this, for that, or this, or that, hundreds of excuses come up. But the truth is, there is a will to live at any price. There is a desire to live, because you live, because the whole world lives, and everything that has savour, everything that is bound up with anything, is in the first place bound up with life. (36.4–11)

This is a rough-hewn piece of writing in some ways, and powerful because of it, but it also acquires some of its power from its rhetorical patterning. As with Gradowski and Langfus, these patterns serve to express, and to keep under control, difficult emotions, but they also permit Lewental to write at speed. The rhetorical structures operate as scaffolding which enables the construction of sentences, providing a form into which words can be fitted as quickly as possible. Rhetoric here is essential simply to being able to testify, necessary precisely in Lewental's circumstances of being restricted and pressed for time.

Equally, once he begins to write the story of the resistance movement within the Sonderkommando, Lewental needs to have means with which he can build the narrative. As he shows in the middle of his account, he chooses aspects that he believes are historically important: the personal traits demonstrated by those around him.

> No one has the right to take away anything from the moral height and courage, bravery and heroism which our friends showed, even in the unsuccessful case, which has not yet had any equal in the history of Auschwitz-Birkenau and overall in the history of oppressions, persecutions, sorrow and agony, which the Germans carried out in the whole occupied world. (70.2–7)

Hayden White's insistence that all histories have to be emplotted is entirely appropriate here.[28] Lewental's account is not just a witness statement. He is attempting to give a history, focusing on what he sees as the significant facts of the case, and explaining why it is important. The personality and feelings of the individuals are features he wants to focus on. Much more than Langfus or Gradowski, he is interested in giving an account of the psychology of the 'special squad', asking the questions of them that the other two scribes encode rather more indirectly into their work. These questions are important and valid, and we do not wish to suggest that his work cannot be examined to answer them, but we also want to suggest that the modes of writing make certain topics possible. Lewental necessarily has to use some set of tools to be able to tell his account. He uses the category of personality as one of those tools.

It is only when he has a cast of characters that he can endow with agency that he is able to marshal them into a narrative, in which they are constrained and constantly held back, but are actually in a position to make plans, to carry them out, and to assess to what extent they have succeeded. The order we have established brings out more clearly how he went about telling that story. Firstly, it shows that he signed off his testimony twice, and that in both cases he finished with the names of those people who were prominent in the revolt. Secondly, it shows a tighter cluster of named individuals being introduced towards the beginning of the account. Although he only occasionally breaks from talking about the Sonderkommando in general, the fact that he begins and ends with individuals shows their importance for him.

The description of how resistance comes about starts with particular people standing out from the mass, especially Leyb Langfus, the dayan of Maków Mazowiecki.

> But there were individual <people> who did not in any way allow themselves to be influenced by the habit, did not allow it to become completely easy, did not get carried away [*mitgerisn*]. Of course, educated elements [*barufene elementen*] that there were among us, for example the very religious Jews such as the dayan from Maków Maz. and others somewhat similar, such noble men who did not in any way want to join in the game of Today I live, tomorrow I die. I have kept going at any price. At first their influence was very small in the Kommando, simply because their numbers were small, and smaller to recognise, because they were not organised. They did not form one unity, and so disappeared in the general *****. (38.12–39.11)

Although it precludes them from being able to have much influence at first, the fact that people such as Langfus are individuals who do not form part of a 'mass' is what makes them valuable for Lewental. Indeed, he goes on to name other people before he starts to discuss how the revolt came about: Jankiel Handelsman, Elusz Malinka and Zalman Gradowski. Lewental has no doubt that organisation was important for the revolt, but he needs to recognise the participants as people with distinct personalities before he can tell the story of how they began to fight back.

Resistance itself seems to begin at an individual level, in what he calls the 'psychosis of running away'. Individuals are named as people who might be prepared to try to escape, including Lewental himself. 'The thought for me ***** was older than the thought of collective action' (49.15–16). Others try to stop him, for reasons that are not entirely clear,[29] but while there seems to be some resentment against 'our own brothers' and 'my comrades' (50.1 and 50.4), the movement does seem to be towards acting collectively. What might be termed the first plan seems to be the thought of a group breakout of the SK: possibly little more than a thought, but one that starts to evolve into more elaborate plans as connections are made with the camp resistance.

One of the most vital connections is with the small Russian element within the SK, who are given a clear personality. They, however, seem to be pretty much of a piece: ready for action, eager, brave, but with little ability to reflect or be patient. Their part in the revolt is key. They come to Birkenau from Lublin (presumably Majdanek) with an account of how they were responsible for disposing of the bodies of the two hundred men selected in February. Their 'ferocity and strength' ('*blutikeyt un shtarkeyt*') (56.4) make them suitable to join in the resistance, but they cannot be fully trusted. The phrase 'political maturity' (56.13) appears further down the page, and would certainly seem to be what these prisoners lack. Lewental characterises the Russians in general as not worrying about consequences or thinking their actions through too much, by virtually taking on their voices: 'Their old system, well known to us, of not pondering too much, just act, and that's all! whether thought through or not, with a chance or without, act, and that's all!' (66.10–13). And this set of personality traits comes out in the lead up to the revolt and in the revolt itself. When an Unterscharführer tries to beat a drunken Russian, the Russian tries to run away, is shot and wounded, then attacks the SS-man before finally being killed. On the basis of this incident the SS decide to include the Russians with the other three hundred due to be selected (70). Because of this, when the revolt breaks out in front of Crematorium IV, the Russians are far more eager to act than the others in Crematoria II and III, who want to wait until the evening to use their weapons. It is the Russians who attack and burn the Kapo, and then break out through the wire (74–75).

All of what happens to the Russians, then, can be explained by the personality that Lewental gives them in his initial description. Because of their rashness, one of them is prepared to drink, run away, and then attack an SS-man without thought of the consequences. Because of those consequences, and because of their own rashness, the other Russians are prepared to act straightaway once the revolt breaks out. Their personality is used as a historical category: it enables Lewental to write that part of his history. As a piece of writing, Lewental's account presents the Russians as 'flat' characters, according to E.M. Forster's famous formulation. Their personalities serve the plot; their characters fail to develop and they do not surprise the reader. In James Phelan's terminology, their dimensions translate straightforwardly into their functions.[30]

As far as the Jewish members of the Sonderkommando are concerned, at least those whom Lewental knew as friends, their personalities have a rather more complicated place in the account. In the main, they are presented as a 'we', and there is not a great distinction to be drawn amongst them psychologically. Nonetheless, there are some differences that Lewental presents: the younger members are more eager to fight, the religious men are less prepared to live for the day. There is also a degree of complexity in the fact that they do not fall easily into one category or another. The Russians as a group are always in favour of acting. The 'allies' in the rest of the camp always want to delay. The Sonderkommando shift between the two positions. In addition, they sometimes want to make links with the rest of the camp, and sometimes feel the best thing to do is to act on their own. Their feelings respond to the changes in circumstance. They are, therefore, the most rounded individuals in his account.[31]

Some of them are presented as individuals with their own personalities, which map on to some of the differentiations within the group. Yossel Warszawski is 'a truly intelligent man with such a fine character by nature. A quiet man, but with the ardent soul of a fighter' (44.7–9). Elusz Malinka seems to stand for the younger members of the SK: 'himself an average youth, but therefore with much t<oo> m<uch> energy and lust for life, a wild risk-taker, and full of temperament, with bright ideas, brave to the utmost' (51.1–3).[32] Leyb Langfus represents the more religious members: 'the dayan himself an intelligent man ***** to be with him, but far from understanding the whole situation straightforwardly because of his attitudes, which stayed within the framework of Jewish law' (79.15–18).[33]

The character sketches are striking when compared with the writings of Langfus and Gradowski, who leave the Sonderkommando anonymous. They are written in a note-like form, but attentive to some complexities in the people, attempting to convey some of the paradoxes of their personalities. Each of these three contains a 'but', suggesting that there is more than one side to them, that the different aspects of their personalities are somewhat surprising in their combination. It might even suggest some level of interiority: they give one impression, but actually there is more to them than might at first be thought.

This is important, because so much of this story is effectively about the interior life of the Sonderkommando: less on what they did; more on what they felt, thought, and intended to do. Interiority is also important because much of the history Lewental discusses is not what happened but rather what they planned would happen. This element shows more clearly that they were resisting. Rather than chronicling what was actually done, or explaining why the SK only acted at the last minute, he provides an account of various plans that they worked on. Doing so provides a far more coherent account of the resistance movement in the Sonderkommando. Although most of the planning comes to nothing, the planning itself is a form of resistance, as is the recording of it.[34]

It also means that certain elements are omitted. The initial plan is described in great detail, but what stopped it is dealt with rather cryptically.

> The group [*oylem*] kissed each other for joy, that we had lived to see the minute when we made an end to everything of our own choosing [*umgetsvungen*]. Nevertheless, no one held the illusion that we were going to save ourselves. On the contrary, we had clearly made the assessment that it was a certain death, but everyone was happy with this. But at the last minute, something timely happened with a transport [*geshen iz ober der letster minit epes tsaytiges mit a transport*],³⁵ and we had to put a stop in the zone, and consequently to the whole operation [*un m'hot gemuzt dort in zone obhaltn, un mimeyle di gantse aktsie*]. Truth be told, our youth wept out loud [*geveynt mit trern*], knowing that such events should not be cancelled. If not, it would not happen as we wanted. (60.12–61.5)

What happened with the transport is not explained. No elaboration of this statement is given. What other Sonderkommando testimony tells us is that a group of reinforcements of the SS arrived.³⁶ Far more important are the emotions associated with the plan and its stymieing: joy, kissing each other, crying.

The thread that connects all the elements of the story is the evolving history of the different plans and intentions of the Sonderkommando. The external factors have their place in the narrative through the effect that they have on the feelings and plans of the SK. For example, 'the political situation outside, which improved from day to day, compelled us to wait' (61.10–12). Most strikingly, in discussing the killing of the Hungarian Jews, Lewental simply writes: 'It took so long that over time half a million Hungarian Jews were burnt' (62.1–3), and while there is a fierce despair in contrasting the simplicity of this statement with the complications of the resistance leadership in Auschwitz still asking for delays, it is also evidence that he wants to explain what happened with the plan rather than what happened to the Hungarian Jews. Two lines of this page discuss the deaths of half a million people. Eight lines are given over to the plan. This is not some skating over of the facts of mass murder: he makes it plain what has happened. Rather, Lewental's story is not about who has died and how. It is about the Sonderkommando.

As well as what part these people played in resistance, therefore, Lewental describes who they are. Their personalities both play a part in explaining the revolt and yet are not entirely subsumed into a cause for their actions. Lewental seems to end by saying that the SK's failures do not lie in their character faults: 'But we are not ***** did not succeed as planned, the fault lies with ***** and, however, the greater strength that he had' (80.4–6). In Forster's terms, these might be called 'round' characters.

In James Phelan's schema, in addition to their 'thematic' function (their personality as an explanatory category), they have a 'mimetic' function too: Lewental is trying to give us a sense of what they were like.[37]

So this text has a second purpose in addition to giving a history. It serves as a memorial. On the penultimate page of the first section, Lewental places the acronym תנצבה ('may their souls be bound in the bundle of life') in the middle of the line (82.4). This acronym occurs on the headstones of Jewish graves, usually on the last line. Lewental's manuscript serves as their headstone; it will mark their graves. Although most of what has been written about gravestones tends to see their inscriptions as largely formulaic, Heidi Szpek has suggested that there are histories and biographies that can be discerned in some of them.[38] In trying to provide a memorial for his fellow members of the Sonderkommando, Lewental is attempting to provide some concrete detail of their lives. The importance of testifying to individuals becomes clear here then, and it is something that he does again a few pages later as his second ending. Their individual characteristics are being memorialised in Lewental's text. Named individuals do not seem to appear in the other extant parts of the text.

Lewental has a number of concerns at the end of his account. The allies betrayed them in a number of ways, but the one that he dwells on the most is the fact that they took 'our' story and did not credit 'us'.

> But it turned out that we were betrayed by the Poles, our allies, and everything that they took from us they have used for their own ends. The material which we issued was attributed to them, and completely silenced our name. (87.9–15)

Burying the manuscripts in the ground is a response to the failure of the allies to credit them as much as to the exigencies of the circumstances in which they are held.[39] Lewental wants to give his name as an author, and those of his fellow members of the Sonderkommando as planners and participants in the uprising, and is prepared to risk having his document damaged rather than give it to someone else who may betray it.

Deportation(s) (pp. 93–115)

Since Lewental signed off his manuscript at the end of his account of the revolt, what follows on from it must in some sense be an afterthought. Finding the time, or simply the inclination, to tell other stories, Lewental started to write again (Figure 4.2). The numbering at the top of the next page (93) is not the only significant part of this sheet that previous readers

144 • Matters of Testimony

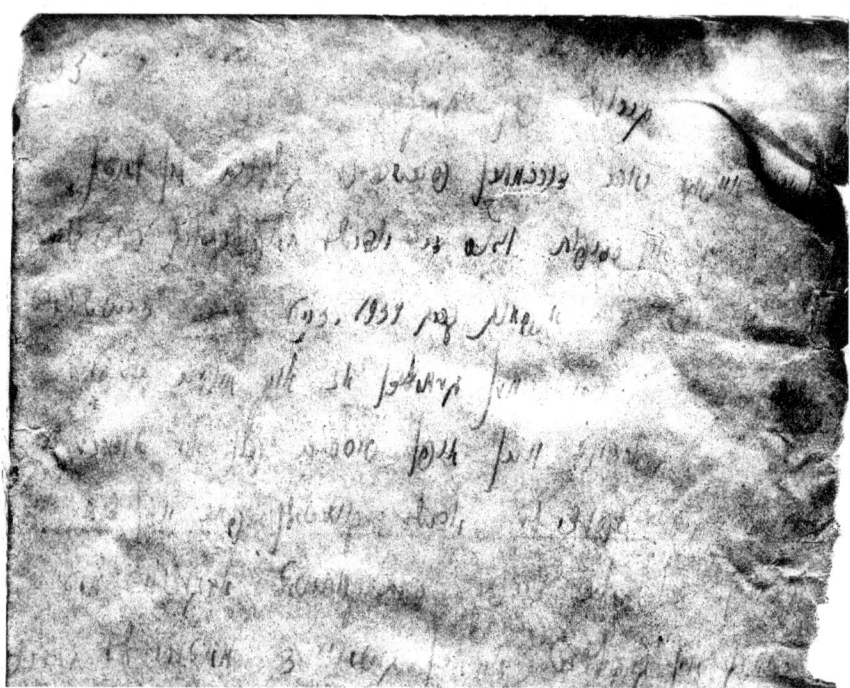

Figure 4.2. Detail from Zalman Lewental's manuscript. The text discusses events in 1939. Part of what seems to be a title is readable at the top. The page number 93 is visible in the top left corner.

have missed. To the right of the page number there are words that are highly likely to be a title, beginning 'Deportation of/from' ('*geyresh fun*') (93.1).[40] These words are written in larger letters and closer to the centre of the page, and ink marks in the top left hand corner, just to the right of the page number, look like rather smaller writing, which could possibly be a date. The final word of this title is hard to make out, but is certainly not Ciechanów. In fact, it looks more like the Hebrew spelling of Maków, Leyb Langfus's home town, which lay about 25 miles away.[41] It is possible that Lewental ended up there during the German occupation. Forced labourers were moved from one place to another, and people fled and found refuge in different ghettos. If this is so, the story told is a condensed version of Langfus's, albeit starting earlier, in 1939, and with an overview of the whole Ciechanów area. Quickly, however, Lewental moves on to the story of the deportation itself, with a transport leaving the ghetto on 17 November 1942. The ending too, is very similar to Langfus's story, with one group being gassed while a second one waiting in a nearby barracks hear their cries. On the last page of this section, Lewental describes how the newly recruited Sonderkommando disposed of the bodies, some of them recognising their own family among the dead. 'In this way there perished our entire settlement, our entire community, our town, our dear parents, children, sisters, brothers on 10/12 1942 late at night, the rest the next day' (108.17–20).

The next page seems to start telling the same story again, describing a train journey, the arrival in Auschwitz, and the taking of people away from the ramp in cars to be gassed. Nonetheless, it may make sense to see it as a separate section. Firstly, the manuscripts themselves do suggest that there may be a break here. The final line of writing on page 108 stops before it reaches the edge of the page. What looks to be the first line of writing on page 109 is much lower down on the page than most of Lewental's first lines. There is some writing at the top, but it does not occupy the whole line (it is on the same line as the written page number), seems somewhat larger, and may therefore be another title. Secondly, there does seem to be a coherent thread to the second part. The constant theme over the seven pages that are legible to any extent is one of deception, false hope and misunderstanding. Lewental writes that they did not know much of what was happening. 'We knew of Auschwitz as a work camp. Harsh camp, very harsh conditions, but even so people there remained alive' (109.9–11). 'As we went along, we were only afraid of ***** Małkinia which led off to' (109.15–17).[42] Małkinia was the station on the main line north-east of Warsaw, from which trains turned to Treblinka. The following word, on the next line, is not completely legible, but it starts 'tr', and in context seems highly likely to be Treblinka. Although the fourth letter in this word looks like a *mem*, and therefore Lewental may have misspelt it as 'Tremblinke', this was a mistake that certainly was made by others writing about this extermination site, about which many details were known, but much was also uncertain in 1942.[43] The end of this page seems to say that the train stopped at Małkinia station (109.18).

On the basis of this page, Danuta Czech surmised that there must have been a transit camp at Małkinia, and that Lewental's transport spent several days there (explaining the difference between the deportation date of 17 November and the arrival in Auschwitz on 10 December).[44] Indeed, in the *Auschwitz Chronicle* she went so far as to record Małkinia as the point of departure of two transports to Auschwitz. However, since there are no other records of such a camp, and since there are certainly prisoners with numbers within the range Czech gives who do not give an account of being in a transit camp in Małkinia,[45] this seems a very extreme move to make sense of what Lewental wrote. For a start, the following page in our ordering, although there are very few words legible, seems (in its current state) to support a reading that the train did not stop here for very long.

Two phrases on that page – 'felt newly revived', and 'found that they were taking us to Auschwitz' (110.5–6) – would certainly fit with a scenario very similar to that described by Zalman Gradowski: the people in the transport feel relieved when they discover that they are not taking the turning to Treblinka, which they know is an extermination site, as opposed to Auschwitz, which they do not.

There is an additional problem, less easily resolved, that no known transport from the Ciechanów region to Auschwitz went via Małkinia.[46] As things stand, there is too much of the manuscript that has not been deciphered for certain conclusions to be made about this portion, but it would seem sensible not to assert the existence of places for which there is no other documentation. A number of other possible answers exist at the moment: the recollections of other survivors from the Ciechanów region are wrong or incomplete, and some trains did take this route (although it would have been circuitous in the extreme); Lewental mistakenly believed that they had stopped there in the middle of the night; he said that he stopped there even though he knew he did not (although we do not regard this as likely).

But we want to raise another possibility: that he was telling somebody else's story, or even two different people's stories. As we have noted, the two stories each seem to start with a title, and the first does not name his home town, but he still calls it 'our community', and mourns 'our parents'. Could it be that even here he is speaking in someone else's voice, someone whose home town was Maków? Someone such as Leyb Langfus, or one of the many other men from Maków recruited into the SK? Equally, is it possible that the story of the transport through Małkinia is the story of someone such as Zalman Gradowski, who came from north-east Poland along that route? Once the narrative of the uprising was finished, Lewental seems to have realised he had more time to tell other stories. Might it be that he decided to gather and record stories from other people, and not just tell his own? This can of course only be a possibility, but the fact that it is conceivable has an effect on the way that we imagine the Sonderkommando. It requires thinking beyond Primo Levi's claim that their testimony could be nothing other than self-justification.[47] Lewental was interested in other people, and wanted to record their names and describe their personalities. He even, as we have shown, took on some of their voices, both the Russians, and the men playing the game of 'Today I live, tomorrow I die'. He collected other people's documents and artefacts, and sometimes commented on them. Perhaps his manuscript is an archive of stories in the same way as his caches of documents are. This would be one other way in which he served as a historian of the Sonderkommando.

The Addendum to the Łódź Manuscript

In his addendum to the Łódź diary, Lewental had already outlined in compressed form what we have seen to be his major concerns. This text sheds valuable light on how Lewental would later approach his account of the uprising. In this short text, his awareness of psychology and his concern about history are repeatedly referenced. The longer document echoes these interests. It is, in part, motivated by a desire to comprehend and share the mind-sets of victims. It is also a work of local history that seeks to give an insider account of the genesis of the uprising and its frustrating aftermath. Lewental looks to the future, seeks to shape how his actions, and those of his fellows, will retrospectively be viewed and understood.

In the addendum Lewental also shows familiarity with the bigger picture. He realises the history of the destruction of Europe's Jews extends beyond the horrific confines of Birkenau. It is this foresight that enables him to recognise the historical and testimonial worth of the Łódź diary. He even provides an assessment of the specific kinds of insights he believes it will provide for historians. The diary gives 'a <c>lear picture of everything, including the economic, the spiritual and even the sanitary situation' of the ghetto.[48] He acknowledges the importance of Warsaw, yet claims that 'u<n>doubtedly Łódź' gives an 'accurate mirror of Polish ghetto life' (434).

The evaluation Lewental makes regarding which of the two ghettos is representative of a particular kind of Jewish existence under Nazi occupation in Poland shows that he is acting as a historian should. He is assessing source material, foreseeing how a story of the past might be written, and determining what evidence might best be employed to support it. His observation also reinforces the reality that the extermination camp was not hermetic. Although he arrived at Auschwitz in December 1942, he was clearly well aware of what transpired in Warsaw in 1943. He also shows knowledge of Russian advances, of how the war is progressing, of current affairs. The Sonderkommando received a steady influx of information from arriving transports from various countries that, coupled with other forms of communication such as messages from the Polish resistance, would give them a strong sense of the unfolding situation in Europe.

As a putative historian in the addendum, Lewental also attends to gaps in his account. He acknowledges the limitations of his testimony, its lacunae, writing: '<I> cannot permit [*derloybn*] myself to describe what I would like for various reasons' (433). Chief among these reasons is the surveillance he is subject to by the camp guards. There is not sufficient opportunity to give a 'full' account because the SK are under near constant observation. There may also be a fear present here that, were the document to be discovered by the Nazis, it would place anyone mentioned in it by name who was from the special squad at risk of reprisals. There are, however, evidently other reasons motivating this reticence which we can only speculate about. What is clear is that there are deliberate gaps introduced in the manuscript (as well as ones produced by contingency later on) which Lewental felt were necessary. Whether he still thought this way when he wrote his later, lengthier document we do not know.

In addition to the lacunae derived from the hostile circumstances in which it was written, Lewental obliquely refers to another gap towards the end of the addendum. He writes that, despite the insights into the ghetto provided by the diary, 'the whole truth is even more tragic and terrible' (434). Here he is again evaluating his historical source material. This time he finds it wanting. He knows that any history is, of necessity, incomplete. The focus on calamity and horrendousness, however, as what an account cannot convey also suggests a recognition of the limits of language, an awareness of the gap between words and the catastrophe they seek to describe and which Lewental lives through.

Despite this appreciation for what any history writing cannot do, the addendum closes with an imploration for the reader to search for further buried documents. If language is inadequate for Lewental, he still appreciates its power. The lacunae that haunt any account require acknowledgment, merit careful consideration – yet writing still does invaluable work. The words consigned to the grounds of the crematoria stubbornly resist Nazi efforts to efface all trace of their crimes. Lewental is acutely aware of how effective their contribution to recording and communicating the horrors of the ghetto and the death factory will be. The text ends: 'Keep looking! You <will> ***** find still more' (434). It closes with a sentence riven by a gap inviting the reader to continue searching for words.

Notes

1. Elie Wiesel, 'Preface', in Ber Mark, *Des voix dans la nuit*, trans. Esther Fridman, Joseph Fridman and Liliane Princet (Paris: Plon, 1982), v.
2. ***** indicates missing text of varied length. See the Preface for a full key to textual symbols.
3. The author for the Łódź diary has not been satisfactorily identified, although a number of suggestions have been made for him. The Marks accepted the claim by Chaim Leib Fox that the writer was Emanuel Herszberg, a Reform-minded rabbi who had published some Yiddish poetry in the 1920s, and who was head of the

Kunstresort in the Łódź ghetto (*Megiles Oyshvits*, 274 n. 14). Fox's reasons for this attribution are not completely clear. His main argument seems to be that Herszberg had published books under the name 'Willi Gottlieb', and the diary is written in the form of letters to a 'Dear Willi'. Chaim Leib Fox, *Lodzsh shel Mayle: Dos Yidishe gaystike un derhoybene Lodzsh (100 yor yidishe un oykh hebreishe literatur un kultur in Lodzsh un in di arumike shtet un shtetlekh)* (Tel Aviv: I.L. Peretz, 1972) 184–85. However, the attribution to Herszberg does not seem secure to us. The diarist writes about having three daughters who seem to be living with him and adopting a male child in the ghetto. The ghetto records show Herszberg to have lived with only two daughters (Beruria and Zimrat-ia), along with his wife. Łódź ghetto records available at: <http://www.jewishgen.org/databases/Poland/LodzGhetto.html> [accessed 29 October 2014].
4. Ber Mark, *Megiles Oyshvits* (Tel Aviv: Yisroel-Bukh, 1977), 272. APMO Tom 51b.
5. Alexandre Prstojevic, 'L'indicible et la fiction configuratrice', *Protée*, 37(2) (2009): 36. Dan Stone, 'The Harmony of Barbarism: Locating the Scrolls of Auschwitz in Holocaust Historiography', in *Representing Auschwitz: At the Margins of Testimony*, ed. Nicholas Chare and Dominic Williams (Basingstoke: Palgrave Macmillan, 2013), 24. This may not have been a role exclusive to Lewental. The foreword to a putative collection of writings by prisoners that was going to be buried suggests that others also wanted to assemble groups of documents. See David Suchoff, 'A Yiddish Text from Auschwitz: Critical History and the Anthological Imagination', *Prooftexts* 19(1) (January 1999): 59–69.
6. Pavel Polian, 'Svidetel', khronist, obvinitel'. Zalman Leventalʹ i yevo teksty', *Ab Imperio* 3 (2012): 229–31.
7. Mark, *Megiles Oyshvits*, 267. Mark only credits Gostyński. Kapczyc-Gostyńska is mentioned in Jadwiga Bezwińska and Danuta Czech, 'Wstęp edytorski', in *Wśród koszmarnej zbrodni: Notatki więźniów z Sonderkommando odnalezione w Oświęcimiu*, ed. Bezwińska and Czech (Oświęcim: Wydawnictwo Państwowego w Oświęcimiu, 1971), 8.
8. Three different versions of Lewental's text have been put together: one by Adam Rutkowski of the Jewish Historical Institute, published in 1968; one in an edition produced by the Auschwitz museum in 1971; and the edition published by the Marks in 1977. Zelman Lewental, 'Pamiętnik członka Sonderkommando Auschwitz II', trans. Adam Rutkowski and Adam Wein, *Biuletyn Żydowskiego Instytutu Historycznego* 65–66 (1968): 211–33; Załmen Lewental, '[Pamiętnik]', trans. Roman Pytel, in *Wśród koszmarnej zbrodni: Notatki więźniów z Sonderkommando odnalezione w Oświęcimiu*, ed. Jadwiga Bezwińska and Danuta Czech (Oświęcim: Wydawnictwo Państwowego w Oświęcimiu, 1971), 126–71; Zalman Leventalʹ, 'Fartseykhenungen', in Ber Mark, *Megiles Oyshvits* (Tel Aviv: Yisroel-Bukh, 1977), 377–421. Czech and Bezwińska make a number of valid objections to Rutkowski's edition, based on the fact that it arranges some passages without any regard for the pages that they appear on. But there also seem to have been some other elements in this criticism: Rutkowski and his fellow translator Adam Wein are accused of possibly having a misplaced national solidarity, and of using Lewental's text to falsely attack the Polish resistance for failing to help the Sonderkommando (8–16). These criticisms of Rutkowski and Wein, included in 1971, but not in the 1973 edition, are clearly marked by the so-called anti-Zionist campaign of March 1968. See our discussion of this in the Introduction. Czech and Bezwińska do not give any examples of how this edition falsified the part

played by the Polish resistance. Indeed, in their own edition, they have to add an apparatus claiming that Lewental was wrong about the Poles (e.g. 168 n. 94).
9. Adam Rutkowski wrote that 'the pages are not numbered' ('Pamiętnik', 211). Bezwińska and Czech also talk about the lack of pagination (*Wśród koszmarnej zbrodni* (1971), 8), but nuance this when they say that 'the majority of pages are unpaginated', adding that the author 'may not have numbered the pages' (121). Ber Mark says that 'Lewental did not number his pages' (*Megiles Oyshvits*, 267).
10. MS page 37a. Note that we work from the manuscript numbers used for the digital copies in the Auschwitz archive. An earlier set of photocopies in the archive uses a slightly different way of identifying different sides of each sheet, and applies it inconsistently. It usually gives a bare sheet number for one side and the number plus 'a' for the other (there is no consistent correspondence between the 'a' sides of the digital images and the photocopies). However, sheet 20 has its verso misnumbered as 21 instead of 20a. Publications of the Auschwitz museum sometimes use the photocopy numbers, hence the mismatch between some of their numbers and ours.
11. In fact, there appears to be writing on all four sides of the cover as well, although it has not yet been possible to read any of it. We would suggest that these were the last pages upon which Lewental wrote.
12. MS sheets 17–23. The order we give for these sheets, from outermost to innermost in the signature, is 17, 18, 19, 21, 20, 22, 23.
13. MS pages 9b and 8b. What the Auschwitz museum identifies as sheet 8 does not fit easily into any group. From the page numbers and text that are decipherable on it, and the stains that match other sheets, it is actually most likely to be two separate half-sheets that formed the outer sheets of the first and last signatures in the book. This would indicate that the first and last pages of the book were torn out before Lewental began writing and numbering the pages of his account. In the jumble of pages caused by the restoration process, the museum probably assumed that these two half-sheets formed one sheet together.
14. MS pages 24a and 9a.
15. MS pages 7, 17a, 18b, 19b.
16. To see how these page numbers correspond to the other three editions produced and to the manuscript held in the Auschwitz archive, consult the table in Appendix C.
17. With approximately nine words to each line, and nineteen lines to each page, the eighty-two and a bit pages come to something like 14,000–15,000 words. To produce this in three days is feasible – a number of writers have claimed to write 1,000 words an hour (famously, Anthony Trollope), and the SK worked 12-hour shifts when they were working. Gideon Greif, *We Wept without Tears: Testimonies of the Jewish Sonderkommando from Auschwitz*, trans. Naftali Greenwood (New Haven, CT, and London: Yale University Press, 2005), 106.
18. E.g. '*samokhod*' for 'car' (*samochód* in Polish, *oyto* in standard Yiddish); '*samolyot*' for 'aeroplane' (*samolot* in Polish, *(a)eroplan* in Yiddish); and '*podobne*' for 'similar' (*podobny* in Polish, which also occurs in some Yiddish dialects).
19. See 54.4 and 64.5 for 'end the game' and 72.3–4 for 'start the game'. For 'material', see 51.19, 55.15 and 87.12.
20. Cesare Brandi, *Theory of Restoration*, ed. Giuseppe Basile, trans. Cynthia Rockwell (Florence: Nardini Editore, 2005), 57–59, 90–93. Translation of *Teoria del restauro*, 1977. Brandi's emphasis was on making lacunae recede into the background, so that they simply became structural elements in an artwork, whereas we are of course arguing that the lacunae need to be made more prominent. This reflects the different

ways lacunae operate in images and texts. Fundamentally, the idea that they should play a part in giving the work a structure is comparable.
21. From this point on we will give references to Lewental's longer text using the system of page numbers we have established. The number(s) after the full stop indicate the line number(s) on the manuscript page. The table in Appendix C shows how our page numbers correspond both to manuscript pages and to the section numbers assigned by the other editions. The line numbers help to give an indication of how large the lacunae are, as there are on average about nine words per line.
22. The final few pages are also illegible for the most part, except for one page on which phrases describing horrific sexual violence can be made out. We briefly discuss this page in Chapter 6.
23. In this they differ from the 'white worries', *blancs soucis*, gaps in testimony which signal when a witness cannot name something. See Georges Didi-Huberman, *Blancs soucis* (Paris: Éditions de Minuit, 2013), 92–93.
24. Charles Hedrick Jr, *History and Silence: Purge and Rehabilitation of Memory in Late Antiquity* (Austin: University of Texas Press, 2000), 246.
25. The first few pages of Gradowski's text are also treated as a kind of silence by the Auschwitz museum. They do not communicate information, and so constitute a part that can be omitted. See Chapter 2.
26. Reading *visen* instead of *hobn* for 23.12.
27. David Nencel's testimony tells what seems to be a similar story. He arrived on a transport from Mława in early December 1942, was taken at first to Buna, and then when an epidemic broke out he was sent to Birkenau and drafted into the Sonderkommando, apparently with others. <http://www.google.com/culturalinstitute/asset-viewer/testimony-of-david-nencel-born-in-rypin-1916-regarding-his-experiences-in-german-captivity-ghettos-in-poland-sonderkommando-in-auschwitz-and-mauthausen/jgHuY64vC0kWzA?hl=en&l.expanded-id=XAE5LAJAcIq5zQ> (Tape 3, 43:00–45:00). The other complication with Lewental's manuscript is that he writes, carefully, and including *nekudot* (vowel points), either 'בענאו' ('benau') or, just possibly, 'בונאו' ('bunau') (10.2). There was a small German town Benau, now Bieniów in western Poland, but it was not a subcamp of Auschwitz. Lewental probably misspelt it. The list of people killed in October 1944, which was found with this document, spells it 'Bunau'. If Lewental did spell it this way in his manuscript, that would count as evidence in favour of him being the author of this list as well.
28. Hayden White, *Metahistory: The Historical Imagination in Nineteenth-Century Europe* (Baltimore, MD: Johns Hopkins University Press, 1973), 7–11.
29. Tzipora Halivni suggests that it was the Polish ZOW (Związek Organizacji Wojskowej), but the sense is more that it was done by fellow members of the Sonderkommando. Tzipora Hager Halivni, 'The Birkenau Revolt: Poles Prevent a Timely Insurrection', *Jewish Social Studies* 41(2) (Spring 1979): 133.
30. E.M. Forster, *Aspects of the Novel* (London: Penguin, 1990), 73–77; James Phelan, *Reading Characters, Reading Plots* (Chicago and London: University of Chicago Press, 1989), 9.
31. There is no interest at all in the psychology the SS, understandably perhaps, although there are some examples of prisoners taking some interest in them. Gradowski uses free indirect discourse to portray their thoughts in *In the Heart of Hell: In harts fun gehenem* (Jerusalem: Wolnerman, n.d.), esp. 82–91. MM's sketchbook from Auschwitz is interested in the kinds of poses that SS-men strike, in the way tyranny

is embodied. Agnieszka Sieradzka (ed.), *Szkicownik z Auschwitz/The Sketchbook from Auschwitz* (Oświęcim: Państwowe Muzeum Auschwitz-Birkenau, 2011), 42, 52.
32. The Auschwitz museum edition reads his name as 'Majerko', the Marks' edition as 'Malinka'. The name seems clearly to me to be Malinka; see especially 79.19 [DW].
33. Gradowski is introduced on page 53: '*Gradowski Zalman, aleyn*' – the same wording that introduces Lewental's other descriptions of people, which would suggest that he too was given some kind of character sketch.
34. We will discuss this idea more in Chapter 6.
35. Reading '*tsaytiges*' instead of '*vikhtiges*' ('important').
36. David Nencel, Yad Vashem interview (Tape 4, 1:25–3:20); 'Vernehmung des Zeugen Milton Buki', 127. Verhandlungstag (14.01.1965), *Der 1. Frankfurter Auschwitz-Prozess*, 27890; Greif, *We Wept without Tears*, 226; Marcel Nadjary, *Khroniko 1941–1945* (Thessaloniki: Etz Khaim, 1991), 57. The dates given vary between July and September, but they seem to be talking about the same incident. See Erich Friedler, Barbara Siebert and Andreas Killian, *Zeugen aus der Todeszone: Das jüdische Sonderkommando in Auschwitz* (Munich: Deutsche Taschenbuch, 2008), 262. Tzipora Hager Halivni suggests that it was the placing of a transport of Hungarian women, including Halivni herself, in the zone which prevented the uprising taking place. While this cannot be dismissed out of hand, she does provide a rather skewed translation from Lewental to support it: 'something serious happened with a transport in the zone and we were forced to halt there and, consequently, to halt the entire action' ('The Birkenau Revolt', 136). Lewental's sentence is rather awkward, and could perhaps be resolved by taking *obhaltn* to have a missing or assumed reflexive pronoun, but there is no reason to think that the phrase '*in zone*' qualifies the transport. (The translation I give here is also in line with Maurice Pfeffer's French translation. [DW])
37. Forster, *Aspects of the Novel*, 77–81. Phelan, *Reading Characters*, 2–3.
38. Heidi Szpek, 'Jewish Epitaphs from Białystok, 1892–1902: Embracing the Spirit of Dubnow', *East European Jewish Affairs* 42(2) (August 2012): 129–58.
39. Halivni, 'The Birkenau Revolt', 142.
40. The phrase '*geyresh fun*' is more commonly used to mean 'deportation of' people. 'Deportation from' a town is more commonly expressed as a compound noun: e.g. '*Geyresh Shpanie*', '*geyresh Mlave*', '*geyresh Plotsk*'. However, it is sometimes possible to use it to mean deportation from a place.
41. This is the spelling Lewental uses for the town elsewhere in the manuscript: מאקוב (39.1). He also uses the Hebrew spelling for Ciechanów: ציהנוב (45.3).
42. Reading '*aropgefirt*' instead of '*arayngefirt*'.
43. See, for example: the letter quoted in Simone Gigliotti, *The Train Journey: Transit, Captivity, and Witnessing in the Holocaust* (New York: Berghahn Books, 2009), 118; the JTA report quoted in Donald Bloxham, *Genocide on Trial: War Crimes Trials and the Formation of Holocaust History and Memory* (Oxford: Oxford University Press, 2001), 116 n. 125; Ogólny Żydowski Związek Robotniczy 'Bund' w Polsce, *Geto in Flamen: Zamlbukh* (New York: Amerikaner Representants fun Bund, 1944), 22, 24, 53; Kh. Shushkes, *Bleter fun a Geto-Tog-Bukh* (New York: H.H. Glants, 1943), 40, 58, 117.
44. The date that Lewental gives for his departure, 17 November 1942, is later than most of the accounts of when transports left Ciechanów (5 and 6 November north to the transit camp and rail hub of Mława). Michał Grynberg, *Żydzi w rejencji ciechanowskiej* (Warsaw: Państwowe Wydawnictwo Naukowe, 1984), 107–8. The date does fit the liquidation of the ghetto in Nowe Miasto, and 1,200 Jews from Ciechanów had

been transferred to Nowe Miasto in 1941. It is one of the towns Lewental mentions when he discusses the institution of ghettos. However, the deportees only stayed for one night in Płońsk before being transported to Auschwitz (VHF interviews 17375, 1260, 2110, 2242). The closest match in dates is in accounts of the liquidation of the Maków ghetto. According to Mordechai Ciechanower, they were taken on 18 November to Mława, and arrived in Auschwitz on 10 December. *Der Dachdecker von Auschwitz* (Berlin: Metropol Verlag, 2007), 103, 109.

45. Danuta Czech lists two transports arriving in Auschwitz from Małkinia: one on 10 December 1942 (for which she lists the camp numbers as 81400–81923), and one on 12 December 1942 (with numbers 82047–82462 for the men selected, and 26800–26805 for women). Danuta Czech, *Auschwitz Chronicle*, trans. Barbara Harshav, Martha Humphreys and Stephen Shearier (New York: Henry Holt, 1990), 283, 284. However, Mordechai Ciechanower (camp number 81434), Stanley Glogover (81481), Hersch Unger (81843), Moishe Silberman (81920), Sam Itzkowitz (82190) and David Nencel (82321) all give accounts of going from Maków to Mława, and from Mława to Auschwitz (VHF archives, nos. 19721, 28862, 10853, 29430, 15815; Nencel interview, op. cit.). There is no mention of a Małkinia camp in the encyclopedia of camps produced by the Commission for Investigating Nazi Crimes in Poland. Główna Komisja Badania Zbrodni Hitlerowskich w Polsce, *Obozy hitlerowskie na ziemiach polskich 1939–1945: Informator encyklopedyczny* (Warsaw: Państwowe Wydawnictwo Naukowe, 1979). In Czech's earlier version of the Calendar, the transport was simply listed as coming from Ciechanów. Danuta Czech, 'Kalendarium der Ereignisse im Konzentrationslager Auschwitz-Birkenau', *Hefte von Auschwitz* 3 (1960): 106–7. The likelihood is, therefore, that the discovery of Lewental's text in 1962 was the reason for the change.

46. There are some reports of transports from Mława going to Treblinka, although even these have been questioned by historians. Katrin Reichelt and Martin Dean, 'Maków Mazowiecki', in *USHMM Encyclopedia of Camps and Ghettos, 1933–1945*, Vol. II, Part A, ed. Martin Dean (Bloomington: Indiana University Press, 2012), 16. Małkinia was used as a euphemism for Treblinka. Langfus says that the people in the ghetto at Maków were told that this is where the women and children were going to go (see Chapter 3). None of the interviewees from Maków, Nowe Miasto or Ciechanów for the USC Shoah Foundation Video Archive mentions going to Auschwitz via Małkinia. Most say that the journey took two or three days.

47. Primo Levi, *The Drowned and the Saved*, trans. Raymond Rosenthal (London: Abacus, 1989), 36–37.

48. Zalman Lewental, 'Hesofe tsum Lodzher ksav-yad', in Ber Mark, *Megiles Oyshvits* (Tel Aviv: Yisroel-Bukh, 1977), 432. References to this text will be given in the main body of this chapter from now on.

Chapter 5

Characters and Letters

Chaim Herman and Marcel Nadjary

Living Letters

During his retrospective account of the discovery of Chaim Herman's letter in February 1944, Andrzej Zaorski drew attention to what struck him as important in both the form and the content of the document.[1] He was clearly intrigued by its shape, mentioning repeatedly the way that it was constructed, 'folded up in the form of a letter', with the outermost sheet serving as a 'makeshift envelope'. Herman had used his ingenuity to protect the document as best he could. He also rolled the rough envelope and its cherished contents into a scroll, which he then stashed in a bottle and buried. Evidently his various efforts to safeguard the letter met with some success, as Zaorski notes that it was 'superbly preserved'. The rudimentary wrapping sheltering the letter included a superscription. With unnerving premonition, Herman had addressed the cover to the Polish Red Cross, of which Zaorski, its finder, was a member.

Zaorski's description suggests, perhaps, that some effort had been put into making the outer sheet look like an envelope. Herman did not simply want his document to be protected, but to take on the actual form of a letter. In addition, the envelope attempted to conceal the address of his wife, as well as the words that he wrote to her. This attempt was not entirely successful: clearly Zaorski thought the fact that it was not a real, sealed envelope excused his looking inside. The materials did not quite live up to the task given to them. Herman had been forced to make use of what he had to hand: sheets of graph paper. Squared paper was originally designed to be used to plot coordinates with ease, to draw graphs. It was first marketed in scientific circles and retains an association with factuality and objectivity. Here, it was adapted to meet the very different requirements and rules of letter writing: attempting to observe a degree of privacy, to create a space in which familial relationships could be asserted and heartfelt personal emotions could be expressed.

Herman's message to his wife is memorable for the way it articulates a complex series of emotions – love, guilt, fear, hope, pride – in short order. The letter forms a painfully condensed stream of consciousness, jumbled and desperate, scribbled against a graphic backdrop of neatness and uniformity. The rawness of the evidently hastily written communication means it gives significant and moving insight into the character of a particular individual. This may explain why the letter so affected an author such as David Lodge, who refers to it in his novel *Deaf Sentence*. In Lodge's novel, the central character, Desmond Bates, a retired academic coming to terms with his loss of hearing, makes reference to Herman who he has read about in 'a paperback about Auschwitz and the Final Solution' purchased at a station bookstall.[2] This paperback is presumably Laurence Rees's *Auschwitz: The Nazis and the Final Solution*, which became a bestseller.[3] Bates learns of the inmates at Auschwitz that 'many of them, knowing they would never survive, left letters to their loved ones buried in jars or canteens in the camp, hoping these documents might one day be discovered and delivered, or at least read by somebody'.[4]

In *Auschwitz*, Rees mistakenly identifies all the manuscripts composed by members of the Sonderkommando as taking the form of letters.[5] Through Bates's summary, Lodge's novel repeats Rees's inaccuracy, retransmitting and perpetuating it. There are actually only two known documents, by Herman and Marcel Nadjary, that can be straightforwardly classified as epistolary writings.[6] Herman's correspondence is preserved in the archives of *L'Amicale des déportés d'Auschwitz Birkenau*.[7] Nadjary's letter is in the Auschwitz museum.

Rees's characterisation of all the documents as letters, despite his having obviously read the collection of manuscripts published as *Amidst a Nightmare of Crime*, is initially perplexing. In fact, it is common for the literary genre of the Sonderkommando manuscripts to be misidentified. Nathan Cohen, for example, refers to the manuscripts written by Gradowski, Langfus and Lewental as consisting of 'diaries and notes'.[8] Others who have referred to the documents as diaries include Saul Friedländer and Susie Linfield.[9] Cohen suggests that 'these diaries were written by men who knew that they had no hope of remaining alive'.[10] He provides an early, sensitive analysis of the documents and is obviously well aware that they are not diaries in the usual sense of the term. Diaries are traditionally compilations of individual dated entries, as the title of Alexandra Garbarini's nuanced exploration of diaries and the Holocaust, *Numbered Days*, suggests.[11] In this context, Sigmund Freud's one line a day diary, which he kept between 1929 and 1939, forms a schematic example. It is a diary Griselda Pollock suggests was kept for the sole purpose of affirming that 'death has not come this day'.[12] Through penning a few characters a day, Freud took the time to record the passage of time and affirmed that he continued to live. For this reason the minimal jottings comprised a vital activity for him. In this vein, James Young (who also describes the Scrolls as diaries) states that for the Holocaust diarist, 'the words he inscribed on a page seemed to be living traces of his life at that moment'.[13] Ink here is conceived of as a kind of lifeblood.

The diaries Garbarini discusses were produced for varied reasons yet the majority involved regular dated entries. David Paterson also writes in the context of Holocaust testimony that 'in contrast to other literary genres, the significance of what the diarist records is definitively related to the time when she records it: the entries in a diary are *dated*'.[14] There are occasional references to key dates (including when particular manuscripts were completed) in the Sonderkommando manuscripts, yet none adhere to the diary format.[15] The closest to a daily record of events is the list of transport arrivals written in Polish. Cohen's decision to frame these writings as diaries, despite his obvious familiarity with their form and content, is therefore, like Rees's imprecision, puzzling at the outset.

There are, however, similarities between the two literary genres. Diaries, like letters, are often highly individual. They are not usually intended for publication and are for limited circulation. Garbarini describes the examples she examines, collectively, as 'the personal reactions of individuals who lived in a moment of radical disarray'.[16] Cohen, who provides 'thumbnail biographical sketches' of the three authors he analyses in his first essay on the writings, is interested in the differing characters of the men who wrote the accounts.[17] In this context, he decision to call the writings 'diaries' works to foreground their personal dimension.

Cohen does not discuss the letters by Herman and Nadjary. They presumably do not fit his criteria for what comprises a diary or are viewed as unimportant as testimonies. Given the diversity and richness of the manuscripts in Yiddish, this stance is understandable. The letters, much shorter, far less writerly, do not compare as works of literature and there is a temptation to slur over them. Nevertheless they possess a particular power that sets them apart from these other documents. In Rees's case, the composition which has impacted him the most, to the extent that it becomes representative of all the Sonderkommando writings, is Herman's letter. This text, placed last in the Auschwitz museum edition and given the status of a postscript, has, for Rees, overwritten all the other Sonderkommando writings. This is a telling, if atypical, response. Many, like Cohen, disregard Herman's letter, failing to acknowledge its existence. It was not included in Ber Mark's *Megiles Oyshvits* or in the English translation *The Scrolls of Auschwitz*, although it does appear in the French translation *Des voix dans la nuit*. It is also not a part of *Des voix sous la cendre*, which includes new French translations of *Megiles Oyshvits*.[18]

Herman's message was evidently produced at speed in what he believed to be his final days or hours. As he is composing its conclusion, he refers directly to the form of his holograph: 'Forgive this dazed [*étourdi*] text and also my French if you only knew in what circumstances I am writing'.[19] Lewental's history of the Sonderkommando was also composed quickly, yet it is far greater in scale and scope than Herman's effort.

Herman, originally from Poland, was deported to Auschwitz from the French internment camp at Drancy on 2 March 1943, arriving there on the night of 4 March. When he put pen to paper he deliberately rejected composing his letter in Yiddish or Polish. It is obvious, nonetheless, that he spoke (if not wrote) these languages. The letter draws attention to the difficulties faced by a French compatriot, David Lahana, who is unable to communicate in Yiddish, Polish or German, implying that Herman did not share this predicament.[20] Herman, however, opted to compose his missive in French. From the clumsy syntax of the letter, preserved in the transcription provided in *Des voix dans la nuit*, it was evidently a language he was not yet fully proficient at writing in.

Despite being a Polish Jew (born in Warsaw on 3 May 1901), he deliberately refrained from writing in Yiddish although this would undoubtedly have been easier for him.[21] The extra effort expended in writing in French therefore assumes considerable significance. Through his refusal to assume his 'mother tongue', Herman demonstrates his animosity towards Poland. This animosity is, revealingly, remarked upon by Zaorski during his reminiscences about the letter's content. The absence of Herman's correspondence from the volume produced by Ber and Esther Mark might therefore be attributed to his decision to write in French despite being of Polish Jewish extraction. Ber Mark draws attention to solidarity between French Jews, 'many of whom were in fact immigrants from Eastern Europe'.[22] In this context, to Mark, Herman's adoption of France may have seemed a betrayal, either of his Polish roots or of East European Yiddish culture. After the war, Mark remained fiercely proud of being a Polish Jew (as his numerous activities in Poland attest). Herman's ambiguous relationship towards his East European background, also expressed in his description of Poland as an accursed country, potentially complicated his inclusion alongside the Yiddish authors discussed in previous chapters.[23] Mark's presumed ambivalence towards Herman existed despite the Frenchman's otherwise strong resistance credentials, particularly his reference to the potentially heroic death that awaited him.[24]

The form adopted by Herman may also have contributed to his subsequent marginalisation. His composition lacks the self-conscious literariness that Gradowski and Langfus brought to their writings. Letters do not comprise a major genre in literature and are not conventionally considered as historiographical in themselves, although they are frequently used as evidence by historians (as Rees's decision to refer to Herman in *Auschwitz* demonstrates).[25] Despite this, for Rees, contra Mark, Herman assumes greater importance than Gradowski, Langfus or Lewental. The reason behind his assessment may be bound up with the nature of the letter as a medium.

The remainder of this chapter will explore differences and similarities between the letters and the other Sonderkommando manuscripts. Paying attention to Nadjary and Herman's frequently overlooked letters provides evidence of how varied the experiences of members of the Sonderkommando were. The band of men working in the SK comprised distinct groups, cliques even. Those who did not come from Poland had quite different experiences, both within Auschwitz-Birkenau and in their relationship with their countries of origin. With Greece and France less under German control than Poland, there were still family members to whom Herman and Nadjary could write. The choice to pen letters, therefore, reflected their different circumstances. Letters also encouraged writing of a particular form, giving their authors the space to imaginatively reassert their family ties, and express certain emotions, as well as requiring them perhaps to suppress others, or at least veil some of the worst aspects of their lives. Greece and France, countries with which they strongly identified, could also be envisioned as having a future existence. Polish Jewry, by contrast, had been almost entirely wiped out. This chapter focuses on what the letters, as a distinct literary genre, reveal about the frequently interconnected issues of emotion, group dynamics, masculinity and temporality. It also briefly examines written testimonies produced at Chełmno. These are particularly illuminating in the context of reading the letters and other writings from Birkenau as a vital form of resistance.

Emotional Reality

Final Letters from Victims of the Holocaust collects together in a single volume a number of letters held in the Yad Vashem archive which were written by Jews during the Holocaust.[26] It reproduces one page of Nadjary's letter. In his foreword to the book, Chaim Herzog draws attention to the varied nature of the compositions: 'Some record data – names, events – for coming generations; others are deeply personal messages to family and friends. Some are philosophical; others almost mundane. All show dignity and courage'.[27] Taken together, the letters by Herman and Nadjary encompass many of the qualities Herzog identifies. They both contain personal content. Compositions of this kind form private spaces for the sharing of intimate thoughts, although Amanda Gilroy and W.M. Verhoeven caution that 'the most historically powerful fiction of the letter has been that which figures it as the trope of authenticity and intimacy'.[28]

The touching character of Herman's letter is clear from its opening paragraph, in which he movingly asserts how much he cherishes a note he received from his wife and daughter in early July of 1944. He again refers to this correspondence later on, stating, 'since I got your letter with the writing of both of you, which I often kiss, since that time my contentment is complete'.[29] The letter appears to embody Herman's wife for him, to carry a part of her with it. Rebecca Earle argues that, in some quasi-sexual textual encounters, 'the physicality of the letter might stand for the body of the letter-writer'.[30] Herman's description gestures towards such a doubling. The letter forms a medium through which to connect with his wife.

For Herman, form is evidently as important as content, if not more so. It is crucial that the letter is in his wife's hand and that it also includes script that is recognisably by his daughter. These calligraphies function indexically, the handwriting exhibiting familiar characters, specific gestures, physical pressures which point to two deeply cherished people. Herman's words here foreground how important the substances that support the words also are, the personal touches provided by penmanship, the tangible signs of his loved ones. Letters form objects 'passed from one set of hands to another'.[31] Handwritten missives image 'actual bodily presence'.[32]

In this context, the use of graph paper, a use imposed on Herman by his dismal circumstances, produces a disjunct between form and content. Graphs can involve plotting pairwise relationships between points, but these connections are cold, abstract. The relationship Herman is striving to revitalise through penning the letter is of a different order – warm, tangible, compassionate. The pristine condition of the letter (its seemingly unsullied paper), something remarked upon by Zaorski, might also come across as at odds with the sickening milieu in which it was produced and discovered.

In Chapter 1 we examined how the media that were used to produce the Scrolls, the varied inks and papers, often reinforce and supplement the content of the writings, lending them additional emotional intensity. Here, the opposite occurs. The medium, with its immaculate grids, conflicts with the emotional turmoil of the message. Zaorski's testimony picks up on this inharmoniousness.

Despite this, Herman's letter endeavours to establish comparable contiguity to that generated by his wife's correspondence. The writing is designed to maintain and renew relations, relationships. The theme of separation is one that is common in letters in general. William Merrill Decker suggests that the most prominent genre-reflexive themes 'are those of separation, loneliness, and apprehension that death will intervene before the parties can reunite – a fear that letter sheet, mail, and language are inadequate to the task of maintaining relations'.[33] Awareness of mortality is a regular theme in letter writing. But in the letters of Herman and Nadjary it is massively amplified and death is accepted as imminent (rather than regarded as an event that only might intervene between the time of writing and the letter's receipt). This imparts a powerful emotional charge to their compositions.

Both letters show considerable feeling. This emotiveness may have contributed to the questionable status they seem to be accorded as documents, their marginalisation as historical evidence. Letter writing in general, as Jenny Hartley observes, is commonly regarded as comprising a 'warm' literary genre, intimate and sincere, privileging feelings over facts.[34] It is obvious that there are powerful emotions directing the content of Herman's and Nadjary's letters. This could be perceived to potentially call into question their value as historical documents. We will argue here, however, that the emotional content, in common with the attention to feelings in Langfus and Lewental, actually enhances our knowledge of life for the men in the Sonderkommando.

Herman's message gives a sense of the diverse feelings to which members of the squads were subject. He begins by recounting his exhilaration at receiving his wife's letter, which provided solace where usually there was sadness. Later he expresses regret for quarrelling with her in the past. He also declares that his most pleasurable memories from his time at Auschwitz have been fantasies of being with her. Towards the end of the letter, Herman expresses his hope that his friends will revenge their 'brothers and sisters thrown upon the pyre for no guilt of theirs'.[35] Nadjary's letter also refers to revenge, repeatedly. Of the legible parts, two pages make reference to the desire for vengeance.[36] His thoughts also turn to love, to his loved ones, his friends, and his sister's love for a man called Elias.³⁷ Additionally, Nadjary expresses pleasure at learning of the liberation of Greece (Athens was liberated on 14 October 1944).³⁸

In Herman's letter the account of his experiences at Birkenau is of secondary importance to the articulation of feelings. The poor condition of Nadjary's letter makes judgements about content difficult. It does seem closer to the manuscripts discussed in previous chapters in terms of its aims. Attesting to what happened at Birkenau is evidently a major motivation for the Greek. The form of his composition is that of a letter, with the final page possibly even serving as a makeshift envelope, yet several pages were seemingly dedicated to a chronological account of his experiences since leaving Athens on 2 April 1944. Herman devotes only four paragraphs in the middle of his letter to a similar chronology.

The emphasis on emotion in Herman (and, to a lesser extent, Nadjary), the affect that line these missives, is easily dismissed as lacking in insight by historians who privilege fact over the 'felt'. Rebecca Schneider suggests that historiography conventionally favours 'hard' facts over 'softer' ephemeral traces of the past.³⁹ The ephemeral traces described by Schneider are 'felt' traces, forming an affective engagement with the past. Encounters with feeling of this kind are open to coding as feminine within the traditional Western cultural logic of historiography.

In the context of Holocaust testimony, Primo Levi ostensibly takes a comparable hard line against emotion, favouring unfeeling fact.⁴⁰ Hayden White has drawn attention to Levi's desire in his testimony 'to maintain a power of objective observation, a rationality of judgement, and clarity of expression'.⁴¹ Levi, White explains, regarded style as an ethical issue. He privileged pared forms of writing over those which were overtly stylised and regarded as obscuring. Levi's examples of writers of the latter approach were Ezra Pound, Georg Trakl and Paul Celan. Celan's poetry 'is not a communication, it is not a language, or at most it is a dark and truncated language precisely like that of a person who is about to die and is alone'.⁴² For Levi, 'if one is not clear there is no message at all'.⁴³ The perceived opacity in Celan is therefore anathema. Levi would, arguably, have also viewed Gradowski's literary flourishes with mistrust as he apparently favours bare, factual accounts. He is describing how testimony should be written yet, by extension, he is also gesturing towards which forms of testimony should be read.

In Levi's opinion, rhetorical or figurative language in testimony or history gets in the way of the facts. White, however, argues forcefully, and convincingly, that Levi's own accounts of Auschwitz fail to fulfil the plain-speaking template he advocates. By contrast, 'far from being void of literary flourishes and adornments, [Levi's writing] constitutes a model of how a specifically literary mode of writing can heighten both the referential and semantic valences of a discourse of fact'.[44] In a move 'that runs counter to the positivist demand that language act only and transparently to convey the facts', the literary, as Judith Butler explains in her perceptive engagement with White's essay, enables 'the emotional reality' of events to be communicated.[45] White draws on Levi's work to argue for the value of the figurative as providing a means of access to the feel of past events. He is, by extension, arguing against the partiality accorded to hard historicising.

The letters do not make complex use of figuration. As a literary genre, however, they are well suited to providing an understanding of the emotional reality of the Sonderkommando, supplementing the insights into emotion provided by Langfus and Lewental. The reality signalled by the letters is one in which feelings other than revenge are evidently suspect. Herman twice makes a point of repeating that he is calm.[46] He also affirms that he will be calm at the moment of his death.[47] These repeated references to composure can be interpreted as Herman seeking to reassure his wife and daughter that he is not anguished. He wants to project a comforting (calming, even) image to them of his last days despite the dire circumstances in which he is writing. His figuring of himself as 'at ease' is, nonetheless, initially coupled with a mention of his potential future heroism. This connection of qualities may be interpreted as implying that calmness is itself a form of courageousness, an expression of it.

There is therefore a tension operating within the letter between acknowledgments of intense emotion and efforts to deny or suppress its existence. This strain is less obvious in Lewental's history, for instance, which gives in to feeling far more. Although both Herman and Lewental wrote rapidly, it is the author of the letter who seems better able to contain his emotions. This may be because Herman's letter is directed at particular recipients, his wife and daughter, rather than a general audience. He wants to protect their feelings through suppressing his own. The kind of responsibility Herman feels for his readers is therefore of a different kind to that of Lewental or, indeed, Gradowski or Langfus. Langfus makes no effort to spare the reader's pain as they are anonymous to him. His style, though, like Herman's, is controlled. He does not betray the effusiveness, the literary exuberance, the close to 'joy' in horror, of Gradowski, or the barely controlled anger and frustration of Lewental. In the context of emotion, Gradowski's lively style can be attributed to the massive pressures he was subject to, the intense feelings he was striving to control and process. For all the authors, writing was therefore bound up with feeling, although they approached this relationship in markedly different ways.

Men of Letters

That Herman is also occasionally prey to strongly painful feelings is most apparent in a brief section of the letter relating to his daughter Simone. He describes the enduring image he has of her departing with a Mr Vanhems (presumably for her own safety) on 17 February 1943. He then recounts:

> often, walking about the large hall of the crematorium (empty) I would say Simone's name aloud as if I was calling her and I listened to my voice, in which the beloved name had sounded, which, alas, I will never be able to use anymore, this is the greatest punishment which our enemy could inflict on us.[48]

The vision of a father calling out his missing daughter's name within the crematorium, attending to its echo, is both chilling and poignant. Herman addresses an absence here, speaks to a void. His voicing of Simone's name seems, on some level, to be motivated by a desire to instantiate her. She is present as voice, returned to him somehow through the echo. The act is reminiscent of Langfus crying out his son's name, Shmuel, which was discussed in Chapter 3. Both men use the voice to articulate their pain and also draw on its vitalising ability to materialise their loving relationship to their children. Presumably Herman penning Simone's name serves a similar purpose. She becomes a person of substance through the ink. Herman's spoken words, however, go unheard. He is not using her name to attract her attention. He will never be able to use her name usefully again. Herman addresses only the indifferent walls of the crematorium. The soliloquy he repeatedly delivers to these desolate surrounds serves to reinforce the tragic separation of a father from his child, embodies disconnection and solitude. The letter, by contrast, offers a possibility of posthumous reconnection.

In general in the Sonderkommando there was seemingly no place for expressions of misery, of vulnerability, of the kind contained in Herman's account of his grief at being unable to speak to his daughter in person again. One reason for this would seemingly be that their horrendous situation generated an emotional numbness. As appendages to the machinery of death, subject to the daily routine of mass murder, members of the Sonderkommando were rendered insensible, unfeeling.[49] Kraus and Kulka state that they became 'apathetic and insensitive'.[50] Herman's letter and the other writings, however, challenge assumptions that the men became like automata. They demonstrate a continuing sensitivity, even if feelings are reserved for concealed pages. Emotion may, however, have been suppressed because of unspoken pressures to conform to a particular image of masculinity. In patriarchal ideology, the theme that 'men are rational while women are emotional' is a familiar one.[51] The letters and other writings therefore perform an important role as spaces through which to articulate and process feelings that could not outwardly be displayed. If they wept, the Sonderkommando did so without tears. It is a man, a father, who Lewental refers to in his writings as weeping without tears in relation to the murder of his wife and five children (101.19).[52]

The idea of a concern over self-image, of anxieties about being man enough arising at the heart of hell, may seem incredible. But Herman's letter provides significant evidence that some men were attentive to their manliness. His expression of pride in his physical appearance – he describes himself as thin and muscular with only his grey hair betraying his age, otherwise looking thirty – might be interpreted as an expression of satisfaction that he is resisting the emasculating effects of ageing.[53] The description of his physique, of course, also contrasts with his account of himself as being in a skeletal state in the summer of 1943 and works to reinforce the privileged position accorded the Sonderkommando. The remark about his age, however, implies that there is also an element of vanity present. Additionally, it may have been consciously included by Herman to reassure his wife he was all right, to provide her with an image of his vitality.

The pressure to continue to be a man in Herman's letter is more obvious from the way in which he tries to assert his continuing mastery over his wife and daughter from afar. Given that he foresees his impending demise, he evidently wishes to exert posthumous influence over them. He gives his wife (who is never mentioned by name in the letter) permission to remarry, and suggests she secure employment with a hosier. Herman also directs her not to return to Poland. In relation to Simone, he asks his wife to ensure she marries a Jewish man and (as he does not wish her to have a stepfather) that this be arranged quickly even if it necessitates her abandoning her higher education.[54] He wants Simone to have many children to ensure the continuation of his name. Nadjary is also concerned with his family name, instructing the reader to inform his relatives abroad that the European branch of the Nadjary family has been 'eliminated'.[55]

Later in his letter, Herman gives his wife instructions to contact the family of a companion from the same transport, David Lahana, who is deceased. Nadjary also includes instructions in his letter, charging that his sister's piano be given to Elias in memory of her: 'now this piano will remain with him so he can remember her'.[56] These directives can be interpreted as efforts to reassert agency from within circumstances in which both men are enslaved, deprived of their freewill. To many members of the Sonderkommando, their relative helplessness may have been experienced as emasculating. The grey zone of moral ambiguity within which Levi located the Sonderkommando in the camps was also a grey zone in terms of gender. The Special Squad was composed of men who remained alive because they were men, yet men deprived of authority and autonomy. This even applied to those religious Jews who may not have been particularly invested in such 'masculine' virtues as the physical capacity to fight. They would have felt keenly their inability to protect their families or control their destinies, as Leyb Langfus's anguish shows.[57] Herman had made every effort to assimilate to French culture and presumably to its norms of gender; Nadjary had served as a soldier and regretted bitterly being unable to participate in the uprising. Their self-image as men would clearly have been undermined in this environment. In such a context, the sets of instructions bequeathed by both writers to future readers may be understood, on one level, as unconscious efforts to reassert a measure of control, to act in and upon the world.

The action of writing, of course, also forms a resistance to Nazi disciplinary practices. In a broader context, Decker examines how letters can sometimes form 'scenes of subversion and insurgency, a claiming of power that may or may not achieve effective social form'.[58] The letters by Herman and Nadjary can both be understood in this way. Herman draws attention to the 'great risk and danger' that accompanies composing his missive.[59] Among other motivations, acts of insurrection (and fantasies of them) constituted a vital means by which to reaffirm masculinity. Putting pen or pencil to paper, recording events, lives, was a way to rebel. In this situation, acts of figuration and narration, as a means of exercising agency in relation to the events that were being experienced, add another layer to this writerly form of revolt. Organising words, composing a form of writing, shaping and adapting it, is an act of defiance. Gradowski, Langfus and Lewental employ this form of stylistic resistance more than the authors of the letters.

Groups within the Group

The differing approaches adopted by the authors of the Scrolls reinforce the varied personalities that were grouped together in the Sonderkommando. The relative paucity of texts comprising this archive (with the ideas and values of Russian or Hungarian members, for example, completely absent) means any exploration of group dynamics, of factional squabbles as well as of broad uniformities of feeling and opinion, must, of necessity, be tentative. The manuscripts do, nevertheless, provide a unique set of local accounts, a nascent history written 'from below'. It is clear even from the few documents we possess that members had differing priorities and perceptions of their situation.

Each of the writers of the Scrolls was, for example, seeking to shape the form that his literary resistance would take in specific ways. In his letter, Herman is worried that he will be judged poorly for participating in the running of the death factory. He is critically reflexive about his actions in a way Nadjary does not appear to be. Herman comments: '[I]f there were good and bad men among our folk I have certainly never been among the latter'.[60] This implies that the Sonderkommando formed a heterogeneous community, with judgements made about the conduct of some by others, supporting Gideon Greif's assertion that 'it seems impossible to portray the community of Sonderkommando prisoners as a homogeneous group'.[61] It also problematises Greif's assertion that the actions of the Sonderkommando are beyond judgement.[62] The members evidently felt able to judge each other morally. Some within the squads were perceived as unscrupulous.

Comparing Herman's and Nadjary's letters brings out differences and similarities between the two writers that are informative in relation to thinking through the complex constitution of the Sonderkommando as a whole. Both authors exhibit passionate nationalism, for France and Greece respectively. Nadjary, for example, states that his last words will be 'Long live Greece'.[63] Herman advises his wife that 'the French soil is that which one should love and replenish'.[64] From these proclamations it becomes possible to envision groups of varying sizes bound by shared national identities coexisting within the Sonderkommando. These groups would obviously have interacted yet, potentially, also maintained a degree of distance and difference from each other. In his retrospective testimony, *Inside the Gas Chambers*, Shlomo Venezia suggests that the Greek Jews, although religious, were probably less stringent than those from 'little villages of Poland'.[65] Venezia, however, reveals that within the Greek Jewish community his Italian heritage made him stand apart, which demonstrates that simply grouping members by their countries of origin is also too simplistic.[66]

Language, however, would have divided many of the men. Venezia confesses he did not know Hebrew.[67] Most of the Greek Jews did know Hebrew but were unfamiliar with Yiddish or Slavic languages.[68] Venezia spoke Ladino at home and Greek in public.[69] Nadjary evidently also spoke Greek. Gradowski begins his 1943 composition with an address to historians in five different languages. He was evidently therefore thinking about issues of communication and translation, unsurprising given the linguistic diversity of Auschwitz. Greek is not one of the languages Gradowski uses. The Greek prisoners, as Steven Bowman recounts, 'were in a special situation, denigrated by the Polish and other northern Ashkenazi Jews, who called them "cholera" and "korva" (whores)'.[70] Given this situation, it is unlikely that Gradowski, Langfus or Lewental would have been in regular communication with many of the Greek Jews. Nadjary, however, appears to have been exceptional in this respect. His gifts as a mime artist seem to have overcome some of these prejudices.[71] Daniel Bennahmias attests that 'even the Poles, who were not compassionate … and who ridiculed the Greek Jews for not knowing how to speak Yiddish, wept when they saw Marcel'.[72] Positioning Herman is also difficult. He was one of only two members of the transport from France still alive at the time he was writing, and may therefore have gravitated towards Jews from Poland.

There is, however, a postscript to Herman's letter which is revealing in this respect. It is addressed to a named person, Germaine Cofen, the wife of Leon Cofen, with news of her husband. Cofen or Cohen is a Greek Jew from Salonika.[73] The letter becomes a space through which another member of the Sonderkommando seeks to transmit information. It is possible to speculate that Cofen interrupted Herman as he was finishing the letter, imploring him to add the final lines.[74] The French Jew and the Greek Jew shared paper, a precious commodity, transforming it into a collaborative act of communication, both thinking of their wives. In this instance, letter writing assumes a collective, rather than individual, character. The paper forms a space in which social interaction is recorded, multiple subjectivities acknowledged if not expressed, demonstrating how national identities did not dictate allegiances although they may have informed them.

While the Greek Jews evidently had an uneasy relationship with their East European counterparts, the content of Nadjary's letter places him closer to the three Yiddish writers of the Scrolls than Herman's does. Bearing direct witness is of peripheral import to Herman, yet it is crucial to Nadjary (Figure 5.1). It seems likely that five or six pages were devoted to describing his experiences at Birkenau. The letter was obviously intended to be a witness account, to serve a similar purpose to the writings of Gradowski, Langfus and Lewental, even if it is truncated in comparison. Nadjary's narrative is intentionally insurrectionary in a way that Herman's is not. The Greek Jews were evidently active in resistance efforts within the Sonderkommando. Their contribution took many forms, from active fighting, escape attempts and the refusal to serve in the special squads to the production of varied forms of testimony.[75] These included Nadjary's letter, the four photographs discussed in the next chapter, and the composition of songs.

Berry Nahmia, from Kastoria, recounts that a member of the Sonderkommando who worked in Crematorium IV and was billeted near

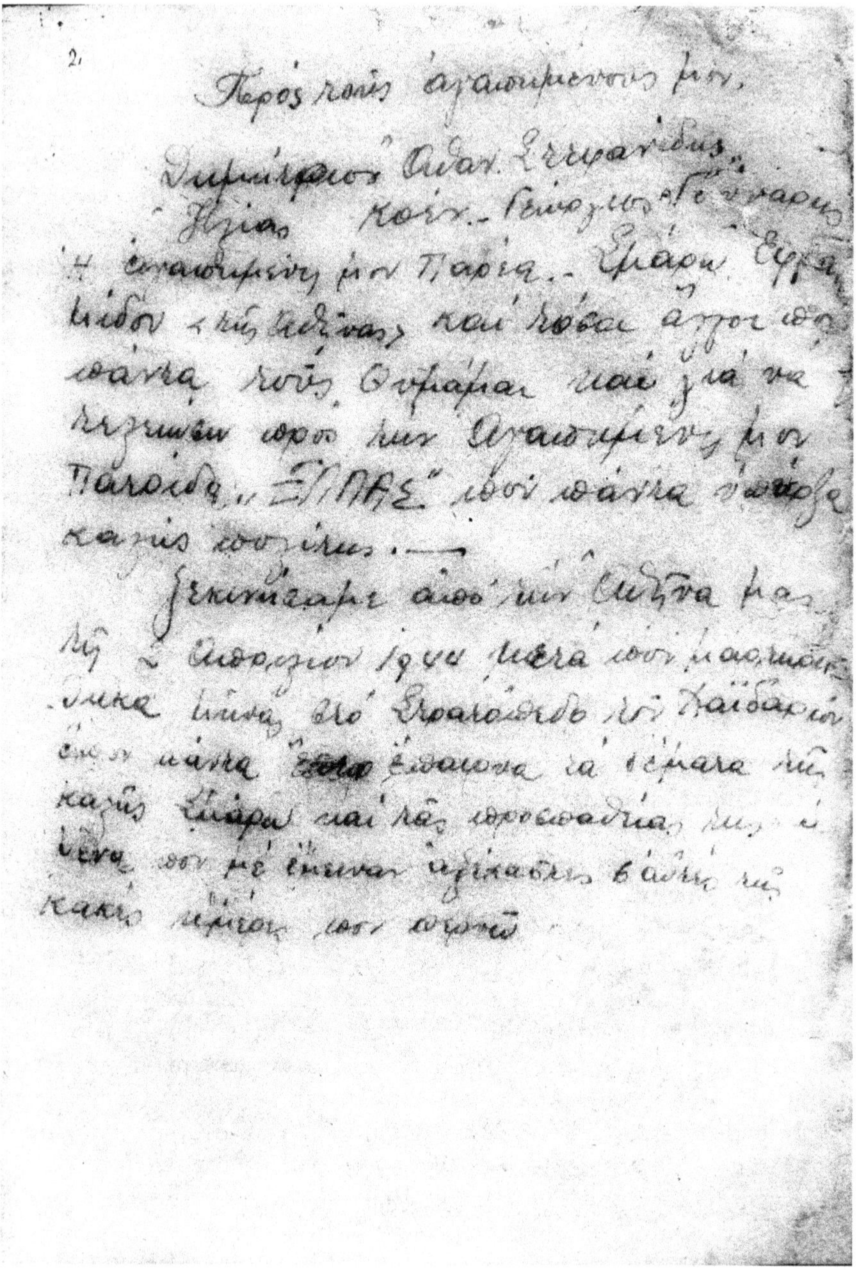

Figure 5.1. Page 2 of Marcel Nadjary's manuscript.

where she was staying would sing in a loud voice every night for almost two months about the horrors he had witnessed, ending with the plea: 'Girls – Greeks – I beg you, if you get out of here alive, tell the entire world the story that I sing to you'.[76] Here the voice is used to carry information across boundaries, lyrics in the Greek language used to smuggle an account to other parts of Birkenau. A man addresses a group of women he hopes will in turn repeat the lines of his song. There is unfortunately no transcription of his composition. The act of resistance is remembered, yet not the content.

Bowman has drawn attention to how the contribution of the Greek Jews to the uprising of October 1944 has been downplayed because 'the predominant historiography of the revolt is by Polish Gentile and Polish Jewish survivors'.[77] In this context, Nadjary's letter might be read as being in competition with the manuscripts discussed in the three preceding chapters. His fervent nationalism is plain from the repeated references he makes to Greece, his 'beloved country'.[78] He is evidently also extremely proud of his Jewishness and, in spite of everything he has endured, reaffirms his religious faith in the letter. Herman also asserts that improvised ceremonies, particularly in relation to the feast day of Yom Kippur, were performed by the Sonderkommando, drawing attention to an ongoing religiosity at the heart of hell.[79] Nadjary's Greek heritage is obviously key to his sense of identity. The tensions between the Greek and Polish Jews may therefore be being played out across all insurrectionary activities. Conflict within groups is commonplace. Donelson Forsyth suggests intragroup conflict frequently derives from competition over resources or, as seems more relevant in the context of the Sonderkommando, status.[80] The differing nationalities in the special squads were allied, sharing a common hatred for the Nazis, yet their cooperation was uneasy and, at times, possibly rivalrous. The content of Nadjary's letter can be understood as informed by these tensions.

Shared Experiences

Despite the major differences that exist between the authors of the Sonderkommando manuscripts, divergences that are, at times, embodied in the forms and contents of their accounts, there are also unifying characteristics, one of which is the sense of impending doom, of a particularly marked sense of time running out. There are repeated assertions in writings that death is pending. The time of writing is therefore distinct from ordinary, everyday progressive time. At Birkenau, a dwindling of time was intensely, painfully obvious. In such extraordinary circumstances, time was materialised, made tangible. It emerged through the urgency of the writings. All the Sonderkommando manuscripts demonstrate elements of this phenomenon, their pages marked by desperate times, yet in Herman's and Nadjary's letters and Lewental's history, which were seemingly composed especially hastily, this pressing, palpable temporality is rendered particularly apparent.[81]

Eva Hoffman has movingly described the way time in the concentration camps was curtailed to a persistent present, such that there was a temporal as well as a physical incarceration. She writes of inmates:

> The past, for them, was cruelly severed, with no hope of return; the future was foreshortened by the looming wall of probable death. The exit from temporal confinement was blocked in both directions, making 'living in the present' a form not of liberation, but of terrible psychic imprisonment.[82]

The letters are written in the shadow of this wall. Nadjary, for example, signs off his letter's coversheet/envelope with the statement: 'This is my last will. I am sentenced to death by the Germans because I am of the Jewish religion'.[83] Herman states, 'my letter is coming in my final hours, so I am sending you my last farewell forever'.[84] As their lives seem about to end, Herman and Nadjary, like Langfus, turn to writing for succour. This is because, like all the other Sonderkommando manuscripts, the letters form a means to break with the oppressive presentness of the camps identified by Hoffman. Possessing the time and means to construct narratives of arrival and of subsequent experiences permit the Sonderkommando authors a moving through time denied to most of the prisoners, who lived day to day. Part of this movement is towards a post-war future. The letters and other writings therefore reclaim the temporal, envisaging a time beyond Nazi control.

Letters are always addressed to an elsewhere, be it an actual geographical location, a metaphysical realm, or a future time. Herman's and Nadjary's compositions look beyond the present to the liberation of Birkenau and to the end of the war. Being able to conceive of time to come, looking beyond the present, brought cruel hope. Although Herman suggests that, since arriving, 'all connection with the other world was broken', his words provide a means by which to mend the temporal dimension to that rupture.[85] They possess the potential, at a time ahead, to cross from his current world to another. This prospect may be what rekindles optimism in Herman that he too might one day return to the world he knew before, restore the past in the future. He writes: '[B]ut in spite of everything I keep up from time to time a tiny spark of hope that perhaps by some miracle I, who have had so many chances, one of the oldest here, who have surmounted so many obstacles … perhaps I shall reach you before this buried letter is found'.[86]

Wolfgang Sofsky suggested that part of the Nazi order of terror in the camps was to seize 'hold of biographical time'.[87] Herman, however, revitalises his time, he thinks ahead, moving beyond what Sofsky calls the 'endless duration' of camp time by foreseeing the camp's end and his liberation.[88] Time as experienced by the Sonderkommando in the exterminatory universe was qualitatively different to time as it was known by many in the concentration camp. The letter allows Herman to transcend his circumstances, to travel temporally, and this awakens hopefulness in him, a hope that it is painful to recognise retrospectively. Herman survived for less than a month after he wrote the letter. Nadjary is not solidly forlorn in his missive either. He states: 'I wanted and want if I live to revenge the death of my father, my mother and my dear sister'.[89] Here Nadjary betrays a comparable glimmer.

In the Greek's case, the optimism was justified. Although Rees states of the Sonderkommando authors that 'every one of those who recorded their experiences was subsequently murdered', Nadjary survived the war.[90] In 1947 he would write a memoir of his time in the Sonderkommando, which would only be published in 1991. The memoir affirms the valiant role played by the Greeks in the Sonderkommando uprising.[91] Greif lists Nadjary as one of only four former members of the Sonderkommando to have published an account of their experiences.[92] This act demonstrates how important the Greek felt bearing witness to be as an activity, both during and subsequent to events at Birkenau.

Nadjary and Herman, however, also draw attention to language's inability to convey what they have lived through. Words cannot carry the horrors of the death factory to the reader. Herman asserts 'it is wholly impossible to give you proof in writing of everything that I have experienced here'.[93] In what remains legible of Nadjary's text, he twice refers to how indescribable the horrors are that surround him. This recurring theme exhibits his frustration with his literary endeavours. The first reference to the failure of written language occurs after a description of the destruction and disposal of physical remains.

Nadjary suggests that what his eyes have seen cannot be reproduced for the reader. It is beyond words: '<the dramas that> my eyes have seen are indescribable'.[94] The observation shows his dissatisfaction with what he perceives to be a lack of symmetry between world and word. There is disjuncture between what he has seen and what he is able to write. His choice of style is noteworthy in this context. The letter, unlike his powerful and sophisticated retrospective account, is pared; from what remains legible it seemingly focuses on bare specifics, numbers, mode of death, time taken to die, disposal of human remains.

Given the basic nature of what survives of Nadjary's description of the mass murders perpetrated at Birkenau, he seems to be expressing frustration with his efforts at documenting, with his own factual language. At the heart of the death factory, under the most pressing circumstances, he appears to recognise that dispassionate factuality does not do justice to the horror. Demonstrating fidelity to facts is not displaying fidelity to feeling. Nadjary, however, does not have the time to try and create a framework of the kind embodied in the longer manuscripts, particularly Gradowski's, in which fact and feeling are combined, feeling brought to fact. Despite this restriction, even in the rapidly composed letter there is more than raw data. As part of his summary of an instance of mass murder, Nadjary uses only a few words to detail the number of people killed and the time it took for them to die. There is, however, a descriptive genitive. Those murdered were tormented, 'of torture they die [μαρτιρίων ἀποθνήσκουν]': the six or seven minutes it took to die in the gas chamber is therefore conceived of as an inordinate amount of time to be suffering.[95] This minimal, this sparing, approach possesses its own power, one that should be recognised even if its author failed to see it.

Herman also exhibits frustration with figuration's failings. Like many, including most famously Levi, he draws on Dante Alighieri's vision of hell as a comparison. He argues, however, that 'Dante's hell is incomparably ridiculous in comparison with this real one'.[96] Dante is simultaneously summoned and rejected. In both letters it seems that during their composition a stream of consciousness in relation to the possibility, or not, of adequately bearing witness was taking place. Debates which still preoccupy Holocaust scholars today were hurriedly, yet thoughtfully, engaged in. Nadjary also did not believe that any form of communication would be able to prompt an adequate envisioning in his reader. He states, 'it is impossible to imagine what my eyes have seen'.

The writers do attest, nevertheless. They carry on with their accounts despite avowing a lack of belief in them. Nadjary mentions Nazi efforts to destroy evidence of their crimes: '[T]hey forced us to sift and pass <ashes> through a coarse sieve'.[97] This information demonstrates the threat that material testimony was perceived to pose. The actions of destroying bodily remnants, the need to do so, must also have reinforced to Nadjary that the Germans were losing the war. They were afraid of post-war retribution for their crimes. For him, the letter may not have adequately captured what he witnessed, yet he obviously felt it would contribute to holding the perpetrators to account.

Nadjary's letter is not devoid of rhetorical complexity either. There is an echo of Gradowski's more refined reference to barbarity in civilisation when the Greek observes that his family has been erased 'by those civilized

Germans (New Europe) they call them'.⁹⁸ The sentence is also reminiscent in its ironic tone of the sardonic edge developed by Langfus in his later compositions. This crossover between the writings of members of the Sonderkommando with their different backgrounds gives insight into what may have been general outlooks and modes of coping with their horrible situation. There are similarities as well as differences. Another connection between all the writings is a shared belief in language as providing a means for the authors to escape Birkenau, even if posthumously. Nadjary did not mention his buried letter in his memoir. He died in 1971, nine years before its discovery. Like the other manuscripts, it therefore granted its author a kind of afterlife.

Writing as Life

The concern with feeling that is conventionally associated with letter writing as a literary form is displayed in Herman's missive and, albeit less so, in Nadjary's. The category of the letter, however, like all genres has uncertain boundaries. Rebecca Earle suggests that the letter can be thought of as 'a protean, all-inclusive genre, whose very shapelessness is its strength, allowing it to adapt to any expressive requirement'.⁹⁹ Decker also draws attention to how 'letter writers themselves struggle hard to define the epistolary genre, conflating it with other forms and rhetorical frames of reference'.¹⁰⁰ Conflations of this kind occur in Herman's and Nadjary's compositions. Herman, for example, expresses concern with how his actions as a member of the Sonderkommando will be perceived retrospectively, thereby lending some sections of his letter the status of autobiography. Nadjary's correspondence undertakes to be letter, autobiography and will.

Personal letters of the kinds penned by Herman and Nadjary might usually be expected to form private spaces, passages to intimacy. The horrific conditions in which these letters were composed meant, however, that their authors knew they would circulate among strangers before, hopefully, reaching their intended readers. There does therefore seem to be a degree of censorship at work in Herman's letter, which never refers to his spouse by name and makes cryptic reference to lessening the suffering of those sent to the gas chamber.¹⁰¹ He is evidently worried about causing distress to his wife and that the letter might still fall into the wrong hands. Herman is also concerned with his legacy, with how his life will retrospectively be perceived. He therefore still cautiously refers to his altruism: 'Fearing neither risk nor danger, I was doing in the course of this work all that was in my power to alleviate the fate of the unhappy ones'.¹⁰²

The two men both provide stories of their lives, specifically of their deportation and then internment. The letters, as autobiographies, are vital endeavours to endure, if not in person then in ink. Decker has suggested that 'to the extent that the geographic separation of correspondents prefigures their mutual death to one another, a letter anticipates the life that persists beyond the body's deprivation'.[103] For members of the Sonderkommando, this is palpably the case and a prime motivation for writing. Letters form a means by which to try and secure an afterlife for their authors. Nadjary, for instance, wills his self as well as his sister's piano. He leaves aspects of his personality on paper, entrusts them to the vacuum flask. Given his recognition that the piano, a material object, will provide a powerful locus of memory because of the associations it has with his sister, it is possible to speculate that he views the letter he is composing in the same way. It is in his hand. It holds something of him for any who read it who have known him (and, indeed, for any who are strangers).

The letters, like the other manuscripts, form a way to posthumously escape the death factory. The document Miklós Nyiszli refers to, the 'manifesto of accusation' penned by 'a painter from Paris' (possibly a reference to David Olère) and signed by all the roughly two hundred members of the Sonderkommando working at Crematorium II, may have served a similar purpose.[104] The manifesto, which was concealed in a recamier that the SS officer Eric Muhsfeldt had forced the squad to construct for him, was primarily intended to record details of the perpetrators and their crimes. The names of the Sonderkommando appended to it therefore act to vouchsafe the account. These names would leave Birkenau as the recamier was to be sent to Mannheim. Butler has drawn attention to the importance of knowing the names of the dead if their lives are to be grievable.[105] Names grant a sense of identity and hypostatise the dead. In the context of Auschwitz, in which numbers replaced names, asserting your given name (not the number given to you) was also an act of revolt. Depriving inmates of their names and personal possessions is identified as an important part of the assault on their egos perpetrated at concentration camps.[106] The names joined to the document Nyiszli references and to the letters therefore have multiple functions – they persist, they resist, they verify.

The importance of the survival of the name, its escape from erasure, is also evident in the seventeen pages of a notebook consigned to a Polish farmer by a prisoner from Chełmno. This document, dated 9 January 1945, was a collaborative effort.[107] It begins with a number of accounts by different authors. The writers came from among the last forty-seven forced labour workers at the camp. They were part of a contingent of Jewish prisoners tasked with removing all evidence of the mass murders committed at Chełmno. Their work was therefore comparable to some of the activities the Sonderkommando at Auschwitz. They were nearly all shot close to a week later, on 17 January. Two, Mordechai Żurawski and Simon Srebnik (who would subsequently testify to his experiences in Claude Lanzmann's *Shoah*) survived the executions.

The notebook contains a reference to Srebnik. Hauptsturmführer Hans Bothmann is recorded as threatening him with death whenever he paused in his work. It forms part of a section at the end of the document which follows on from a list of German officers and privates who participated in the crimes at Chełmno. The section is called 'Statements', and mainly details different methods by which specific soldiers killed victims. The notebook concludes with a description of a Jew from Pabianice, Finkelstein, who threw his own sister into the oven thinking she was dead: 'She screamed: "My brother! I am still alive, my own brother throws me into the fire!"'[108] Recounting this event appears to have been deliberately left to the last as if it sums up the worst of the atrocity the men had experienced, that Jews must aid in the murder of other Jews, of their own families. It forms a shocking, powerful conclusion. There is therefore a care in the compilation of the testimonies: their ordering is not random.

The first account in the notebook seeks to detail the process of genocide at Chełmno. Its writer, seemingly speaking for all the men rather than as an individual, describes the operation of a gas van. He also recounts the psychological pressures of working in the midst of mass murder. The emotional numbness that is usually associated with the special squads is referenced. He suggests that an outsider would regard the men as having 'nerves … made of steel' because of their 'indifference' to their labours.[109] The coda to the notebook, however, illustrates that this indifference was never unmitigated. Like the letters by Herman and Nadjary, there is also a call for revenge: 'We ask everyone to avenge us, because meanwhile there is nothing we can do, and we wait for liberation'.[110]

Additionally, there are shorter testimonies by named individuals, sixteen in total. One account, the first by Israel Zygelman, describes losing his child in an 'Akzia' in the ghetto and then implores readers: 'People! Imagine this pain, these torments'.[111] This style of direct address is repeated later in Zygelman's brief overview of his experience. He asks, after describing finding remains of his own child at Chełmno: 'What have you to say about this?'[112] This style of writing differs from the other testimonies in the notebook. Taken collectively, the Chełmno testimonies therefore reveal comparable differences in style, in ways of recounting, to the Sonderkommando testimonies from Auschwitz, albeit in a significantly condensed form. Zygelman also berates England and the United States for their apathy. Like Lewental, he shows an awareness of general as well as local events. He is evidently conscious of the failed efforts by Szmul

Zygielbojm and others to persuade England and the United States to help Europe's Jews.

The accounts in the manuscript grow shorter at times. Shmul Nasadzki, Natan and Icek Rappaport, and Pawel Akin write only one or two sentences.[113] They record barely more than their names and the details of any relatives living outside Nazi-occupied Europe.[114] Dawid Bendkowski's entry is similar. He writes simply: 'Dawid Bendkowski, who lived in Łódź at Brzezińska St. My sister, Fela Krasn (née Bendkowska), lives in Montevideo. My brother, Israel Bendkowski, lives in Russia'.[115] Bendkowski records who he is, where he is from, and where his relatives live. These few words, this minimal information, were intended to survive Bendkowski's death. They did so.

Two other testimonies from Chełmno which have been discovered, both much shorter than the seventeen-page one, include lists of names. One account refers to a group of men who have worked in the 'slaughterhouse for human beings' and 'who will live for only a few more hours'. Its anonymous author writes: 'There were 17 craftsmen there [illegible word], I can give you their names'.[116] The seventeen names are then listed and also where each man was from. The first name on the list is Pinkus Grun, from Włocławek, who may have composed the document given that his details are given at its start. The other account, also anonymous, begins: 'These are the Jews who have worked in Kulmhof (Chełmno) between Koło and Dąbie in the death camp'.[117] It then lists the names of twelve men and where they were from. The names have been laid out carefully in a hastily crafted table comprising four columns. There is an obvious desire to communicate this information as clearly as possible. The script here and throughout the document is even and clear, steadily urgent. The account concludes with the hope that through it relatives might one day receive news of the fate of the men, and that the list will provide closure. It also calls for vengeance: 'So you shall know all Jews who were sent away from Litzmannstadt were killed in a very cruel manner they were tortured and burnt goodbye if you survive you must take revenge'.[118] The lack of punctuation may be evidence that the writer had little time to take: that this is precipitous writing produced in great haste in fear of immediate death. The abrupt farewell, the most minimal of leave takings, is incongruous, hanging mid-sentence. It is a painfully human gesture. The goodbye prefigures another separation, the pen leaving the paper. This ending marks the end of the writer's presence.

The two shorter Chełmno accounts are included in *Final Letters from the Yad Vashem Archive*, immediately prior to Nadjary's. They are, however, hardly letters unless the medium is understood in the broadest possible sense as a written message communicating information between people. Unlike Herman's and Nadjary's compositions, the two Chełmno 'letters' do not possess the form usually associated with the genre. They are truncated records designed to preserve events and detail fates. In fact, the third Chełmno testimony, which is not reproduced in the collection, is more like a letter in that the particulars of specific relatives of many of the men are included. This collaborative composition addresses both a general and an individual readership. It is written for both strangers and family members.

The first account in the notebook of Chełmno testimony includes a reference to the Nazi practice of forcing those about to be murdered at the camp 'to write postcards to the ghetto, saying they fared well, had been given a good job, were well fed, and so on'.[119] Those in the ghetto who received postcards 'had no idea, at the time they received a postcard, that their relatives had long since disappeared without a trace'.[120] The postcards therefore produced a kind of grotesque life after death for those murdered. The composers of the accounts in the notebook, by contrast, actively want to harness the written word's capacity to survive the death of the author. All three accounts from Chełmno list names and places, essentials that form the core of each man's identity. Writing permits these minimal, yet crucial, details, traces, of existences to persist. In this context, Gradowski's dedication to his family, each member named individually at the start of all his texts, can also be regarded as ensuring a kind of continued existence for his kin. The dedications, in fact, frame his accounts as a whole as written in their memory, as their memory, words refusing to grant the erasure of lives, of worlds, desired by the Nazis. Similarly, Cofen's request to be included in Herman's letter, to be named in it, does not solely enable him to potentially communicate with his wife. It provides a way to endure. In all the testimonies from Birkenau and Chełmno, words and names prevent total destruction.

Nadjary's letter, the most damaged of the Sonderkommando documents, the most ruined, fragmented and ambiguous overall, is no different in this respect. What remains legible of the Greek's composition displays a continual doubt. As discussed earlier, there is explicit uncertainty in relation to his seemingly impending death. He writes to his multiple addressees 'perhaps my only last <desire is for you to receive>'.[121] We do not know what he wishes them to receive, possibly his words, the chronicle of his experiences and of his feelings of hate, love and loss. The insertion of 'perhaps', however, creates uncertainty about his desire's finality. These are not necessarily his last wishes. There are also remembrances of past doubts. Nadjary writes: 'Birke<nau> ***** where we remained for about a month and from there they sent us ***** where? where? *****'.[122] These passages seem to describe his move from the main camp to the crematorium, his joining of the Sonderkommando, as they are followed immediately by a description of a gassing. The repeated interrogative reinforces the sense of confusion and, possibly, signals the fear accompanying the move. Spiritual doubts also surface: 'Every day we think about whether God exists'.[123] Additionally there are qualms about Nadjary's ability to communicate the horrors he has seen to others. What is never in doubt throughout the letter, however, is Nadjary's overall faith in the power of words. His belief in them persists. He writes down his intended last utterance: 'Long live Hellas', followed by his name, 'Marcel Na<dja>ry'.[124] His words reaffirm how important Greece is to him. The concluding words of the main body of the letter are, however, his signature.[125] At the last, he again affirms himself through writing. The characters of the autograph are now illegible yet the trace of the name, the substance of it, endures.

Notes

1. This account is discussed in detail in the Introduction.
2. David Lodge, *Deaf Sentence* (London: Penguin, 2009), 279.
3. Rees's book is listed by Lodge in his Acknowledgments to *Deaf Sentence*, 308–9.
4. Ibid., 279.
5. Laurence Rees, *Auschwitz: The Nazis and the 'Final Solution'* (London: Random House, 2005), 291.
6. Steven Bowman claims that Leon Cohen also buried a letter, which was later dug up, and that 'on the basis of it, his wife in Salonika received condolences from the Italian consul there': Bowman, 'Introduction: The Greeks in Auschwitz', in Rebecca Fromer, *The Holocaust Odyssey of Daniel Bennahmias* (Tuscaloosa: University of Alabama Press, 1993), xxii. But it is much more likely that this was Herman's letter. As we discuss below, Herman included a message from Cohen in his own missive. See also n. 74.
7. Ber Mark, *Des voix dans la nuit* (Paris: Plon, 1972), 325.
8. Nathan Cohen, 'Diaries of the Sonderkommando in Auschwitz: Coping with Fate and Reality', *Yad Vashem Studies* 20 (1990): 274.
9. See Saul Friedländer, *The Years of Extermination: Nazi Germany and the Jews 1939–1945* (London: Phoenix, 2008), 580; Susan Linfield, *The Cruel Radiance: Photography and Political Violence* (Chicago: University of Chicago Press, 2010), 89.
10. Nathan Cohen, 'Diaries of the Sonderkommando', in *Anatomy of the Auschwitz Death Camp*, ed. Yisrael Gutman and Michael Berenbaum (Bloomington: Indiana University Press, 1994), 522.
11. Alexandra Garbarini, *Numbered Days: Diaries and the Holocaust* (New Haven, CT: Yale University Press, 2006).
12. Griselda Pollock, 'Art as Transport Station of Trauma? Haunting Objects in the Works of Bracha Ettinger, Sarah Kofman and Chantal Akerman', in *Representing Auschwitz: At the Margins of Testimony*, ed. Nicholas Chare and Dominic Williams (Basingstoke: Palgrave Macmillan, 2013), 195.
13. James Young, 'Interpreting Literary Testimony: A Preface to Reading Holocaust Diaries and Memoirs', *New Literary History* 18(2) (1987): 413.

14. David Patterson, *Along the Edge of Annihilation: The Collapse and Recovery of Life in the Holocaust Diary* (Seattle and London: University of Washington Press, 1999), 18.
15. Despite this lack of regular dating, Patterson includes references to Gradowski in his consideration of the Holocaust diary as a form of spiritual resistance. Ibid., 274.
16. Garbarini, *Numbered Days*, 162.
17. Cohen, 'Diaries of the Sonderkommando in Auschwitz', 276.
18. Georges Bensoussan, Philippe Mesnard and Carlo Saletti (eds), *Des voix sous la cendre* (Viborg: Calmann-Lévy, 2005).
19. Chaim Herman, 'The Manuscript of Chaim Herman', in *Amidst a Nightmare of Crime*, 190 (translation amended).
20. Ibid., 188.
21. As someone who reached adulthood before Polish independence, Herman would probably not have had a Polish education, so he may not have written the language particularly well, but would almost certainly have spoken it. Jadwiga Bezwińska and Danuta Czech (eds), *Wśród koszmarnej zbrodni: Notatki więźnów z Sonderkommando w Oświęcimiu*, 2nd edn (Oświęcim: Wydawnictwo Państwowego Muzeum w Oświęcimiu, 1973), 181.
22. Ber Mark, *The Scrolls of Auschwitz*, trans. Sharon Neemani (Tel Aviv: Am Oved, 1985), 49.
23. Herman, 'The Manuscript of Chaim Herman', 182.
24. Ibid., 181.
25. Susan Sontag lists letters alongside diaries, court records and psychiatric case histories as sub-literary documents. Susan Sontag, *On Photography* (London: Penguin, 1977), 74.
26. Reuven Dafni and Yehudit Kleinman (eds), *Final Letters from the Yad Vashem Archive* (London: Weidenfeld and Nicholson, 1991).
27. Chaim Herzog, 'Foreword', in *Final Letters*, 7.
28. Amanda Gilroy and W.M. Verhoeven, 'Introduction', in *Epistolary Histories: Letters, Fiction, Culture*, ed. Amanda Gilroy and W.M. Verhoeven (Charlottesville: University of Virginia Press, 2000), 1.
29. Herman, 'The Manuscript of Chaim Herman', 188.
30. Rebecca Earle, 'Introduction: Letters, Writers and the Historian', in *Epistolary Selves: Letters and Letter-Writers, 1600–1945*, ed. Rebecca Earle (Aldershot: Ashgate, 1999), 6.
31. William Merrill Decker, *Epistolary Practices: Letter Writing in America before Telecommunications* (Chapel Hill: University of North Carolina Press, 1998), 39.
32. Ibid., 40.
33. Ibid., 22.
34. Jenny Hartley, '"Letters are *Everything* these Days": Mothers and Letters in the Second World War', in *Epistolary Selves*, 184–85.
35. Herman, 'The Manuscript of Chaim Herman', 190.
36. MS pages 8 and 11.
37. Ibid., page 11.
38. Ibid.
39. Rebecca Schneider, *Performing Remains: Art and War in Times of Theatrical Reenactment* (New York: Routledge, 2011), 14.
40. Primo Levi, 'On Obscure Writing', in *Other People's Trades*, trans. Raymond Rosenthal (London: Abacus, 1991), 157–63.
41. Hayden White, 'Figural Realism in Witness Literature', *parallax* 10(1) (2004): 115.

180 • Matters of Testimony

42. Levi, 'On Obscure Writing', 161.
43. Ibid., 162.
44. White, 'Figural Realism in Witness Literature', 116.
45. Judith Butler, *Parting Ways: Jewishness and the Critique of Zionism* (New York: Columbia University Press, 2012), 183.
46. Herman, 'The Manuscript of Chaim Herman', 181, 190.
47. Ibid., 188.
48. Ibid., 185.
49. Gideon Greif briefly discusses feelings in relation to the Sonderommando, drawing on the testimonies of Gradowski, Langfus and Lewental to suggest the men became emotionally detached. The writings, however, through their varied styles, if not content, demonstrate that this detachment was not total or perpetual. See Greif, *We Wept without Tears*, 20–22.
50. Ota Kraus and Erich Kulka, *The Death Factory*, trans. Stephen Jolly (Oxford: Pergamon, 1966), 152.
51. R.W. Connell, *Masculinities*, 2nd edn (Cambridge: Polity, 2005), 164.
52. Mark, *Megiles Oyshvits*, 382.
53. Herman, 'The Manuscript of Chaim Herman', 185.
54. Ibid., 182.
55. MS page 11.
56. Ibid.
57. Daniel Boyarin discusses the difference between Orthodox Jewish masculinity and the '*goyim naches*' ('goyish pursuits') valorised for non-Jewish men. *Unheroic Conduct: The Rise of Heterosexuality and the Invention of the Jewish Man* (Berkeley and Los Angeles: University of California Press, 1997), 33–80. Nechama Tec mentions a number of men, including religious ones, who felt broken by their loss of status and powerlessness. Nehama Tec, *Resilience and Courage: Men, Women and the Holocaust* (New Haven, CT, and London: Yale University Press, 2003), 24–29.
58. Decker, *Epistolary Practices*, 14.
59. Herman, 'The Manuscript of Chaim Herman', 181.
60. Ibid., 184.
61. Greif, *We Wept without Tears*, 56–57.
62. Ibid., 70.
63. MS page 11.
64. Herman, 'The Manuscript of Chaim Herman', 182.
65. Shlomo Venezia, *Inside the Gas Chambers: Eight Months in the Sonderkommando of Auschwitz* (Cambridge: Polity, 2009), 5.
66. Leon Welbel also testifies that among Polish Jews there were bad feelings between Litvaks ('Lithuanian' Jews, but including those from north-east Poland) and 'Galitsyaner' (here used to mean Jews from the rest of Poland, not just those from Galicia). VHF1770 seg. 78.
67. Venezia, *Inside the Gas Chambers*, 5.
68. Bowman, 'Introduction: The Greeks in Auschwitz', xv.
69. Venezia, *Inside the Gas Chambers*, 7.
70. Bowman, 'Introduction', xxii. 'Cholera!' and 'kurwa!' are both exclamations in Polish, and while the latter, a strong swear word, is an insult to women, it is not often used against men. While it is unlikely that the Greek Jews thought they were being insulted when they were not, the fact that they probably misunderstood the words indicates the difficulty of communication.

71. However, even Nadjary's relationship with the Polish and French Jews of Polish origin could be a complex one. In his post-war memoir, he mentions being very good friends with Lemke Strassenvogel, and says that the Oberkapo of Crematoria II and III, Jakób Kamiński, was always good to the Greeks. But he also blames the French and Polish Jews in Crematorium III for not joining the uprising, and is bitterly critical of the Polish Jews in Crematorium V for their failure to warn others. Marcel Nadjary, *Khroniko 1941–1945* (Thessaloniki: Etz Khaim, 1991), 48–49, 59–60.
72. Fromer, *The Holocaust Odyssey of Daniel Bennahmias*, 56.
73. Cofen is a derivative of Cohen. Herman is almost certainly referring to Leon Cohen, whose wife was the daughter of the owner of the Union Bank in Salonika (the address to which this brief postscript is directed).
74. Leon Cohen makes reference to burying a letter in a glass bottle in the 'crematoria courtyards' in his memoir. This is presumably actually his addition to Herman's correspondence as he states that the letter was discovered and published in France. See Leon Cohen, *From Greece to Birkenau: The Crematoria Workers' Uprising*, trans. Jose-Maurice Gormezano (Tel Aviv: Salonika Jewry Research Centre, 1996), 60.
75. Isaak Venezia from Salonika, for instance, escaped to the Kanada commando on 9 October 1944 and was able to give an account of the Sonderkommando uprising after the war ended: Michael Matsas, *The Illusion of Safety: The Story of the Greek Jews during the Second World War* (New York: Athens Printing Company, 1997), 249. In the summer of 1944 a group of Greek Jews took the unprecedented step of refusing to serve in the Sonderkommando, which led to their immediate execution. Steven Bowman, *The Agony of Greek Jews, 1940–1945* (Stanford, CA: Stanford University Press, 2009), 95. Michael Matsas draws attention to two instances, involving four hundred stevedores from Salonika and one hundred Athenians respectively, in which Greek Jews refused to work as members of the Sonderkommando. *The Illusion of Safety*, 241.
76. Matsas, *The Illusion of Safety*, 265.
77. Bowman, 'Introduction', xx.
78. MS page 2.
79. Herman, 'The Manuscript of Chaim Herman', 185.
80. Donelson R. Forsyth, *Group Dynamics*, 6th edn (Belmont, CA: Wadsworth Publishing, 2013), 433–68.
81. The haste in which the manuscripts were written contrasts markedly with how they are now read. We became aware of the slowness of our reading, the protracted attentiveness we gave the letters – a consideration which, upon reflection, was not motivated solely by a search for significance but also formed an unconscious sign of respect, a recognition of the fraught circumstances that impress every word, each character shaped in spite of everything.
82. Eva Hoffman, *Time* (London: Profile, 2009), 100.
83. MS page 13.
84. Herman, 'The Manuscript of Chaim Herman', 190.
85. Ibid., 185.
86. Ibid. Translation amended.
87. Wolfgang Sofsky, *The Order of Terror: The Concentration Camp*, trans. William Templer (Princeton, NJ: Princeton University Press, 1997), 73.
88. Ibid., 74.
89. MS page 8.
90. Rees, *Auschwitz*, 291.

91. Nadjary, *Khroniko 1941–1945*, 58–59.
92. Greif, *We Wept without Tears*, 80.
93. Herman, 'The Manuscript of Chaim Herman', 184.
94. MS page 5.
95. Ibid., page 3.
96. Herman, 'The Manuscript of Chaim Herman', 185.
97. MS page 5.
98. Ibid., page 11.
99. Earle, 'Introduction: Letters, Writers and the Historian', 8.
100. Decker, *Epistolary Practices*, 17.
101. Herman, 'The Manuscript of Chaim Herman', 184.
102. Ibid.
103. Decker, *Epistolary Practices*, 41.
104. Miklós Nyiszli, *Auschwitz: A Doctor's Eyewitness Account*, trans. Tibère Kremer and Richard Seaver (London: Penguin, 2013), 85–87.
105. Judith Butler, *Precarious Life: The Powers of Mourning and Violence* (London: Verso, 2004), 32–33.
106. Henry Krystal, 'Studies of Concentration-Camp Survivors', in *Massive Psychic Trauma*, ed. Henry Krystal (New York: International Universities Press, 1968), 23–46; 32.
107. Jakob Szlamkowicz et al., 'Death Camp in Koło County', in Shmuel Krakowski and Ilya Altman, 'The Testament of the Last Prisoners of the Chelmno Death Camp', *Yad Vashem Studies* 27 (1991): 105–23. This English translation is based upon a Russian-language manuscript held by Yad Vashem, a translation from the Polish original.
108. Ibid., 123.
109. Ibid., 112.
110. Ibid., 113.
111. Ibid., 116.
112. Ibid.
113. Ibid., 118–19.
114. Gradowski, of course, also indicates that he has an uncle in New York and other relatives in Israel and the United States (Mark, *Megiles Oyshvits*, 346).
115. Szlamkowicz et al., 'Death Camp in Koło County', 119.
116. Dafni and Kleinman (eds), *Final Letters from the Yad Vashem Archive*, 121.
117. Ibid., 119.
118. Ibid., 120.
119. Szlamkowicz et al., 'Death Camp in Koło County', 111–12.
120. Ibid., 112.
121. MS page 8.
122. Ibid., page 3.
123. Ibid., page 11.
124. Ibid.
125. Ibid., page 11. It seems likely that the last page formed an envelope rather than the last page of the letter itself, as an address features prominently on the page.

Chapter 6

The Camera Eye
Four Photographs from Birkenau

> In each testimonial production, in each act of memory, language and image are absolutely bound to one another, never ceasing to exchange their reciprocal lacunae. An image often appears where a word seems to fail; a word often appears where the imagination seems to fail.[1]

Images in Spite of All

In August 1944 a member of the Sonderkommando managed to use a camera to take four exposures of events in the vicinity of Crematorium V. The film was then smuggled out to the Polish resistance by Helena Datoń to be developed. It reached them on 4 September. The man formed part of a group who worked together to make the conditions for taking the pictures possible. This band of men consisted of at least five individuals: the photographer (known as Alex), the brothers Shlomo and Abraham Dragon, Alter Fajnzylberg and David Szmulewski.[2] Two of the pictures Alex took show bodies being burned in an incineration pit in the grounds of the crematorium, the third portrays a transport of women on their way to the gas chamber and the final one is of silver birch trees in bright sunlight. The first two photographs were taken from within one of the gas chambers of Crematorium V, looking out through a doorway.³ The second two were taken outdoors, on the other side of the crematorium near a copse of birches. The open air snapshots were likely secured with a concealed camera, secreted either in a cupped hand, clothing or a bucket. Alex had a sense of what the film would show when it was developed. He would, however, never come to *know* what pictures he had taken. He never observed the product of his labours. These photographs have provoked considerable debate. This extends to the identity of their author.

Credit was given initially to David Szmulewski, but Szmulewski himself denied having taken them.⁴ Eric Friedler, Barbara Siebert and Andreas Kilian identify the photographer as Alberto Errera.⁵ Errera, a Greek Jew and former army officer, attained considerable renown within Auschwitz for an escape attempt he made whilst on a work detail to dispose of ashes in the Vistula. He successfully overpowered two guards and swam across the river but was caught the next day and executed. Errikos Sevillias, a Greek inmate at Auschwitz, recounts in his memoir *Athens – Auschwitz* that Errera was a man 'about whose bravery they spoke for weeks in the camp'.⁶ Alekos Alexandridis was Alberto Errera's codename in the camp resistance movement, which is how this attribution has arisen.⁷ We are unconvinced, however, by this ascription of authorship. In his account of the taking of the photographs, for example, Alter Fajnzylberg states that Alex was 'a Greek Jew whose surname I do not remember'.⁸ It seems unlikely that Fajnzylberg would forget Alex's identity if he was Errera, given the latter's notoriety. Our own belief is therefore that Alex is an unknown Greek Jew from the Sonderkommando.⁹ If this is indeed the case, then the only remaining trace of his presence at Auschwitz is the four pictures.

The photographs first attracted significant critical attention in 2001 when Georges Didi-Huberman wrote a catalogue essay about them for the exhibition 'Mémoire des camps: Photographies des camps de concentration et d'extermination nazis (1933–1999)', and Dan Stone published an article, 'The Sonderkommando Photographs', in *Jewish Social Studies*.¹⁰ Didi-Huberman would subsequently expand his discussion of the pictures into a book, *Images malgré tout*, which was published in 2003 and translated into English as *Images in Spite of All* in 2008. The insularity of French scholarship, however, means that *Images in Spite of All* makes no mention of Stone's highly noteworthy analysis of the photographs. Despite independently recognising their crucial importance for, and as, Holocaust testimony, there is, as will become apparent, considerable crossover between the interpretations of Didi-Huberman and Stone.

In *Images in Spite of All*, Didi-Huberman suggests that the four photographs and the Sonderkommando writings operate in a symbiotic relationship: each is revealing about the other. He states, '[S]hould we not acknowledge that these narratives allow us ... to take a better look at the four archival photos ... just as they allow us to better *picture* for ourselves what the narratives, attempting the impossible, strive to describe'.[11] The photographs are situated within the broader resistance efforts of the Sonderkommando. He suggests that 'the photographic scroll ... participates directly in [the] attempt to broaden the channels – and the voices – of testimony'.[12] Here the four images are framed as another 'Scroll of Auschwitz', another hitherto neglected manuscript. We also believe the photographs should be viewed as generated by a parallel impetus to the written documents, and therefore as complementing them. Neither the writings nor the images should be studied in isolation although there are, on occasion, marked differences between the aims governing the two modes of bearing witness. Didi-Huberman, like-minded, recommends reading the photographs in tandem with the other documents and also additional forms of testimony, particularly Filip Müller's retrospective written account, as a means to understand them and to aid the process of imagining he believes they invite and facilitate. This chapter examines Didi-Huberman's efforts to cultivate such a reading and, at times, diverges from and seeks to extend it. It also considers the critique Gérard Wajcman levelled at Didi-Huberman's interpretation of the photographs, a scathing assessment that is engaged with at length in *Images in Spite of All*.

The chapter argues that a consideration of gender is crucial to making sense of the photographs. In this context, Didi-Huberman does not adequately address the significance of Alex's efforts to record the naked women on the way to their deaths. We also draw out Didi-Huberman's remarks on iconicity and indexicality as a means to consider the general importance of exploiting indexical signs for Sonderkommando efforts at resistance. Didi-Huberman views Alex's actions, the testimony he produced, as being of the same order as the Sonderkommando writings. Through an analysis of Gradowski and Langfus, however, we suggest that words and photographic images were conceived of as possessing distinct properties in relation to their status as testimony. Additionally, there has been a tendency to focus on whether or not the photographs show the gas chambers. We argue that although this question has assumed great retrospective importance, the presence of the gas chamber in two of the pictures was tangential. The main aim of Alex, what he wished to bear witness to, was to record other aspects to the process of mass murder, especially the attempt to eliminate corpses.

Altered States

Didi-Huberman and Stone both explore the motivations behind the ways reproductions of the images have been manipulated. These interventions occur in relation to the first three images. Didi-Huberman identifies two reasons for the frequent alterations, cropping, reframing and retouching that these images are subject to. The first consists of the desire 'to see everything in them'.[13] The wish to render the images iconic, to enhance their clarity as a means by which to increase their prominence, is made most apparent in the tampering regularly done to the third photograph of the women undressing and moving towards the crematorium. Prior to cropping and retouching, this photograph is, in Didi-Huberman's words, 'no more than movement, blur, event'.[14] The practice of zeroing in on the group of indistinct figures beside the tree line and then giving faces and breasts to two women in the foreground stills this image, distils it, extracting stability where previously there was none.[15] The essence of the photograph becomes two faces, two bodies, made to stand for mass murder. Their enhanced appearance, restored visages, makes them easier to identify with. Didi-Huberman, however, does not pursue the potential implications at the level of gender of the decision to make these alterations.

The seeming desiccated, sagging body of the woman on the right has, in particular, evidently been cosmetically rejuvenated, uplifted.[16] Breasts, a traditional marker of femininity, are returned to her. The illusion of youth and vigour is implanted to enhance the horror of her impending murder. The blurred figure is remade woman. She becomes representative of Woman – what Griselda Pollock refers to in a different context as 'ideal and icon'.[17] In this instance of creative retouching, a vision of Woman is constructed. She is made to symbolise all those murdered in the Holocaust, becoming the picture-perfect figure to portray death. This woman is alive yet dead. Elisabeth Bronfen has explored how femininity is frequently linked with death in art and literature. These forms of representation often function to stabilise death and femininity, traits which Bronfen views as powers of excess within culture, pointing to a reality that is beyond figuration and 'disruptive of all systems of language'.[18] The acts of retouching are therefore open to being understood as symptoms of anxiety relating to these excesses. The marks made over the woman's body, representations made on her behalf, form an effort to recuperate order.

Bronfen argues that death and femininity involve 'the uncanny return of the repressed'.[19] The uncanny 'always involves the question of visibility/invisibility, presence to/absence from sight, and the fear of losing one's sight serves as a substitute in western cultural myth and image repertoire for castration anxiety'.[20] Retouching the image, making it clearer to see, is a means to assuage anxiety. Transforming the hazy figure on the right into Woman is to evacuate femininity as Bronfen conceives of it. It is to steady the visual field and empty it of its uncanny potency. For Bronfen, uncanny materials such as the corpse are associated with the Real, as Jacques Lacan conceives of it. The Real is a register of psychic reality that Lacan 'defines as beyond semiotic, imaginary or symbolic categories'.[21] The Real is therefore seemingly beyond representation. The practice of retouching the dead yet alive body is consequently designed to refuse the Real, to anchor the image firmly to the Symbolic, the realm of language and representation.

Didi-Huberman, however, suggests that the writings and images produced by the Sonderkommando were snatched 'from the harrowing Real of their experience'.[22] For him, Alex managed 'in a few minutes to capture incompletely, fugitively, some aspects of that Real'.[23] These capitalised Reals reveal that his reading of the photographs is in dialogue with Lacan's work and, by extension, with theories of trauma derived from it. He believes that the Real can be communicated, if not represented. The modelling that was done to the bodies of the women in the third photograph works to suppress the image's uncanny qualities, smothering its capacity as a vehicle of the Real. That Didi-Huberman believes the Real can be conveyed through language, if not as language, is made clear as part of his riposte to criticisms levelled at his work on the Sonderkommando photographs by Wajcman.

Wajcman's essay, published in the journal *Les Temps modernes* edited by Claude Lanzmann, is entitled 'Photographic Belief'.[24] It casts Didi-Huberman's approach to the images, his faith in their testimonial value, as a Christian response to the issue of Holocaust representation. Wajcman describes Didi-Huberman as a fetishist who uses the photographs to make good the lack of images of the Shoah, specifically of the gas chamber in operation. Wajcman observes that 'denial ... is the response of the child noting his mother's lack of a penis and refusing this fact, without completely repudiating it'.[25] He adds: '*I know, but all the same*, canonical formulation of the fetishist, he who works to cover up absence, the lack of anything to see, with all kinds of things that he will display and worship like relics of the missing phallus, shoes, stockings, or small panties'.[26] Through his blind faith in images, Didi-Huberman therefore reduces Birkenau to a reliquary, the photographs forming some of the sanctified remains he venerates. The psychoanalytic fetish, as Laura Mulvey explains, 'includes a trace of indexicality in its function as "memorial"'.[27] Wajcman is well aware of this aspect to fetishism. He is claiming that Didi-Huberman's fetishising of the photographs is a retrospective response to an undeniable, yet disavowed, lack. Didi-Huberman's actions reinforce the absence of images of the Shoah if only he would confront this reality. Instead, however, he uses the images as a salve: they provide the illusion of something where there is nothing.[28] In the context of the 'touched up' bodies of the women, however, Didi-Huberman is striving to reintroduce lack rather than avoid its absent-presence.[29] He is arguing for the undoing of manipulations to the image of the women and is therefore striving to trouble its iconic status in Charles S. Peirce's sense of the term: its resemblance to the object it refers to. The iconic aspect of a photograph is, as Marianne Hirsch explains, one that enables it to exhibit 'a mimetic similarity to [its] object'.[30] Iconic photographs look like what they take as their subject. The photograph of the women in its blurriness and graininess resists the medium's usual iconicity. The figures in the foreground are semblances of women rather than resemblances. It is only with the intervention of the manipulator that their mimetic capacity strengthens sufficiently for a survivor to believe he had found the countenance of his wife in her final moments.[31] It is, nevertheless, a constructed face, virtual rather than taken from life, artificially made to meet the gaze of photographer and viewer.

The iconic status of the image is engineered retrospectively. It is this later impetus to iconicity that Didi-Huberman strives to reverse. He views images such as the original, unmodified print of the women as embodying his conception of the 'rending-image' (*image-déchirure*). It is this conception that underpins his reading of the Sonderkommando photographs. He suggests that, 'like the signs of language, images in their own way – and this is the problem – are able to produce an effect *along with* its negation' and form 'a dialectic stirring together *the veil with its rip* [*qui agite ensemble* le voile avec sa déchirure]'.[32] The image provides both blindness and insight. Didi-Huberman finds the idea of this dual system already extant in works by Georges Bataille and Lacan. A lengthy quotation from Lacan's second seminar on 'The Ego in Freud's Theory and in the Technique of Psychoanalysis' is used to illustrate that the rending-image is an image 'from which a fragment of the real escapes'.[33] Here is the quotation:

> The phenomenology of the dream of Irma's injection has allowed us to distinguish the sudden appearance of the terrifying, harrowing image of this true Medusa's head ... a revelation of something that is unnameable ... There is therefore a harrowing apparition of *an image that sums up what we can call the revelation of the real* in what is least penetrable, of the real without any possible mediation, of the last real, of the essential object that is no longer an object but, rather, something before which all words stop and all categories fail, the object of anxiety par excellence ... It is an essential dissimilar, neither the supplement nor the complement of the similar, which is the very image of dislocation, of the essential tearing of the subject.[34]

In this extract from Lacan's seminar, the dream, specifically the image that Freud is presented with when he looks inside Irma's mouth, a vision which Lacan compares to the Medusa's head, provides a means by which to access the unnameable, the Real. Primo Levi famously described the *Muselmänner*, prisoners weakened to such an extent that they were barely alive, as 'those who saw the Gorgon', complete witnesses who were either dead 'or have returned mute'.[35] Later, Giorgio Agamben, echoing Levi, would write that 'it is as if there were in Auschwitz something like a Gorgon's head, which one cannot – and does not want to – see at any cost'.[36] Seeing the Gorgon is therefore encountering the unspeakable Real.

Lacan states earlier that it is this open mouth which presents Freud with 'a horrendous discovery ..., that of the flesh one never sees, the foundation of things, the other side of the head, the face, the secretory glands *par excellence*, the flesh from which everything exudes, at the very heart of the mystery, the flesh in as much as it is suffering, is formless'.[37] Didi-Huberman, however, is reluctant to join Freud and Lacan in altogether contemplating this form of formlessness. He looks selectively. The gaps in the quotation from *Images in Spite of All*, Didi-Huberman's elisions, are therefore what we wish to draw attention to here. In the seminar, after suggesting that the unnameable has been revealed, Lacan states that this unnameable is 'the abyss of the feminine organ' and connects it with an illness of Freud's daughter Mathilde, and also with the death of a patient.[38] It becomes clear that Lacan's discussion of the emergence of the unmediated Real is one that draws attention to how it is bound up with femininity and death. The specific rending-image of the women running, we would argue, is also linked with these qualities. There is an anxiety towards the feminine as excess, as an unspoken formlessness, underpinning the decision to retouch the image and provide it with greater contour, clearer figures. This anxiety also informs Didi-Huberman's reluctance to engage with Lacan's text about Irma in its entirety.

The acts of touching up the photograph of the women transform the image into a representation and therefore a '*point de capiton*' in Lacan's terms. The *point de capiton*, or quilting point, is discussed in Lacan's third seminar on 'The Psychoses'. It is 'the point at which the signified and the signifier are knotted together'.[39] Bronfen writes of the representation of the expiring and dead feminine body as an attempt 'to attach the dying, decomposing body, destabilising in its mobility, to a fixed semantic position'.[40] Didi-Huberman may share the retoucher's anxiety about formlessness, yet his interpretation still acts to pick apart the quilting point, to rumple the fabric of significance, unfixing the clarity of meaning ascribed to the image.

The Imperative to Imagine

Didi-Huberman's second reason for why three of the Sonderkommando images have been interfered with in the past is to enhance their informational content: 'seeing in [them] no more than a *document* of horror'.[41] This process of purification removes material considered to possess no documentary weight. Much of Didi-Huberman's phenomenological analysis of the four photographs, his sensory and kinetic imaginings, are designed to demonstrate that this seemingly extraneous material, such as the often-cropped shadow that is a doorway to the gas chamber featured in the first two images, performs a crucial documentary function. It records the conditions of production of the image, conditions that are vital to reconstructing, recalling the actions and emotions of the photographer. The cropping deprives the images of their eventfulness. Stone reads this cropping as driven, on one level, by a need 'to get closer to the "thing itself," possess it, render it amenable to the senses and cognizable'.[42] The thing itself, placed in scare quotes, is the horrifying product of the death factory, the pile of bodies. This rationale for the manipulation of the pictures is therefore in keeping with that of Didi-Huberman. The shadows are pared to facilitate knowledge transfer. They are removed to ensure that what is informative within each image is easily perceived.

The drive to zoom in on the information within the images requires first locating the facts within each of them, and then working on each picture to render this data as clear as possible. The desire to treat the pictures as sources of information is in keeping with the intention behind their taking. Fajnzylberg discusses the photographs as efforts to document the crimes the Nazis were committing at the crematoria. These were intended as substantiation, conceived of, burdened with, providing proof of the committing of mass murder. Those who condemn engagement with photographs because they function as a form of proof therefore do violence to the actions of Alex and his companions as they strive, courting death, to produce visual documentation of mass murder.[43] Wajcman writes: 'There is evidence, but we know the Shoah took place, without evidence, and everyone should know this, without evidence'.[44] To turn to evidence is to enter into 'the logic of negationism'.[45] Wajcman, however, calls the photographs 'traces of a crime', demonstrating that he recognises their evidentiary potential.[46]

In reality Didi-Huberman does not interpret the images as evidence in the way Wajcman suggests. He does not use them to 'prove' something about the crematoria. But the members of the Sonderkommando were intent on providing proof. They were not to know how much evidence would survive; they could not envisage that the Shoah would become unquestionable knowledge. The material – ruins, documents, photographs, written and oral testimonies – that has rendered the Holocaust indisputable has also indirectly led to the condemnation of their local efforts at attestation.[47] A surfeit of proof has removed any need to acknowledge proof. Jacques Rancière suggests that Wajcman has sought to 'establish a radical opposition between two kinds of representation – the visible image and spoken narrative – and two sorts of attestation – proof and testimony'.[48] Wajcman's criticism of Didi-Huberman is, by extension, one of the Sonderkommando: '[T]hey are criticised for having believed that the reality of the process [of extermination] was in need of proof and that the visible image afforded such proof'.[49] If we want to properly understand why these images were generated we have to accord weight to Fajnzylberg's testimony and respect the terms by which he explains their endeavour.

The Sonderkommando knew of the magnitude of the crimes they were seeking to attest to, yet they still felt they could potentially bear witness through images, provide proof that way. For them, testimony and proof were coterminous rather than divergent activities. The decisions about what events to photograph would have been informed by a wish to capture, as ably as possible, the aftermath and build up to crime. These are images that Fajnzylberg's remarks make clear should be viewed as a distinctive kind of crime scene photography. The usual objectives of such photography include: 'to record the condition of the scene before alterations occur ..., document the point of view of principals and potential witnesses, and document spatial relationships of pertinent items'.[50] Crime scene photography also 'plays an important role in the efforts to reconstruct the events of the crime'.[51]

The scene of the crime in this instance is continually being altered because the murders are ongoing, still unfolding. This state of affairs also places Alex in the position of both photographer and witness. He sees the crimes being committed and records their aftermath. Documenting his own point of view is to document the point of view of an eyewitness. The photographs do, at times, also give a sense of spatial relationships, not between items but between the scene and its perimeter.[52] It is possible to see a boundary fence in the background of the two shots of the incineration pits and, behind, a bank of birch trees, another border. The distance between the fence and the doorway to the gas chamber is not huge. This scene of genocide, of destruction, is terrifyingly compact. In this small space groups of people are murdered, their bodies are burned. The photographs taken from the doorway approximate the principal's, the murderer's perspective. No victim from a transport or from the main camp could possess this look, could contemplate the aftermath of a gassing. There is, however, in the furtiveness of this viewpoint, in the anxiety underpinning it, also evidence of Alex's victimhood. He cannot look with impunity. He fails to convincingly assume the position of the principal. Something of his own ambiguous status as a member of the Sonderkommando is therefore inadvertently registered in the two shots.

Crime scene photographs are also intended to aid the reconstruction of the events of a crime. They therefore invite imaginative responses, being used as the foundations for a mental re-enacting of the crime that has been perpetrated. Didi-Huberman's response to the four images, his reconstruction of the process which resulted in the bodies being laid on the ground in the first two pictures and of the fate of the women shown in the third, shows that this dimension of crime scene photography interests him. He extends the idea of reconstruction to the figure of the photographer as well. As Alex is, after all, a part of the crime rather than arriving belatedly at the scene, his own actions are also potentially informative. Didi-Huberman therefore sets out to envision Alex's moods and movements, and, at times, those of the people he photographs.

By attending to this vital aspect of the images, Didi-Huberman forcefully demonstrates how a narrow conception of information (one concentrated on what there is to see, rather than to feel, in the pictures) leads to crucial aspects of the image being overlooked, excised. The way Didi-Huberman approaches the photographs, his attentiveness to emotion within them, resonates with Langfus's foregrounding of the affective aspects of events discussed in Chapter 3 (particularly in relation to the story of the three thousand women). It is the usual privileging of fact over feeling, of information over emotion (as if emotions are not informative), that leads to the fourth picture not being reproduced.[53] In the display of the photographs (each replicated in a manipulated form) that is sited where Crematorium V used to be at Birkenau, for example, the fourth picture is absent. Its existence is also not referenced in the text that accompanies the other images, which claims that 'these three photographs are the only remaining pictures of Auschwitz actually to have been taken clandestinely by prisoners'. The omission of this image and the way that the other photographs are reproduced at Auschwitz is discussed by Didi-Huberman in *Écorces*.[54]

For Didi-Huberman, all four photographs in their unaltered states are important as each provides material through which to imagine the conditions of their taking. The capacity of the photographs to stimulate imagination, the obligation they place on the spectator to imagine, is their major strength.[55] What Didi-Huberman understands by imagination only gradually becomes clear. Late in *Images in Spite of All* we learn via a discussion of Lanzmann's disdain for photography that imagination is linked with emotion, memory and testimony. It is also psychically fecund.⁵⁶ The imaginings prompted by the photographs can therefore be expected to provide insight into Alex's mental states, his thoughts and feelings. If, following Lanzmann, the photographs are conceived of as without imagination, then they are also regarded as without feeling. They are reduced to bare, or brutal, fact. They do not possess the rhetoric, the narrative dimensions, Hayden White identifies in testimony, in works of history. White regards these narrative dimensions and figurative elements that refer to the real world as possessing truth-value.⁵⁷

As well as gradually revealing what he means by imagination, Didi-Huberman also provides insight into what he believes imagination is *not*. It is not, for example, 'identification, and even less hallucination'.⁵⁸ He is here rebutting Wajcman's claim that he is a narcissist. Wajcman contends that empathy relies upon what the viewer knows and the viewer cannot know Auschwitz. If Didi-Huberman therefore empathises with what he sees in the images taken by Alex then it is because he is using the pictures as a mirror.⁵⁹ Didi-Huberman sees himself reflected in the members of the Sonderkommando. Didi-Huberman, however, strongly resists this charge, arguing that the 'images will never be *reassuring images of oneself*; they will always remain *images of the Other*'.⁶⁰ For Didi-Huberman, imagination is an approximation of feelings and thought processes, not an appropriation of them.⁶¹ The empathic response that Didi-Huberman believes is imperative when confronted by the picture of the running women is therefore not conceived of in the way early theorists of empathy understood the process, as 'the experience of merging with the object of one's contemplation'.⁶² Imagination rather fosters empathy that can be characterised as generating a knowing distance. This empathy provides imperfect, yet invaluable, kinetic and sensible insights.

The material in the photographs that encourages imaginative empathy of this kind comprises gestures, motions and, linked with this, the photographer's positioning.⁶³ Gestures, utterances either visible in the images or made visible through extrapolating the physical actions behind producing the images, are referred to repeatedly in *Images in Spite of All*. The gestures of the members of the Sonderkommando in the first two photographs, for example, signal 'human banality at the service of the most radical evil'.⁶⁴ The horror of these gestures, otherwise mundane physical actions such as lifting an arm to maintain one's balance over uneven terrain, bending the back to lift and drag, placing hands on hips to pause and plan, is contained in the context in which they are 'uttered'. Didi-Huberman also notes the downcast eyes of the men in the second photograph, interpreting this as signalling their concentration 'on the work of death'.⁶⁵ They also look down 'because the earth is their destiny'.⁶⁶ Their heads are bent in resignation (or, as seems more likely to us, conversation).

Didi-Huberman writes of his efforts to conserve the 'gestural character' of the picture within his interpretation. These gestures are, on the whole, not conscious or intentional communications. They are accidental utterances. The forward motion of Alex within the gas chamber, his coming closer to the doorway to take the second photograph, forms an utterance that, for Didi-Huberman, indexes his becoming emboldened. The final photograph he takes, sunlight-dappled trees, is described as 'pure gesture'.[67] There is no content to be used as material for reconstruction, only action, the physical depression of the shutter-release button. This hasty, aimless act 'gives us access to the condition of urgency in which four shreds were snatched from hell'.[68] The physical motions of Alex and the people depicted in the pictures are treated as signifiers of a specific kind. Their visible utterances index states of mind. Peirce lists the pointing finger as an example of the index in his 1885 'Algebra of Logic'.[69] The gestures in the photographs function like a pointing finger, indicating feelings and thoughts. Peirce described indexes of this kind as exerting 'a real physiological *force* over the attention'.[70]

Indexing Destruction

The viewer with imagination can reconstruct the physical motions signalled by the people portrayed in the photographs, and thus access the moods these actions index. In relation to Alex, the photographs also act as indices to his movements. The fuzziness of the entire image of the women, for instance, bespeaks his being in motion. Analogue photographs are also usually conceived of as possessing a general indexicality, manifesting a physical link with what they depict. As Kaja Silverman explains, for Peirce there was an 'existential bond between the indexical sign and its object'.[71] This bond is essential for Didi-Huberman. It is the photograph's status as index that, he argues, gives it its capacity to act as 'a possible point of *contact*' between 'the *image* and the *real*'.[72] The index points towards the Real. In *Camera Lucida*, Barthes argues something similar, writing that 'the Photograph always leads the corpus I need back to the body I see …, the *This* …, in short, what Lacan calls the *Tuché*, the Occasion, the Encounter, the Real'.[73]

In her impressive study of Peirce, *The Machinery of Talk*, Freadman suggests that the role of the index is 'fixing and individuating; backward reference; arresting for a moment the essential mobility of the objects of knowledge'.[74] The index achieves this seizure of the Real through contiguity: it connects apprehension and the thing meant.[75] Our sense of Birkenau is linked to the place itself by way of the Sonderkommando photographs. In this conception, the photograph arrests the crime: securing the viewer to it as Real by way of its thin pellicle. Crucially here, however, the photograph as index is not the Real. The Real is on the other side of it, signalled by it yet not equivalent to it, nor to be conflated with it.

Didi-Huberman praises 'the photographic medium' for linking the mental images conjured by apprehension of the four pictures, the imaginings they prompt, with Crematorium V on an August day in 1944.[76] The photograph as index enables this bond. Wajcman's critique of Didi-Huberman overlooks this reliance on the index as conduit, this acknowledgment within *Images in Spite of All* that the insights the images provide are mediated. The image as index, as Didi-Huberman recognises, is not the same as the thing it points towards. It may look like the thing, possessing an iconic aspect, yet its status as indication rather than object acts to distance what it depicts. Mary Ann Doane ably summarises this odd status of the index, writing that:

> As photographic trace or impression, the index seems to harbour a fullness, an excessiveness of detail that is always supplemental to meaning or intention. Yet, the index as *deixis* implies an emptiness, a hollowness that can only be filled in specific, contingent, always mutating situations. It is this dialectic of the empty and the full that lends the index an eeriness and uncanniness not associated with the realms of the icon or the symbol.[77]

The index, full yet empty, a space of plenitude and lack, gives the viewer Birkenau while simultaneously withholding it. Doane also draws attention to the recurring linking of the index with death in literature on the topic.[78] She is here referring specifically to the writings of André Bazin and Roland Barthes. For Barthes, the photograph indexes death through its own gradual physical decomposition and, particularly in relation to historical images, through defeat of time inherent in them, depicting the now dead as still living: '*that* is dead and *that* is going to die'.[79] Barthes also allies photographs with the feminine. Using a maternal metaphor, he writes that 'a sort of umbilical cord links the body of the photographed thing to my gaze: light, though impalpable, is here a carnal medium, a skin I share with anyone who has been photographed'.[80] The index is here figured as the umbilical, linking viewer and viewed. The photograph for Barthes is aligned with death and the feminine. This explains the uncanniness Doane identifies in it. The index may seemingly function to hold fast the mutable world, yet it is itself unstable.

Barthes and Didi-Huberman share the conception of photography as a kind of skin. In *Images in Spite of All*, as Hannah Mowat and Emma Wilson draw attention to, the four photographs taken by Alex are described as *lambeaux*, translated as 'shreds' by Shane Lillis yet in French carrying multiple connotations not contained in that word: 'fragments, paper scraps, material rags, [and] in more ghastly imagery, … flaying and the shaving off of flesh and skin'.[81] Didi-Huberman's skin is therefore not luminous like Barthes's, it is scourged. As Mowat and Wilson suggest, he foregrounds a 'fleshy, mortal relation to signification' in which 'the evidence produced is written with the lifeblood of the deportees … on fragments torn from their flesh'.[82] The skin of the photograph he envisions is one that lacks corporeal integrity. Barthes's unifying skin is the skin as index. The skin Didi-Huberman is describing here is the skin of the photograph as icon. He is drawing attention to the lacunae in these images pregnant with horror.

The iconic aspect of the photograph is bound to the indexical. The gaps in the former therefore permeate the latter, like a knot in the umbilical, obstructing, without stopping, the flow of material feeding the viewer's imagination. Didi-Huberman's recognition of the imperfect communication manifested by each of the images explains why Lewental's assertion that Auschwitz is unimaginable is referenced in *Images in Spite of All*.[83] Lewental wrote, seemingly of historians seeking to understand the past, that '<they> will certainly not reach the truth because no one is capable of imagining it'.[84] He subsequently reiterates, 'no man's imaginings can match these events accurately'.[85] This assertion is one in keeping with Wajcman's contention that the Shoah is beyond imagining.[86] Wajcman argues that it is instead our duty not to imagine.[87] Didi-Huberman acknowledges the lacunae present in imaginative acts but does not concur with Wajcman that they should not take place. He calls instead for 'an internal critique so as to deal with [the] *lacunary necessity*' of the images.[88] Didi-Huberman's position seems close in spirit to Lewental's. Lewental, as discussed in Chapter 4, rejected any totalising claims for history yet still recognised its value. He too embraced internal critique, recognising the gaps in the history of the Łódź ghetto he archived and, presumably, in his own history of the Sonderkommando revolt.

This discussion of the indexical qualities of the photographs may seem tangential to advancing understanding of the Sonderkommando and their activities, yet in reality it was their recognition of the power and potential of indexicality that motivated some of their efforts at resistance even if they would not have described what they were doing as indexing. The first two photographs taken by Alex, for example, point an accusatory finger at the Nazis. The pile of bodies forms an index as Peirce understood it. In his 1867 paper on signs, 'On a New List of Categories', Peirce lists murder as one of his examples of the index.[89] It is indexical because 'the existence of a murdered person is a sign that there exists a murderer' or because the existence of a murderer signals that someone has been murdered.[90]

The bare, parched earth in the foreground of the first two photographs also forms an index, one overlooked by Didi-Huberman. The absence of vegetation indexes the regular passage of feet across this patch of ground, points towards the murders as an ongoing process rather than a singular event.

The teeth buried in the grounds of the crematoria discussed in Chapter 1 can also be seen as indices of murder. Peirce calls the index 'a fragment torn away from the Object'. The teeth, as physical remnants of those murdered, invite the reconstitution of the whole of which they had once been part. Some of the Sonderkommando seem to have consciously sought to exploit this indexical quality as a means to resist Nazi efforts to destroy all evidence of their crimes. The words the Sonderkommando composed to describe the death factory are symbolic in Peirce's sense of the term; they are formed of signs 'whose relation to [their] conceptual object is entirely arbitrary'.[91] The Sonderkommando evidently felt that these written accounts therefore required supplementing with other forms of sign, of evidence: material traces such as the photographs (also iconic) and teeth. They did not foresee that one day their writings, the inks and papers they used, would also be recognised as possessing indexical qualities.

Images and Texts

Wajcman chastises Didi-Huberman for devoting consideration, drawing attention, to a set of photographs that do not depict the gas chambers. This is because, he claims, on one level the gas chambers are, and will remain, unrepresentable (whether or not photographs exist of them). Wajcman writes: '[T]he gas chambers are an event which in itself forms a kind of aporia, an unbreakable real which pierces and places in question the status of the image and puts at risk all thinking concerning images'.[92] Despite this observation, however, Wajcman is still troubled by Didi-Huberman's claim that the shadow framing the acts of incineration in the first two photographs is formed by masonry belonging to the gas chamber, by its outer wall. This assertion, which Didi-Huberman supports with evidence, suggests to Wajcman that somehow the gas chamber has been rendered visible. It is, of course, the claimed absence of eyewitness accounts of the gas chamber that the denier Robert Faurisson uses to buttress his negationist position.[93]

Wajcman writes later:

> Along with the bodies in the process of burning in the centre of the photograph, an image of the destiny of all inmates, the surrounding 'black

mass' shows something, it shows mortal danger, it shows the great courage of the members of the Sonderkommando. Not the gas chamber.[94]

It is obvious that for Wajcman, the gas chamber *is* the Shoah. It is the shard of unrepresentability that transpierces any and all representations of the Holocaust, revealing their lack. The centrality of the gas chambers to the horrors of the Holocaust, their facilitation of murder on an industrial scale, is indisputable. For the Sonderkommando, however, the gas chambers were part of a lengthy process of the destruction of 'worlds', as Gradowski called individuals. This process, as Simone Gigliotti has powerfully demonstrated, was already well advanced on the transports.[95] The Łódź ghetto diary preserved by Lewental, and Langfus's depiction of Maków, show that dehumanisation began before deportation. The special squads, however, entered the process for the first time at the undressing routine, the debasing removal of clothes in the presence of strangers designed to produce a sense of naked humiliation.

The administering of Zyklon B, the act of murder, was perpetrated by a member of the SS. The gas chamber as a technique of mass murder, the so called 'Brack method', was adopted because of the psychological strain experienced by the *Einsatzgruppen* as they shot large groups of people.[96] It enabled thousands to be killed simultaneously through a simple action, the deaths occurring out of sight of the murderer. The ghastly aftermath of a gassing is, as discussed in chapters 2 and 3, described in graphic detail by Gradowski and Langfus. Yet for the Sonderkommando, it is clear that it was not the method of murder that was most hellish for them. The heart of hell was the burning of bodies. Their role in the obliteration of all traces of the dead was what caused them the greatest anguish. The chapter titled 'The Heart of Hell' in Gradowski's *In the Heart of Hell* is not about the operation of the gas chambers. The description of opening the doors of the gas chamber to reveal its victims occurs earlier and is titled 'In the Bunker'. The centre of the inferno was the ovens. Alex's photograph shows the outdoor equivalent. The ovens and the incineration pits were used to void all traces of a life. For Alex and for Gradowski this was Birkenau's repellent core.

Our sense of the horror of the Holocaust, acquired retrospectively, predictably centres on the mode of murder settled on by the Nazis. In the death camp at Auschwitz, however, it is clear that those actually working within the crematoria found the sweltering, stinking, crackling destruction of bodies to be the Nazi's most infernal crime. Langfus's *The Deportation* is informative here. The description of the burning of people discussed in Chapter 3, which forms the conclusion to the account of the fate of the Jews from the Maków ghetto, reinforces that this process was at the nucleus of the horrible. That it forms the culmination of the account, rather than ending with the gassings, is revealing. The burning of the bodies was, of course, the last indignity inflicted on the victims. Nonetheless, as the scrap of address book attests, Langfus appears to exhibit particular concern over this passage. On the draft composition, it is the Sonderkommando who must destroy the evidence, enabling the murderer to 'wash his bloody hands' by removing all traces of the crime. This clean-up operation causes the Sonderkommando to become tainted by the crime: 'The frying and roasting of people made the air in the entire area greasy'.[97] It was they who formed, who worked, and who lived within this odious environment. This, for them, was the heart of hell.

In one sense, Wajcman is therefore right to insist that the most important aspect of Alex's first two photographs is the act of incineration they record. For Wajcman, however, this is a lesser event than what occurred in the gas chambers. He does not address the context of the photograph, does not attend to how the photographer might have viewed things, conceived of these shots. Alex's purpose was to record what, for him and his companions, formed the worst features of Nazi crimes. Filip Müller, who devotes considerable attention to the incineration pits in *Eyewitness Auschwitz*, writes that the team tasked with pulverising ashes after an incineration 'were almost without exception Greek Jews'.[98] He adds that 'they accompanied their monotonous activity by non-stop cheerful singing'.[99] The ash team, he states, had a job that 'was surely the worst of all'.[100]

For the Sonderkommando, as chapters 2 and 3 make clear, encounters with women were also amongst the most distressing and disturbing events they experienced.[101] Didi-Huberman identifies a 'troubling complementarity between the photograph of women walking toward the gas chamber and Gradowski's narratives – but also Leib Langfus's – [of] this particularly ignoble phase of the criminal process'.[102] He might also have made reference to Lewental's description of the violence, possibly perpetrated in the Ciechanów ghetto, which draws attention to the fate of 'naked young women' and makes reference to rape.[103] Although Lewental does not seem to be documenting events at Birkenau in this passage, he is demonstrating how humiliation of, and brutality towards, women was taken to be particularly shocking and in need of recording.

Langfus's account of 'The 3000 Naked Women' about to be gassed highlights the anguish of the Sonderkommando and the women. In 'Particulars' he also draws attention to Oberscharführer Voss's practice of 'stand[ing] by the doorway of the undressing room and feel[ing] the genitalia of each young woman going through as they went naked into the gas chamber'.[104] These acts of sexual violation were practised by SS men of all ranks.[105] Gradowski writes of the arrival of women in the undressing room: 'The moment they take off their clothes and are left stark naked, they will lose their last support, they will lose their last foundation, by which their life is still held'.[106] To be naked in the grounds of the crematoria at Birkenau was to be on the way to death and, if a young woman, potential violation.

The women Gradowski and Langfus describe could not provide their own accounts of the horrors they experienced. A distant sense of what their experience might have been like can be gathered, however, from other kinds of testimony. The Ringelblum archive contains a report of the Mława ghetto, where 'at night (every night) SS-men would come and photograph young women (naked)'.[107] Olga Lengyel, a survivor from Birkenau, provided testimony of her arrival there, which gives insight into how horrible the experience was.[108] She writes of the humiliation she experienced having to undress in front of guards and of having to endure 'a thorough examination in the Nazi manner, oral, rectal, and vaginal. ... We had to lie across a table stark naked while they probed. All that in the presence of drunken soldiers who sat around ... chuckling obscenely'.[109] Lengyel's account, leaving nothing to the imagination, is remarkable given that it was published in 1947.[110] In her discussion of sexual humiliation during camp induction processes, S. Lillian Kremer draws attention to Sara Nomberg-Przytyk's account of her arrival at Auschwitz as foregrounding the experience of 'the shame of public nudity' and 'the sense of being objectified, dehumanised and defeminised by disdainful men'.[111]

The accounts by Gradowski and Langfus, coupled with survivor accounts of the concentration camp of Auschwitz-Birkenau, place these photographs in context, providing insight into what they depict and prefigure. It is a context that Wajcman refuses to countenance. He suggests, 'if we did not know where this image came from, it would not be incongruous to see in it a country scene of German naturists'.[112] It is obvious that Wajcman has never looked at the image (or at any of the images). He twice refers to it as having been taken from a window rather than *en plein air*.[113] Wajcman's shocking assertion, his effort to situate the image, albeit in fantasy, as representative of *Freikörperkultur*, appears symptomatic of anxiety, of a refusal to look. Wajcman twice also references the hostile reception that the picture generated from some quarters when it was displayed at Yad Vashem.[114] From his second reference to this event, it becomes clear his working knowledge of the image is derived from Annette Wieviorka's discussion of it, which appears to be based on the manipulated version. Wajcman quotes her, stating that 'the bodies of the women could have been photographed in a hamam'.[115]

The manipulated image, as discussed, strives to bring clarity to a disturbance in the field of vision. Wajcman appears to wish to do the same: to find form, to make good, albeit fantastically through naturism, the lack of intelligibility that characterises the original print. The image of women being driven to their deaths is too troubling for him. The naked dead of the first two photographs, however, do not cause him concern. For the Sonderkommando, by contrast, the unclothed bodies were also a source of anxiety. Gradowski writes in 'In the Bunker', a section discussed in Chapter 2, of the initial moments after opening the gas chamber doors: 'Our eyes are riveted, hypnotised by this sea of naked dead bodies that have appeared before us'. He goes on repeatedly to reference nakedness. In the space of five sentences he describes 'this deep naked sea', 'this naked world', 'this vast sea of nakedness', 'these naked waves', and 'this deep naked abyss'. The closing line of 'In the Bunker' is: 'These heads, dark, fair, brown, are the only parts that stand out from the universal nakedness'.[116]

Comparing this final sentence with Gradowski's initial description of the arrival of these victims is informative. When they first appear, the hair on their heads is described as black, brown and blonde, with the occasional grey-haired head also visible.[117] These older heads have disappeared in the later depiction. The sea of dead bodies is rendered more youthful. Gradowski is almost 'retouching' his imagery here. Like the anonymous manipulator of Alex's photograph, he constructs a vision of death as youthful femininity. In the description of these young-looking dead in the gas chamber, bare skin assumes overwhelming proportions, a swell of undifferentiated, exposed bodies seemingly threatening to engulf the Sonderkommando. The repetition of 'naked' works to detach this word from the other words in the passage, foreground it. Gradowski constructs a wave of references to nakedness so his reader, like the Sonderkommando, is overwhelmed by this feature. The sea of bodies primarily signifies nakedness.

The first two photographs taken by Alex, when read alongside Gradowski's account, assume another import. The nakedness of the bodies that are being burned adds to the horror of what is taking place. The bodies still register as degraded. Their humiliation, at least as far as the Sonderkommando were concerned, persisted beyond death. An explanation for this can be found in *Eyewitness Auschwitz*. Müller writes that 'because of our constant handling of the dead we seemed to forget they were corpses'.[118] Müller goes on to state of the murdered: 'We would talk to them as if they were still alive, and even though there was no reply it appeared to worry no one, for we supplied our own answers'.[119] For those working in the crematoria, the living were viewed as already dead, the dead as still living. In Alex's photographs, the eyes of the supine corpses still met the gaze of the Sonderkommando. The conversations with the dead detailed by Müller were, of course, coping mechanisms. In the trenches in the First World War, comparable exchanges between dead and living took place. The living gave voice to the dead. This is what Alex is doing in all the photographs. Wajcman's refusal to hear what the dead have to say does a grave injustice to both them and Alex. He is, however, far from alone in condemning photographic testimony.

The Camera Eye

Geoffrey Hartman, for instance, accords the Sonderkommando photographs evidential value yet contends that 'they cannot make the dead testify more forcefully by that kind of visibility than the thousands whose witness, instead of assaulting the viewer with brutal, mechanically frozen images, opens onto a potentially non-traumatizing reception'. Hartman acknowledges that 'I have not seen' the photographs, yet he *imagines* them to be brutal.[120] They are envisaged to be unreasoning, cruel. This characterisation is linked to the means of their production, the mechanical. Photographs unthinkingly assault the viewer. Stone states of each of these images: '[E]verything is always all at once bursting out of the photograph, carving a path of terror through our senses'.[121] Like Hartman, he views the images as doing more than depicting, as acting. For Hartman, their action is specifically to violate. For Stone, it is to powerfully convey an aspect of the horror of Birkenau.

Hartman interprets photography as possessing a violent physicality which other forms of witnessing potentially do not. He contrasts the images with testimony that is human, humane. He presumably has video testimony in mind, given his deep involvement in the Yale Video Testimony Project. Hartman's move here is reminiscent of Wajcman's in that both men privilege particular forms of testimony, specifically the oral testimony of survivors, over others. Rancière rightly points out, however, that 'he who testifies in a narrative as to what he has seen in a death camp is engaged in a work of representation, just like the person who has sought to record a visible trace of it'.[122]

Hartman's contrasting of modes of bearing witnessing ignores the crossover between them. Video testimony and photography are both forms of representation. Admittedly it cannot be ignored that the means of production of photography and video testimony (and, indeed, photography and written testimony) are, at least on the surface, different. This view was seemingly held by members of the Sonderkommando as well. Didi-Huberman twice quotes Gradowski's reference to a camera as a means to lend support to his reading of the photographs and their consequence.

He does not appear to have carefully attended to the meaning Gradowski ascribes to this technology. Here is the epigraph that opens *Images in Spite of All*:

> Tell them, your friends and acquaintances, that if you never return, it will only be because your blood has frozen in your veins and ceased to flow, on beholding the fearsome horrors of the slaughter of the innocent, helpless children, the children of my tortured people.
> Tell them that even if your heart turns to stone, your brain to a cold thinking machine, and your eye into a camera, you will not return to them.[123]

In this section, Gradowski links the camera as mechanical apparatus with a lack of emotion. It forms part of the lengthy appeal that opens his first manuscript. The narrator is here foreseeing the impact upon the friend/reader/listener/viewer that the horrific sights which will be revealed will have. In the passage, through association, photography is aligned with heartlessness and impassivity. Optical technology is credited with the capacity to bring things into view ('through microscopic lenses we will observe [*beobakhtn*] everything'),[124] but the camera is detached in a way that a human, a humane witness cannot be. Leyb Langfus in particular offers other modes of witnessing. We have read his refusal to 'observe' ('*beobakhte[n]*') the final moments of the three thousand naked women as an ethical choice. Gradowski can also be read as demanding that his reader 'feel' as well as 'see'. He too conceives of testimony as a practice that should consist of more than sheer observation.

Didi-Huberman uses the passage in *Images in Spite of All* against the grain of Gradowski's intention. This is evident in his second reference to it. He interprets the section as an extension of Gradowski's writing project, of his invitations to envision and imagine. He writes: '[I]n order to sustain the imagination of these images, [Gradowski] then says, "your heart must turn to stone ... and your eyes must be transformed into a camera"'.[125] The reality of the passage, however, is that becoming a camera is not a way of preserving the images that will be revealed to the witness. It is a way of becoming emotionally numb. The camera is employed negatively as metaphor: it is 'a mere camera' ('*bloyz a fotografishn aparat*') in the original.[126] From this passage, we can deduce that Gradowski would not necessarily have embraced Alex's actions. By implication, writing provides a way of regulating testimony that cold machinery cannot. Didi-Huberman fosters a unity of intention between writing and photography that is not obviously present in Gradowski's text.

The way Gradowski views the camera, as a heartless witness to the heart of hell, is revealing in the context of the account of the women in their final moments in the undressing room, discussed in Chapter 2. He evidently felt that imagistic writing provided an appropriate mode of testimony. He certainly recognised writing to be a form of representation yet he also evidently viewed it as being of a different order to photography. He was happy to exploit writing's capacity to shock, to call for vengeance, yet he conceived of the upset it could cause as being unlike that of a photograph. The privileging of the symbolic dimension of signification in writing is one key difference that Gradowski may have appreciated. Symbols evoke images rather than 'being' images. This may render them more palatable as testimonial material.

The Fourth Photograph

Reading Gradowski in tandem with the photographs demonstrates that viewing the Sonderkommando writings in their entirety as part of the same project as Alex's is problematic. As we have shown in Chapter 5 especially, the Sonderkommando should not be considered as of one piece. Didi-Huberman claims that the photographs form the Special Squad's self-portrait.[127] Gradowski and, potentially, Langfus and Lewental may not have recognised themselves in it. The photographer and all the writers, however, shared in the striving to resist. The photographs performed resistance in their taking: recording the act of insurrection through their production as record. The writers resisted through each word, each character, they composed. Alex and the writers all sought to counter the Nazi policy of obliteration, of erasing every trace of the dead, through their material testimony.

The images taken by Alex differ from other photographs produced at extermination camps in their quality as acts of resistance. As a form of revolt against Nazi oppression, they are perhaps closest in spirit to the French film *Sous le manteau* made by POWs in 1940 at the Oflag 17a camp in Austria. The motion picture, a documentary made using a camera concealed in a dictionary, records the daily life of officer inmates in the prison camp. Parts of the camera were smuggled into the camp in food parcels sent from France and it was then assembled. The camera used by the Sonderkommando was sneaked in to them in a soup bucket with a false bottom.[128] *Sous le manteau*, of course, does not depict the daily horror of mass murder. It emerges, nonetheless, from a comparable spirit of resistance.

Sous le manteau also records the actions of preparing to escape, such as the remarkable shots of officers digging a tunnel and the use of a camera as an aid to producing false identity papers. These actions of resistance, digging, forging, were important not just as means to ends but as ends in themselves. Similarly, the acts of the group who produced the Sonderkommando photographs, while aimed at documenting atrocity, were also of value in themselves to the men. As discussed in the previous chapter, resistance of any kind had a valuable role in preserving a sense of self, and of self-worth. Langbein writes of Auschwitz that 'again and again an inmate was shown in drastic fashion how impotent he was'.[129] In this context, the photographs produced by Alex and his compatriots were a display of their potency. Didi-Huberman suggests the act of resisting comprised maintaining a self-image as human – which, at base, meant keeping 'upright'.[130] The stand taken by the Sonderkommando, the erect stance of Alex as he snatched his images, formed an embodied defiance of the SS which had value in, and of, itself.

Sous le manteau derived its name from the method by which much of the footage was sourced. The camera was concealed in a hollowed out dictionary which was sometimes hidden under the cape officers were permitted to wear. It is also likely that Alex secreted the camera in his clothing as he set out from the crematorium to the birch copse. Didi-Huberman draws attention to the constraints of visibility created by 'hiding the camera in one's hand or clothes'.[131] In the context of the crematorium, of course, having clothes identified you as one of the living rather than someone marked for death. Alex is able to record the nakedness of the women who are soon to die because of his privileged position. He does not have nudity imposed on him. His clothes form another thread, alongside his agency as resistor, linking him to humanity.

The last two photographs, the women running and the treetops and light, presumably form another pair, like the first two: two pictures of death, two pictures of death in life, a group of four pictures of nakedness. The final photograph, however, shows no undressed bodies. It shows very little … almost nothing. For Stone, the three images preceding the photograph of shadows and light provide sufficient material to see beyond its nothingness: '[W]hat lies behind those black depths is both unknown and, thanks to the other three photographs, only too imaginable'.[132] Here, like Didi-Huberman, he treats the photograph as 'practically abstract'.[133] There is nothing to figure out here. In its abstraction, the image comes to affirm the limits of representation.

Stone avers of the four images, 'we do not want to fall into the trap of seeing in the photographs privileged moments of time rescued from oblivion, making them stand metonymically for the genocide as a whole, as "Auschwitz" already does'.[134] Didi-Huberman agrees with this, clearly sensible, position. He cautions against asking too much of the images.[135] He acknowledges their inadequacy, their lack. Neither of them regards the photographs as making good the lack of representations of the death factory, neither fetishises them. Nonetheless, they do both agree that the pictures provide insights through their indexicality. The sense of urgency indexed in the photographs is palpable.[136] It is urgency with historical import.[137] In the fourth photograph, however, the poor framing is solely ascribed to the difficulty of rapidly and surreptitiously capturing images at Birkenau.

This is certainly a factor. It is nevertheless possible to imagine another, additional motivation in Alex's gesture. Given the difficulty with confronting nakedness experienced by many members of the Sonderkommando, might it not be embarrassment that unconsciously contributes to Alex's fumble with the camera? This slip-up would then index a refusal to replicate the logic of objectification, of degradation embraced by the SS in their treatment of women. In the image preceding this one, although Didi-Huberman describes two women in the foreground there is a third, adjacent to the tall woman to the left. This woman has her head seemingly bowed, her arms clasped to her breasts. Her body closes in on itself. She is hiding herself. The fourth image hides her and those with her. It turns away, upwards. Alex therefore records the difficulty of attesting, the ethical dilemma it poses him. This dilemma is embedded in the sequence. The fourth image, in its looking away from – rather than at – nakedness, breaks the series.

Bronfen suggests that the repetitions of the image of the dying and dead feminine body exemplify 'how the violence of the real is translated only precariously into representations'.[138] She suggests that 'the aporia of representation seems to be that part of putting the real under erasure means articulating it, enacting that is not only how representations falter and stumble before the real but how the real must also fail before representation'.[139] Here, however, there is a refusal of repetition. The image breaks with precedent. It does not duplicate the previous perspective. We are therefore left with an image of birch boughs, their trunks and branches malformed in the light, close to formless. Sean Cubitt asserts that the sun 'cannot be seen, cannot be looked at, without loss of sight', and is a 'manifestation of an extreme where vision and blindness, warmth and pain intersect'.[140] This luminous photograph can therefore be read as providing the 'rending-image' referred to earlier, the torn depiction through which the Symbolic veil is rent and the Real is revealed. It is here, more than in any of the other photographs, that what Didi-Huberman refers to as the 'naked horror' is exposed.[141] This is a horror that cannot be faced, that no face can be put to.

The image shows us Alex's horror: the breakdown of his process of recording, documenting a limit to what he could endure in spite of the necessity to attest. To view the fourth photograph purely as disorientation indexing anxiety and urgency is to ignore the context in which it was seemingly produced, an encounter with a group of women, forcibly made to undress, on their way to the gas chamber. Reading the image as evidence of distress, of the persistence of powerful negative emotions in Alex, is to suggest there was a conflict over the limits of testimony, over what to record and how to record it. In his encounter with the naked women Alex may have reached his moral limit. Once acknowledged, it is possible to read this unease in the blurred photograph that precedes it. There is already a pulling upwards of the camera towards the sky evident in it, a desire to look elsewhere. The Sonderkommando writings, particularly Gradowski's complex response to comparable subject-matter, suggest that such an empathic reading (although not countenanced by Didi-Huberman) is not out of place.

The fourth photograph exhibits a reluctance to see, to record. This unwillingness, however, still produces testimony of a painful kind. The lens flare in the effulgent image establishes the strong sun on that day. The bright light swallows the surrounding foliage, disrupts the photograph's iconicity, creating an image of abstract beauty. The flare indexes the camera mechanism, foregrounds the testimony as technologically mediated. It also indexes the sun. It reinforces that this particular day, this moment at the heart of hell, is a sunny one. The camera, twisted to point upwards, heavenwards, rather than forwards, registers an image that, on one level, forms a visual counterpoint to Gradowski's address to the moon. In this accidental address to the sun, a similar shining indifference is identifiable. On this beautiful day, beneath the warmth of the sun, mass murder has already occurred and is in the process of continuing. It is difficult to imagine. Yet the fourth photograph, when read together with the others, forcibly brings home this terrible reality.

Notes

1. Georges Didi-Huberman, *Images in Spite of All*, trans. Shane B. Lillis (Chicago: University of Chicago Press, 2008), 26.
2. This is the account given by David Szmulewski, which is drawn upon in Clément Chéroux (ed.), *Mémoires des camps: photographies des camps de concentration et d'extermination Nazis 1933–1999* (Paris: Marval, 2001), 86. Szmulewski appears to have misremembered Abraham Dragon's name and called him Josel. Fajnzylberg is referred to as Alter Foincilber throughout *Images in Spite of All*.
3. Didi-Huberman examines arguments that the photographs may have been taken in a different order in *Images in Spite of All* (116). He draws attention to Clément

Chéroux's discovery of the remains of an image of birch trees in the margin of the photograph usually identified as the first in the sequence. This would indicate that the exterior shots were taken prior to those shot from within the gas chamber looking out. Didi-Huberman asks, '[I]s the *margin of the image* questioned by Clément Chéroux not emblematic of the *margin of indetermination* with which all research is confronted necessarily in its study of the vestiges of history?' (116, original italics). The reading we have produced also emerges from out of these vestiges and is therefore, of necessity, tentative. Didi-Huberman's preferred sequence, based as it is upon Szmulewski's testimony to Pressac, is persuasive to us and we therefore follow him to produce this alternative interpretation to his own.

4. Janina Struk, *Photographing the Holocaust: Interpretations of the Evidence* (London: I.B. Tauris, 2004), 114. See also Szmulewski's admission to Jean-Claude Pressac that he was not the person who took the photographs, although he did operate as a lookout. Jean-Claude Pressac, *Auschwitz: Technique and Operation of the Gas Chamber* (New York: Beate Klarsfeld Foundation, 1989), 424.
5. Eric Friedler, Barbara Siebert and Andreas Kilian, *Zeugen aus der Todeszone: Das jüdische Sonderkommando in Auschwitz* (Munich: Deutsches Taschenbuch Verlag, 2005), 214.
6. Errikos Sevillias, *Athens – Auschwitz*, trans. Nikos Stavroulakis (Athens: Lycabettus Press, 1983), 42.
7. Steven B. Bowman, *The Agony of Greek Jews, 1940–1945* (Stanford, CA: Stanford University Press, 2009), 271. Filip Müller also refers to him as Alex Errera in *Sonderbehandlung: Drei Jahre in den Krematorien und Gaskammern von Auschwitz* (Munich: Steinhausen, 1979), 125. The name is omitted in the English translation.
8. Teresa Świebocka, *Auschwitz: A History in Photographs* (Indianapolis: Indiana University Press, 1993), 42.
9. Shlomo Dragon's interview with Gideon Greif provided an opportunity to resolve the identity of the photographer. Dragon twice draws attention to the presence of a camera at Crematorium IV in response to questions. Greif, however, fails to follow up this revelation. Greif, *We Wept without Tears*, 166, 170.
10. Georges Didi-Huberman, 'Images malgré tout', in *Mémoire des camps: Photographies des camps de concentration et d'extermination nazis (1933–1999)*, ed. Clément Chéroux (Paris: Marval, 2001), 219–41; Dan Stone, 'The Sonderkommando Photographs', *Jewish Social Studies* 7(3) (2001): 132–48.
11. Didi-Huberman, *Images in Spite of All*, 110–11.
12. Ibid., 110. The word scroll here is 'rouleau' in the original, which is the way megillah was rendered in the main text, although not the title, when Ber Mark's *Megillat Auschwitz* was translated into French as *Des voix dans la nuit* (Paris: Plon, 1982).
13. Didi-Huberman, *Images in Spite of All*, 34.
14. Ibid.
15. Stone also remarks on a tension between stasis and action in the Sonderkommando photographs, although, in this context, he focuses on the first two images and registers this friction outside of any manipulation. For him, photographs inherently have stillness, what he describes as arrest and ossification, which can appear as a paradox when action is their subject. Stone, 'The Sonderkommando Photographs', 135.
16. A version of this image with more obvious retouching than the one reproduced in *Images in Spite of All* is used in the Yiddish version and the English translation of Ber Mark's *The Scrolls of Auschwitz*. In his discussion of these images, Mark mistakenly

refers to only two photographs. He does not attribute the taking of the photographs to a specific person. The photographs are also used in *The Death Factory*, in which the four photographs are credited to Szmulewski. See Ota Kraus and Erich Kulka, *The Death Factory*, trans. Stephen Jolly (Oxford: Pergamon Press, 1966), 92.
17. Griselda Pollock, *Mary Cassatt: Painter of Modern Life* (London: Thames & Hudson, 1998), 39.
18. Elisabeth Bronfen, *Over her Dead Body: Death, Femininity and the Aesthetic* (Manchester: Manchester University Press, 1992), xii.
19. Ibid.
20. Ibid., 113.
21. Ibid., 52.
22. Didi-Huberman, *Images in Spite of All*, 3.
23. Ibid., 60.
24. Gérard Wajcman, 'De la croyance photographique', *Les Temps modernes* 56 (2001): 47–83.
25. Ibid., 81. All translations are by Nicholas Chare.
26. Ibid.
27. Laura Mulvey, *Fetishism and Curiosity* (Bloomington: Indiana University Press, 1996), 6.
28. Wajcman, 'De la croyance photographique', 67.
29. Didi-Huberman, *Images in Spite of All*, 34.
30. Marianne Hirsch, 'The Generation of Postmemory', *Poetics Today* 29(1) (2008): 115.
31. Didi-Huberman, *Images in Spite of All*, 34.
32. Ibid., 79–80. Translation of Georges Didi-Huberman, *Images malgré tout* (Paris: Les Éditions de minuit, 2003), 103. Original italics.
33. Ibid., 80–81.
34. Ibid., 80.
35. Primo Levi, 'Shame', in *The Drowned and the Saved* (London: Abacus, 1989), 64. See also Primo Levi, 'Words, Memory, Hope (1984)', in Levi, *The Voice of Memory: Interview, 1961–1967* (New York: The New Press, 2001), 252.
36. Giorgio Agamben, *Remnants of Auschwitz: The Witness and the Archive*, trans. Daniel Heller-Roazen (New York: Zone Books, 1999), 81.
37. Jacques Lacan, *The Seminars of Jacques Lacan 2: The Ego in Freud's Theory and in the Technique of Psychoanalysis 1954–1955*, trans. Sylvana Tomaselli (New York: Norton, 1991), 154.
38. Ibid., 164.
39. Jacques Lacan, *The Seminars of Jacques Lacan 3: The Psychoses*, trans. Russell Grigg (London: Routledge, 1993), 268.
40. Bronfen, *Over her Dead Body*, 53.
41. Didi-Huberman, *Images in Spite of All*, 34.
42. Stone, 'The Sonderkommando Photographs', 137.
43. Elisabeth Pagnoux, 'Reporter photographique à Auschwitz', *Les Temps modernes* 56 (2001): 84–108.
44. Wajcman, 'De la croyance photographique', 53.
45. Ibid.
46. Ibid., 80.
47. Barbie Zelizer describes how photographs of the liberation of concentration camps, for example, are held to have contributed significantly to an acknowledgment of the

atrocities perpetrated by the Nazis. Barbie Zelizer, *Remembering to Forget: Holocaust Memory through the Camera's Eye* (Chicago: University of Chicago Press, 1998), 12.
48. Jacques Rancière, *The Emancipated Spectator*, trans. Gregory Elliott (London: Verso, 2009), 89.
49. Ibid., 90.
50. Robert R. Ogle, *Crime Scene Investigation and Reconstruction* (Upper Saddle River, NJ: Pearson Prentice Hall, 2004), 35.
51. Ibid.
52. The photographs are all reproduced in *Images in Spite of All*.
53. At times, in fact, the very existence of the fourth photograph is not recognised. In *The Agony of Greek Jews, 1940–1945*, for example, Bowman only refers to the existence of 'three photographs of the Sonderkommando at the burning pits'. Bowman, *The Agony of Greek Jews*, 96.
54. Georges Didi-Huberman, *Écorces* (Paris: Éditions de Minuit, 2011), 48–49. The title would translate in English as *Barks* but also refers to peel and skin. See also Isabel Wollaston, 'The Absent, the Partial and the Iconic in Archival Photographs of the Holocaust', *Jewish Culture and History* 12(3) (2010): 443–45.
55. In a different context, that of the contemporary photographer Mikael Levin, Ulrich Baer explores the power of images that resist the viewer's imagination to attest to the Holocaust. See Baer, *Spectral Evidence: The Photography of Trauma* (Cambridge, MA: MIT Press, 2002), 65.
56. Didi-Huberman, *Images in Spite of All*, 111.
57. See Hayden White, 'Historical Discourse and Literary Writing', in *Tropes for the Past: Hayden White and the History/Literature Debate*, ed. Kusima Korhonen (Amsterdam: Rodopi, 2006), 25–33.
58. Didi-Huberman, *Images in Spite of All*, 88.
59. Wajcman, 'De la croyance photographique', 74.
60. Didi-Huberman, *Images in Spite of All*, 88. Original italics.
61. Ibid.
62. Susan Leigh Foster, *Choreographing Empathy: Kinesthesia in Performance* (London: Routledge, 2011), 127. Andrea Liss expresses reservations about this conception of empathy in the context of Holocaust photography. Liss, *Trespassing through Shadows: Memory, Photography and the Holocaust* (Minneapolis: University of Minnesota Press, 1998), 7.
63. Jan Karski draws attention to the importance of attending to gestures to convey a given testimony as clearly as possible, stating: '[T]he most effective way of getting my material across was not to soften or interpret it, but to convey it as directly as possible, reproducing not merely the ideas and instructions but the language, gestures, and nuances of those from whom the material came'. He may here be unconsciously exploiting gesture's power to promote empathy. Jan Karski, *Story of a Secret State* (Boston, MA: Houghton Mifflin, 1944), 335.
64. Didi-Huberman, *Images in Spite of All*, 81.
65. Ibid., 46.
66. Ibid.
67. Ibid., 37.
68. Ibid., 38.
69. Charles S. Peirce, 'On the Algebra of Logic', *American Journal of Mathematics* 7(2) (1885), 181.

70. Charles S. Peirce, 'An American Plato: Review of Royce's *Religious Aspect of Philosophy* (1885)', in *The Essential Peirce: Selected Philosophical Writings Volume 1, 1867–1893*, ed. Nathan Houser and Christian Kloesel (Bloomington: Indiana University Press, 1992), 232.
71. Kaja Silverman, *The Subject of Semiotics* (New York: Oxford University Press, 1983), 19.
72. Didi-Huberman, *Images in Spite of All*, 75.
73. Roland Barthes, *Camera Lucida*, trans. Richard Howard (London: Vintage, 1993), 4. The pronoun '*This*', as a shifter in language, forms one of Peirce's examples of an index. Peirce's shifters, referential indexical signs the meanings of which shift depending on the context in which they are employed, are, however, different from Barthes's *This*: the unvarying Real.
74. Anne Freadman, *The Machinery of Talk: Charles Peirce and the Sign Hypothesis* (Stanford, CA: Stanford University Press, 2004), 107.
75. Ibid.
76. Didi-Huberman, *Images in Spite of All*, 75.
77. Mary Ann Doane, 'Indexicality: Trace and Sign: Introduction', *Differences* 18(1) (2007): 2.
78. Ibid., 5.
79. Barthes, *Camera Lucida*, 93–97.
80. Ibid., 81.
81. Hannah Mowat and Emma Wilson, 'Reconciling History in Alain Resnais's *L'Année dernière à Marienbad* (1961)', in *Representing Auschwitz: At the Margins of Testimony*, ed. Nicholas Chare and Dominic Williams (Basingstoke: Palgrave Macmillan, 2013), 158.
82. Ibid.
83. Didi-Huberman, *Images in Spite of All*, 63.
84. Zalman Lewental, 'Hesofe tsum Lodzher ksav-yad', in Ber Mark, *Megiles Oyshvits* (Tel Aviv: Yisroel-Bukh, 1977), 433.
85. Ibid.
86. Wajcman, 'De la croyance photographique', 71. For a discussion of the difficulties of imagining as an inmate from within Auschwitz, see Nicholas Chare, 'Symbol Re-formation: Concentrationary Memory in Charlotte Delbo's *Auschwitz and After*', in *Concentrationary Memories: Totalitarian Terror and Cultural Resistance*, ed. Griselda Pollock and Max Silverman (London: I.B. Tauris, 2013), 103–13.
87. Wajcman, 'De la croyance photographique', 73.
88. Didi-Huberman, *Images in Spite of All*, 45.
89. Charles S. Peirce, 'On a New List of Categories', *Proceedings of the American Academy of Arts and Sciences* 7 (1868): 290.
90. Freadman, *The Machinery of Talk*, 14.
91. Ibid., 119. Silverman, *The Subject of Semiotics*, 20.
92. Wajcman, 'De la croyance photographique', 63.
93. Jean-François Lyotard, *The Differend: Phrases in Dispute*, trans. Georges Van Den Abbeele (Minneapolis: University of Minnesota Press, 1988), 3.
94. Wajcman, 'De la croyance photographique', 80.
95. Simone Gigliotti, *The Train Journey* (New York: Berghahn Books, 2009).
96. Dan Stone, *Histories of the Holocaust* (Oxford: Oxford University Press, 2010), 190.
97. Leyb Langfus, *Der Geyresh*, [99] 111. No published Yiddish text exists for this document. I have worked directly from the manuscript, also making use of the Polish

translation: Lejb [—], 'Wysiedlenie', trans. Roman Pytel, *Zeszyty Oświęcimskie* 14 (1972), 15–62 [DW].
98. Filip Müller, *Eyewitness Auschwitz: Three Years in the Gas Chambers*, trans. Susanne Flatauer (Chicago: Ivan R. Dee, 1999), 139 (Trans. of *Sonderbehandlung*, 222).
99. Ibid.
100. Ibid., 138 (Trans. of *Sonderbehandlung*, 222).
101. Richard Glazar says that the only 'dropouts' from the Red commando in Treblinka 'were the ones who couldn't take the undressing, especially the women undressing'. *Trap with a Green Fence: Survival in Treblinka*, trans. Roslyn Theobald (Evanston, IL: Northwestern University Press, 1995), 54.
102. Didi-Huberman, *Images in Spite of All*, 110.
103. Zalman Lewental, 'Fartseykhenungen', in Ber Mark, *Megiles Oyshvits* (Tel Aviv: Am Oved, 1977), 377. This page, page 122 in our order, comes after all the other deciphered pages, and exists at the limits of readability. Since women and children are mentioned, these incidents are unlikely to have happened in Auschwitz. They are consistent with stories about the Ciechanów ghetto, but also with numerous incidents in other locations. The context is hard to tell as the preceding and following pages have not been deciphered at all. Jolanta Kraemer, 'Ciechanów', *USHMM Encyclopedia of Camps and Ghettos, 1933–1945*, Vol. II, Part A, Vol. ed. Martin Dean (Bloomington: Indiana University Press, 2012), 11. *Megiles Oyshvits*, 423 n. 2.
104. Leyb Langfus, 'Eyntselheyten', in Ber Mark, *Megiles Oyshvits* (Tel Aviv: Am Oved), 357.
105. Ibid.
106. Zalman Gradowski, *In harts fun gehenem* (Jerusalem: Wolnerman, n.d. [c. 1977]), 71.
107. 'Geyresh Mlave', 5/6 December 1940, ARG 929 (Ring I 865), 2. Janina Struk notes a number of incidents of Germans photographing naked Jews, Poles and Roma. Struk, *Photographing the Holocaust*, 71–73, 80–81. See also Yvonne Kozlovsky-Golan, '"Public Property": Sexual Abuse of Women and Girls in Cinematic Memory', in *Sexual Violence against Jewish Women during the Holocaust*, ed. Sonja M. Hedgepeth and Rochelle G. Saidel (Hanover, NH: University Press of New England, 2010), 235.
108. Her testimony is used by Elie A. Cohen as part of his exploration of *Human Behaviour in the Concentration Camp* (London: Free Association, 1988), 120.
109. Olga Lengyel, *Five Chimneys* (Chicago: Ziff-Davis, 1947), 17–19.
110. Zoë Waxman has drawn attention to how 'the perceived "appropriateness" of experiences' can impact on whether they are published. See Zoë Vania Waxman, *Writing the Holocaust: Identity, Testimony, Representation* (Oxford: Oxford University Press, 2006), 128.
111. S. Lillian Kremer, 'Sexual Abuse in Holocaust Literature', in *Sexual Violence against Jewish Women during the Holocaust*, 179.
112. Wajcman, 'De la croyance photographique', 78.
113. Ibid., 49, 66.
114. Ibid., 49, 77.
115. Ibid., 77.
116. Gradowski, *In harts fun gehenem*, 101–2.
117. Ibid., 70.
118. Müller, *Eyewitness Auschwitz*, 100 (Trans. of *Sonderbehandlung*, 158).
119. Ibid.
120. Geoffrey Hartman, 'The Struggle against the Inauthentic', *parallax* 10(1) (2004): 77.
121. Stone, 'The Sonderkommando Photographs', 138.

122. Rancière, *The Emancipated Spectator*, 90.
123. Didi-Huberman, *Images in Spite of All*, no page number. Translation amended to reflect the original French.
124. Gradowski, 'Fartseykhenungen', 292.
125. The ellipsis in the Gradowski quotation is Didi-Huberman's. Didi-Huberman, *Images in Spite of All*, 32.
126. Gradowski, 'Fartseykhenungen', 291.
127. Didi-Huberman, *Images in Spite of All*, 45.
128. Herman Langbein, *People in Auschwitz*, trans. Harry Zohn (Chapel Hill: North Carolina Press, 2004), 255. The English translation describes it as a food pail.
129. Langbein, *People in Auschwitz*, 240.
130. Didi-Huberman, *Images in Spite of All*, 43.
131. Ibid., 32.
132. Stone, 'The Sonderkommando Photographs', 138.
133. Didi-Huberman, *Images in Spite of All*, 16.
134. Stone, 'The Sonderkommando Photographs', 133.
135. Didi-Huberman, *Images in Spite of All*, 33.
136. Stone, 'The Sonderkommando Photographs', 131.
137. Didi-Huberman, *Images in Spite of All*, 38.
138. Bronfen, *Over Her Dead Body*, 53.
139. Ibid.
140. Sean Cubitt, 'The Sound of Sunlight', *Screen* 51(2) (2010): 118–20.
141. Didi-Huberman, *Images in Spite of All*, 81.

Conclusion

Crossing the Circle of Flame

> The Holocaust is unique because it created a circle of flame around itself, a boundary not to be crossed, since horror in the absolute degree cannot be communicated.¹

Claude Lanzmann's rancorous dispute with Georges Didi-Huberman concerning the appropriateness of using archival images as testaments to the Shoah, detailed in the last chapter, would lead many to believe that the filmmaker was entirely hostile to material such as the Sonderkommando writings. Their works seek to represent the death factory. The representations they provide are designed to act as evidence of Nazi genocide, to provide proof of it. Gradowski, in particular, seeks to harness the capacity of the written word to conjure images, to prompt imaginings. He wants words to carry the sights, sounds, textures of the processes of the death factory, from inside the event to its geographical and temporal outside. He, like the other authors, seeks to cross these boundaries and communicate the horror. Lanzmann's relation to the Sonderkommando archive is, however, more complex than might be expected. As is made clear by out-takes from the film *Shoah*, he is familiar with the 'Scrolls' and their authors and, seemingly, with Alex's photographs. He refers to Zalman Lewental explicitly during his recording of the testimony of Filip Müller.² We want to conclude by analysing the uses Lanzmann makes of Sonderkommando testimony produced from within the event, as we believe his actions reveal much about the power of these documents, a power he has subsequently sought to disavow.

During their interview, Lanzmann and Müller look through a book of photographs together, and one of these is almost certainly the picture taken by Alex of the bodies that were lying in the courtyard outside Crematorium V. The photograph, as becomes clear from the conversation that develops around it, is used as a prompt for Müller's subsequent recollections.

> La: The backyard, that is, how many metres from the crematorium?
> Mü: Oh, that was about 10, 20 metres. Here in the backyard, yes. And there were those five pits. In each pit, you could incinerate 1,200 to 1,400 people in 24 hours. Just imagine, if there are only five…
> La: Those are these…
> Mü: …five pits.
> La: That's this photo.
> Mü: That's the photo we're looking at. That's the backyard of Crematorium V.
> La: Where is the pit?
> Mü: The pit is here, where the smoke is coming out. And these corpses were thrown out of, out of…
> La: …the gas chambers.
> Mü: The gas chambers. And before that, the women had their hair shorn.[3]

In this exchange, Lanzmann ostensibly uses the photograph to solicit information, to clarify details regarding location and process. He is also, however, preparing Müller and, perhaps, himself for the telling of the former Sonderkommando member's story. The photograph is an aide-memoire and a spur to (re-)imagining.

Square brackets have been placed round one of the sentences in the copy of transcript in the United States Holocaust Memorial Museum (USHMM): 'these corpses were thrown out of'. In most other cases where square brackets like this appear, these words have been spliced into the voice-over track.[4] This suggests that the editor, Ziva Postec, selected it as potentially part of some voice-over. It does not appear to have been used, but the bodies in the photograph ('these corpses') might, then, have been referred to by the film. Ultimately it was left out, yet for a time its inclusion was contemplated. Lanzmann's relationship to this image is therefore by no means as absolute or as straightforward as the articles in *Les Temps modernes* condemning Didi-Huberman's engagement with it might suggest. The Sonderkommando photographs have a ghostly presence within *Shoah*, certainly not quite there, but not quite excluded either.

The 'Scrolls of Auschwitz' were also present in footage shot for the film, although their once being there is obviously not well known.

Philippe Mesnard has recently stated that the written testimonies of the Sonderkommando have never been accorded importance by Lanzmann and 'never entered into his project'.[5] Again in the interviews with Müller, however, Lanzmann asks at one point about the kind of person Zalman Lewental was.[6] In his ensuing description of Lewental, Müller emphasises how the young man felt the Sonderkommando (and, perhaps, by extension all Jews at Auschwitz) had been abandoned by the world, by humanity. This sense of rejection was nevertheless coupled with a desire to reach out to the world outside Auschwitz. Immediately after detailing the sense of isolation Lewental experienced, Müller recounts the man's sense of having a duty to document the atrocities he was immersed within. Writing is therefore perceived as a means of reconnecting with humanity, as an affirmation of humanity in inhuman circumstances. As the preceding chapters have sought to demonstrate, writing was conceived of as a powerful means to resist the dehumanising efforts of the Nazis.

Lanzmann's invitation to recall Lewental in the present is a simultaneous prompt for Müller to return to Auschwitz. The act of remembrance is indexed through Müller's shifting posture as he talks to Lanzmann.[7] After relating Lewental's sense of obligation to bear witness, Müller turns away from Lanzmann, breaks eye contact with him, and looks in the direction of the camera. He continues: 'As I've already said, he was very conscientious'. These words are not directed at Lanzmann. They are spoken at the same time as Müller seemingly strives to visualise Lewental again, to imagine him, someone he may only have known slightly. In this moment the camera is positioned in the location where Müller is, on the face of it, looking for Birkenau. His eyes are elsewhere, looking towards the camera yet not into it. His address at this point is to a companion's memory rather than to his interviewer. The moment is one of radical disconnection. Lanzmann is not invited 'in' to this recollection, and nor are the audience.

Müller then goes on to discuss the pressures Lewental was under as he wrote, providing an explanation for the perceived concision of his account, and also detailing how the descriptions written by members of the Sonderkommando were buried and preserved. Müller makes a brief but noteworthy hand gesture during his discussion of the documents, bringing both hands together and then, fingers fanned, pulling his hands apart. His palms are facing the camera. The visible utterance seems designed to reinforce the scale of the efforts at writing. The descriptions of the death factory that were produced are, in Müller's mind, considerable. His gesture covers a lot of screen space. It is encompassing. His eyes are again not directed at Lanzmann as he speaks and gestures. They look to the past. It is therefore possible to read the gesture as indicating the writings of the Sonderkommando cover Birkenau, form an overview. The gesture represents the representative capacity of the writings.

After establishing who Lewental was and how the documents survived, Müller offers to read an extract aloud. The extract is the story of 'The 600 Boys', by Langfus, an account of the murder of a group of adolescents. The boys, who appear in rude health despite their ragged clothes, realise early on that they are about to die, and therefore panic and try to run away. The camera pulls back as Müller prepares to read the tale. He is given space, the space of his imagined audience. The camera operator envisions how Müller will be observed later when the documentary is screened. The move to a more distant viewing position indicates that an emotional response is not expected at this instant. Lanzmann and his crew liked to use close-ups as emotional cues.[8] Proximity often signals a moment of heightened feeling in *Shoah*, as is the case with the famed interview with Abraham Bomba staged in a barber's shop.

Lanzmann claims that with 'Filip Müller I did not stage anything, it was impossible'; but the reading of Langfus's text is a form of staging, not just the use of documents including the photograph to prompt memory and discussion which occurs in an earlier reel, but here the calling upon him to give a kind of performance.[9] Müller has clearly agreed with Lanzmann beforehand that he will read the story: it lies ready to hand next to him (in what seems to be a well-worn edition of the *Hefte von Auschwitz*, Special Edition 1), and glances towards it several times while they are discussing Lewental.

He begins to read with the kind of intonation one might give to a children's story, making its introductory phrase especially seem like a 'once upon a time'. He breaks off at several points to expand and explain with some enthusiasm, although not always sure what he wants to say. 'Here is a piece of evidence!' he proclaims, only to be able to do no more than repeat what the text says. Perhaps these instances hint of a reluctance to read the story, signalling attempts at maintaining the relationship with Lanzmann (who answers one question minimally '*Ja, genau*') in order to avoid becoming absorbed in the text in front of him. In the middle of the performance, he ends with a meaningless sentence: 'The Kommandoführer and his helpers'. The falling intonation shows he has decided to conclude here rather than going on to the verb '*schlugen*' – 'beat'. Instead, he tries to sum up what he has read: 'Yes, *Wehlage* [lit. a situation of suffering; his mispronunciation or misreading of *Wehklage*: "lamentation"], it ends with that. That was the story…'

Lanzmann, sensing, perhaps, in the tension between the performance and the hesitations the possibility of a moment of 'incarnation', gently, quietly (he seems to want the logic of the reading to play itself out without an intrusive presence from him) insists that he carry on ('*Weiter, weiter*').[10] Müller launches back into the story, stumbling occasionally as he reads out parts, and with tears showing in his eyes, but only at one point does the flow of his reading stop for a moment, as he finds it difficult to read about one boy offering to do the hardest work if his life is spared. With a handful of sentences to go, the reel runs out; once it is replaced Müller has to reread one sentence before going on to the final three. Finally he is able to sum it up: 'That is the story of the 600 children'. He has managed to reach the end and remain in control. The break in the reel may have helped.

It seems clear to us why Lanzmann chose not to include this part in the film. Aside from the possible problems with sound recording, the moment of incarnation does not quite take place and Müller's performing self is never fully punctured. The moment that was included, where Müller, describing his emotional reaction to the members of the family camp singing the Czech national anthem and *HaTikvah*, breaks down and asks Lanzmann to stop, shows him reaching something more unspeakable (although, in the next reel, he is able to retell exactly the same moment in a decidedly flatter fashion). It also resonates with other elements of the film in much clearer ways: reacting to song, to the voices of women, and also with Müller actually entering the gas chamber in order to die with them. Many of these elements resound with Abraham Bomba's point of unspeakability. It also, like Glazar in Treblinka, like Vrba also in Auschwitz, describes the need to resist and to bear witness.

Nonetheless, it also seems clear that Lanzmann saw possibilities here. It is, he says himself, a 'terrible' story, whose emotional effects are difficult to deal with, as Müller's demeanour demonstrates. It describes what happens to children, and this concern is what prompts the two suicides referred to in the film, of Fredy Hirsch in the Czech family camp, and of Adam Czerniaków in the Warsaw Ghetto. For Müller particularly, it recalls times of powerless witnessing by members of the Sonderkommando, and the impossibility, at points, of having fellowship with the victims. One might expect the story to cause him a great deal of emotional pain – indeed, Langfus seems to have selected it as an incident that would have a powerful effect on the reader. The way it is written too, forcefully rhetorical even if occasionally clumsily phrased, is quite suited to Müller's own hypnotic tones ('the voice of bronze', as Lanzmann called it).[11] For Lanzmann, therefore, there was a strong possibility that manuscripts written by the Sonderkommando would enable the kind of moments that he was interested in.

However, there are also features of this scene which have the potential not merely of not fitting into the schema of the film that Lanzmann (and Ziva Postec) later worked out, but of calling it into question, or at least questioning what it is that Lanzmann now claims the film is doing. Müller's stumbles are not simply some index of psychological difficulty. They are caused by the way that the text has been edited and laid out on the page. Each page of the original document is treated as a separate block of text, regardless of whether a sentence runs on from one manuscript page to another. Müller stops at the end of the first manuscript page surely because it is printed as a self-contained block of text. This layout of the text is the result of the history of what happened to the manuscript. Since these pages are fairly well preserved, the fact that it is printed in separate sections like this can only be because the Auschwitz museum treated it as part of Zalman Lewental's manuscript, which was much more extensively damaged, and whose order was deemed irrecoverable.

And yet it is hard to think that his stopping there has nothing to do with the fact that the next word is '*schlugen*' (hit). There seems, therefore, to be a psychic dimension to this moment. Lanzmann has reminded him that it is a story of terrible violence. The book looks well worn. If it is his own copy, then he has clearly read this story before. He picks up very quickly on Lanzmann's instruction to keep going, and is able to read the full sentence immediately. There is a kind of interplay between the material resistance of this text and of the psychological reluctance he has to discuss this violence. The halting is not a straightforward moment of incarnation; it does not give us access to Birkenau as missed experience (of trauma as Cathy Caruth conceives of it) or the reliving of history (as Lanzmann thinks of the witness turned actor).[12] The 'narrative voice' is interrupted, rendered unsettled and marked by the affective and material histories contained in the pages that are being read. In this sense, Müller's reading attests to historical trauma. It is a kind of historiography, yet not one produced consciously. It therefore resonates with, yet differs from, the kind of empathically unsettled history Dominick LaCapra calls for.[13]

It is also, as we have said, a performance, which is at points punctured. Just as the puncturing is more than a way of breaking through to the truth, the performance is not just a means of controlling the feelings raised by this episode. Performing this story is a kind of reanimation of the writer: not at the moment of witnessing this incident, but at the moment of writing it down. Eerily – even more eerily than at other points when he speaks in the film – Müller is reliving a moment of creativity that took place within the crematorium. He shows that Langfus was able to interpret and shape what he saw. He also shows that this shaping can have a powerful and painful effect on its readers, even if they are only secondary witnesses. Although there was clearly some commonality between the experiences of Müller and the author of this piece, it is not something he lived through – 'I don't remember this episode', he says. And yet it clearly seems to be some of the hardest material for him to perform.

These engagements with Langfus and with the photographs by Alex, although they did not make the final cut, certainly challenge Lanzmann's avowed antipathy to the archive. During the making of *Shoah* he showed no qualms in exploiting the capacities of words and images to clarify and to cause and convey emotion. In these out-takes it is obvious that Lanzmann appreciates the potential for these archival sources to nurture moments of incarnation (if not to actually incarnate the horrors they refer to or, perhaps, embody). As he is a major critic of archival materials and a powerful advocate of the Holocaust's non-representability, Lanzmann's actions here are particularly revealing. They show that despite his subsequent public stance, there was a period of time when the director recognised the testimonial power of the manuscripts in particular. It is this power that we have striven to convey aspects of in this book.

Gillian Rose suggested that to argue that the Holocaust is unrepresentable is '*to mystify something we dare not understand*, because we fear that it may be all too understandable, all too continuous with what we are – human, all too human'.[14] Lanzmann's circle of flame forms such an act of mystification. His conduct during the making of *Shoah*, however, demonstrates that something of the humanity of the Sonderkommando touched him, crossing the boundary from inside to outside. Their writings are not, as we hope we have demonstrated, simply sources of information (although they are this), but are also archives of feelings, memorials to fellows and loved ones, acts of resistance against the odds, assertions of self. For these purposes and more, they continue to merit our careful and sustained attention.

Notes

1. Claude Lanzmann, 'From the Holocaust to "Holocaust"', in *Claude Lanzmann's 'Shoah': Key Essays*, ed. Stuart Liebman (Oxford: Oxford University Press, 2007), 30.
2. Selected clips from the out-takes can be streamed, and PDFs of the original German transcipt and an English translation can be downloaded from: <http://www.ushmm.org/online/film/display/detail.php?file_num=4745>.
3. Translation of transcript, 51; German transcript, 51.
4. For example, pages 3, 33 and 87 of the German transcript. The words in these passages were spliced together to form the voice-over for First Era (Part 1) 2:25:12–2:26:01 (DVD1, ch. 56). See Postec's account of her working process at <http://www.zivapostec.com/Shoah.php>.

5. Philippe Mesnard, 'Le fiction et ses dispositifs à l'épreuve des Sonderkommandos', in *La Shoah: Théatre et cinéma aux limites de la représentation*, ed. Alain Kleinberger and Philippe Mesnard (Paris: Éditions Kimé, 2013), 258.
6. This part is recorded on Camera Rolls 17 and 18. German transcript 77–82; Translation of transcript, 77–82.
7. For a general discussion of the importance of gesture in *Shoah*, see Nicholas Chare, 'Gesture in *Shoah*', *Journal for Cultural Research* 19(1) (2015), 30–42.
8. Aaron Kerner, *Film and the Holocaust: New Perspectives on Dramas, Documentaries and Experimental Films* (New York: Continuum, 2011), 209.
9. Marc Chevrie and Hervé Le Roux, 'Site and Speech: An Interview with Claude Lanzmann about *Shoah*', in *Claude Lanzmann's 'Shoah': Key Essays*, 45.
10. Incarnation, for Lanzmann, signals a moment when the past is relived rather than conceived of as distant and different from the present. See Dominick LaCapra, *History and Memory after Auschwitz* (Ithaca, NY: Cornell University Press, 1998), 104.
11. Claude Lanzmann, *The Patagonian Hare*, trans. Frank Wynne (London: Atlantic, 2013), 422.
12. The witnesses must 'act' if they are to incarnate. See Chevrie and Le Roux, 'Site and Speech', 45. Cathy Caruth, *Unclaimed Experience: Trauma, Narrative and History* (Baltimore, MD: Johns Hopkins, 1996).
13. Dominick LaCapra, *Writing History, Writing Trauma* (Baltimore, MD: Johns Hopkins University Press, 2001), 108–9.
14. Gillian Rose, *Mourning Becomes the Law: Philosophy and Representation* (Cambridge: Cambridge University Press, 1996), 43.

Bibliography

Aaron, Frieda W. *Bearing the Unbearable: Yiddish and Polish Poetry of the Ghettos and Concentration Camps*. Albany, NY: SUNY Press, 1990.
Abramovitsh, S.Y. (Mendele Moykher Sforim). *Fishke der Krumer*. In *Ale shriftn fun Mendele Moykher Sforim*, vol. 1. New York: Hebrew Publishing Company, n.d.
Abrams, M.H. *The Mirror and the Lamp: Romantic Theory and the Critical Tradition*. Oxford: Oxford University Press, 1971.
Agamben, Giorgio. *Remnants of Auschwitz: The Witness and the Archive*. Trans. Daniel Heller-Roazen. New York: Zone, 1999.
Ankersmit, Frank. *Sublime Historical Experience*. Stanford, CA: Stanford University Press, 2005.
———. *Meaning, Truth, and Reference in Historical Representation*. Ithaca, NY: Cornell University Press, 2012.
Asch, Sholem. *Geklibene verk* vol. 1: *Dos shtetl*. New York: Ykuf Ferlag, 1947.
Baer, Ulrich. *Spectral Evidence: The Photography of Trauma*. Cambridge, MA: MIT Press, 2002.
Ball, Karyn. *Disciplining the Holocaust*. New York: SUNY, 2008.
Balloffet, Nelly. *Preservation and Conservation for Libraries and Archives*. Chicago: American Library Association, 2005.
Bar-Itzhak, Haya. 'Women in the Holocaust: The Story of a Jewish Woman Who Killed a Nazi in a Concentration Camp: A Folkloristic Perspective'. *Fabula* 50(1–2) (2009): 67–77.
Barthes, Roland. *Camera Lucida*. Trans. Richard Howard. London: Vintage, 1993.
Bartosik, Igor. *Bunt Sonderkommando: 7 października 1944 roku*. Oświęcim: Państwowe Muzeum Auschwitz-Birkenau, 2014.
Bennett, Jane. *Vibrant Matter: A Political Ecology of Things*. Durham, NC: Duke University Press, 2010.
Bennett, Jill. *Empathic Vision: Affect, Trauma, and Contemporary Art*. Stanford, CA: Stanford University Press, 2005.
———. *Practical Aesthetics: Events, Affects and Art after 09/11*. London: I.B. Tauris, 2012.
Bensoussan, Georges, Philippe Mesnard and Carlo Saletti (eds). *Des voix sous la cendre: Manuscrits des Sonderkommandos d'Auschwitz-Birkenau*. Paris: Calmann Lévy/Mémorial de la Shoah, 2005.
Bernshteyn, Ignats. *Yidishe shprikhverter*. New York: Alveltlekhe Yiddisher Kultur-Kongres, 1983.
Bezwińska, Jadwiga, and Danuta Czech (eds). 'Wstęp edytorski'. In *Wśród koszmarnej zbrodni: Notatki więźniów z Sonderkommando odnalezione w Oświęcimiu*, 1st edn., 5–16. Oświęcim: Wydawnictwo Państwowego Muzeum w Oświęcimiu, 1971.
——— (eds). *Wśród koszmarnej zbrodni: Notatki więźnów z Sonderkommando odnalezione w Oświęcimiu*. Oświecim: Wydawnictwo Państwowego Muzeum w Oświęcimiu, 1971.

―――― (eds). *Wśród koszmarnej zbrodni: Notatki więźnów Sonderkommando*. 2nd edn. Oświęcim: Wydawnictwo Państwowego Muzeum w Oświęcimiu, 1973.

―――― (eds). *Amidst a Nightmare of Crime: Manuscripts of Members of Sonderkommando*. Trans. Krystyna Michalik. Oświęcim: State Museum at Oświęcim, 1973.

Bloxham, Donald. *Genocide on Trial: War Crimes Trials and the Formation of Holocaust History and Memory*. Oxford: Oxford University Press, 2001.

Blumental, Nachman. *Shmuesn vegn der yidisher literatur unter der daytsher okupatsye*. Buenos Aires: Tsentral Farband far Poylishe Yidn in Argentine, 1966.

Bowman, Steven. 'Introduction: The Greeks in Auschwitz'. In Rebecca Fromer, *The Holocaust Odyssey of Daniel Bennahmias*, xi–xxv. Tuscaloosa: University of Alabama Press, 1993.

――――. *The Agony of Greek Jews, 1940–1945*. Stanford, CA: Stanford University Press, 2009.

Boyarin, Daniel. *Unheroic Conduct: The Rise of Heterosexuality and the Invention of the Jewish Man*. Berkeley and Los Angeles: University of California Press, 1997.

Braham, Randolph L. 'Hungarian Jews'. In *Anatomy of the Auschwitz Death Camp*, ed. Yisrael Gutman and Michael Berenbaum, 456–68. Bloomington: Indiana University Press, 1994.

Brandi, Cesare. *Theory of Restoration*, ed. Giuseppe Basile, trans. Cynthia Rockwell. Florence: Nardini Editore, 2005. Translation of *Teoria del restauro*, 1977.

Bronfen, Elisabeth. *Over her Dead Body: Death, Femininity and the Aesthetic*. Manchester: Manchester University Press, 1992.

Brown, Adam. *Judging 'Privileged' Jews: Holocaust Ethics, Representation, and the 'Grey Zone'*. New York: Berghahn Books, 2013.

Butler, Judith. *Bodies that Matter: On the Discursive Limits of 'Sex'*. New York: Routledge, 1993.

――――. *Precarious Life: The Powers of Mourning and Violence*. London: Verso, 2004.

――――. *Parting Ways: Jewishness and the Critique of Zionism*. New York: Columbia University Press, 2012.

Candlin, Fiona. *Art, Museums and Touch*. Manchester: Manchester University Press, 2010.

Čapková, Kateřina. 'Das Zeugnis von Salmen Gradowski'. *Theresienstädter Studien und Dokumente* (1999): 107.

Caruth, Cathy. *Unclaimed Experience: Trauma, Narrative, and History*. Baltimore, MD: Johns Hopkins University Press, 1996.

Chare, Nicholas. 'The Gap in Context: Giorgio Agamben's *Remnants of Auschwitz*'. *Cultural Critique* 64 (Fall 2006): 40–68.

――――. *Auschwitz and Afterimages: Abjection, Witnessing and Representation*. London: I.B. Tauris, 2011.

――――. 'On the Problem of Empathy: Attending to Gaps in the Scrolls of Auschwitz'. In *Representing Auschwitz: At the Margins of Testimony*, ed. Nicholas Chare and Dominic Williams, 33–57. Basingstoke: Palgrave Macmillan, 2013.

――――. 'Symbol Re-formation: Concentrationary Memory in Charlotte Delbo's *Auschwitz and After*'. In *Concentrationary Memories: Totalitarian Terror and Cultural Resistance*, ed. Griselda Pollock and Max Silverman, 103–13. London: I.B. Tauris, 2013.

――――. 'Gesture in *Shoah*'. *Journal for Cultural Research* 19(1) (2015): 30–42.

Chatwood, Kirsty. 'Schillinger and the Dancer: Representing Agency and Sexual Violence in Holocaust Testimonies'. In *Sexual Violence against Jewish Women during the Holocaust*, ed. Sonia Hedgepeth and Rochelle G. Saidel, 61–74. Hanover, MA, and London: University Press of New England, 2010.

Chéroux, Clément (ed.). *Mémoires des camps: photographies des camps de concentration et d'extermination Nazis 1933–1999*. Paris: Marval, 2001.
Chevrie, Marc, and Hervé Le Roux, 'Site and Speech: An Interview with Claude Lanzmann about *Shoah*'. In *Claude Lanzmann's 'Shoah': Key Essays*, ed. Stuart Liebman, 37–45. Oxford: Oxford University Press, 2007.
Ciechanower, Mordechai. *Der Dachdecker von Auschwitz-Birkenau*. Trans. Christina Mulolli. Berlin: Metropol Verlag, 2007. Trans. of *Mirakhok kokhav minatsnats*. Tel Aviv: Yad Vashem, 2005.
Cobb, Peter. 'Forensic Science'. In *Crime Scene to Court: The Essentials of Forensic Science*, ed. Peter White, 1–14. Cambridge: Royal Society of Chemistry, 1998.
Cohen, Arthur A. *The Tremendum: A Theological Interpretation of the Holocaust*. New York: Continuum, 1993.
Cohen, Elie A. *Human Behaviour in the Concentration Camp*. London: Free Association, 1988.
Cohen, Leon. *From Greece to Birkenau: The Crematoria Workers' Uprising*. Trans. Jose-Maurice Gormezano. Tel Aviv: Salonika Jewry Research Centre, 1996.
Cohen, Nathan. 'Diaries of the "Sonderkommandos" in Auschwitz: Coping with Fate and Reality'. *Yad Vashem Studies* 20 (1990): 273–312.
———. 'Diaries of the Sonderkommando'. In *Anatomy of the Auschwitz Death Camp*, ed. Yisrael Gutman and Michael Berenbaum, 522–34. Bloomington: Indiana University Press, 1994.
Cohen, Sande. *History Out of Joint: Essays on the Use and Abuse of History*. Baltimore, MD: Johns Hopkins University Press, 2006.
Colebrook, Claire. *Irony*. London: Routledge, 2004.
Confino, Alon. *Foundational Pasts: The Holocaust as Historical Understanding*. Cambridge: Cambridge University Press, 2012.
Connell, R.W. *Masculinities*. 2nd edn. Cambridge: Polity, 2005.
Cubitt, Sean. 'The Sound of Sunlight'. *Screen* 51(2) (2010): 118–28.
Culler, Jonathan. 'Apostrophe'. *Diacritics* 7(4) (Winter 1977): 59–69.
Czech, Danuta. 'Kalendarium der Ereignisse im Konzentrationslager Auschwitz-Birkenau'. *Hefte von Auschwitz* 3 (1960): 47–110.
———. *Auschwitz Chronicle*. Trans. Barbara Harshav, Martha Humphreys and Stephen Shearier. New York: Henry Holt, 1990.
Dafni, Reuven, and Yehudit Kleinman (eds). *Final Letters: From the Yad Vashem Archive*. London: Weidenfeld and Nicholson, 1991.
Dan, Joseph. 'Hasidism: Teachings and Literature'. In *The YIVO Encyclopedia of Jews in Eastern Europe*, Vol. 1, 670–73. New Haven, CT, and London: Yale University Press, 2008.
Daybell, James. *The Material Letter in Early Modern England: Manuscript Letters and the Culture and Practices of Letter-Writing, 1512–1635*. Basingstoke: Palgrave Macmillan, 2012.
Decker, William Merrill. *Epistolary Practices: Letter Writing in America before Telecommunications*. Chapel Hill: University of North Carolina Press, 1998.
Didi-Huberman, Georges. 'Images malgré tout'. In *Mémoire des camps: Photographies des camps de concentration et d'extermination nazis (1933–1999)*, ed. Clément Chéroux, 219–41. Paris: Marval, 2001.
———. *Images malgré tout*. Paris: Éditions de minuit, 2003.
———. *Images in Spite of All*. Trans. Shane B. Lillis. Chicago: University of Chicago Press, 2008.

———. *Écorces*. Paris: Éditions de Minuit, 2011.
———. *Blancs soucis*. Paris: Éditions de Minuit, 2013.
Doane, Mary Ann. 'Indexicality: Trace and Sign: Introduction'. *Differences* 18(1) (2007): 1–6.
Dobroszycki, Lucjan. 'Introduction'. *The Chronicle of the Łódź Ghetto 1941–1944*, ed. Dobroszycki. Trans. Richard Lourie, Joachim Neugroschel et al. ix–lxviii. New Haven, CT and London: Yale University Press, 1984.
Dworkin, Craig. *Reading the Illegible*. Evanston, IL: Northwestern University Press, 2003.
Earle, Rebecca. 'Introduction: Letters, Writers and the Historian'. In *Epistolary Selves: Letters and Letter-Writers, 1600–1945*, ed. Rebecca Earle, 1–12. Aldershot: Ashgate, 1999.
Einhorn, Dovid. *Shtile gezangen*. Warsaw: Ferlag Progres, 1910.
Eliach, Yaffa. *Hasidic Tales of the Holocaust*. New York: Oxford University Press, 1982.
Felman, Shoshana, and Dori Laub. *Testimony: Crises of Witnessing in Literature, Psychoanalysis, and History*. New York: Routledge, 1992.
Forster, E.M. *Aspects of the Novel*. London: Penguin, 1990.
Forsyth, Donelson R. *Group Dynamics*. 6th edn. Belmont, CA: Wadsworth Publishing, 2013.
Foster, Susan Leigh. *Choreographing Empathy: Kinesthesia in Performance*. London: Routledge, 2011.
Fox, Chaim Leib. *Lodzsh shel Mayle: Dos Yidishe gaystike un derhoybene Lodzsh (100 yor yidishe un oykh hebreishe literatur un kultur in Lodzsh un in di arumike shtet un shtetlekh)*. Tel Aviv: I.L. Peretz, 1972.
Frank, Salomon. *Togbukh fun lodzher geto*. Buenos Aires: Tsentral farband fun poylishe yidn in Argentine, 1958.
Frankl, Viktor E. *Man's Search for Meaning: An Introduction to Logotherapy*. 3rd edn. New York: Touchstone, 1984.
Freadman, Anne. *The Machinery of Talk: Charles Peirce and the Sign Hypothesis*. Stanford, CA: Stanford University Press, 2004.
Friedländer, Saul. *The Years of Extermination: Nazi Germany and the Jews, 1939–1945*. London: Phoenix, 2008.
Friedler, Eric, Barbara Siebert and Andreas Kilian. *Zeugen aus der Todeszone: Das Jüdische Sonderkommando in Auschwitz*. Munich: Deutsche Taschenbuch Verlag, 2005.
Fromer, Rebecca Camhi. *The Holocaust Odyssey of Daniel Bennahmias, Sonderkommando*. Tuscaloosa: University of Alabama Press, 1993.
Fulbrook, Mary. *A Small Town near Auschwitz: Ordinary Nazis and the Holocaust*. Oxford: Oxford University Press, 2012.
Gallop, Angela, and Russell Stockdale. 'Trace and Contact Evidence'. In *Crime Scene to Court: The Essentials of Forensic Science*, ed. Peter White, 47–72. Cambridge: Royal Society of Chemistry, 1998.
Garbarini, Alexandra. *Numbered Days: Diaries and the Holocaust*. New Haven, CT: Yale University Press, 2006.
Garrett, Leah. *Journeys beyond the Pale: Yiddish Travel Writing in the Modern World*. Madison: University of Wisconsin Press, 2003.
Gigliotti, Simone. *The Train Journey: Transit, Captivity and Witnessing in the Holocaust*. New York: Berghahn Books, 2009.
Gilbert, Shirli. *Music during the Holocaust: Confronting Life in the Nazi Ghettos and Camps*. Oxford: Clarendon, 2005.

Giles, Audrey. 'The Forensic Examination of Documents'. In *Crime Scene to Court: The Essentials of Forensic Science*, ed. Peter White, 105–32. Cambridge: Royal Society of Chemistry, 1998.
Gilroy, Amanda, and W.M. Verhoeven, 'Introduction'. In *Epistolary Histories: Letters, Fiction, Culture*, ed. Amanda Gilroy and W.M. Verhoeven, 1–25. Charlottesville: University of Virginia Press, 2000.
Glazar, Richard. *Die Falle mit dem grünen Zaun: Überleben in Treblinka*. Frankfurt: Fischer Taschenbuch Verlag, 1992.
———. *Trap with a Green Fence: Survival in Treblinka*. Trans. Roslyn Theobald. Evanston, IL: Northwestern University Press, 1995.
Główna Komisja Badania Zbrodni Hitlerowskich w Polsce. *Obozy hitlerowskie na ziemiach polskich 1939–1945: Informator encyklopedyczny*. Warsaw: Państwowe Wydawnictwo Naukowe, 1979.
Głuchowski, Leszek, and Antony Polonsky (eds). *1968: Forty Years After, POLIN: Studies in Polish Jewry* 21 (2008).
Goethe, Johann Wolfgang von. 'An den Mond'. In *Sämtliche Werke*, ed. K. Richter, vol. 2.1, 35–36. Munich and Vienna: Carl Hanser Verlag, 1987.
Grabowski, Jan. 'The Holocaust in Northern Mazovia (Poland) in the Light of the Archive of the Ciechanów Gestapo'. *Holocaust and Genocide Studies* 18(4) (Winter 2004): 460–76.
Gradowski, Zalman. 'Fartseykhenungen'. In Ber Mark, *Megiles Oyshvits*, 290–352. Tel Aviv: Yisroel Bukh, 1977.
———. *In harts fun gehenem*. Jerusalem: Wolnerman, n.d. [c.1977].
———. 'The Czech Transport: A Chronicle of the Auschwitz Sonderkommando'. Trans. Robert Wolf. In *The Literature of Destruction: Jewish Responses to Catastrophe*, ed. David Roskies, 548–64. Philadelphia: Jewish Publication Society, 1989.
———. *Au cœur de l'enfer: Témoignage d'un Sonderkommando d'Auschwitz, 1944*. Trans. Batia Baum. Paris: Kimé, 2001.
———. *Au cœur de l'enfer: Témoignage d'un Sonderkommando d'Auschwitz, 1944*. Trans. Batia Baum. Paris: Tallandier, 2009.
———. *V serdtsevine Ada: Zapiski, naidennie v peple vozle pechei Osventsima*. Trans. Aleksandra Polian. Moscow: Gamma Press, 2011.
Greenberg, Uri Zvi. *Farnakhtengold*. Warsaw: Farlag 'Di Tsayt', 1921.
Greif, Gideon. *We Wept without Tears: Testimonies of the Jewish Sonderkommando in Auschwitz*. Trans. Naftali Greenwood. New Haven, CT: Yale University Press, 2005.
———. 'Between Sanity and Insanity: Spheres of Everyday Life in the Auschwitz-Birkenau *Sonderkommando*'. In *Gray Zones: Ambiguity and Compromise in the Holocaust and its Aftermath*, ed. Jonathan Petropoulos and John K. Roth, 37–59. New York: Berghahn Books, 2005.
Gross, Jan Tomasz, and Irena Grudzińska Gross. *Golden Harvest: Events on the Margin of the Holocaust*. Oxford: Oxford University Press, 2012.
Grynberg, Michał. *Żydzi w rejencji ciechanowskiej*. Warsaw: Państwowe Wydawnictwo Naukowe, 1984.
Gubar, Susan. *Poetry after Auschwitz: Remembering What One Never Knew*. Bloomington and Indianapolis: Indiana University Press, 2003.
Guyer, Sara. *Romanticism after Auschwitz*. Stanford, CA: Stanford University Press, 2007.
Halivni, Tzipora Hager. 'The Birkenau Revolt: Poles Prevent a Timely Insurrection'. *Jewish Social Studies* 41(2) (Spring 1979): 123–54.

Hartley, Jenny. '"Letters are *Everything* these Days": Mothers and Letters in the Second World War'. In *Epistolary Selves: Letters and Letter-Writers, 1600–1945*, ed. Rebecca Earle, 183–95. Aldershot: Ashgate, 1999.
Hartman, Geoffrey. 'The Struggle against the Inauthentic'. *parallax* 10(1) (2004): 72–77.
Hedrick Jr, Charles. *History and Silence: Purge and Rehabilitation of Memory in Late Antiquity*. Austin: University of Texas Press, 2000.
Heller, Daniel K. *The Rise of the Zionist Right: Polish Jews and the Betar Youth Movement, 1922–1935*. Ph.D. diss., University of Stanford, CA, 2012.
Herman, Chaim. 'The Manuscript of Chaim Herman'. In *Amidst a Nightmare of Crime: Manuscripts of Members of Sonderkommando*, ed. Jadwiga Bezwińska and Danuta Czech. Trans. Krystyna Michalik, 179–90. Oświęcim: State Museum at Oświęcim, 1973.
Herman, Judith. *Trauma and Recovery: From Domestic Abuse to Political Terror*. London: Pandora, 1994.
Hirsch, Marianne. 'The Generation of Postmemory'. *Poetics Today* 29(1) (2008): 103–28.
Hoffman, Eva. *Time*. London: Profile, 2009.
Höß, Rudolf. *Kommandant in Auschwitz: Autobiographische Aufzeichnungen*, ed. Martin Broszat. Munich: Deutsche Taschenbuch Verlag, 2013.
Huener, Jonathan. *Auschwitz, Poland, and the Politics of Commemoration, 1945– 1979*. Athens: Ohio University Press, 2003.
Imber, Naftali. *Vos ikh zing un zog*. Lviv: n. pub., 1909.
Jockusch, Laura. *Collect and Record!: Jewish Holocaust Documentation in Early Postwar Europe*. Oxford: Oxford University Press, 2012.
Kant, Immanuel. *Critique of Judgment*. Trans. Werner Pluhar. Indianapolis: Hackett, 1987.
Kaplan, Eran. *The Jewish Radical Right: Revisionist Zionism and its Ideological Legacy*. Madison: University of Wisconsin Press, 2005.
Kárný, Miroslav. 'The Vrba and Wetzler Report'. In *Anatomy of the Auschwitz Death Camp*, ed. Yisrael Gutman and Michael Berenbaum, 553–68. Bloomington: Indiana University Press, 1994.
———. 'Fragen zum 8. März 1944', *Theresienstädter Studien und Dokumente* (1999): 9–42.
Karski, Jan. *Story of a Secret State*. Boston, MA: Houghton Mifflin, 1944.
Kassow, Samuel. *Who Will Write Our History?: Rediscovering a Hidden Archive from the Warsaw Ghetto*. London: Penguin, 2007.
Kaumkötter, Jürgen, et al. (eds). *Kunst in Auschwitz/Sztuka w Auschwitz*. Bramsche: Rasch Verlag, 2005.
Keenan, Thomas, and Eyal Weizman. *Mengele's Skull: The Advent of a Forensic Aesthetics*. Frankfurt: Sternberg Press, 2012.
Kerner, Aaron. *Film and the Holocaust: New Perspectives on Dramas, Documentaries and Experimental Films*. New York: Continuum, 2011.
Kirshenblatt-Gimblett, Barbara. 'The Concept and Varieties of Narrative Performance in East European Jewish Culture'. In *Explorations in the Ethnography of Speaking*, 2nd edn, ed. Richard Bauman and Joel Sherzer, 283–310. Cambridge: Cambridge University Press, 1989.
Klibansky, Ben-Tsion. 'Unique Characteristics of the Łomża Yeshiva Students after WWI'. *Landsmen: Quarterly Publication of the Suwalk-Lomza Interest Group for Jewish Genealogists* 19(1–2) (2009): 6–14.
Königseder, Angelika, 'Das Sonderkommando'. In *Der Ort des Terrors: Geschichte der nationalsozialistischen Konzentrationslager*, ed. Wolfgang Benz and Barbara Distel. Vol. 5: *Hinzert, Auschwitz, Neuengamme*, ed. Königseder, 152–53. Munich: Verlag C.H. Beck, 2007.

The Koren Sacks Siddur. Trans. and commentary Jonathan Sacks. Jerusalem: Koren, 2009.

Kozlovsky-Golan, Yvonne. '"Public Property": Sexual Abuse of Women and Girls in Cinematic Memory'. In *Sexual Violence against Jewish Women during the Holocaust*, ed. Sonja M. Hedgepeth and Rochelle G. Saidel, 235–51. Hanover, NH: University Press of New England, 2010.

Kraemer, Jolanta. 'Ciechanów'. In *USHMM Encyclopedia of Camps and Ghettos, 1933–1945*, Vol. II, Part A, vol. ed. Martin Dean, 876. Bloomington: Indiana University Press, 2012.

Krakowski, Shmuel, and Ilya Altman. 'The Testament of the Last Prisoners of the Chelmno Death Camp'. *Yad Vashem Studies* 21 (1991): 105–24.

Kraus, Ota, and Erich Kulka. *The Death Factory: Document on Auschwitz*. Trans. Stephen Jolly. Oxford: Pergamon Press, 1966.

Kremer, S. Lillian. 'Sexual Abuse in Holocaust Literature'. In *Sexual Violence against Jewish Women during the Holocaust*, ed. Sonja M. Hedgepeth and Rochelle G. Saidel, 177–99. Hanover, NH: University Press of New England, 2010.

Krystal, Henry. 'Studies of Concentration-Camp Survivors'. In *Massive Psychic Trauma*, ed. Henry Krystal, 23–46. New York: International Universities Press, 1968.

Kulbak, Moishe. *Shirim*. Vilnius: Farayn fun di Yidish Literatorn un Zhurnalistn in Vilne, 1920.

Kulka, Otto Dov. *Landscapes of the Metropolis of Death: Reflections on Memory and Imagination*. Trans. Ralph Mandel. London: Penguin, 2013.

LaCapra, Dominick. *History and Memory after Auschwitz*. Ithaca, NY: Cornell University Press, 1998.

———. *Writing History, Writing Trauma*. Baltimore, MD: Johns Hopkins University Press, 2001.

———. *History, Literature, Critical Theory*. Ithaca, NY: Cornell University Press, 2013.

Lacan, Jacques. *The Seminars of Jacques Lacan 2: The Ego in Freud's Theory and in the Technique of Psychoanalysis 1954–1955*. Trans. Sylvana Tomaselli. New York: Norton, 1991.

———. *The Seminars of Jacques Lacan 3: The Psychoses*. Trans. Russell Grigg. London: Routledge, 1993.

Lang, Berel. 'The Representation of Limits'. In *Probing the Limits of Representation: Nazism and the 'Final Solution'*, ed. Saul Friedländer, 300–17. Cambridge, MA: Harvard University Press, 1992.

———. *Holocaust Representation: Art within the Limits of History and Ethics*. Baltimore, MD: Johns Hopkins University Press, 2000.

Langbein, Herman. *People in Auschwitz*. Trans. Harry Zohn. Chapel Hill: North Carolina Press, 2004.

Langer, Lawrence. *Holocaust Testimonies: The Ruins of Memory*. New Haven, CT: Yale University Press, 1991.

Langfus, Leyb. (Anon.) 'W otchłani zbrodni'. *Biuletyn Żydowskiego Instytutu Historycznego* 9–10 (1954): 303–9.

———. (Lejb [—]). 'Wysiedlenie'. Trans. Roman Pytel. *Zeszyty Oświęcimskie* 14 (1972): 15–62.

———. 'In groyl fun retsikhe'. In Ber Mark, *Megiles Oyshvits*, 351–61. Tel Aviv: Yisroel-Bukh, 1977.

———. (Lejb [Langfus]). 'Aussiedlung'. Trans. Herta Henschel and Jochen August. In *Inmitten des grauenvollen Verbrechens: Handschriften von Mitgliedern des Sonderkommandos*, ed. Teresa Świebocka, Franciszek Piper and Martin Mayr, 73–129. Oświęcim: Verlag des Staatlichen Auschwitz-Birkenau Museums, 1996.

Lanzmann, Claude. 'Le lieu et la parole'. In *Au sujet de 'Shoah': Le film de Claude Lanzmann*, ed. Michel Deguy, 407–25. Paris: Belin, 1990.

———. 'From the Holocaust to "Holocaust"'. In *Claude Lanzmann's 'Shoah': Key Essays*, ed. Stuart Liebman, 27–36. Oxford: Oxford University Press, 2007.

———. *The Patagonian Hare*. Trans. Frank Wynne. London: Atlantic, 2013.

Laqueur, Renata. *Schreiben im KZ*. Bremen: Donat Verlag, 1991.

Laqueur, Walter. *The History of Zionism*. 3rd edn. London: Tauris Parke, 2003.

Laub, Dori, and Nanette C. Auerhahn. 'Failed Empathy: A Central Theme in the Survivor's Holocaust Experience'. *Psychoanalytic Psychology* 6(4) (1989): 377–400.

Lawson, Tom. *Debates on the Holocaust*. Manchester: Manchester University Press, 2010.

Leivick, H. *Ale Verk*, vol. 1. New York: Posy-Shoulson Press, 1940.

Lengyel, Olga. *Five Chimneys*. Chicago: Ziff-Davis, 1947.

Levi, Primo. *I sommersi e i salvati*. Turin: Einaudi, 1986.

———. *The Drowned and the Saved*. Trans. Raymond Rosenthal. London: Abacus, 1989.

———. 'The Grey Zone'. In *The Drowned and the Saved*. Trans. Raymond Rosenthal. 22–51. London: Abacus, 1989.

———. 'On Obscure Writing'. In *Other People's Trades*, trans. Raymond Rosenthal. 157–63. London: Abacus, 1991.

———. 'Words, Memory, Hope (1984)'. In Levi, *The Voice of Memory: Interview, 1961–1967*, ed. Marco Belpoliti and Robert Gordon, 250–57. New York: The New Press, 2001.

Lewental, Zalman. 'Rękopis Zełmana Lewentala'. In *Szukajcie w popiołach*, ed. Janusz Gumkowski and Adam Rutkowski. Trans. Szymon Datner. 125–30. Łódź: Wydawnictwo Łodzkie, n.d. [1965].

———. 'Pamiętnik członka Sonderkommando Auschwitz II'. Trans. Adam Rutkowski and Adam Wein. *Biuletyn Żydowskiego Instytuta Historycznego* 65–66 (1968): 211–33.

———. (Załmen Lewental). '[Pamiętnik]'. Trans. Roman Pytel. In *Wśród koszmarnej zbrodni: Notatki więźniów z Sonderkommando odnalezione w Oświęcimiu*, ed. Jadwiga Bezwińska and Danuta Czech, 126–71. Oświęcim: Wydawnictwo Państwowego Muzeum w Oświęcimiu, 1971.

———. 'Fartseykhenungen'. In Ber Mark, *Megiles Oyshvits*, 377–421. Tel Aviv: Am Oved, 1977.

———. 'Hesofe tsum Lodzher ksav-yad'. In Ber Mark, *Megiles Oyshvits*, 430–35. Tel Aviv: Am Oved, 1977.

Leys, Ruth. *Trauma: A Genealogy*. Chicago: Chicago University Press, 2000.

Linfield, Susan. *The Cruel Radiance: Photography and Political Violence*. Chicago: University of Chicago Press, 2010.

Lipszyc, Rywka. *The Diary of Rywka Lipszyc*, ed. Alexandra Zapruder. San Francisco, CA: Jewish Family and Children's Services Holocaust Center, 2014.

Liss, Andrea. *Trespassing through Shadows: Memory, Photography and the Holocaust*. Minneapolis: University of Minnesota Press, 1998.

Locard, Edmond. 'The Analysis of Dust Traces: Part 1'. *The American Journal of Police Science* 1(3) (1930): 276–98.

Lodge, David. *Deaf Sentence*. London: Penguin, 2009.

Lustigman, Michael M. *The Kindness of Truth and the Art of Reading Ashes*. New York and Bern: Peter Lang, 1988.

Lyotard, Jean-François. *The Differend: Phrases in Dispute*. Trans. Georges Van Den Abbeele. Minneapolis: University of Minnesota Press, 1988.

———. *Heidegger and 'the jews'*. Minneapolis: University of Minnesota Press, 1990.

Mandel, Naomi. *Against the Unspeakable: Complicity, the Holocaust and Slavery in America*. Charlottesville: University of Virginia Press, 2007.

Marcus, Ruth. 'Lunna-Wola during the Second World War and the Holocaust' <http://kehilalinks.jewishgen.org/lunna/German.html> [accessed 1 March 2014].

Marinkova, Milena. *Michael Ondaatje: Haptic Aesthetics and Micropolitical Writing*. New York: Continuum, 2011.

Mark, Ber. (Bernard Mark) 'O rękopisie Załmena Gradowskiego'. In *Wśród koszmarnej zbrodni: Notatki więźniów z Sonderkommando odnalezione w Oświęcimiu*, ed. Jadwiga Bezwińska and Danuta Czech, 1st edn, 69–72. Oświęcim: Wydawnictwo Państwowego Museum w Oświęcimiu, 1971.

———. *Megiles Oyshvits*. Tel Aviv: Yisroel-Bukh, 1977.

———. *Des voix dans la nuit*. Trans. Esther Fridman, Joseph Fridman and Liliane Princet. Paris: Plon, 1982.

———. *The Scrolls of Auschwitz*. Trans. Sharon Neemani. Tel Aviv: Am Oved, 1985.

———. 'Dziennik (grudzień 1965 – luty 1966)'. Trans. Joanna Nalewajko-Kulikov. *Kwartalnik Historii Żydów* 226(2) (2008): 156–92.

Mark, Esther. 'Dergentsung tsu di yedies vegn dem mekhaber "anonim" un zayne ksavyadn'. In Ber Mark, *Megiles Oyshvits*, 276–82. Tel Aviv: Yisroel-Bukh, 1977.

Matsas, Michael. *The Illusion of Safety: The Story of the Greek Jews during the Second World War*. New York: Athens Printing Company, 1997.

Mesnard, Philippe. 'Ecrire au-dehors de soi'. *Des voix sous la cendre: Manuscrits des Sonderkommandos d'Auschwitz-Birkenau*, ed. Georges Bensoussan, Philippe Mesnard and Carlo Saletti, 215–43. Paris: Calmann-Lévy/Mémorial de la Shoah, 2005.

———. 'Le fiction et ses dispositifs à l'épreuve des Sonderkommandos'. In *La Shoah: Théatre et cinéma aux limites de la représentation*, ed. Alain Kleinberger and Philippe Mesnard, 233–62. Paris: Éditions Kimé, 2013.

Mesnard, Philippe, and Claudine Kahan. *Giorgio Agamben: À l'épreuve d'Auschwitz*. Paris: Éditions Kimé, 2001.

Mickenberg, David, Corinne Granoff and Peter Hayes, (eds). *The Last Expression: Art and Auschwitz*. Evanston, IL: Mary and Leigh Block Museum of Art, Northwestern University, 2003.

Miron, Dan. 'Uri Zvi Grinberg's War Poetry'. In *The Jews of Poland between Two World Wars*, ed. Yisrael Gutman, 368–82. Hanover, NH: University Press of New England, 1989.

———. *A Traveler Disguised: The Rise of Modern Yiddish Fiction in the Nineteenth Century*. Syracuse, NY: Syracuse University Press, 1996.

———. *The Image of the Shtetl and Other Studies of Modern Jewish Literary Imagination*. Syracuse, NY: Syracuse University Press, 2000.

Miron, Guy (ed.). *Yad Vashem Encyclopedia of the Ghettos during the Holocaust*, co-ed. Shlomit Shulhani. 2 vols. Jerusalem: Yad Vashem, 2009.

Moseley, Marcus. *Being for Myself Alone: Origins of Jewish Autobiography*. Stanford, CA: Stanford University Press, 2006.

Mowat, Hannah, and Emma Wilson. 'Reconciling History in Alain Resnais's *L'Année dernière à Marienbad* (1961)'. In *Representing Auschwitz: At the Margins of Testimony*, ed. Nicholas Chare and Dominic Williams, 151–73. Basingstoke: Palgrave Macmillan, 2013.

Müller, Filip. *Sonderbehandlung: Drei Jahre in den Krematorien und Gaskammern von Auschwitz*. Literary collaboration with Helmut Freitag. Munich: Steinhausen, 1979.

———. *Eyewitness Auschwitz: Three Years in the Gas Chambers*. Trans. and ed. Susan Flatauer. Chicago: Ivan R. Dee, 1999.
Mulvey, Laura. *Fetishism and Curiosity*. Bloomington: Indiana University Press, 1996.
Munslow, Alun. *Narrative and History*. Basingstoke: Palgrave, 2007.
———. *A History of History*. Abingdon: Routledge, 2012.
Nader, Andrés. *Traumatic Verses: On Poetry in German from the Concentration Camps, 1933–1945*. Rochester, NY: Camden House, 2007.
Nadjary, Marcel. *Khroniko, 1941–1945*. Thessaloniki: Etz Khaim, 1991.
Nalewajko-Kulikov, Joanna. 'Trzy kolory: szary: Szkic do portretu Bernarda Marka'. *Zagłada Żydów* 4 (2008): 263–84.
———. 'The Last Yiddish Books Printed in Poland: Outline of the Activities of Yidish Bukh Publishing House'. In *Under the Red Banner: Yiddish Culture in the Communist Countries in the Postwar Era*, ed. Elvira Grözinger and Magdalena Ruta, 111–34. Wiesbaden: Harrassowitz, 2008.
Niethammer, Günther. 'Beobachtungen über die Vogelwelt von Auschwitz/Ost-Oberschlesien', *Annalen des Naturhistorischen Museums in Wien* 52 (1942): 164–99.
Nyiszli, Miklós. *Im Jenseits der Menschlichkeit: Ein Gerichtsmediziner in Auschwitz*. Trans. Angelika Bihari. Berlin: Karl Dietz, 2005.
———. *Auschwitz: A Doctor's Eyewitness Report*. Trans. Tibère Kremer and Richard Seaver. London: Penguin, 2012.
Ogle, Robert R. *Crime Scene Investigation and Reconstruction*. Upper Saddle River, NJ: Pearson Prentice Hall, 2004.
Ogólny Żydowski Związek Robotniczy 'Bund' w Polsce. *Geto in Flamen: Zamlbukh*. New York: Amerikaner Representants fun Bund, 1944.
Oleksy, Krystyna. 'Salman Gradowski: Ein Zeuge aus dem Sonderkommando'. *Theresienstädter Studien und Dokumente* (1995): 121–35.
Pagnoux, Elisabeth. 'Reporter photographique à Auschwitz'. *Les Temps modernes* 56 (2001): 84–108.
Patterson, David. *Along the Edge of Annihilation: The Collapse and Recovery of Life in the Holocaust Diary*. Seattle and London: University of Washington Press, 1999.
Peirce, Charles S. 'On a New List of Categories'. *Proceedings of the American Academy of Arts and Sciences* 7 (1868): 287–98.
———. 'On the Algebra of Logic'. *American Journal of Mathematics* 7(2) (1885): 180–96.
———. 'An American Plato: Review of Royce's *Religious Aspect of Philosophy* (1885)'. In *The Essential Peirce: Selected Philosophical Writings Volume 1, 1867–1893*, ed. Nathan Houser and Christian Kloesel, 229–41. Bloomington: Indiana University Press, 1992.
Pentlin, Susan L. 'Testimony from the Ashes: Final Words from Auschwitz-Birkenau Sonderkommando'. In *The Genocidal Mind*, ed. Dennis B. Klein et al., 245–62. St Paul, MN: Paragon House, 2005.
Perlman, Elliot. *The Street Sweeper*. London: Faber, 2012.
Phelan, James. *Reading Characters, Reading Plots*. Chicago and London: University of Chicago Press, 1989.
Piper, Franciszek. '*Sonderkommando* Prisoners: Details of their Living Condition and Work'. In *Auschwitz 1940–1945: Central Issues in the History of the Camp*, 5 vols, ed. Wacław Długoborski and Franciszek Piper. Trans. William Brand. Vol. 3, 180–97. Oswiecim: Auschwitz-Birkenau State Museum, 2000.
Polian, Pavel. 'I v kontse tozhe bylo slovo (vmesto predisloviya)'. In Zalman Gradowski, *V serdtsevine Ada: Zapiski naidennie v peple vozle pechei Osventsima*. Trans. Aleksandra Polian, 12–53. Moscow: Gamma Press, 2011.

———. 'Svidetel', khronist, obvinitel'. Zalman Levental' i yevo teksty', *Ab Imperio* 3 (2012): 229–31.
Pollock, Griselda. *Vision and Difference: Feminism, Femininity and the Histories of Art*. London: Routledge, 1988.
———. *Mary Cassatt: Painter of Modern Life*. London: Thames & Hudson, 1998.
———. 'Art as Transport Station of Trauma? Haunting Objects in the Works of Bracha Ettinger, Sarah Kofman and Chantal Akerman'. In *Representing Auschwitz: At the Margins of Testimony*, ed. Nicholas Chare and Dominic Williams, 194–221. Basingstoke: Palgrave Macmillan, 2013.
Pollock, Griselda, and Max Silverman. 'Introduction. The Politics of Memory: From Concentrationary Memory to Concentrationary Memories'. In *Concentrationary Memories: Totalitarian Terror and Cultural Resistance*, ed. Pollock and Silverman, 1–28. London: I.B. Tauris, 2013.
Południak, Jan. *Sonder: An Interview with Sonderkommando Member Henryk Mandelbaum*. Trans. Witold Zbirohowski-Kościa. Oświęcim: Frap-Books, 2009.
Pressac, Jean-Claude. *Auschwitz: Technique and Operation of the Gas Chamber*. New York: Beate Klarsfeld Foundation, 1989.
Prstojevic, Alexandre. 'L'indicible et la fiction configuratrice'. *Protée*, 37(2) (2009): 33–44.
Pytel, Roman. 'Od tłumacza'. *Zeszyty oświęcimskie* 14 (1972): 11–14.
Rancière, Jacques. *The Emancipated Spectator*. Trans. Gregory Elliott. London: Verso, 2009.
Rees, Laurence. *Auschwitz: The Nazis and the 'Final Solution'*. London: Random House, 2005.
Reichelt, Katrin, and Martin Dean, 'Maków Mazowiecki'. In *USHMM Encyclopedia of Camps and Ghettos, 1933–1945*, Vol. II, Part A, ed. Martin Dean, 15–17. Bloomington: Indiana University Press, 2012.
Rogers, Spencer L. *The Testimony of Teeth: Forensic Aspects of Dentition*. Springfield, IL: Charles C. Thomas, 1988.
Rose, Gillian. *Mourning Becomes the Law: Philosophy and Representation*. Cambridge: Cambridge University Press, 1996.
Rosen, Alan. *The Wonder of their Voices*. Oxford: Oxford University Press, 2010.
———. (ed.). *Literature of the Holocaust*. Cambridge: Cambridge University Press, 2013.
———. 'Introduction'. In *Literature of the Holocaust*, ed. Rosen, 1–11. Cambridge: Cambridge University Press, 2013.
Rosenfeld, Alvin H. *A Double Dying: Reflections on Holocaust Literature*. Bloomington: Indiana University Press, 1980.
Roskies, David. 'The Pogrom Poem and the Literature of Destruction'. *Notre Dame English Journal*, 11(2) (April 1979): 103–7.
———. *Against the Apocalypse*. Cambridge, MA: Harvard University Press, 1984.
———. *The Literature of Destruction: Jewish Responses to Catastrophe*. Philadelphia: Jewish Publication Society, 1989.
———. 'Wartime Victim Writing in Eastern Europe'. In *Literature of the Holocaust*, ed. Alan Rosen, 15–32. Cambridge: Cambridge University Press, 2013.
Rothberg, Michael. *Traumatic Realism: The Demands of Holocaust Representation*. Minneapolis: University of Minnesota Press, 2000.
Rothenberg, Jerome. *Khurbn and Other Poems*. New York: New Directions, 1989.
Rozental, Ben-Tsion. 'Makov shel mayle'. In *Sefer zikaron lekehilat Makov-Mazovyetsk*, 388–402. Tel Aviv: Komitet fun makover landsmanshaftn in Yisroel un Amerike, 1969.
Ryman, Shloime. 'Betar'. In *Yizker-bukh Suvalk*, 405–8.

Sakowicz, Kazimierz. *Ponary Diary 1941–1943: A Bystander's Account of a Mass Murder*. Trans. uncredited. New Haven, CT and London: Yale University Press, 2005.
Saletti, Carlo. 'À propos des manuscrits des membres du *Sonderkommando* de Birkenau'. In *Des voix sous la cendre*, 21–30. Paris: Le Livre de Poche, 2005.
——— (ed.). *La voce dei sommersi: Manoscritti ritrovati di membri del Sonderkommando di Auschwitz*. Venice: Marsilio, 1999.
Schivelbusch, Wolfgang. *The Railway Journey: The Industrialization of Time and Space in the Nineteenth Century*. Trans. uncredited. Leamington Spa, Hamburg and New York: Berg, 1986.
Schlesak, Dieter. *Capesius, der Auschwitzapotheker*. Bonn: Dietz, 2006.
Schneider, Rebecca. *Performing Remains: Art and War in Times of Theatrical Reenactment*. Abingdon: Routledge, 2011.
Schwarz, Jan. *Imagining Lives: Autobiographical Fiction of Yiddish Writers*. Madison: University of Wisconsin Press, 2005.
Scott, Joan W. 'The Evidence of Experience'. *Critical Inquiry* 17(4) (Summer 1991): 794.
Segal, Hanna. *Dream Phantasy and Art*. Hove and New York: Brunner-Routledge, 1991.
Sevillias, Errikos. *Athens – Auschwitz*. Trans. Nikos Stavroulakis. Athens: Lycabettus Press, 1983.
Sfard, Dovid. 'Eynike zikhroynes vegn Zalman Gradowski'. In Gradowski, *In harts fun gehenem*, 6–8. Jerusalem: Wolnerman, n.d. [c.1977].
———. 'Prof. B. Mark'. *Mit zikh un mit andere: Oytobiografishe un literarishe eseyen*, 375–79. Jerusalem: Farlag 'Yerushalayim Almanakh', 1984.
Shallcross, Bożena. *The Holocaust Object in Polish and Polish Jewish Culture*. Bloomington and Indianapolis: Indiana University Press, 2011.
Shapiro, Robert Moses. 'Diaries and Memoirs from the Lodz Ghetto'. In *Holocaust Chronicles: Individualizing the Holocaust through Diaries and Other Contemporaneous Personal Accounts*, ed. Shapiro, 95–115. Hoboken, NJ: Ktav, 1999.
Shavit, Yaakov. 'Politics and Messianism: The Zionist Revisionist Movement and Polish Political Culture'. *Studies in Zionism* 6(2) (1985): 233–35.
Shushkes, Kh. *Bleter fun a Geto-Tog-Bukh*. New York: H.H. Glants, 1943.
Sieradzka, Agnieszka (ed.). *Szkicownik z Auschwitz/The Sketchbook from Auschwitz*. Oświęcim: Państwowe Muzeum Auschwitz-Birkenau, 2011.
Silverman, Kaja. *The Subject of Semiotics*. New York: Oxford University Press, 1983.
Smith, Mark L. 'No Silence in Yiddish: Popular and Scholarly Writing about the Holocaust in the Early Post-War Years'. In *After the Holocaust: Challenging the Myths of Silence*, ed. David Cesarani and Eric L. Sundquist, 55–66. London: Routledge, 2012.
Sofsky, Wolfgang. *The Order of Terror: The Concentration Camp*. Trans. William Templer. Princeton, NJ: Princeton University Press, 1997.
Sontag, Susan. *On Photography*. London: Penguin, 1977.
Stafford, Fiona J. *The Last of the Race: The Growth of a Myth from Milton to Darwin*. Oxford: Clarendon Press, 1994.
Stanislawski, Michael. *Zionism and the Fin-de-Siècle: Cosmopolitanism and Nationalism from Nordau to Jabotinsky*. Berkeley and Los Angeles: University of California Press, 2001.
Stanley-Price, Nicholas. 'The Reconstruction of Ruins: Principles and Practice'. In *Conservation: Principles, Dilemmas and Uncomfortable Truths*, ed. Alison Richmond and Alison Bracker, 32–46. Oxford: Elsevier, 2009.
Steinbacher, Sybille. *Auschwitz: A History*. Trans. Shaun Whiteside. London: Penguin, 2005.

Steiner, George. *Language and Silence: Essays on Language, Literature and the Inhuman*. New Haven, CT: Yale University Press, 1998.
Stone, Dan. 'The Sonderkommando Photographs'. *Jewish Social Studies* 7(3) (2001): 132–48.
———. *Histories of the Holocaust*. Oxford: Oxford University Press, 2010.
———. 'Introduction: The Holocaust and Holocaust Methodology'. In *The Holocaust and Holocaust Methodology*, ed. Dan Stone, 1–19. New York: Berghahn Books, 2012.
———. 'The Harmony of Barbarism: Locating the Scrolls of Auschwitz in Holocaust Historiography'. In *Representing Auschwitz: At the Margins of Testimony*, ed. Nicholas Chare and Dominic Williams, 11–32. Basingstoke: Palgrave Macmillan, 2013.
Struk, Janina. *Photographing the Holocaust: Interpretations of the Evidence*. London: I.B. Tauris, 2004.
Strzelecki, Andrzej. *The Evacuation, Dismantling and Liberation of Auschwitz*. Oświęcim: Auschwitz-Birkenau State Museum, 2001.
Stutshkov, Nokhem. *Der oytser fun der yiddisher shprakh*. New York: YIVO Institute for Jewish Research, 1950.
Suchoff, David. 'A Yiddish Text from Auschwitz: Critical History and the Anthological Imagination', *Prooftexts* 19(1) (January 1999): 59–69.
Surminski, Arno. *Die Vogelwelt von Auschwitz*. Munich: Langen Müller Verlag, 2008.
Świebocka, Teresa. *Auschwitz: A History in Photographs*. Indianapolis: Indiana University Press, 1993.
Świebocka, Teresa, Franciszek Piper and Martin Mayr (eds). *Inmitten des grauenvollen Verbrechens: Handschriften von Mitgliedern des Sonderkommandos*. Trans. Herta Henschel and Jochen August. Oświęcim: Verlag des Staatlichen Auschwitz-Birkenau Museums, 1996.
Szczepański, Janusz. *Dzieje społeczności żydowskiej powiatów Pułtusk i Maków Mazowiecki*. Warsaw: Pułtuskie Towarzystwo Społeczno-Kulturalne and Towarzystwo Miłośników Makowa Mazowieckiego, 1993.
Szlamkowicz, Jakob, et al. 'Death Camp in Kolo County'. In Shmuel Krakowski and Ilya Altman, 'The Testament of the Last Prisoners of the Chelmno Death Camp', *Yad Vashem Studies* 27 (1991): 105–23.
Szlengel, Władysław. *Poeta Nieznany*, ed. Magdalena Stańczuk. Warsaw: Bellona Spółka Akcyjna, 2013.
Szpek, Heidi. 'Jewish Epitaphs from Białystok, 1892–1902: Embracing the Spirit of Dubnow'. *East European Jewish Affairs* 42(2) (August 2012): 129–58.
Tapper, Colin. *Cross & Tapper: On Evidence*. 10th edn. London: Reed Elsevier, 2004.
Taub, Shmuel. 'A bintl troyerike zikhroynes'. In *Sefer zikaron lekehilat Makov-Mazovyetsk*, 283–90. Tel Aviv: Komitet fun makover landsmanshaftn in Yisroel un Amerike, 1969.
Tec, Nehama. *Resilience and Courage: Men, Women and the Holocaust*. New Haven, CT, and London: Yale University Press, 2003.
Tomasik, Wojciech. *Ikona nowoczesności: Kolej w literaturze polskiej*. Wrocław: Wydawnictwo Uniwersytetu Wrocławskiego, 2007.
Trezise, Thomas. *Witnessing Witnessing: On the Reception of Holocaust Survivor Testimony*. New York: Fordham University Press, 2013.
Venezia, Shlomo. *Inside the Gas Chambers: Eight Months in the Sonderkommando of Auschwitz*. Trans. Andrew Brown. Cambridge: Polity, 2009.
Wajcman, Gérard. 'De la croyance photographique'. *Les Temps modernes* 56 (2001): 47–83.
Waxman, Zoe. *Writing the Holocaust: Identity, Testimony, Representation*. Oxford: Oxford University Press, 2006.

Wells, Leon W. *The Death Brigade (The Janowska Road)*. New York: Holocaust Library, 1978.
White, Hayden. *Metahistory: The Historical Imagination in Nineteenth-Century Europe*. Baltimore, MD: Johns Hopkins University Press, 1973.
———. 'Figural Realism in Witness Literature', *parallax* 10(1) (2004): 113–24.
———. 'Historical Discourse and Literary Writing'. In *Tropes for the Past: Hayden White and the History/Literature Debate*, ed. Kusima Korhonen, 25–33. Amsterdam: Rodopi, 2006.
Wiesel, Elie. 'The Holocaust as Literary Inspiration'. In Wiesel et al., *Dimensions of the Holocaust*, 5–19. Evanston, IL: Northwestern University Press, 1977.
———. 'Preface'. In Ber Mark, *Des voix dans la nuit*, Trans. Esther Fridman, Joseph Fridman and Liliane Princet, i–v. Paris: Plon, 1982.
Williams, Dominic. 'The Dead Are My Teachers: The Scrolls of Auschwitz in Jerome Rothenberg's *Khurbn*'. In *Representing Auschwitz: At the Margins of Testimony*, ed. Nicholas Chare and Dominic Williams, 58–84. Basingstoke: Palgrave Macmillian, 2013.
———. 'Figuring the Grey Zone: The Auschwitz Sonderkommando in Contemporary Culture'. *Holocaust Studies*, forthcoming.
Wollaston, Isabel. 'The Absent, the Partial and the Iconic in Archival Photographs of the Holocaust'. *Jewish Culture and History* 12(3) (2010): 443–45.
Wolnerman, Chaim. 'Araynfir'. In Zalman Gradowski, *In harts fun gehenem*, 1–5. Jerusalem: Wolnerman, n.d. [c.1977].
Wygodzki, Yehoshua. 'A vort fun a gevezenem asir'. In Zalman Gradowski, *In harts fun gehenem*, 9–15. Jerusalem: Wolnerman, n.d. [c.1977].
Yerushalmi, Yosef. *Zakhor: Jewish History and Jewish Memory*. Seattle and London: University of Washington Press, 1996.
Young, James. 'Interpreting Literary Testimony: A Preface to Reading Holocaust Diaries and Memoirs'. *New Literary History* 18(2) (1987): 403–23.
Zawoznicki, Yehoyesh. 'Portretn fun lomdim, askonim un nedivim in Suvalk'. *Yizker-bukh Suvalk*, 431–74.
———. 'Di toyre-yugnt in Suvalk'. *Yizker-bukh Suvalk*, 365–72.
Zelizer, Barbie. *Remembering to Forget: Holocaust Memory through the Camera's Eye*. Chicago: University of Chicago Press, 1998.
Żółkiewska, Agnieszka (ed.). *Słowa pośród nocy: Poetyckie dokumenty Holokaustu*. Warsaw: Żydowski Instytut Historyczy, 2012.

Appendices

238 • Appendices

Appendix A Leyb Langfus's *The Deportation*

Page	Chapter	Yiddish title	Translated title	Place	Events
[1] 6	1	der ershter onzog	The first announcement	Top of page	Group of Jews hanged; announcement of deportation: those fit for work to Auschwitz; women, children, and unfit-for-work to Malkinia
[10] 19	2	dezorientatsye un endgiltige xxx	Confusion and final xxx	Top of page	Reaction; preparation for escape for/with children; call for resistance
[14] 9	3	<in der heym>	<At home>	Top of page	Leyb and his wife and child; he lies to his son that they can escape; cries out in despair
[22] 27	**kapitel 4**	falsher shvindel	Fake trickery	line 7	Steinmetz's deception; there will be a commission; fit-to-work will go to a coal mine and can take children with them; stymies resistance; some believe, some not; gendarmes treat them politely – also a deception
[26] 31	5	in gas	In the street	line 6	Some preparations: burying things, uncertainty keeps everyone awake; they stream out onto the street to discuss whether they should believe first or second version given by Steinmetz; suicides; escapees come back to ghetto; news that Ciechanów ghetto has been liquidated
[30] 35	**kapitel 6**	der tilim	The psalm	line 17	Children told what is happening; they recite a psalm; their crying gives way to finding words for their pain in the psalm; children and adults mourn together
[34] 39	7	<di> komisye	Commission	line 14	Commission comes, divides them into fit and unfit
[37] 42	[8]	in di tsvishen tsayt	In the mean time	Top of page	Families: children, mothers, fathers; workers forced to work for the Germans; children from Płońsk come into the ghetto
[42] 47	[9]	g<eze>g<e>nung	Leavetaking	Top of page	date for deportation set; meeting to discuss details; Gurfinkiel and Ehrlich speak, then rabbi from Krasnosielc, and the dayan of Maków; everyone returns home to say farewell, pack up and wait

Appendices • 239

[46] 51 **kapitel 10** fortogs	The day before	line 11	repeats end of last chapter, then people go out on the streets, approach the ghetto gate, which feels like threshold of death, women taking their children to their deaths; only the beginning
[49] 54 **kapitel 11** dos trayben	Expulsion	line 22	day begins, police appear on street, people chased out of their homes and shot, father beaten before children, they line up to get on carts, more beatings, Gestapo take their valuables off them, thrown on carts, anyone who falls off is shot
[55] 60 **kapitel 12** in Mlava	In Mława	line 17	arrive at Mława, only recently liquidated, Polikart, people assemble, executions?, dismissed
[61] 66 [13] in di gefinene teg	In the days left	top of page	(many parts of the text difficult to decipher) time spent in Mława
[64] 69 *14* <f>ehiger	<f>it	top of page	community ordered to gather together and then put into two deserted mills, where they mourn their fate
[69] 74 [15] hertsraysender un *****	heartrending and *****	top of page	their grief, relationships between mothers and children,
[76] 81 [16]		title at top of page?	thoughts and feelings of the men while they sit in the mill
[83] 88 **kapitel 17** tsum bahn	To the train	line 18	they assemble in the square before the ghetto gate and are marched to the train

A summary of the first 17 chapter divisions of Langfus's manuscript. It is not clear whether the chapters continue after Chapter 17. The placing of chapters 3, 15 and 16 is somewhat speculative and very much open to revision, but the divisions of the others are clear either by the fact that there is a clear chapter number and/or title.

Chapter: as it is written in the manuscript. Numbers in bold (e.g. **1**) are completely legible; numbers in italics (e.g. *7*) are not completely legible but could plausibly be read this way; numbers in square brackets (e.g. [9]) are not legible.

Place: line number gives the line of handwriting.

Appendix B Leyb Langfus's 'Particulars'

	Opening phrase	Date	Incident	Link
1	ven es iz gekumen	Between 3 & 6 Aug 1944	Rabbi from Będzin dies singing and dancing	ends: 'kidesh ha shem'
2	tsvey ungarishe idn hoben gefregt	After May 1944	Hungarian Jews drink L'Chaim with a member of the Sonderkommando	ends: 'kidesh ha shem' Hungarian
3	es iz gevezen in miten zumer	'midsummer' 1944	Hungarian Jews – run naked from Crem. 2 to 3 and are shot	Hungarian shot one by one
4	men hot gebrakht a grupe iden fun a lager	?	Prisoners fed and die happy when they are shot	shot one by one
5	es iz gevezen umgefehr far di ende 1943	'about the end of 1943'	Members of the Polish underground and Dutch Jews gassed together. Poles sing their national anthem; Jews sing *HaTikvah*. They sing the Internationale together.	self-deception?
6	es iz gevezen sof zumer 1944	'end summer 1944'	Woman from Slovakia hopes for a miracle while entering the gas chamber	self-deception?
7	es iz geven far sof zumer 1943	'end summer 1943' (after 1–2 Sept)	People from Tarnów come to terms with death, one man refuses to believe they will be killed	self-deception
8	dos is gevezen pesakh 1944	'Passover 1944'	Rabbi from Vittel speaks to Oberscharführer	Defiant rabbi

Appendices • 241

9	se iz gevezen a Kashoyer transport ende mai 1944	'May 1944'	Rebbetsin from Košice speaks out	Defiant rebbetsin
10	es iz gevezen vinter sof 1943	'winter end 1943'	Children from Šiauliai (Lithuania) denounce Sonderkommando	Children
11	es iz gevezen onhoyb 1943	'beginning 1943'	Child clubbed, then shot	Children
12	der hoyptsharfihrer Moll flegt	N/A	Moll's habits	SS Habits
13	obersharfihrer Forst flegt	N/A	Voss's habits Other SS habits	SS Habits
14	ende zumer 1942 iz gekumen	'End summer 1942' [actually 1943]	Przemyśl – resistance betrayed by leader	

Appendix C Zalman Lewental's Manuscript

Page	MS	SA	ANC	BŻIH
[1]	17a^L			
2	18b^L			
3	19b^R			
4	21b^L			
5	20b^L			
6	22b^L			
7	23a^L			
8	23b^L			
9	22a^L			
[10]	20a^L			
11	21a^L			
12	19a^R	22	20	213:5
13	18a^L			
14	17b^L			
15	8a^L			
16	9a^R			
17	10a^R	93		
18	11a^L	92		
19	12b^L			
20	13a^R			
21	14a^R	90	47	232:5
22	15b^L	40	48	233:2
23	16a^L	41	49	
24	16b^L	91	36	232:1
25	15a^L	23	25	214:1
26	14b^R	27	24	233:1
27	13b^R	30	23	222:2a
[28]	12a^L	28	13	232:4
29	11b^L	32	22	232:3
30	10b^R	24	26	214:2-3
31	9b^R	29	14	
[32]	24a^R			
33	29b^L	25	27	214:4a
34	28a^L	26	28	214:4b
[35]	27b^L	31	29	
36	26a^L	33	30	232:2; 222:1-2a
37	25b^L	34	31	221:5a
38	32a^R	35	32	221:5b
39	31b^R	36	33	221:5c
40	31a^R	37	34	
41	32b^R	38	35	
42	25a^L	39	54	220:3
43	26b^L	46	55	220:4
44	27a^L	44	52	231:6
45	28b^L	45	53	221:3-4
46	29a^L	42	50	215:1a
47	24b^R	43	51	215:1b
48	8a^R	53	63	223:1
49	30a^L	47	56	220:5
50	33b^R	48	58	221:1
51	35a^L	49	59	221:2; 222:3b
52	34b^L	54	64	222:3c
53	38a^L	50	60	215:2; 219:2a
54	36a^R	51	61	219:2b 220:1a

Page	MS	SA	ANC	BŻIH
55	37a^L	52	62	220:1b-2
56	37b^L	55	65	223:2
57	36b^R	56	66	227:1
[58]	38b^L	57	67	233:5; 223:3a
59	34a^L	58	68	223:3b
60	35b^L	59	69	223:3c-224:2a
61	33a^R	60	70	224:2b-3a
62	30b^L	61	71	224:3b
63	30a^R	62	72	224:3c-225:2a
64	33b^L	63	73	225:2b-3a
65	35a^R	64	74	225:3b-4a
[66]	34b^R	65	75	225:4b-226:1
67	38a^R	66	76	226:2-3a
68	36a^L	67	77	226:3b
69	37a^R	68	78	226:3c-4
70	37b^R	69	79	227:3b-4
71	36b^L	70	80	227:5-6a
72	38b^R	71	81	227:6b-228:1a
73	34a^R	72	82	228:1b
74	35b^R	73	83	228:2-229:1a
75	33a^L	74	84	229:1b-2a
76	30b^R	75	85	229:2b-4a
77	8b^L	76	86	229:4b-5
78	24a^L	77	87	230:1a
79	29b^R	78	88	230:1b
80	28a^R	79	89	230:1c-2a; 230:3a
81	27b^R	80	90	
82	26a^R	81	91	226:5a; 230:3b 226:5b
83	25b^R	94	92	231:1
84	32a^L	82	93	231:2-3a
85	31b^L	83	94	231:3b-5
[86]	31a^L	84	96	233:3a
87	32b^L	85	97	233:3b
[88]	25a^R	86	95	
[89]	26b^R			
[90]	27a^R	88	57	
[91]	28b^R	87	98	
[92]	29a^R	89	99	233:4; 233:6
93	24b^L	1	1	212:1
[94]	9a^L	3	2	212:2
[95]	10a^L	6	3	
[96]	11a^R	4		
[97]	12b^R	9	9	
[98]	13a^L	5		
[99]	14a^L			
100	15b^R	7	4	
[101]	16b^R	10	5	
[102]	16a^R	8	8	
[103]	15a^R			
[104]	14b^L	16		
[105]	13b^L			
[106]	12a^R	19	19	213:1

Page	MS	SA	ANC	BŻIH	Page	MS	SA	ANC	BŻIH
107	11b[R]	20	16	213:4	[116]	22b[R]			
[108]	10b[L]	21	15	213:3	[117]	23a[R]			
109	9b[L]	11	6	212:3	[118]	23b[R]			
[110]	8b[R]				[119]	22a[R]			
[111]	17a[R]	15	21		[120]	20a[R]			
112	18b[R]	17	12		[121]	21a[R]			
[113]	19b[L]	12	10	212:4	[122]	19a[L]	2	7	212:5
[114]	21b[R]	13	18	212:7	[123]	18a[R]			
[115]	20b[R]	18	17	212:6	[124]	17b[R]			

Thicker lines indicate breaks between signatures. 'MS Sheet 8' is most likely two separate half-sheets, part of the first and last signatures. **Page**: number in bold (e.g. **7**): page number legible on MS; number in italics (e.g. *6*): page number not completely legible, but could plausibly be read this way; number in square brackets (e.g. [1]): no page number legible. **MS:** the numbering follows that given by the Auschwitz museum to its digital files, with the addition of superscript L and R indicating left and right sides of the page (from each file's original orientation). **SA:** Ber Mark, *Scrolls of Auschwitz*. **ANC:** *Amidst a Nightmare of Crime*. Page numbers 37–45 and 100–102 do not appear in this table. They are 'The 3000 Naked Women' and the 'The 600 Boys', which we believe to be by Leyb Langfus. **BŻIH:** *Biuletyn Żydowskiego Instytuta Historycznego*. Unlike the Marks' and the Auschwitz editions, this version does not preserve MS pages as separate paragraphs. The number given here is the page number followed by paragraph number; parts of paragraphs are indicated by letters. Not included: 213:2 is the last paragraph of 'The 3000 Naked Women'; the rest of the story, followed by 'The 600 Boys', is on 216:1–219:1. Unidentified: 222.3a; 226.4c; 227.2–3a; 230.2b.

Index

A
Abramovitsh, S.Y. 72, 73
aesthetics 18, 52, 80
affect. *See* emotions
Agamben, Giorgio 19, 28n85, 189
'Alex' (Greek Jewish prisoner, surname unknown) 10, 18, 25n45, 41, 183–207, 208n7, 214–215, 220
Amidst a Nightmare of Crime. See editions of the Scrolls
Angel of Death 66, 133
Ankersmit, Frank 49–53, 58n91, 59n110
anonymity 4, 32, 47, 93–95, 96, 141, 162, 176, 201
anti-Zionist campaign in Poland, March 1968 4, 22n14, 149n8
archives 10, 15–16, 21n8, 31–32, 34, 42, 50, 92n81, 119n8, 119n9, 127, 146, 155, 159, 165, 196, 200, 214, 220
art 11, 18, 51, 52, 77, 78, 80, 151–152n31
Asch, Sholem 72
ash 2, 5, 31, 42, 50, 64, 80, 83, 84, 88n27, 93, 107, 172, 184, 199
Auerhahn, Nancy 104, 122n38
Auschwitz I, the Stammlager 1–2
Auschwitz museum 3, 4, 29n112, 34, 35, 41, 43–45, 65, 96, 99, 115, 120n16, 121n22, 128, 135, 150n10, 150n13, 151n25, 155, 157, 219
authorship, questions of 4–5, 93–96, 103–104, 115, 118, 119n4, 119n6, 119n8, 148–149n3, 151n27, 184, 208n9

B
Bacon, Yehuda 23n24, 80
beobakhten. See witnessing
Barthes, Roland 194, 195–196, 211n73

Bełżec 12
Bennahmias, Daniel 167
Bennett, Jane 43
Bennett, Jill 105, 123n41
Berezovskaya, Zinaida 21n7
Betar 62
Bezwińska, Jadwiga 103, 149–150n8, 150n9
Białystok 12, 68,
Birkenau
  Block 13 6, 116
  Block 25 110
  Bunkers 6, 89n45, 130
  crematoria 1, 2, 3, 5, 6–7, 8, 11, 14, 18, 21n7, 30, 31, 32, 35, 41, 42, 47, 49, 56n41, 57n61, 61, 63, 72, 75, 76, 81, 86, 93, 95–96, 98, 109, 110, 112, 114, 116, 117, 118n2, 120n16, 125, 126, 130, 140, 148, 163, 177, 181n71, 181n74, 183–184, 186, 190, 192, 195, 197, 198, 200, 201, 205, 208n9, 215, 219
  Crematorium II ('1') 2, 3, 7, 75, 81, 93, 95–96, 110, 140, 174, 181n71
  Crematorium III ('2') 2, 3, 7, 24n30, 42, 81, 93, 95–96, 126, 140, 181n71
  Crematorium IV ('3') 7, 24n30, 63, 130, 140, 167, 208n9
  Crematorium V ('4') 7, 24n30, 41, 117, 130, 181n71, 183–184, 192, 195, 205, 215
  Czech family camp 11, 61–62, 64, 71, 75–84, 91n67, 218
  Kanada 5, 10, 181n75
  Sauna 117
Blumental, Nachman 4, 12, 26n70, 27n71, 90n57

Bomba, Abraham 217, 218
Borowczyk, Gustaw 3, 4
Borowczyk, Wojciech 3, 4
Bowman, Steven 166, 169, 178n6, 210n53
bracelet from the Łódź ghetto 3, 42, 125, 126
Brandi, Cesare 133, 150n20
Bronfen, Elisabeth 186–187, 189, 206
Brown, Adam 9
Butler, Judith 50, 58n91, 162, 174

C

Caruth, Cathy 15, 28n92, 219
Celan, Paul 161
Chełmno 12, 20, 158, 174–177
children 12–13, 21n4, 79, 101–102, 103, 106–107, 112, 114, 115, 145, 163, 164, 175, 187, 203, 217–220
chronology 16, 33, 49, 64, 112, 114–115, 127, 131, 161
Ciechanów 121n25, 125, 131, 144, 146, 152n41, 152–153n44, 153n45, 199, 212n103
Ciechanower, Mordecai 23, 97, 114, 119n8, 122n35, 123n58, 152–153n44, 153n45
clothes 5, 6, 77, 79–80, 198, 200, 205, 217
Cohen, Arthur 52
Cohen, Elie 79, 212n108
Cohen, Leon 24n27, 25n45, 57n61, 167, 178n6, 181n73, 181n74
Cohen, Nathan 13, 102, 122n35, 155–157
Cohen, Ya'acov 63
Colebrook, Claire 113
collaboration 7, 33, 132
concentration camps 11, 12, 19–20, 70, 93, 170, 171, 174
Confino, Alon 51–52, 53, 59n100, 59n110
conservation 35, 43–46, 133
containers of the Scrolls 2, 34, 40–42, 43, 44, 57n52, 61, 93, 125, 126, 127, 155, 174
corpses 1, 5–6, 80, 185, 201–202, 215
creativity 20, 36, 84, 219
cremation. *See* burning bodies
crime
    calling to account for 172
    concealment of 20, 31, 117, 148, 172, 199
    evidence of 20, 30–31, 44, 47, 70, 174, 175, 190, 191, 199
    and forensics 34, 44, 54–55
    separation from 8, 110
    traces of 20, 44, 45, 54–55, 190
crime scene 54, 191–192
Czech, Danuta 103, 120n11, 145, 149–150n8, 150n9, 153n45

D

damage to manuscripts 39, 43, 45, 55, 70, 98–100, 119n7, 126, 127–131, 132, 133–136, 143, 177, 219
Dante Alighieri 172
Daybell, James 34
dead bodies. *See* corpses
death camps 12, 176, 198, 202
deception 103, 137, 145
Decker, William Merrill 160, 165, 173, 174
dehumanisation 14, 108, 198, 200, 216
Des voix dans la nuit. *See* editions of the Scrolls
Des voix sous la cendre. *See* editions of the Scrolls
diaries 8, 12, 13, 14, 16–17, 21n7, 27n76, 28n89, 56n38, 59n110, 60, 118–119n2, 122n36, 179n15, 179n25
    diary from the Łódź ghetto, buried by Zalman Lewental 3, 42, 125, 126, 132, 147–148, 148–149n3, 198
    diaries as opposed to the Sonderkommando mansucripts 17, 100–101, 155–156
Didi-Huberman, Georges
    Blancs soucis 151n23
    Écorces 192, 210n54
    empathy 193–194, 207
    Images malgré tout 10, 184
    Images in Spite of All 184–185, 189, 192, 193, 195–196, 203
    use of Zalman Gradowski's writings 202–204
Doane, Mary Ann 195
drafting 35, 65, 70, 100, 114, 199

Dragon, Shlomo 3, 90n60, 120n11, 183, 208n9
Drancy 157
Dutch Jews 112
Dworkin, Craig 39

E
Earle, Rebecca 159, 173
East Prussia 62, 98
editions of the Scrolls of Auschwitz
  Amidst a Nightmare of Crime (Auschwitz museum) 4, 155
  Des voix dans la nuit (Mark, B.) 157, 208n12
  Des voix sous la cendre (Saletti, C. & Mesnard, P.) 157
  Megiles Oyshvits (Mark, B.) 4, 150n9, 157
  Scrolls of Auschwitz, The (Mark, B.) 157
  V serdtsevine Ada (Polian, P.) 22n19, 88n29
emotions
  affect and 17, 20, 38, 39, 40, 41, 50, 52–53, 58n91, 82, 97, 105, 123n41, 161, 192, 219
  doubt 97, 177–178
  fear 20, 31, 69, 70, 75, 100, 101, 121n25, 147–148, 155, 160, 176, 178, 186, 203, 220
  guilt 64, 67, 79, 112, 137, 155, 160
  joy 64–65, 142, 162
  lack of 7, 9, 38–39, 163, 180n49
  mood and 50–53, 192, 194
  shame 3, 12, 13, 116, 137, 200
empathy 40, 64, 68, 78, 97, 193–194, 207, 210n62, 210n63, 219
Errera, Alberto 25n45, 184, 208n7
escape 2, 3, 7, 11, 12, 20, 71, 101, 130, 139–140, 167, 173, 174, 181n75, 184, 204–205
ethical judgement 17–18, 86, 97, 108, 110–111, 115, 203, 206
ethics 7, 20, 78, 92n79, 122–123n38, 161. *See also* ethical judgement
evidence. *See* proof
executions 49, 98–99, 175, 181n75, 184

F
Fajnzylberg, Alter 183, 184, 190, 191, 207n2
fantasy 4, 7, 71, 76–79, 160, 165, 200–201
feelings. *See* emotions
femininity 73–74, 75, 77, 80, 161, 186–187, 189, 195, 200, 201, 206
fetishism 187, 206
figuration 8, 45, 49–50, 73, 74, 81, 104, 159, 162, 165, 172, 186, 195
Forster, E.M. 140, 142
Forsyth, Donelson 169
France 2, 157, 158, 166, 167, 181n74, 204
Frankl, Viktor 15
Freimark, Yaakov 63
French Jews 6, 157, 167, 181n71
French Revolution 51–52, 53, 59n100
Freud, Sigmund 156, 189
Friedländer, Saul 13, 53, 155
Friedler, Eric, Barbara Siebert and Andreas Kilian 9, 25n45, 184
Furman, Kalman 80

G
gaps 16, 43, 45, 46, 51, 52, 53, 126, 132, 133–136, 147–148, 151n23, 189, 196
Garbarini, Alexandra 13, 56n38, 156
gas chambers 5, 6, 8, 9, 41, 62, 80–82, 106–107, 109, 112–113, 120n16, 172, 173, 183–184, 185, 187, 190, 191, 194, 197–201, 207, 207–208n3, 215, 218
gassing 7, 9, 106, 131, 177, 191, 198, 199
gender 61, 74, 165, 185, 186
gesture 39–40, 54–55, 69, 159, 193–194, 206, 210n63, 216–217
  cut throat 69
ghettos 11–13, 26n60, 32, 42, 63, 98, 101, 102, 105, 121n25, 122n36, 125, 127, 144, 147–148, 175, 177, 196, 198, 199, 200, 212n103, 218
Gigliotti, Simone 57n57, 68, 198
Giles, Audrey 37
Glazar, Richard 79–80, 212n101, 218
Goethe, Johann Wolfgang von 73
Gradowski, Sara (née Złotojabłko) 62–63

Gradowski, Zalman
  family 3, 62–63, 67, 68, 85, 87n14, 87n15, 87–88n21
  In the Heart of Hell 40, 72, 85, 151–152n31, 198,
  life 62–63, 84–86, 86–87n9, 87n14, 88n24
  part in the revolt of 7 Oct 7, 62, 63, 84, 85, 88n24, 126, 139
  politics 62–63, 73, 85
  St. Petersburg manuscript 35, 36, 41, 56n28, 61, 64–71, 84, 135
Greece 6, 25n45, 158, 161, 166, 169
  liberation of 161
Greek Jews 6, 166–169, 171, 180n70, 181n71, 181n75, 184, 199
Greenberg, Uri Zvi 63, 72, 73
Greif, Gideon 8–9, 13, 24n27, 24n32, 76, 88n24, 89n39, 116, 166, 171, 180n49, 208n9
grey zone 7–8, 54, 165
Grodno 62, 67
Grossman, Meir 62
group dynamics 20, 141, 158, 165–166
guilt. *See* emotions

H
handwriting 36–40, 47, 54, 88n31, 96, 114, 119n6, 159
Hartman, Geoffrey 202
Hasidism 97, 114, 119–120n10, 120n18, 123n55
headstones, Jewish 72, 143
hearing. *See* senses
Hebrew 5, 9, 22n19, 36, 63, 96, 110, 119n5, 120n13, 144, 152n41, 166
Hedrick, Charles 136
Heine, Heinrich 73
hell 66–67, 77, 82–84, 164, 169, 172, 194, 198–199, 203–204, 207
Herman, Chaim
  emotion 155, 157, 159, 160–162, 163–164, 173
  family 42, 155, 158, 163–164, 173
  judgment of actions 17, 166, 173
  masculinity 20, 164–165
  nationalism 157–158, 166
  relationship to Poland 157–158, 179n21
  style of writing 157, 170, 172, 173
Herman, Judith 17
Herzog, Chaim 159
Hirsch, Marianne 188
historians 11, 12, 24n27, 26n60, 32–34, 36, 38, 40, 46–47, 50, 51, 98, 124n60, 126, 146, 147–148, 153n46, 158, 161, 166, 196
histories
  affective 17, 38, 39, 40, 41, 50, 52, 97, 105, 161, 192, 219
  material 41–42, 45–46, 50, 135, 219
historiography 33, 46–47, 49–53, 147–148, 161–162, 196
Hoffman, Eva 170
Höss (Hoess), Rudolf 21n2, 24n27, 25n46
Hungarian Jews 6, 130, 142, 152n36, 165

I
iconicity 185, 186, 188, 195, 196, 197, 207
illegibility 39, 43, 108, 128, 151n22, 176, 178
imagination 10, 14, 19, 31, 36, 42, 61, 67, 80, 83, 89n35, 101, 105, 107, 118, 136, 146, 158, 172, 175, 185, 190, 192–196, 200, 202, 203, 205, 206, 207, 210n55, 211n86, 214, 215, 216, 217
improvisation 100, 154, 169
incarnation 10, 16, 28n101, 54, 90n59, 217–218, 219, 220
incineration pits 5, 6, 18, 183, 191, 197, 198, 199, 215
indexicality 18, 31, 36, 38, 39, 44, 49, 54, 59n119, 59n120, 132, 159, 185, 187, 194–197, 206–207, 211n73, 216, 219
intonation 217
irony 97, 113–114, 118, 173

J
Jabotinsky, Vladimir 62, 63
Jewish Historical Institute 3, 4, 119n8
Jewish liturgy 55n7, 63, 72, 100, 114–115, 169
Judaism 97, 123n55

K
Kahan, Claudine 19
Kant, Immanuel 91n73
Keats, John 73
Keenan, Thomas 34
Kiełbasin 63, 65, 66, 67, 105
Kirshenblatt-Gimblett, Barbara 114
Klüger, Ruth 11
knowledge of events
  among Jews 14, 69–70, 145, 146, 147, 175–176
  among others 136–137, 169, 175–176, 183
  among the Sonderkommando 14, 32–33, 52, 83, 98, 130, 136–137, 141, 147, 156, 161, 169, 175–176
Krasnosielc 103, 122n33
Kraus, Ota 7, 55n2, 88n24, 163
Kulka, Erich 7, 11, 55n2, 88n24, 163

L
Lacan, Jacques
  point de capiton (quilting point) 189
  Real 187–189, 194–195, 206, 211n73
  Symbolic 187, 204, 206
  'The Ego in Freud's Theory and in the Technique of Psychoanalysis' 188–189
LaCapra, Dominick 14, 17, 18, 40, 45, 46, 97, 219
lacunae 45–46, 133–136, 147–148, 150–151n20, 151n21, 184, 196. *See also* damage to manuscripts; illegibility
Lang, Berel 16–17
Langbein, Herman 79, 205
Langer, Lawrence 15–16
Langfus, Dvoyre, née Rozental 95, 96, 97, 101, 106–107
Langfus, Leyb
  'The 3000 Naked Women' 76, 109–111, 116, 199
  'The 600 Boys' 109–110, 217–218
  biography 5, 95, 96–97, 115, 117, 119n7
  date of death 7, 24n31, 117, 120n16
  The Deportation 4, 5, 35, 37–38, 40, 44, 45, 93, 95, 96, 97–108, 109, 110, 111, 115–116, 126, 198
  differences from Gradowski 105–108, 115, 116
  disputed authorship of 4, 95–96, 119n6, 119n8
  ethical approach to writing 18, 20, 108, 110–111, 116, 203
  family 95, 97, 101–102, 115, 119–120n10, 163
  irony, use of 97, 113–114, 118, 173
  'The Manuscript by the Unknown Author' 4, 47, 96, 111–115, 115, 116, 117–118, 119n6, 119n8, 199
  'Notes' 47, 117–118
  part in the revolt of 7 Oct 120n16, 130
  'Particulars' 111–115, 115, 116, 199
Langfus, Shmuel 95, 96, 97, 101–102, 106–107
language, limits of 17–18, 50–51, 54, 147–148, 160, 171–172, 186
Lanzmann, Claude 9–10, 16, 24n27, 25n36, 28n101, 31, 54, 88n24, 175, 187, 192–193, 214–220, 221n10
Laub, Dori 14–16, 36, 70, 104, 122n38
Lawson, Tom 13, 27n80
legibility 43, 44–45, 128, 133
Leivick, H. 72–73
Lengyel, Olga 200
'Leon' (cook for the Sonderkommando, surname unknown) 55n7
letters 12, 20, 34, 57n61, 154–178, 179n25
Levental, Yisroel 11
Levi, Primo 7–9, 10, 25n45, 38, 53, 107, 146, 161–162, 165, 172, 189
Lewental, Zalman
  addendum to the Łódź diary 3, 19, 32, 35, 41, 44, 147–148
  biography 6, 7, 24n30, 130–131, 137
  commentary on the Łódź diary 3, 32, 126, 147–148, 196
  differences from Gradowski and Langfus 125–126, 132, 136, 138, 141
  disputed authorship of 96, 119n4, 119n6, 151n27
  as a historian 16, 33, 36, 126, 146, 147–148
  longer manuscript by 35, 44, 45–46, 96, 111, 115, 127–146

memorialist 20, 132, 141, 143, 152n33
part in the revolt of 7 Oct 130–131,
 139–140, 141, 143
and psychology 137, 138, 147, 151–
 152n31
Liebeskind, Aron 13, 27n71
Lipszyc, Rywka 21n7, 118–119n2
literature
 comparisons of Scrolls with 13, 18,
  20, 33, 60–61, 71–74, 82, 83, 84, 85,
  86–87n9, 87n10, 97, 102, 113–115,
  135, 156, 161, 162, 171, 173
 references to by the Scrolls 63–64,
  72-74, 114–115
Lodge, David 155, 178n3
Łódź 176
Łódź ghetto 8, 12, 21n7, 32, 122n36,
 bracelet from, buried by Zalman
  Lewental 3, 42, 125
 diary from, buried by Zalman
  Lewental 3, 41, 42, 125, 126, 132,
  147–148, 148–149n3, 196, 198
Łomża yeshiva 62, 85, 87n14
Łososna 68
Łunna 62–63
Lyotard, Jean-François 52

M
Maków Mazowiecki 95, 96–97, 98–99,
 103, 106, 120n12, 121n24, 139, 144,
 146, 152–153n44, 153n46, 198
Małkinia 69, 98, 145–146, 153n45,
 153n46
Mark, Ber 4–5, 22n16, 22n19, 33, 47,
 56n33, 62, 96, 119n8, 128, 132, 133,
 135, 148n3, 149n7, 150n9, 157–158,
 208n16
Mark, Esther 4–5, 22n14, 22n15, 22n19,
 96, 119–120nn4–10, 120n16, 128,
 133, 135, 148n3, 157
masculinity 20, 85, 158, 163–165, 180n57,
 205
materiality 17, 34, 43, 45–46, 50, 54,
 56n30, 59n110, 59n120, 61, 83, 93,
 102, 126, 155, 163, 170, 172, 197, 204,
 219
Mauthausen 7

Medical and Military Museum, St
 Petersburg 35, 40, 56n28,
Megiles Oyshvits. *See* editions of the Scrolls
memorial books. *See* yizker bikher
memorials 9, 20, 71, 72, 73, 84, 85, 96–97,
 132, 143, 187, 220
Mesnard, Philippe 13, 19, 61, 216
Mickiewicz, Adam 73, 90n59
Mława 97, 98, 106, 120n11, 151n27,
 153n46, 200
Modernism 63, 73, 122n32
moon, images of 71–78, 81, 82
morality 7–8, 9, 18, 64–65, 78, 108, 113,
 138, 165, 166, 207. *See also* ethics
Mowat, Hannah 195–196
Müller, Filip 7, 9–10, 23n21, 24n30, 76,
 88n24, 90n64, 97, 120n12, 120n14,
 185, 199, 201–202, 208n7, 214–220
Mulvey, Laura 187
Munslow, Alun 33–34, 46–47, 53
Murmelstein, Benjamin 25n36
Muselmänner 19, 189
music 53, 70, 89n41. *See also* song

N
Nadjary, Marcel
 emotion 37, 39, 47, 160, 161
 family 160–161, 164, 174
 Khroniko, 1941–1945 29n112, 171
 nationalism 39, 161, 166, 169, 178
 revenge, desire for 160, 175
 style of writing 36, 37, 47, 172–173
Nahmia, Berry 167
nakedness 78, 81–82, 201, 205, 206
names
 as memorials 11, 84–85, 139, 143, 146,
  174, 177, 178
 as resistance 143, 174, 177, 178
 concealing 85, 95, 96, 104, 147–148,
  164, 173, 184
 of family members 84–85, 101–102,
  163, 164, 167, 176
 revealing 85, 95
narrative devices
 chapters 74, 75–77, 81, 99–104, 106,
  121–122n26,

enabling connection with outside, other prisoners 65, 73, 79, 97
first-person narrator 66–67, 102, 103–104
third-person narrator 102, 103–104, 137
narrative voice 10, 103–104, 113–114, 146, 219
self-image as ghost 66–68
See also rhetoric
national identity 39, 73, 149–150n8, 166–167, 169, 178, 218
negationism 31, 190, 197
Nencel, David 122n35, 122–123n38, 151n27, 152n36, 153n45
Niethammer, Günther 21n2
non-representability 14, 16–19, 28n85, 52, 187, 197–198, 220
Nyiszli, Miklós 7–8, 24n26, 97, 120n14, 174

O

observing. *See* witnessing
Oleksy, Krystyna 86n9, 92n80
Olère, David 91n75, 174
organising 10, 93
Oświęcim, town of 1, 3, 21n4
Oyneg Shabes 12, 26n60, 119n9, 200

P

page numbers 29n112, 121n22, 128–131, 137, 143–144, 145, 150n9, 150n13, 150n16, 151n21
page order 74, 90n62, 121n22, 126, 127–137, 139, 145–146, 150n12
Patterson, David 27n76, 179n15
Peirce, C.S. 54, 59n119, 188, 194, 196–197, 211n73
Pentlin, Susan 13, 87n10
perpetrators 8, 11, 14, 71, 79, 115, 172, 174
personalities, descriptions by SK writers
 of guards 91n75, 114, 151–152n31, 175, 199–200
 of prisoners 118, 138–141, 143, 146, 174
Phelan, James 140, 143

photographs
 by 'Alex' 10, 18, 41, 183–207, 214, 215, 220
 blurring 186, 188, 207
 cropping 41, 186, 190
 and the gas chambers 183–184, 185, 187, 190, 191, 194, 197–199, 207
 and ethics 203–204, 207
 lens flare 207
 and the heart of hell 198–199, 203–204, 207
 by perpetrators 11, 25n53, 200, 212n107
 retouching 186–187, 189, 208–209n16
poetry 11, 63, 72–73, 90n59, 148–149n3, 161
Polian, Aleksandra 56n34, 88n29,
Polian, Pavel 13, 60, 85
Polish Jews 3, 157–158, 169, 180n66, 181n71
Polish Red Cross 1–2, 154
Pollock, Griselda 33, 156, 186
Ponar 12
Postec, Ziva 215, 218, 220n4
proof
 material 31–32
 photographic 190–191
Prstojevic, Alexandre 13, 61, 89n35, 115, 124n60, 126
Pytel, Roman 4, 119n6, 121n20, 122n29, 122n33, 123n39, 132,

R

Rancière, Jacques 191, 202
reader
 position of 63, 65–68, 74, 79, 82, 84, 85, 95, 97, 100–101, 102, 105, 112, 113–114, 116, 135, 175, 201, 203, 218
 reaction 19, 39–40, 53, 54–55, 60–61, 80, 92n79, 105, 121n20, 140, 219–220
 responsibility of 19, 95, 108, 111, 148
Red Army 1, 64, 130
Red Cross 1–2, 154
Rees, Laurence 155–157, 158, 171, 178n3
remains, physical 1, 2, 30–32, 42, 47, 54, 55n7, 117, 171, 175, 197

representation 16–19, 29n114, 33, 34, 45, 46, 50, 53, 58n91, 186–189, 191, 198, 202, 204, 205, 206, 214
representability 14, 18–19, 198, 220
resistance 12, 19, 20, 32, 36, 60, 63, 75, 101, 126, 127, 130–131, 138, 139–143, 147, 149–150n8, 158, 165, 166, 167, 169, 179n15, 183, 184, 185, 196, 204–205, 220
restoration 43, 44–46, 133, 150n13, 150–151n20, 186
revenge 7, 12, 14, 31, 32, 84, 92n80, 160, 162, 171, 175, 176, 204
revolt of 7 October. *See under* Sonderkommando.
rewriting 94–95
Revisionist Zionism 62, 63, 73, 85
rhetoric
  apostrophe 73, 81
  chiasmus 65, 88n30
  prosopopoeia 34, 81, 91n77
Ringelblum, Emmanuel 26n60
Rogers, Spencer 32
Romanticism 67, 73, 90n53
Rose, Gillian 220
Rosenfeld, Alvin H. 79
Roskies, David 13, 27n83, 86n9, 90n53
Rousset, David 19, 29n114
Rozental, Shmuel Yoysef 96, 119n9, 119n10
ruptures, in history 51–53
Russians in Sonderkommando. *See under* Sonderkommando.
Rutkowski, Adam 22n14, 149n8, 150n9

S
sadism 64–65, 80, 199
Schillinger, Josef 75, 91n65
Schneider, Rebecca 40, 161
senses
  hearing 15, 52, 66, 67, 81, 83, 106, 114, 135, 144, 155, 163, 202, 203
  seeing 66, 68, 80, 82, 83, 110–111, 116, 171, 189, 190, 206
  smell 68, 79, 108, 198
  touch 43, 49, 68, 72, 78, 108, 159, 188
  See also witnessing

Sevillias, Errikos 184
sex 78–81, 85, 159
sexual desire 78–81
sexual violence 151n22, 199–200, 212n107
Sfard, Dovid 22n14, 22n16, 62, 87n14,
shame. *See* emotions
Shenker, M. 12–13
Shoah (Claude Lanzmann) 9–10, 25n36, 90n64, 175, 214–220
Shoah Foundation Visual History Archive 153n46
signatures in code 3, 85, 96, 119n5
silences 135–136, 151n25
Silesia 1, 69, 98, 121n25
Silverman, Kaja 194
siman (sign) 30, 31, 55n4
Slovak Jews 5, 35, 112
Slovakia 35, 112
Słowacki, Juliusz 73
smell. *See* senses
Sofsky, Wolfgang 171
Sonderkommando
  agency of 13, 18, 61, 164, 165, 205
  divisions among 25n45, 139–141, 165–167, 169, 180n70, 181n71
  history of 5–7, 16, 23n22, 24n27, 47, 127, 132, 136–143, 157, 196
  isolation from other prisoners 6, 10, 93, 116, 169, 183
  later portrayals of 9–10, 24n32, 214–220
  living conditions 7, 10, 37, 38, 45, 47, 61, 63, 113–114, 130–131, 137, 173
  living quarters 6, 10, 114, 116
  psychological damage/suffering 67, 70, 86, 104, 175, 219
  recruitment 5–6, 63, 130, 144–145, 146
  revolt of 7 Oct 6–7, 16, 25n45, 45, 49, 62, 63, 97, 130–131, 136–143, 169, 196
  Russian members 130–131, 140–141, 146, 165
  self-image 79, 165, 166, 205
song
  as testimony 11, 12, 26n59, 27n71, 167–169
  Czech Anthem 81, 218

HaTikvah 81, 218
Partisan Song 81
the Internationale 81, 112
Sous le manteau (Anonymous) 204–205
Srebnik, Simon 175
SS 7, 38, 61, 80, 91n75, 131, 137, 140, 147, 174, 184, 199–200
stains on manuscripts 44, 53, 96, 127–130, 150n13
Steiner, George 13
Steinmetz, Wolfgang, ghetto commissar of Maków 98, 102–103
Stone, Dan 10, 13, 33, 38, 45, 89n41, 126, 184, 186, 190, 202, 205, 208n15
storytelling 97, 114–115, 123n55, 132
style
  literary 13, 16, 18, 61, 63–64, 70, 71, 84, 86–87n9, 115, 116, 131–132, 161–162, 171, 175, 180n49
subjectivity 15, 36–37, 50, 85, 104, 118, 167, 188
sublime 49–53
sun, the 18, 183–184, 194, 206–207
Suwałki 62–63, 87n14, 87n15, 87–88n21
symbols 69, 76, 105, 125, 186
syntax 111, 131–132, 157
Szeps, Fela 12
Szlengel, Władysław 12, 26n69
Szmulewski, David 183–184, 207n2, 207–208n3, 208n4, 208–209n16

T
Taub, Shmuel 23n24, 119n4, 119n8, 120n16, 122n35
teeth 5, 30–32, 34, 42, 47, 54, 55n7, 197
temporality. *See* time
testimony
  oral 9–10, 15–16, 88n24, 123n44, 191, 202, 214–219
  material 34–35, 37–40, 42, 44, 54–55, 159–160, 172, 204
  video 15–16, 80, 122–123n38, 202
  written 15–16, 158, 202, 216
Theresienstadt, Terezín 25n36, 35, 49
time
  chronology 16, 33, 49, 64, 112, 114–115, 127, 131, 161

futurity 8, 11, 16, 19–20, 32, 34, 47, 63, 97, 117, 118, 147, 158, 162, 165, 170
past 9, 15–16, 17–18, 33, 34, 40, 42, 46–49, 50–53, 54, 71–72, 74, 117, 147, 160, 161, 162, 170, 177, 196, 216, 221n10
present 15–16, 34, 40, 46–49, 50, 51, 52, 54, 68, 71, 72, 82, 118, 170, 216
touch. *See* senses
train journeys 67, 68–70, 71–72, 88n32, 89n37, 98, 100, 106, 145–146. *See also* transport to Auschwitz
translation 4–5, 22n19, 34, 36, 92n79, 96, 121n22, 152n36, 157, 166
transports to Auschwitz 6, 35, 41, 48–49, 65, 67–68, 70, 74–82, 87–88n21, 92n79, 96, 112, 113, 114–115, 119n4, 120n11, 127, 130–131, 137, 142, 144–146, 147, 152n36, 152–153n44, 153n45, 153n46, 156, 164, 167, 183, 191, 198
trauma 15, 17–18, 40, 45–46, 51, 52, 53, 97, 104, 105, 187, 202, 219
Treblinka 12–13, 69–70, 79, 90n57, 145–146, 153n46, 212n101, 218
'tremendum' (Arthur Cohen) 52

U
uncanny, the 186–187
unfinished writing 65, 70
unknown author of the Sonderkommando. *See* Langfus, Leyb
unrepresentability 14, 197–198, 220
uprising of 7 October. *See under* Sonderkommando

V
Venezia, Shlomo 80, 166
visuality 39, 47, 68, 107, 116, 187, 190, 207, 216
voice 10, 15, 34, 101–102, 106, 163, 168–169, 202, 215, 218, 220n4. *See also* narrative voice

W
Wajcman, Gérard 185, 187, 190–191, 193, 195–202

Warsaw 2, 3, 4, 12, 13, 26n60, 69, 96, 147, 157, 218
Warsaw Ghetto Uprising 4, 147
Waxman, Zoë 13, 27n76, 212n110
Wein, Adam 22n14, 149n8
Weizman, Eyal 34
Welbel, Leon 23n25, 23n26, 24n30, 180n66
Weliczker Wells, Leon 12
White, Hayden 38, 138, 161–162, 193
Wiesel, Elie 71
Wilson, Emma 195–196
witnessing
   observing (*beobakhten*) 67, 110–111, 203
   possibility of 11, 14–15, 18, 19, 36–37, 61, 73, 85, 86, 109, 110, 123n41, 151n23, 172, 191, 217–218
   totality, completeness 70, 107
   See also senses; testimony; unrepresentability
Wolf, Robert 91n78, 92n79
Wolnerman, Chaim 3, 4, 21n4, 57n53, 64, 71, 74
work camps 98, 136–137, 145
writing materials
   exercise book, notebook or ledger 3, 4, 35–36, 38, 40, 44, 56n41, 64, 88n27, 95, 96, 99, 100, 107, 117, 127, 128, 174–176, 177
   ink 10, 34, 35, 36, 37–38, 43, 45, 47, 50, 51, 93, 96, 100, 108, 127, 128, 144, 156, 160, 163, 197
   paper 2, 3, 10, 15, 34, 35, 37–38, 41, 42, 43, 44–45, 49–50, 54, 56n41, 65, 93, 96, 127, 128, 155, 159–160, 167, 174, 176, 197
   pencil 35
Wygodzki, Yehoshua 22n14, 60–61, 92n80,

Y

Yad Vashem 64, 74, 84, 85, 159, 200
Yale Video Archive 15–16, 202
Yiddish 3, 4, 12, 20, 36, 37, 60, 72–73, 74, 89n37, 96, 97, 110, 113, 119n5, 122n32, 132, 148–149n3, 156, 157–158, 166, 197
yizker bikher (memorial books) 62, 87n14, 119n4, 120n16
Young, James 46, 59n120, 156

Z

Zaorski, Andrzej 1–3, 21n2, 21n4, 42, 154–155, 157, 159–160

www.ingramcontent.com/pod-product-compliance
Lightning Source LLC
Chambersburg PA
CBHW072148100526
44589CB00015B/2143